Patrick A. Desplat, Dorothea E. Schulz (eds.)
Prayer in the City

global local Islam

Patrick A. Desplat, Dorothea E. Schulz (eds.)

Prayer in the City

The Making of Muslim Sacred Places and Urban Life

[transcript]

Bibliographic information published by the Deutsche Nationalbibliothek
The Deutsche Nationalbibliothek lists this publication in the Deutsche Natio-
nalbibliografie; detailed bibliographic data are available in the Internet at
http://dnb.d-nb.de

Cover layout: Kordula Röckenhaus, Bielefeld
Cover illustration: © Patrick Desplat, The recitation of religious songs at
 the shrine Aw Shulum Ahmad during Shuwwal 'Id, Harar/Ethiopia 2003
Typeset by Carolin Maevis
Printed by Majuskel Medienproduktion GmbH, Wetzlar
ISBN 978-3-8376-1945-4

Global distribution outside Germany, Austria and Switzerland:

Transaction Publishers
New Brunswick (U.S.A.) and London (U.K.)

Transaction Publishers   Tel.: (732) 445-2280
Rutgers University   Fax: (732) 445-3138
35 Berrue Circle   for orders (U.S. only):
Piscataway, NJ 08854   toll free 888-999-6778

Contents

PART III EVERYDAY PRAYER AND URBAN TOPOGRAPHY

Acknowledgments

The thematic focus of this book grew out of a series of scholarly debates and events organized at the Berlin Graduate School of Muslim Societies and Cultures (BGSMSC) during Patrick Desplat's time as a research fellow at the institution in 2008/2009. Several chapters of the book were initially presented to the workshop 'Prayer in the City. Islam, Sacred Space and Urban Life', organized by Patrick Desplat and Eliza Bertuzzo at the BGSMSC in June 2009. We gratefully acknowledge the many ways in which colleagues who participated in the workshop contributed to the success of the workshop. We particularly want to thank Eliza Bertuzzo for her input into the thematic focus of the book.

To broaden the regional and thematic scope of the volume, we invited additional contributions (Hawkins, Stauth, Thielmann, Willemse). The article by Georg Stauth has been printed in *Scritture e interpretazioni. DOST Critical Studies 8*, edited by Allessandro Monti and Flavio Gallucci (Alessandria: Edizioni dell'Orso, pp.17-31). We thank Alessandro Monti, the editor-in-chief of Edizioni dell'Orso, for granting permission to reprint the article.

The BGSMSC provided generous funding for the workshop, the final publication, and an extended visiting fellowship for Dorothea Schulz at the institution in 2010. The members of the BGSMCS executive committee, Gudrun Krämer, Michael Bongardt and Ingeborg Baldauf, and the managing director, Katharina Nötzold, provided important scholarly input and logistical support at different stages of the project.

Patrick Desplat would like to thank Ute Luig and the excellence-in-research cluster TOPOI (The Formation and Transformation of Space and Knowledge in Ancient Civilizations) in Berlin for supporting him with a senior scholarship to refine his conceptual approach to key themes covered in this volume. We thank Joy Adapon for her careful language editing work and Carolin Maevis, Lena Herzog and Katarina Fritzsche for their editorial work.

Any edited volume that brings together essays covering historically and ethnographically diverse Muslim societies and languages poses considerable challenges with regard to uniform transliteration of the different dialects of Arabic and other languages spoken in these societies (a.o. Wolof, Bengali, Kiswahili, Bamanakan and Hindu). To ensure consistency in transliteration, we adopted simplified Arabic transliteration. Diacritics have been left out. The plural of words has been formed by the addition of an 's' to the singular, except in such cases as *ulama* in which the transliterated plural form has become standard.

Patrick Desplat and Dorothea E. Schulz, Cologne, December 2011

Introduction

Representations of Space, Place-making and Urban Life in Muslim Societies[1]

PATRICK DESPLAT

In 2009 a referendum that led to a ban of minarets in Switzerland stirred a heated public debate about Islam and religious freedom in Europe. The controversy brought to the open old-standing fears about Islam, but also, in some factions, outrage about this vivid demonstration of xenophobic sentiment. To substantiate their claims against or in favor of the Muslim call for prayer, politicians, journalists and others involved in the debate referred to various manifestations of increased Muslim presence in European societies, most notably female 'veiling' in public. By taking the ban in Switzerland as a starting point, the British Muslim writer Shelina Zahra Janmohamed reviewed a seminar held by the Arts and Islam Initiative of Arts Council England and makes a different point through illustrating the aesthetic qualities of religious buildings and their specific spatial relationship towards their community and their urban environment.[2] Quoting a workshop participant, she asked "What makes the brick of the butcher's shop across the road, less sacred than the brick in the religious building?" The answer

---

I am especially grateful to Dorothea Schulz who patiently commented on and criticized several stages of the draft of this introduction. Her invisible voice has undoubtedly played a part in shaping this chapter. Similarly, I would like to thank Martin Zillinger and Jörn Thielmann for their helpful suggestions and comments on earlier versions. The discussions with students during a graduate seminar in 2010 on 'Place Matters' provided a fertile ground for several trains of thought.

2 http://artsandislam.com/wp-content/uploads/2010/06/Faithbuildings.pdf (last accessed 15.12.2010).

she suggested was that a locality's sacred significance results from the actions of people who imbue the physical structure of a locality with specific meanings and functions.

What practices turn spaces, sites and buildings in Muslim societies into a Muslim sacred place? How do Muslims transform abstract and empty space into a place that is invested with particular social and symbolic meanings? In what broader cultural understandings are Muslims' practices of sacred place-making grounded? Who controls Muslims' diverse sacred places and who contests the claim for their sacredness? And how do Muslims' diverse practices of rendering places 'sacred' intertwine with the opportunities and constraints of urban space?

Prayer in the City takes social practices surrounding mosques, shrines and public spaces in urban contexts as a window onto the diverse ways in which Muslims in different regional and historical settings imagine, experience, and inhabit places and spaces and invest them with sacred meaning. Unlike most studies on Muslim communities, this volume concentrates on social practices and expressions of urban everyday life rather than on the political issues that dominate today's headlines. These practices are conceived of as specific modes of place-making and the authors seek to understand them in their semantic and contextual complexity. This collection thereby moves beyond interpretations that focus exclusively on the ritual character of these places. The religious meaning of places, often initiated and maintained by Islamic scholars, ritual specialists and common visitors, is mostly accompanied by more subtle and routinely everyday activities and interpretations by people who may not participate in ritual activities but they live, work and interact at these places. Some of these actors might be in charge of picking up garbage in front of a shrine; others might sell sweets or audio-cassettes with Qur'anic recitations; yet others might simply hang out in front of the mosque to relax from overcrowded and busy street life; these activities are done without any peculiarly religious intent; they belong to the realm of everyday routines and occupations. All these practices help construct a physical space as a place that bears particular, religious and mundane meanings.

A place is not only a site where Muslims live. It is also a site of struggle and contestation over the use and significance of this place. Muslim sacred places constitute spatial nodes in a wider network of religious, socio-political, cultural or economic flows in which different ideas, claims and interests intersect and sometimes converge. Sacred places are contested sites because opinions of their uses may differ, just as the meaning of 'sacredness' may be questioned. In urban settings, with their historically and regionally specific backgrounds, their density and heterogeneity offer various possibilities for the making of sacred places. At the same time, the urban physical structure and centralized administration may impose various constraints on Muslim ritual as well as on their ways of conducting everyday life. For instance, projects by politicians and or state officials to renovate and refashion a mosque building or to use its surrounding property for new purposes often collide with the resistance of those who actually frequent these sites. Considerable disagreement over proper attitude, comportment, dress and religious conviction may exist among believers and visitors who flock to a well-known mosque or shrine. New Islamic reform movements may contest existing understandings and claims about the sacredness of particular places, and simultaneously promote their own domiciles as sites of proper behavior and moral piety. Throughout Muslim history, shrines and correlating practices of worship and veneration have often constituted a bone of contention among competing religious groups. Controversies centered not so much on the special, sacred character of these sites but on questions of proper religious practice.

Stretching from Morocco, Mali, Senegal, Tanzania, Sudan, Tunisia, Germany, and Egypt to Pakistan, India and Bangladesh, the contributions to this volume explore different modes of place-making in Muslim societies with a focus on urban settings. Drawing on a range of analytical and disciplinary perspectives, the chapters examine how the cultural, material and sensuous architectonics of religious practice, on one side, and everyday experience and activities in town on the other constitute and affect each other. The contributions examine spatial practices in Islam from an interdisciplinary and trans-regional perspective, and thus move beyond approaches that have been commonly advanced in Islamic studies and in the social sciences. The place-making activities examined in the different chapters range from practices of Senegalese Sufi pilgrims, female Malian Muslim activists, and traders engaged in the Tunisian tourist industry, to activities in different mosque and shrine congregations, and finally to festivities that partake in the visual and aural construction of sacred place in urban environments.

The different chapters in this volume pursue three guiding concerns. First, conventional scholarship on Islam treated space (and place) as meta-categories without defining them explicitly. Space was taken for granted or understood as a 'container' of human action, filled with a specific Islamic order of norms, values, and practices. In search of a definition of Islam on the grounds of proper religious practice and conduct, studies of Islam mapped Muslim societies according to their specific methodologies: from the early Orientalist notion of centre and periphery to the dichotomy of rural and urban Islam and the assumption of fragmented *islams* of local contexts in anthropology. How Muslims themselves construct space and place has been comparatively neglected.

Second, space and place within Muslim societies had either been treated as being interchangeable concepts or as dichotomies. Although this book takes place-making of Muslims as an initial starting point, space has to be included in the overall analysis. Both terms are complementary and it is a comprehensive theme of most contributions to illustrate that Muslim sacred places are always made of diffusion, appropriation and movement in space.

Third, the practice of transforming something into a sacred place is explicitly related to the question of how sacredness is constituted in different Muslim contexts. Sacredness is related to a social practice of investing specific meaning to physical structure. This process is both guided by religious references as well the context-related everyday life of social actors with their specific economic, socio-political dimensions. Everyday life in urban settings is particularly shaped by the interaction of heterogeneous actors with their respective life styles, practices, and attitudes that produces both routines as well as cultural creativity. Against this background, Muslim practices of place-making are often intensified to maneuver through the complexities of urban life. However, the increasing presence of even temporary Muslim sacred places often results in tensions over their legitimacy and use.

REPRESENTATIONS OF SPACE IN SCHOLARSHIP ON ISLAM AND MUSLIM SOCIETIES

Until the 1980s, scholarship on Muslim societies and cultures did not treat 'space', 'place' and 'landscape' as analytical categories. Very often, these terms were used interchangeably and applied to geographical locations and regions that were treated as timeless and static. This endeavor of categorizing reflected a colonial thinking to assume the existence of separate cultures that are rooted in isolated, unique and bounded territories. To subdivide the world into a mosaic of cultures was helpful to understand complex differences. In early anthropology geographical regions became containers, in which constrained cultures were connected with surfaces of institutionalized social knowledge as 'gate keeping concepts' or 'theoretical metonyms' (Appadurai 1986; Rodman 1992). Arjun Appadurai (1988), for example, criticized that caste became the substitute for Indian society while India became the predominant region for anthropologists to study hierarchy which produced a region-specific school of structuralism. In this sense, space is treated as an external but undefined meta-category that reflects knowledge and power while excluding actor-centered perspectives. In the same way, the Middle and Near East was conceived of primarily in terms of segmentation, Islam and the harem (Abu-Lughod 1989). In an isomorphic perception of a geographical region (Middle and Near East), its social structure (Arab segmented society) and its underlying culture/religion (Islam), Islam became the explanatory framework for European imperialism to understand the 'Arab mind'. In this sense, the image of the Middle and Near East produced knowledge of an abstract spatial frontier which has to be explored, traversed and controlled. This point has been criticized in Edward Said's famous *Orientalism* (1978), which shook many scientific disciplines to the core. For Said, Orientalism is a body of theory and practice about the 'Orient' and about Islam, which form a set of representations based on power hegemonies of European scholars and their subject.

The claim that 'Muslim society' has been homogeneous and timeless goes back to the shallow Orientalist imaginations of the 19th century and earlier.[3] The search of early Islamic studies for an essence through the analysis of Islamic texts and theology resulted in a categorization of a territorial bounded Islamic centre and its peripheries. These categories are based on the normative perception of different expressions of Islam: the Middle and Near East were perceived as the heartland of an assumed Islamic orthopraxy, which served as a scale to evaluate 'nonstandard' practices as 'syncretic' or 'pre-Islamic'. Since most religious texts were produced in centers of Islamic learning in the Arab world, other regions like Africa or Asia were defined by Islamic studies as Muslim peripheries. They regarded Muslim societies at the assumed fringe as passive receivers and not as producers of Islamic religion while presuming at the same time that these Muslims must be considerably shaped by their cultural context and local religions like Animism, Hinduism and Buddhism, thus practicing a 'syncretic' or mixed Islam. The search for and definition of a normative essence on the basis of analyzing Islamic texts resulted in a general disregard of the peripheral regions as locations of research, even though many Muslim societies in Africa or Asia developed a rich tradition of Islamic literature. This gap was filled later on by the works of anthropologists, who tried to avoid complex historical depth and literal legacies and searched for rituals and face-to-face interactions.

From the 1950s onwards, increasing anthropological research on Islam and Muslim societies resulted in a paradigmatic shift. The Islamicist scholar Gustav E. von Grunebaum (1956) and the anthropologist Robert Redfield (1955) sought to overcome the hierarchical and categorical opposition of orthodox and syncret-

---

3   An example for the continuity of this notion is Ernest Gellner's *Muslim Society* (1981). Despite Gellner's sophisticated amalgamation of Hume's oscillation theory with the sociology of Ibn Khaldun and the impact of modernity on Muslim society, his work portrays Muslims as rather behaving in a fixed and timeless system than acting as individual social actors.

ic Islam by proposing an alternative, the conceptual contrast of 'Great' and 'Little Traditions'. Initially developed with regard to peasant studies and urban migration (with the intent of studying the folk-urban continuum), both terms were meant to refer to contrasting forms of practicing Islam. The 'Great Tradition' was understood as 'orthodox' Islam, to be based on scriptural scholarship and cultivated in urban mosques and urban institutions of education by an urban elite. 'Little Tradition' in contrast referred to what von Grunebaum and Redfield understood as 'heterodox' forms of Islam, practiced by mostly non-literate rural populations and manifesting itself in demotic versions like mysticism, saint veneration or maraboutism.

One could argue that by positing a contrast between a Great and a Little Tradition, von Grunebaum and Redfield were asking valid questions yet offered only partial answers that brought with them new challenges. The Great vs. Little Tradition dichotomy organized differences within a religious tradition in spatial terms, by opposing a rural to an urban Islam. The strength of the categorical divide posited by von Grunebaum and Redfield was that it accorded equal value and importance to different expressions and practices of Islam, instead of ordering them in a fixed hierarchy, with 'orthodox' Islamic knowledge prevailing over aberrant and un-Islamic beliefs and practices. By treating both traditions as equal, the conceptual duality overcame the hierarchical categorization in Islamic studies in orthodox practices and inferior deviants.

Still, a shortcoming of the Great vs. Little Traditions categorization was that it arranged a great variety of Muslim practices, conventions and interpretations into a neat and, one could argue, rigid and ahistorical interpretational scheme. Moreover, the claim of this model to overcome normative hierarchies was only partial fulfilled. According to Redfield, the mosque was (always) the place of 'orthodox' Islam practiced in town, whereas the shrine stood for various manifestations of a 'popular' Islam practiced by believers with little erudition and knowledge in the countryside. This view contains at least two significant problems. First, it strengthens an inner-Islamic discourse of normative assertion concerning the rightfulness of certain practices. Second, it neglects the various overlapping and confluences of the distinctive forms of social organization.

According to Abdul Hamid el-Zein (1977: 248), the anthropological dichotomy of folk and elite Islam is congruent with methods of Islamic theology. He argues, that social sciences merely mirror an Islamic discourse dominated by Muslim elites. This discourse reflects the hegemony over interpretation and therefore takes the right to articulate a vision of proper Islamic conduct as being orthodox. While an urban Islam is always equated with religious orthodoxies, rural concepts change continually according to their diverse contexts of social formation. Although anthropology claims to have a more reflective, systematic and objective approach than Islamic theology, the discipline tries to capture Islamic diversity by the same means and principles of a hegemonic Islamic elite, therefore, strengthening existing hierarchical relationships within Muslim societies.

A second problem with Redfield's dichotomy is its rigidity. Its perspective disregards that many important shrines are located in urban environments, and that many of those who engage in practices associated with mystical Islam and the veneration of saintly figures are models of Islamic erudition. Thus what Redfield considered as little 'folk' tradition is not little at all, since all rituals and religious practices make references to the 'Great Tradition', be it the everyday prayer or the reciting of the Qur'an by rural peasants. On the other hand the urban middle class may very well be attached to Islamic mysticism. To neatly separate urban and rural spheres as different locations of religious practice is impossible because these sites intertwine through people who move back and forth between them and whose practices frequently link these different domains of religious and mundane practice. As early as 1955, McKim Marriot (1955) suggested to replace the Great vs. Little Traditions dichotomy with the twin concepts of universalization and parochialization, and to conceive of different religious traditions as complementary and as existing in a mutually constitutive relationship. Marriot's early and innovative corrective did not find a broad echo. As a result, Redfield's dichotomous classification helped perpetuate an already existing disciplinary division of labor. Philological approaches in Islamic studies and in history continued to focus on texts produced in urban centers; anthropologists and those from other disciplines concentrated on detailed empirical research located in the village as the center of an allegedly traditional and untouched rural life.

In the 1970s, Abdul Hamid el-Zein (1977) conceived of Islam in the plural to comprehend the heterogeneous collection of different practices and beliefs that he illuminated existed. His main argument was that anthropology should detach itself from assumptions of the existence of one Islamic orthodoxy and to assess different religious expressions in equal terms. The explanation of Muslim's diversity became less normative, however, more and more fragmented from a spatial perspective: early attempts to categorize the Islamic world in a center and its surrounding peripheries have been superseded by a localized division into an urban and rural Islam, while anthropologists from the 1960s on understood Islam in its spatial plurality as bounded unities related to their cultural field sites. When Clifford Geertz (1968) heralded an 'anthropology of Islam', he first compared a 'Moroccan Islam' and 'Indonesian Islam' as having the same religious affiliation, although a culturally different religious expression developed.[4] This highly influential work explained diversity in Islam from an angle of cultural diversity as dominating religious expression. This approach echoes the anthropological idea of the ethnographic field as a spatial bounded entity, which is epistemologically central but has been rarely questioned before the early 1990s (Gupta and Ferguson 1992). In a similar manner as the 'field', space in Islamic studies has been treated as an undefined meta-category up till today. Common terms like 'Moroccan Islam' (Eickelman 1976) or 'South Asian Islam' (Ewing 1988), 'African Islam' (Rosander and Westerlund 1997), 'American Islam' (Barrett 2007), or 'Euro-Islam' (AlSayyad and Castells 2002) underline the local distinctiveness of Muslim identities and have the tendency to reproduce a close spatial relationship between a geographical site and specific religious expressions. These spatial terms, implicitly or explicitly, disregard two important dimensions. First, they rather neglect mobilities, movements and historical networks of pilgrimage or trade which crosses regional boundaries and triggered religious, economic and cultural exchange between Muslim communities. Against the background of globalization studies and transnational Islamic movements many authors today turn towards the interconnections and translocal space of Muslims. Engseng Ho (2006), for instance, takes the Yemeni region of Hadramaut as a starting point to illustrate travel, mobility and Hadrami communities dispersed over the Indian Ocean. John Bowen (2004), on the other hand, asks if French Islam is or should be limited culturally, linguistically, and geographically to France. He highlights the field of tension of French Muslims to be part of the global Muslim community and the normative pretensions of the French state to domesticate Islam at the same time.

However, these and earlier studies often neglect – Bowen's study is a rare exception – that Muslims perceive themselves as being part of a universal and global Islam. Only few Muslims would relate their religious belief to a geographical region, such as following an 'Ethiopian Islam', although the term 'Ethiopian Muslim' would be commonly accepted. Spaces inhabited by Muslims have multiple meanings and are socially constructed, not only by studies of Islam but also by Muslims themselves. The division of the world in different territories likes *dar al-Islam*, 'the house of Islam', and *dar al-harb*, 'the house of war', seems to be common theological fact in Islam. However, this mode of mapping the world is in fact not related to passages in the Qur'an or Hadith, but

---

4 "Moroccan Islam became activist, rigorous, dogmatic and more than a little anthropolatrous and why Indonesian Islam became syncretic, reflective, multifarious, and strikingly phenomenological lie, in part anyway, in the sort of collective life within which and along with which they evolved" (Geertz 1968: 20).

is the result of interpretation by Islamic scholars (Bennett 2005). The contributions of this volume de-essentialize notions of sacred places as timeless manifestations of religious power, but take socially constructed places as the starting point to elaborate an actor-centered perspective on practices of place-making.

PRACTICES OF MAKING-PLACE (AND SPACE). MUSLIMS' MOVEMENT AND SENSE OF BELONGING

Despite the role that space had for studies on Muslim societies and cultures, only few scholars have actually specified what they perceive as 'place' and 'space'. Since both categories are everywhere, they seem to stand for themselves and have been misconceived as unquestioned constants of social reality. However, since the 'spatial turn' in the 1980s, it has become more and more fashionable in studies on Islam to use spatial categories and to emphasize the social construction of places and spaces as important aspects of cultural production. This turn is mostly related to contemporary sociological and anthropological scholarship which tend to address spatial aspects relating to lived 'spaces' as being parts of various aspects of Muslims' everyday life: gendered spaces (Falah and Nagel 2005; Göle 1997, 2002), media spaces in the public sphere (Eickelman and Anderson 1999), bodies as sites of embodied piety (Mahmood 2005; Starrett 1995) or the making of Muslim spaces in Europe and North America (Metcalf 1996).

The philological discipline of Islamic studies, in contrast, inclines to focus on remembered 'places'. These are sacred places which are often related to acts of remembrance, the creation of continuity and of imagining the past in an idealistic way. These are places such as mosques, shrines, public places or landscapes which are remembered by Muslims as being related to important figures or events in Islamic history, while being often imagined as an interrelated sacred topography which is inhabited and lived by Muslims (Bennett 1994; Schimmel 1991).

These different perceptions of spatiality in Muslim societies and cultures echo a tendency in the social sciences to treat space and place not necessarily as dichotomous but as differently evaluated concepts of one social reality. On the one hand, there are spaces of modern life which stand for rapid social change and compete with the fixity of places, and on the other hand, there are historic places which stabilize the chaotic surrounding space. These different foci on the relationship of place and space go back to different epistemological traditions. While approaches to study space have been prominent in Marxist inspired sociology, human and social geography has been preferably interested in places. In a general way, Agnew summarized that sociology analyzed space as an abstract grid and object, which could be crossed and lived but also observed, controlled and formed, while the geographical discipline perceived places mostly as subjective, embodiments of meaning and locations of cultural memory. As a consequence, space has been associated with development, change and the global, while place was labeled with nostalgia, continuity and the local (Agnew 2005: 82-83).

There is the need to conceptually distinguish these perspectives on 'place' and 'space'. For both disciplines, space is first of all conceived as a structure or domain uninhabited by people and to which actors have not (yet) inscribed any social meaning. The concept of space is also more abstract than place, and more difficult to apply to empirical investigations. More theoretical understandings of 'space' have been advanced mostly by Marxian inspired approaches in (urban) sociology (Harvey 2006; Jaret 1983; Wallerstein 1976). These studies treat 'places' largely as points of reference in a wider, abstract space, in which power relations are inscribed. Space becomes first of all a capital-induced space. Capitalism was seen as the root of the fragmentation of the world in different states or cities and particular property rights. This perspective is a top-down approach in the sense that spaces have comprehensive influence on places and dominate the everyday life of their inhabitants. The main problem of this approach of space is that it tries to explain political power without reference to situated power relations. Instead, space itself becomes an abstract, all-embracing power, detached from any human agency.

In a more sophisticated way, the social philosopher Henri Lefebvre (1991 [1974]) developed a dialectical relation between space and place. Similar to other studies on space, he presumes that capitalism transformed abstract and empty space into space that colonizes and exploits the everyday life of its inhabitants through control, planning, gentrification or commodification. However, these incapacitated inhabitants may reclaim space by its naming or remembering, thus transforming space into space with a particular and specific meaning beyond its capitalist characteristics. Lefebvre therefore defines space as socially constructed which could be experienced, imagined and acted upon by its inhabitants. Although Lefebvre's amplifications most importantly do focus on uneven economic conditions and dominant practices (and he does not use the term 'place'), the activities of potential resistance imply a place-related agency of people insofar as it gives meaning to space.

'Place', therefore, had its role in sociology, even if it was secondary to space and not named as such. However, the transformation of empty into meaningful space is a distinct form of place-making. A city as such is an urban space, meaningless and abstract, designable and controllable, but cities such as Fez or Islamabad are places conjuring specific histories and identities. Where the early Portuguese explorers of the Indian Ocean may have seen an empty space of wide water which had to be conquered and traversed, Arab and Swahili sailors read the sea as a set of places inhabited by various spirits and fraught with dangers (Sheriff 2010).

In contrast to sociology which favored the perspective on space and perceived place as an abstract position (in space), early human geography was engaged in the explanations of place as a location to which actors attributed particular social meanings or cultural significances (Relph 1976; Tuan 1979). These approaches have been influenced significantly by the phenomenology of Maurice Merlau-Ponty (1962). According to him, life is grounded in perception, an ontological grounding that implies an 'emplaced' knowledge about place and about our own movement in space. Because we are always localized through our 'being in the world', everything we do is in fact emplaced. This approach implies that early approaches in human geography were not necessarily interested in how places were made and constructed in their unique cultural or social setting. Rather they tried to explain the essence of human existence as being 'emplaced'. Tuan for example uses the term 'topophilia', love of place, and explains the perception and emotional ties people have with their environmental surroundings (Tuan 1974). Feelings towards a place may vary, but 'home' and other places of positive memories or nostalgia were perceived as being fixed entities of value and belonging opposed to space as an arena of action, mobility and movement. Edward Relph took this dualism as a starting point to draw a sharp line between 'authentic' places, loaded with identity, experience, belonging and a feeling of home, and of 'inauthentic' places which are the product of increasing mobilities, change and the resulting loss of relationship to place (Relph 1976). Placelessness finally is a nostalgic assertion that more and more places in the modern world are assumed to lose their meaning through developing the same features like airports or motorways as standardized landscapes.

Later on, the contribution of social philosopher Edward Casey (1996) became quite popular in anthropology. Drawing on earlier phenomenological approaches in geography, Casey criticized widely held assumptions about the unproblematic and taken-for-granted existence of space, and their contrast to place as something that requires the active making and signification practices of human actors. Instead of space, according to Casey, it is place which is much more significant for human life and "to live is to live locally and to know is first of all to know the places one is in" (1996: 18). However, Casey departs from earlier approaches that perceived place as a spatial entity fixed with an unchanging self-identity and stressed the processual and undetermined nature of place. Referring to Martin Heidegger, Casey argues that places 'gather' experiences, memory, histories, languages and thoughts and they hold them together (1996: 24). Casey's formulations are important for understanding places as sites where practices, experiences and remembrances intensify by a continuous process of place-making.

However, his assumptions do not include gender or social differences that produce different experiences of the same place. Socially constructed or imagined places do maintain and produce social hierarchy and difference through their makers by excluding and separating people by materials and symbols. Mosques or shrines are often strongholds of power. By controlling them, their geographical locations, built-form or symbolic meanings may be instrumentalized to dominate others. The sociologist Thomas Gieryn (2000: 468), therefore, proposes that we explore how places come into being and what they accomplish. Places are socially constituted through practices, cognitive models and material manifestations, and they simultaneously structure action and social life. The social process of place-making as well as their social consequences, the resulting possibilities and constraints for social agency should be given a preferential treatment in the analysis of places. A place is at once a performative act *and* a structuring order. They are a medium through which social life is affected.

Agnew succinctly sums up important insights drawn from the different approaches to space and place that I discussed so far: "space refers to location somewhere and place to the occupation of that location. Space is about having an address and place is about living at that address" (Agnew 2005: 82). Both conceptualizations of place and space are often arranged in a hierarchical relationship, which is reminiscent of the conceptual dichotomies so characteristic of former approaches to the study of Muslim societies and cultures. One side of the dichotomy was represented by scholars interested in theology, both Muslims and non-Muslims, who conceived of Islam as a universal system (space) that determines Muslim everyday life according to an Islamic orthodoxy that is passed on and reproduced at certain institutions of Islamic erudition (places). On the other side of the dichotomy were scholars who stressed the diversity of Muslim religious expressions and understandings across time and cultures, and who thus promoted a view of Islam in the plural (places), highlighting the particularistic elements of local Islam instead of its claim for universality (space). However, in recent analysis, conceptual boundaries between universalistic and particularistic as well as between space and place became more and more blurred.

Geographer Doreen Massey (1991) has made a much-quoted effort to bring together place and space into one framework of analysis. Questioning the function of places ascribed by neo-Marxian studies on space, Massey criticized that places seem to be constructed by people out of fear as reactive and defensive responses which reflect the struggle for authenticity against the power of a global capitalist juggernaut of homogenization. These place-based social movements include identity politics or cultural heritage politics as subaltern strategies against globalism (see Escobar 2001). Massey suggests that, rather than treating place as a fixed entity in a surrounding mobile chaos, scholars should investigate how places emerge out of particular social and political relations and encounters. In Massey's reading, a place is a process, a site on which multiple identities and histories are inscribed. Place is not only defined by its inscribed identity, but this identity itself is a process reliant on interactions and movement of people through a wider space. A place constitutes a moment and a node in a social network where different experiences and translocal ties and movements intersect. Thus, what Massey's notion of 'place' emphasizes are not boundaries or authentic identities, but processes of contestation, of movement and connection, and (the generation of) ambiguous meanings. According to Massey, place is to be understood in relation to factors that exist outside and reach beyond that place. Massey also makes the important point that globalization is not experienced everywhere in the same way. Different configurations of power and politics allow some people to move and migrate, while restricting the mobility of others (see also Cresswell 2001).

As elsewhere in the world, places in Muslim societies are made through mobility, movement and their restrictions. Muslim places are constantly made and remade by travelling, pilgrimage, knowledge networks or trade, activities which are explicitly encouraged by Islam (Eickelman and Piscatori 1990). Obviously, most places in Islam are made by human actors who move through space: Mecca is made a place fraught with ritual meaning through believers who engage in the *hajj*, the annual pilgrimage, or *'umra,* a pilgrimage which could be performed any time. Medina is 'made' into a sacred place by people who, through embodied practices, commemorate the *hidjra*, the flight of the prophet Muhammad with his followers from Mecca. Jerusalem becomes a place with particular (ritual) meanings through ritual practices that invoke and honor the *miradj*, the nocturnal journey of Muhammad. Other sacred places are made through practices dedicated to the commemoration of pious Muslims who, because of their personal biography, ethical conduct or erudition, are considered saints today and whose tombs are the object of 'visits' (*ziyara*), veneration, and supplication.

As in the past transnational ties, mobility and migration have a tremendous effect on contemporary processes of place-making in Muslim societies and cultures. Transnational Muslim communities in the West purposefully inscribe new meanings into spaces by engaging in various ritual practices, such as processions or those surrounding the constructions of mosques (Metcalf 1996; Werbner 1996). Another example of place-making via movement is the Tabligh-i Jama'at, a modern reform group with an explicit focus on travel and mobility (Masud 2000). Their mode of education starts out from their teaching center (*markaz*) and moves on to the missionary tour (*khuruj*) that includes door-to-door-visits or short trips to mosques located in the surrounding rural and urban areas. A missionary tour may last several months and may take its participants, individuals as well as groups of missionaries, to other countries. In addition to their annual congregations (*ijtema*), the Tabligh also gather in mass meetings that bring together hundreds of thousands of their members from all over the world. However, mobility is often constrained by economic and other reasons. During my fieldwork in the town of Harar in Eastern Ethiopia, for instance, the Tabligh had to report to the local Qadi before going to rural areas first. After an interview, the local Sharia court makes out a document for identification that proves that the affected person is not an 'Islamist' who instigates religious intolerance. The lack of these documents usually resulted in arrests by the police.

The contributions to this volume, too, illustrate that movement, migration, mobility and the restrictions imposed on them, are factors that inform modes of place-making in numerous Muslim societies. Many chapters highlight how the transnational connections play into practices of place-making at various moments of everyday and ritual life. Johara Berhane reports on how inhabitants of a popular neighborhood in the Moroccan town of Fez discovered the importance of a shrine dedicated to the Sufi leader Ahmad al-Tijani only once they were confronted with Senegalese pilgrims flocking to the shrine. Simon Hawkins discusses the significance that young Tunisian traders, whose business is geared toward attracting international tourists, attribute to the famous Zeituna mosque in Tunis. In other contributions, movement is more implicit but is often a decisive factor of place-making. Catherine Asher focuses on the symbolic meaning of a staircase and its mosque in colonized Jaipur/India. The struggle of Muslims with the local government over widening the stairs did result into a violent killing and imprisonments at the mosque. In protest of this perceived betrayal, many Muslims migrated to Delhi, where they stayed for several months before the responsible police officer in Jaipur asked the emigrants to come back and finally ordered for the widening of the mosque stairs. Samuli Schielke opts for the form of a photo-essay to account for the extraordinary nature of *mawlids* festivals in

Egypt. These festivals transform the city or a village temporarily into a world of celebration where the everyday order is suspended. However, the *mawlids* is characterized by a constant mode of flux and the mobile structures of its buildings are treated as temporary cities within the city. Every year these constructions are rebuilt and help to reproduce the magic atmosphere of the festivity.

Muslims obviously make their different places by creative interaction, appropriation or movement. Sacred places are the result of a specific mode of place-making; they are the product of people's investments and practices that endow physical space with diverse, religious connotations. This leaves us with the following questions: What makes a Muslim place a sacred Muslim place? How is the sacred in Muslim societies related to Muslims' everyday life? Addressing these questions and specifying how we conceive of the sacred in Muslim societies is of central import to studies on Islam because sacredness is central to the tension between the claim to universal validity of the teachings of Islam and the historically and culturally variable forms in which they are realized and lived.

SACRED PLACES, SACRED BOUNDARIES AND URBAN LIFE

The constructivist character of places incorporates Muslim practices to imbue physical manifestations with sacred meaning. However, what sacredness in different Muslim societies actually means is open to debate. The 'sacred' is probably one of the most controversial concepts in the social sciences, while Muslims themselves often question, compete over or debate different modes of sacredness. It has to be emphasized that the power of the sacred as well as boundaries between the sacred and the profane are often real for the believers and that this distinction usually plays an important role in their everyday life. On the other hand, the continuous debates of Muslims concerning the role of sacredness reveal diversity of meaning as well as transgression and fluidity of boundaries. Although one is easily attentive for essentialist thoughts – since most believers of monotheistic religions usually refer to a universal truth – the sacralization by Muslims should rather be analyzed through the diverse socio-political conditions and cultural contexts, the everyday life of people, than exclusively through essentialist perspectives which define sacredness in Islam in a rather narrow manner.

From a linguistic point of view, the distinction between the sacred and the mundane is originally related to spatial dimensions and goes back to the Latin terms *sacer* and *profanus*, which are linked to specific and distinct locations. While the *sacer* was a place set apart as *sanctum*, usually a temple, the surrounding space was available for profane use. The concept of sacredness, therefore, is often applied to objects, places or spaces as material manifestations of the elsewhere uncertain transcendence of divine forces. Therefore, sacred space is distinguished from the topography of the non-sacred, the everyday and mundane. Whereas everyday life is perceived as being shaped by routes of work, leisure, love, social obligations and fun, sacred topographies could be identified by the scholar in those blank spaces which are left out by daily routines (Hauser-Schäublin 2003). This distinction goes back to Durkheim's suggestion that the primary characteristic of religion is to divide the world into the two fundamentally opposed domains of sacred and profane (Durkheim 1976). His elaborations on contrasting spheres inform most studies on the 'sacred'. However, according to the religious scholar Matthew T. Evans (2003) most studies on the 'sacred' differ fundamentally and could be categorized in two research traditions. On the one hand, there is a substantivistic approach, which denotes a 'transcendent reality', and on the other hand, a situational-constructive one, which refers to the ascription of special meanings and boundary-making.

Some studies may use a substantivistic approach to examine the sacred as a manifest religious experience which involves ambivalent emotions of fear and desire. The philosopher and religious scholar Mircea Eliade (1959), for example, claimed that sacred space emerges out of profane space. Sacredness, therefore, not only transforms but also penetrates everyday life like a symbolic arrow. Sacred space evolves through the manifestation of the transcendence on earth (hierophany) or the mediation of a transcendent message though a human being (theophany). However, Eliade's approach explains sacredness as detached from human agency. Sacredness stands for itself as an essentialistic category and becomes a manifestation of reality with a specific ambivalent quality since it induces emotions of fear and anxiety but also fascination and attraction.

The situational-constructive approach on the other hand is more fruitful to explore sacred places as being made by Muslims. Spearheaded by Claude Lévi-Strauss, who proposed that the sacred is open to the reception of any meaning (Lévi-Strauss cited in Mauss 2001: 5), some scholars on religion dissociate from essentialistic notions of sacredness and rather emphasized the role of human agency in the ongoing work of sacralizing places or objects. According to David Chidester and Edward T. Linenthal, particular built environments depend "not only upon a symbolic conquest or construction of place, but also upon the temporal processes of ritual and practice, memory and narrative, and the ongoing engagement with historical factors and change" (1995: 25). Sacred space, therefore, could be defined as a

"[...] portion on earth's surface which is recognized by individuals or groups as worthy of devotion, loyalty or esteem. Space is sharply discriminated from the non-sacred or profane world around it. Sacred space does not exist naturally, but is assigned sanctity as man defines, limits and characterizes it though his culture, experience and goals" (Jackson and Henrie 1983: 94)

This explanation implies that sacred space is not abstract, but is a distinct and experienced place which contains at least three important features. It is socially constructed, it implies a moral quality and above all it could be identified by its set-apart character, as having special value which has to be protected by material and symbolic boundaries.

Philological approaches in Islam, for instance, extracted three different intrinsic and essentialistic types of sacredness. The terms *qudsi* or *muqaddas* derive from the Arabic letters *q-d-s* and relate to the transcendental and God only, while the letter sequence *h-r-m* reflects the notion of the forbidden, the taboo or the protected like in *haram*, a place which is forbidden for men. The main mosque in Mecca is called *al-masjid al-haram*, the Sacred Mosque, and Mecca and Medina are known as *al-haraman*, places which are forbidden for non-Muslims. A different mode of sacredness indicates the Arabic letter sequence *w-l-y* like in *walayah*. This form of sacredness is exclusively ascribed to human beings as in the most popular notion of *wali Allah* (pl. *awliya' Allah*), the 'friend of God'. These individuals are 'protectors', 'patrons' or 'helpers' and are perceived – being alive or dead – as being near to God.

However, this approach towards sacredness in Islam is a narrow one. Many Muslims involved in making a place sacred may refer to these Islamic terms as they do to other 'Islamic imperatives', narratives related to the prophet or his companions which legitimize the significance of certain places. At the same time, processes of place-making are always embedded in their socio-political and cultural contexts. To imbue a sacred and special meaning to physical structure often implies nuances, metaphors or notions of a specific cultural background.

These may be complementary to definitions of sacredness by philologists, but not necessarily so. The emphasis on boundaries, as well as their transgression, has a long tradition in social anthropology and is often related to the term liminality. Liminality was first developed by Arnold van Gennep (1960 [1909]) and later on appropriated by Victor Turner (1969) in his pioneering work on processual symbolic analysis. A liminal phase occurs during rites des passages and is defined by its liberation from social norms. In liminal spaces a person can stand outside of their normal social roles and embrace alternative social arrangements and values. In sum, the liminal subjects are "neither here nor there; they are betwixt and between the positions assigned and arrayed by law, custom, convention, and ceremonial" (Turner 1969: 95). It is an ambiguous situation where individuals may reinterpret and criticize social order, which makes them potentially dangerous for others, let us say religious authorities, who wish to continue to monopolize knowledge and "orthodoxy". Closely related to liminality is communitas as forms of sociability, solidarity and equality which is strengthened through a communal spiritual experience. It is "a community or comity of comrades and not a structure of hierarchically arrayed positions" (Turner 1967: 100). As with liminality, the communitas marks a challenge for social and cultural order and Turner clearly places it outside the common social structure, the anti-structure. This means an alternative structure of social relationships which are reversed socially acceptable behavior of people through liminal phases. In sacred places, therefore, things become possible, even prescribed, that may be problematic outside. In any case, a shrine might transcend identities and makes interreligious participation possible and practicable.

This more inclusive aspect is highlighted both by the contributions by Geoffrey Samuel and Santi Rozario as well as Linus Strothmann. Both papers use or mention the Foucaultian notion of heterotopia. Heterotopia is a concept to describe places and spaces of otherness, pointing towards its position at the margins of ordered society. These places/spaces have a system of closure and openness and are not accessible to everybody, since they may require permission or a specific state of being to enter. Geoffrey Samuel and Santi Rozario argue that shrines in Bangladesh are a kind of inversion or negation of the society that surrounds them. They are, or claim to be, places, where the laws of ordinary logic can be suspended – at least in principle. Linus Strothmann does use heterotopia in an alleviated form in his exploration of Data Ganj Bukhsh, a shrine-mosque complex in Lahore/Pakistan, a "city within a city". Describing different meanings of the shrine as sacred place as well as place of crime and moral deterioration, he defines the shrine as a public place in a landscape of different representations.

As suggested by N.J. Demerath III et al., "the secrets of both the sacred and the secular are often revealed more in the adumbrations and interpenetrations than in their separation" (1998: vi). Sacred places may be both sacred and non-sacred in different respects or circumstances. One could argue that a mosque is per se not more sacred than any other building – at least not in the Christian sense of the word. With regard to churches, mosques are not consecrated spaces by a ritual performed by a specialist. Yet Muslims speak of a mosque as being 'sacred', since it is a set-apart space for prayer, in which one is not allowed to enter without ablution. It is thus specific, temporal, restricted, ritual practices that demarcates the mosque as a sacred place, and marks it off as separate from sites of mundane activities. Mosques are places of prayer, but also social, political, often even economical centers, where people can meet and go on with their business. The mosque is also the place for travelling for homeless Muslims, a place, where one could relax or discuss important issues. The ascription of sacredness to a mosque by Muslims is in general multivalent and has to be analyzed though its simultaneous, fluctuating and conflict-laden processes, that take into account both mundane and sacred imaginations.

Eric Ross, for example, illustrates in his contribution to this volume the distinctiveness of the spatial design of urban spaces by the Murid Sufi Order in Senegal. One of his main points is that the primary association of urban design with Islam has been rather accidental. Since the dominant grid model of urban space is predominantly organized around the palatial compound of the *Shaykh*, these places are not just places of proper religion, but primary paragons of community-building which generate and represent a larger political order. Since this specific design was applied to political and not religious places, their 'sacredness' becomes the expression of a larger field of authority, nobility and identity.

Another example is the role of shrines for their communities. For example, despite all the lamentation of decline and disappearance of Islamic saint tradition – often related to notions of 'disenchantments' and to debates about reform – saint veneration is still a lively religious practice in many Muslim societies, as presented by many of the contributions in this volume. Karin Willemse sheds light on how a *shaykh* conquered the cityscape through inscribing it with a new moral and cultural meaning. Based on her research in the Sudanese tripartite metropolis of Omdurman/Khartoum/Bahri, she elaborates on the marking of spaces as sacred through movements of the *shaykh*, while at the same time these marked spaces constitute the individual as a *shaykh*. These spaces are interlocking sacred spaces, corporeal, virtual and imagined, and they 'reach out' to other imagined religious communities via travel or internet. However, the *zawiya* remain a central place where the triadic relation of practice (*zikr*), people (Sufi adherents guided by a *shaykh*) and place form an interactive sacralized space as performative force.

The reasons for the continuity (which is not unbroken) of saint veneration could be manifold. One important point might be that saints and their veneration are appropriated in everyday life. In particular, the individual characteristics ascribed to these individuals do not reflect an Islamic theology, but rather worldly needs and cosmological images of Muslims. That means that most practices of saint veneration are embedded in or related to culturally specific patterns, sometimes agricultural rituals and seasons. This kind of relationship leads to a close identification with the place of the saint, who lived, acted, and finally died at the spot of veneration as ancestor, neighbor, teacher, political leader, spiritual advisor, friend or foe. These variations are culturally specific but they offer a point of view which cannot be grasped by a rather narrow definition of sacredness, which reflects a transcendental reality beyond Muslim practices and their everyday life.

In most non-Western cultures, matters of the sacred and the mundane are inextricably interwoven and very difficult to separate. The sociologist Meredith McGuire (2008) argues that sacredness has its source in the everyday life of people. Most individuals select, interpret and use cultural resources in their everyday life in different manners. Accordingly, their definition of religion is not analogous to a theological one. There is no clear-cut boundary which separates practices of being sacred from those which are not. In other words, the cleaning of the house and body before Ramadan is not scientifically appreciated as a sacred act, although the fasting or nightly recitations of the Qur'an during the month definably are perceived as such. McGuire tries to link an everyday sacredness to the influence of reformers who, later on, drew tidy boundaries around the sacred, in order to protect it from pollution by the profane. Those protections also served to make the sacred less accessible to ordinary people. One key feature for the definition and exclusivity of these places has been the plethora of embodied practices by which people relate to the sacred (McGuire 2007).

Georg Stauth (this volume) underlines in the making of places a process where the endeavor of everyday needs and religious purity are intrinsically connected. Focusing on the symbolic and material role of Pharaonic spoils in mosques and shrines of towns in the Nile Delta of Egypt, he shows that the relationship of Muslims towards those objects are more complex than the pure juxtaposition of belief and Islamic law. While some urban communities have a rather positive cultural attitude towards these objects, others are intolerant – they suppress them as pre-Islamic survivals or neglect them as relics of the past. These different understandings of integration or exclusion are the reflection of different and complex modes of authentification, be it a scientific appropriation, purification or integration of the spoils as forms of everyday life and customary behavior.

His contribution shows that rather than defining what the sacred in Islam *is*, the focus should be on the "ideals and aspirations people express and the everyday lives they live", which are "characterized by complexity, ambiguity, reflectivity, openness, frustration and tragedy" (Schielke 2010: 2). This perspective on

Muslim everyday life coincides with the imagination of urban life as an inherently ambiguous condition. In his classical observation *The Metropolis and Mental Life* (1969), Simmel argued that urban life is often associated with deeply ambivalent meanings and evaluations. Urban life may relate to anonymity, individualism, anomie, isolation, shattered dreams, exclusion, exploitation, state control and danger. At the same time urban life could represent diversity, visions and dreams, tolerance, public sphere, cosmopolitan milieus, integration, networks, higher education, (assumed) freedom and cultural creativity (Simmel 1969).

The underlying uncertainty of urban life mirrors the difficulties in conceptualizing urbanism by social sciences. There have been a number of theoretical attempts to generalize urban conditions. However, according to Canclini (1997), all these studies failed in developing a relatively operational definition to further the investigations of urban life. Canclini primary refers to common theories at the beginning of the 20th century, like the confrontation of urban with rural life, implying a dichotomy of primary relations of community life and secondary relations of segmented roles in cities. Similarly, the definition of urbanism as a way of life as proposed by the Chicago School is not satisfactory, since the spatial focus on size, density, and heterogeneity neglect historic and social processes. The third approach has used economic criteria to define urbanism as an outcome of industrial development and the concentration of capital. However, the economic point of view misses cultural aspects and everyday urban life.

These conceptualizations mainly failed because they searched for archetypical conditions and a universally valid theory of urban life. They are characterized by a relentless drift towards an abstract definition of the 'City' which neglects specific historical and cultural settings. Cities are shaped by a diverse set of processes, which are dependent on factors that are unique to individual cities, like their spatial structure, economic activities, and diversity of social groups, size, or position in relation to networks of cities. Any city, therefore, becomes a very specific mode of social organization, a specificity which should be analyzed against their specific historical, political and socio-economic background.

Each of the papers in this volume is concerned with exploring how Muslims negotiate life-worlds in their very specific urban setting. Many contributions underline the field of tension between Muslims' claims to live according to a Muslim society ordered according to the principles dictated by God on the one hand, and on the other hand, to urban conditions which may contradict the aspiration for a 'proper Muslim life'. Katharina Zöller, for example, argues that Muslims in colonial Dar es Salaam transformed a 'public space' into a 'sacred place' where diverse Muslim groups presented themselves as one group in public during Islamic festivals. At the same time, the act of place-making revealed diverging ideas on religious praxis and existing tensions between the festival participants. The transformation of a public space was the prerequisite for the emergence of a public arena, where the different actors involved raised issues concerning the underlying racial and economical divisions of Dar es Salaam's Muslims in urban everyday life as well as religious practice and the common good of the Muslim community. Dorothea Schulz, on the other hand, pleads to include the unexplored aural dimensions of Muslim urban experience as a key element by which religious places are made and unmade. Female supports of Islamic moral renewal in San/Mali seek to control their daily urban environment by creating places that are conducive to their ethical endeavor. Listening to 'moral lessons' provided by the leaders of Muslim women's neighborhood groups became a regular practice of place-making, which fuels already existing controversies over religious authority. Furthermore, Jörn Thielmann focuses on the ban on Muslims from using a chapel's room at a German university that resulted in an agitated correspondence between the representative of a Muslim group, the Church and the administration of the university. Claiming the right to pray at a secular university, the representative of Muslims fiercely challenged both administration and Church on the grounds of making a place for inter-religious encounters.

Urban everyday life may be, but is not necessarily, linked to resistance, subversion – in other words, power. This volume takes the situational and individualistic character of everyday life and their social actors as a starting point, a life which is also influenced by the struggle for economic means, frustrations, love, boredom or fun. Each chapter discusses the relationship between Muslims' place-making and urban everyday lives, both through historical or contemporary perspectives. The variety of socio-cultural contexts and the variety of approaches adopted in these chapters reflect the ambiguities of religious, social, political and economic meanings ascribed to places of 'sacred' significance within diverse Muslim communities. Paying attention to making places as constructed (materiality), imagined (cognition) and lived (everyday life) allows us to shed light on the common ground and differences of Muslim societies and cultures.

REFERENCES

Abu-Lughod, Lila (1989): "Zones of Theory in the Anthropology of the Arab World", in: Annual Review of Anthropology 18, pp. 267-306.
Agnew, John A. (2005): "Space: Place", in: P.J. Cloke and R.J. Johnston (Eds.), Spaces of Geographical Thought. Deconstructing Human Geography's Binaries, London: Sage, pp. 81-96.

AlSayyad, Nezar and Castells, Manuel (2002): Muslim Europe or Euro-Islam. Politics, Culture, and Citizenship in the Age of Globalization, Lanham: Lexington Books.

Appadurai, Arjun (1986): "Theory in Anthropology. Center and Periphery", in: Comparative Studies in Society and History 28:2, pp. 356-361.

(1988): "Putting Hierarchy in its Place", in: Cultural Anthropology 3:1, pp. 36-49.

Barrett, Paul M. (2007): American Islam. The Struggle for the Soul of a Religion, New York: Farrar Straus and Giroux.

Bennett, Clinton (1994): "Islam", in: J. Holm and J. Bowker (Eds.), Sacred Place, London: Pinter, pp. 88-114.

(2005): Muslims and Modernity. An Introduction to the Issues and Debates, London: Continuum.

Bowen, John (2004): "Does French Islam have Borders? Dilemmas of Domestication in a Global Religious Field", in: American Anthropologist 106:1, pp. 43-55.

Canclini, Néstor García (1997): "Urban Cultures at the End of the Century. The Anthropological Perspective", in: International Social Science Journal 49:153, pp. 345-356.

Casey, Edward (1996): "How to get from Space to Place in a Fairly Short Stretch of Time", in: S. Feld and K.H. Basso (Eds.), Senses of Place, Santa Fe: School of Americal Research, pp. 13-52.

Chidester, David, and Linenthal, Edward Tabor (Eds.) (1995): American Sacred Space, Bloomington: Indiana University Press.

Cresswell, Tim (2001): "The Production of Mobilities", in: New Formations 43, pp. 11-25.

Demerath III, N.J., et al. (1998): Sacred Companies. Organizational Aspects of Religion and Religious Aspects of Organizations, New York: Oxford University Press.

Durkheim, Emile (1976): The Elementary Forms of the Religious Life, London: Routledge.

Eickelman, Dale F. (1976): Moroccan Islam. Tradition and Society in a Pilgrimage Centre, Austin: University of Texas.

Eickelman, Dale F., and Anderson, Jon W. (1999): New Media in the Muslim world. The Emerging Public Sphere, Bloomington: Indiana University Press.

Eickelman, Dale F., and Piscatori, James (1990): Muslim Travellers. Pilgrimage, Migration, and the Religious Imagination, Berkeley: University of California Press.

el-Zein, Abdul Hamid (1977): "Beyond Ideology and Theology. The Search for the Anthropology of Islam", in: Annual Review of Anthropology 6, pp. 227-254.

Eliade, Mircea (1959): The Sacred and the Profane, New York: Harcourt Brace Jovanovich

Escobar, Arturo (2001): "Culture Sits in Places. Reflections on Globalism and Subaltern Strategies of Localization", in: Political Geography 20, p. 139-174.

Evans, Matthew T. (2003): "The Sacred. Differentiating, Clarifying and Extending Concepts", in: Review of Religious Research 45:1, pp. 32-47.

Ewing, Katherine P. (1988): Shari'at and Ambiguity in South Asian Islam, Berkley: University of California Press.

Falah, Ghazi-Walid, and Nagel, Caroline (Eds.) (2005): Geographies of Muslim Women. Gender, Religion, and Space, New York: Guilford Press.

Geertz, Clifford (1968): Islam Observed. Religious Development in Morocco and Indonesia, Chicago: University of Chicago Press.

Gellner, Ernest (1981): Muslim Society, Cambridge: Cambridge University Press.

Gieryn, Thomas F. (2000): "A Space for Place in Sociology", in: Annual Review of Sociology 26, pp. 463-496.

Göle, Nilüfer (1997): "The Gendered Nature of the Public Sphere", in: Public Culture 10:1, pp. 61-81.

(2002): "Islam in public. New Visibilities and New Imaginaries", in: Public Culture 14:1, pp. 173-190.

Grunebaum, Gustave E. von (1956): "The Problem. Unity in Diversity", in: G.E.v. Grunebaum, (Ed.), Unity and Variety in Muslim Civilization, Chicago: University of Chicago Press, pp. 17-37.

Gupta, Akhil, and Ferguson, James (1992): "Beyond 'Culture'. Space, Identity, and the Politics of Difference", in: Cultural Anthropology 7:1, pp. 6-23.

Harvey, David (2006): "The Political Economy of Public Space", in: Setha Low and Neil Smith (Eds.), The Politics of Public Space, London and New York: Routledge Chapman & Hall, pp.17-34.

Hauser-Schäublin, Brigitta (2003): "Raum, Ritual und Gesellschaft. Religiöse Zentren und sozio-religiöse Verdichtungen im Ritual", in: B. Hauser-Schäublin and M. Dickhardt (Eds.), Kulturelle Räume - Räumliche Kultur. Münster: LIT, pp. 43-87.

Ho, Engseng (2006): The Graves of Tarim. Genealogy and Mobility across the Indian Ocean, Berkley: University of California Press.

Jackson, Richard H., and Henrie, Roger (1983): "Perception of Sacred Space", in: Journal of Cultural Geography 3:2, pp. 94-107.

Jaret, Charles (1983): "Recent Neo-Marxist Urban Analysis", in: Annual Review of Sociology 9, pp. 499-525.

Lefebvre, Henri (1991 [1974]): The Production of Space, Oxford: Wiley-Blackwell.

Mahmood, Saba (2005): Politics of Piety. The Islamic Revival and the Feminist Subject, Princeton: Princeton University Press.

Marriott, McKim (1955): Village India. Studies in the Little Communities in an Indigeneous Civilization, Chicago: Chicago University Press.

Massey, Doreen (1991): "A Global Sense of Place", in: Marxism Today 35:6, pp. 24-29.

Masud, Muhammad Khalid (2000): Travellers in Faith. Studies of the Tabligh Jamaat as a Transnational Islamic Movement for Faith Renewal, Leiden: Brill.

Mauss, Marcel (2001): A General Theory of Magic, London: Routledge.

McGuire, Meredith B. (2007): "Sacred Place and Sacred Power. Conceptual Boundaries and the Marginalization of Religious Practices", in: P. Beyer and L. Beaman (Eds.), Religion, Globalization and Culture, Leiden: Brill, pp. 57-77.

(2008): Lived Religion. Faith and Practice in Everyday Life, Oxford: Oxford University Press.

Merleau-Ponty, Maurice (1962): Phenomenology of Perception, New York: Humanities Press.

Metcalf, Barbara Daly (Ed.) (1996): Making Muslim Space in North America and Europe, Berkeley: University of California.

Redfield, Robert (1955): "The Social Organisation of Tradition", in: The Far Eastern Quarterly 15:1, pp. 13-21.

Relph, Edward (1976): Place and Placenessless, London: Pion.

Rodman, Margaret C. (1992): "Empowering Place. Multilocality and Multivocality", in: American Anthropologist 94:3, pp. 640-656.

Rosander, Eva, and Westerlund, David (1997): African Islam and Islam in Africa. Encounters between Sufis and Islamists, London: Hurst.

Said, Edward W. (1978): Orientalism, London: Routledge.

Schielke, Samuli (2010): Second Thoughts about the Anthropology of Islam, or How to Make Sense of Grand Schemes in Everyday Life. http://www.zmo.de/publikationen/WorkingPapers/schielke_2010.pdf

Schimmel, Annemarie (1991): "Sacred Geography in Islam", in: J.S. Scott and P. Simpson- Housley (Eds.), Sacred Places and Profane Spaces. Essays in the Geographics of Judaism, Christianity, and Islam, Westport: Greenwoord Press, pp. 163-175.

Sheriff, Abdul (2010): Dhow Cultures and the Indian Ocean: Cosmopolitanism, Commerce, and Islam, New York: Columbia University Press.

Simmel, Georg (1969): "The Metropolis and Mental Life", in: R. Sennett, (Ed.), Classic Essays on the Culture of Cities, New York: Meredith, pp. 47-60.

Starrett, Gregory (1995): "The Hexis of Interpretation. Islam and the Body in the Egyptian Popular School", in: American Ethnologist 22:4, pp. 953-969.

Tuan, Yi-Fu (1974): Topophilia. A Study of Enviromental Perception, Attitudes and Values, New York: Columbia University Press.

 (1979): "Space and Place. A Humanistic Perspective", in: S. Gale and G. Olsson, (Eds.), Philosophy in Geography, Dordrecht: D. Reidel, pp. 387-427.

Turner, Victor (1967): The Forest of Symbols. Aspects of Ndembu Ritual, Ithaca: Cornell University.

(1969): The Ritual Process. Structure and Anti-Structure, Chicago: Aldine.

van Gennep, Arnold (1960 [1909]): The Rites of Passage, Chicago: University of Chicago.

Wallerstein, Immanuel (1976): The Modern World-System. Capitalist Agriculture and the Origins of the European World-Economy in the Sixteenth Century, New York: Academic Press.

Werbner, Pnina (1996): "Stamping the Earth with the Name of Allah. Zikr and the Sacralizing of Space among British Muslims", in: Cultural Anthropology 11:3, pp. 309-338.

PART I Un-/Making Places

Protecting and Selling the Mosque

Secular Salesmen's Pride and Fears in Tunis

SIMON HAWKINS

Gaining acceptance by the people with whom one works is one of the classical problems of ethnography. The Geertzian model of getting caught in a police raid, while impressive, is, as he admits, not generally available to all of us (Geertz 1972). To become accepted by the young men who work in the central plaza of Tunis' medina was a tricky task. Although one half of the plaza where they work is the wall of Zeintuna mosque, the spiritual heart of the city, the salesmen are a profane group, often boasting of their exploits with women and alcohol. These are not topics normally deployed by liberal assistant professors of a certain age, and I was not entirely sure how to construct my own identity in such a setting.

While I had done other work in Tunisia, the project in the medina was a new one for me. The plaza in front of Zeituna is a central feature of the medina, both geographically and symbolically. Various routes through the medina converge at the plaza bringing a rich assortment of passersby, foreign tourists, Tunisian shoppers, bureaucrats and workers on lunch break, worshippers at the mosque, and so on. Six or seven shops (I have changed identifying characteristics of individuals and specific locations) that cater to tourists and a coffee house line one side of the plaza. The men[1] who work there make up the nucleus of the community, although there are many more people who regularly spend time in the plaza and are acknowledged by the salesmen as part of the larger group. These additional members range from hustlers and black market moneychangers to government workers, coffee house regulars, and the occasional foreign language students. Given the eclecticism of the group, it is hardly surprising that I was

---

1   No women work in the plaza, although some women do work in other stores in the medina.

able to find a position within it during the summer of 2006 and the fall of 2007. My research was primarily participant observation. I arrived in the morning, sometimes helping set up some of the shops, sat on the steps of the mosque throughout the day with the rest of the men, and helped to close up shop in the evening.

While none of the salesmen were religiously observant, and they could treat the mosque at times with a callous disregard, still, in their frequent defense of it from boorish tourists, their occasional expressed admiration for it, and their eagerness to share it with others, it is clear that it was a sacred place to them. While its religious nature played a crucial part of its sacredness, also significant was its recognized historical and cultural importance, both nationally and globally. As a site that drew people from around the world, it marked the community as sophisticated and cosmopolitan, in contrast to more parochial perspectives. In order to preserve its sanctity, the salesmen needed to protect it from those who could not respect its values, either religious or cultural. This understanding of sacredness removes the concept from the strictly religious sphere and incorporates the more broad realm of emotional values, social relations, and community history (Chidester and Linenthal 1995; Evans 2003).

Founded in 703 CE, Zeituna has long occupied a central position in Tunisian religious, intellectual, and (more recently under colonialism), nationalist thought. In addition to being the most prominent mosque in the city, for centuries it was also a center of learning, attracting religious scholars from across North Africa and the Middle East. Because of this long and prominent history, it is a highlight of tours of the city, and prominent official visitors must make an obligatory trip to it. Visiting observant Muslims also find power in its antiquity and come to pray within it. While the whole medina is recognized by the United Nations as a World Heritage cultural site, it is the most prominent monument in the medina. The behavior of the tourists covers a wide range of practices. Some are genuinely interested in the mosque and its history. Many, however, seem to treat it as a required, but not very interesting, stop on their tour of Tunis and view it with an air of disregard and indifference. In the eyes of the salesmen, many of the tourists are rude and ill-mannered, and the tourists' indifference to the mosque only confirms this assumption.

While the mosque is a functioning religious institution, filling up for Friday prayers and ritually important events, the state maintains it as a museum piece as much as anything else. The central courtyard and prayer hall are only generally accessible during times of prayer and it does not function as a communal gathering point or public forum. This is in keeping with the state's efforts to modernize Islam, developing it at as a religion focused on private individual worship rather than communal integration into daily life (Hawkins 2011). While state run media feature many images of Zeituna, often this is alongside images of Roman and Punic ruins, emphasizing the importance of the mosque as a historic, rather than religious site, and drawing connections between the mosque and internationally important civilizations.

My social identity was particularly awkward early in my first field trip, as the young men, mostly in their early twenties, tried to get a sense of me. In the midst of one general conversation one of the dominant young men in the group pressed me on my how much I could drink. Specifically, what was my record for cans of beers? I tried to demure, but he pushed. He was really quite curious about an American's drinking capacity. I tried to explain the nature of faculty potluck parties, where there is a mixture of food and drink, making precise measurements tricky. To make my point, I listed the various kinds of alcohol that might be present, and my desire to be clear made the volume of my voice rise, as I recounted the various options. To my surprise and embarrassment, my list was met with great displeasure, not for its content, but for its volume. I was criticized for speaking so loudly and openly about alcohol on the steps of the mosque. Such behavior was unacceptable. I had not picked up on the fact until then that the conversation had been conducted in low tones with minimal expressive body language. It never occurred to me that these seemingly profane young men would worry about protecting the sanctity of the mosque, but indeed they did. While they were explicitly clear that they did not practice their faith (beyond chasing women and drinking alcohol, they certainly did not pray), they deeply valued the mosque and actively defended it from inappropriate intrusions as particularly embodied by the throngs of often-rude tourists. However, at the same time as they were ostensibly protecting the mosque, they were simultaneously marketing it.

While integrating commercial concerns into the mosque is certainly nothing extraordinary, indeed as the preeminent public space, mosques have long been associated with markets and trade, for both the surrounding community and pilgrims from afar (Pinto 2007), the Zeituna example is distinct from this long-standing practice. Normally, the customary inclusion of the commercial in the mosque is focused on worshippers. In this instance, however, the commercialism is directed at those who are excluded from the mosque, rather than those who are included. Rather than the mosque operating as a public space in which individuals and groups can carry out their business, in this instance it is the mosque itself, or rather, views of the mosque that are being marketed. This shares qualities with the marketing of pilgrimages, but again, the crucial difference is that pilgrims may enter the site, while the tourists are always kept at a remove.

These seemingly contradictory activities of marketing the mosque to tourists while also keeping the tourists out highlight the paradoxical nature of its constructed sacredness and their own identity. They positioned it, and themselves along with it, as simultaneously local and global. Indeed, following on the lead of the Comaroffs, the very localness of the mosque – occupying the heart of the medina, itself, the nucleus of a nation stretching back thousands of years – helps create its power as a global cultural entity, and as such a marketable commodity. That is, while it is crucially grounded in the local, its recognition by the larger global community helps demonstrate its sacred power. For the tourists, Zeituna represents an exotic, alien culture. To them it is not part of the imagined homogenous, modern, interconnected world, but rather a symbol of a community that has preserved its identity and difference. As such a symbol, it shares a stage with the other World Heritage sites around the globe, as important manifestations of local culture, they are held to have a global significance.

Their defense of the mosque helped position and define the salesmen in relation to the mosque and to the tourists. This was not a case of protecting a local institution from outsiders, as the mosque was acknowledged as a site that drew interested parties from around the world. The mosque is not protected from outsiders generally, or even simply non-Muslims, but from boorish, unsophisticated tourists who do not understand its significance and appreciate its value. The defense of the mosque constructs the tourists as parochial figures who cannot understand and respect the values of a foreign culture, making the merchants themselves more sophisticated and cosmopolitan. In this context, the identity of local vs. cosmopolitan is not so much a spatial referent as an attitudinal one. The cosmopolitan is marked by an openness to and engagement with the broader world, while the local is primarily attached to standards and mores of their immediate sphere. Thus, the salesmen may style themselves as cosmopolitan because of their engagement with the diverse international populations passing through the medina and characterize the tourists as mere locals who, although they may travel from their home, do not truly engage with other cultures or peoples.

In many ways, Zeituna creates a divide between the two categories (certainly a building may not be said to have attitudes, but its symbolic associations are linked to attitudes and relationships). On the one hand it is a key symbol of Tunisian national identity, an image of the nation for Tunisians. On the other, its antiquity and historic ties give it an international significance. While the tourists may view the mosque as exotic and separate from the interconnected globe, for the salesmen, much of its power stems from its historic and contemporary connections to the wider world. As a sacred place it is cosmopolitan, with ties that span the centuries and the continents. The salesmen embrace this worldly sacredness. They aspire to similarly sophisticated cosmopolitan perspective, suggesting that their construction of it as a sacred cosmopolitan place is also a construction of their own identity. They demonstrate their cosmopolitan knowledge by performing their understanding of the many foreign cultural groups that parade through the plaza. As with all cosmopolitans, the salesmen's identity depends on a contrast with parochial locals (Hannerz 1990), and in their eyes the tourists fit the role of parochial locals admirably. From the salesmen's perspectives, the tourists have very little knowledge about or interest in the world. The salesmen see the tourists as confined within their own cultural bubble, refusing to actually adapt to the world they travel through (Hawkins 2009). Still, the presence of so many visitors helps establish the importance of the place on the global stage, proving that it is important to the world beyond Tunisia. While such an importance marks the place as different from more mundane sites, suggesting a form of sacredness, the presence of Muslim visitors from around the globe, proves the mosque's more straightforward religious sacredness.

While the salesmen's construction of the mosque as sacred draws on its engagement with global cosmopolitan networks, there is a parallel to this experience of sacredness that is more explicitly religious. Suggesting a 'parallel cosmopolitanism' requires a clear definition of an unmarked cosmopolitanism with which it can be contrasted. As Hannerz (2004) concluded, most usage of the term cosmopolitan divides into two distinct, but related categories: that of the individual who wanders the world, but has little sense of a fixed, stable, local culture, and the individual who is ideologically committed to thinking about policy issues on a global scale, eschewing local forms of affiliation. While this later category tends to be used by authors advocating world views (Appiah 2006; Nussbaum 1994) and the former by ethnographers describing groups (Frohlick 2007; Tsing 2005), the two share a sense that, for all its linkages to Greek antiquity, cosmopolitanism is a particularly modern, secular, sophisticated phenomenon. And indeed, much of the contemporary debate about defining cosmopolitanism turns on the extent that it can be defined as an elite phenomenon, as more scholars describe non-elites that fit the description of cosmopolitan (Diouf 2000; Werbner 2006). Nor is this focus on elitism merely the preserve of scholars, as the subjects being studied may also view a cosmopolitan identity in aspirational terms (Ferguson 1999; Weiss 2002). The salesmen's vision of themselves as cosmopolitan, with the aspirational components, draws heavily on their construction of the mosque as a sacred site whose sacredness itself draws on its engagement with cosmopolitan networks.

As more and more groups describe themselves, or are described by observers, as cosmopolitan, there is danger that the term becomes so vague as to be meaningless. In particular, the terms 'cosmopolitan' 'global', and 'transnational' seem at risk of melding into each other. While obviously there is overlap between the categories, what distinguishes 'cosmopolitan' from the others here is self-conscious attitude. The cosmopolitan actively constructs him or herself as a participant with other groups around the world and distinct from locals who remain bound by their specific circumstances and culture. By contrast 'globalization' notes the engagement with global systems and networks, potentially even involuntarily or unknowingly. Cosmopolitanism is a form of differentiation based not so much on practices as beliefs and self-image. It is also always relative. Because the term depends on comparison with a presumed local, any given individual or group that might define itself as cosmopolitan in relation to some set of locals, might well be viewed as locals by separate groups establishing their own cosmopolitan identities. In the example of the mosque, the tourists and merchants each define themselves as cosmopolitans in contrast to the others' localness (Hawkins 2009). This essay suggests, however, that while the contrast with locals is necessary for a cosmopolitan identity, some forms of identity can simultaneously draw on a cosmopolitan and local identity, as groups project their specific localness into a global realm of similar forms of local identity. That is, there is an explicit awareness of the position of the specific local in a global network of other locals, requiring a sophisticated awareness of other forms of culture and patterns. This clearly draws on the Comaroffs' (2009) discussion of the marketing of regional ethnicity on the global stage, which requires both a celebration of the particular culture and an awareness of its position in the global market that values such markers of ethnicity because it views them as occupying the global margins. This is related to also Wilk's discussion of "structures of common difference" (1995: 115).

Further complicating an understanding of cosmopolitan as a category is the possibility that, as with modernity (Gaonkar 2001), there are, and have been, multiple forms of cosmopolitanism (Mignolo 2000). The traditional vision of cosmopolitanism is of a secular category, insofar as cosmopolitan is seen as eschewing parochial interests and requiring a form of cultural relativism sometimes seen as inimical to religion. However some groups within religions with global aspirations can and do have many of the characteristics associated with cosmopolitans (Diouf 2000). To speak of a worldwide Christian or Muslim community is not to suggest homogenous entities, but rather groups that embrace the cultural diversity within a global community[2].

---

2   This is not to say that Christianity or Islam are inherently cosmopolitan. Certainly there are groups within each religion that do strive for homogeneity.

As my status in the plaza changed, so too did my relationship with the mosque, such that I was no longer a figure that the mosque needed to be protected from, but was allowed and even encouraged to enter. It is by patrolling admission to the mosque that the salesmen most actively protect it. According to the rules posted on an often-overlooked weathered notice board, non-Muslims are never allowed entry to the prayer hall proper, nor to the central courtyard. Upon payment of a four-dinar entry fee (a bit less than four dollars), they may enter an outside colonnade and visit part of one of the internal colonnades that rings the courtyard. However, during prayers, they are forbidden entry to any part of the mosque. Patrolling these regulations is tricky, as Muslims can enter at any time without paying an admission fee, and the ticket seller sitting at a rickety table near the entrance is not always sure whether the camera toting visitor is a tourist who must pay or a Muslim who does not have to, even if he or she is also a tourist.

In general, he assumes that anyone who appears to him to be Arabic is Muslim, but he is aware that while this method works fairly well, it inevitably makes mistakes. Occasionally he will demand payment from a presumed non-Muslim, who then invokes an Islamic identity. These are always slightly awkward interactions, and I have never known him to challenge the credentials of anyone claiming an Islamic identity. Sometimes visiting Muslims would be offended by the exclusion of non-Muslims and argue that mosques should be open to all. The caretaker would give an embarrassed shrug and remind them that he did not make the rules. The salesmen on the steps outside are less concerned with the subtle distinctions. They do not care about the ambiguous cases, but the clear-cut ones, the shorts and tank-top wearing, sunburned, and confusedly peering around obvious tourists.

The treatment of the tourists depends on their behavior. The tourist who wanders toward the entrance during prayers will be politely called out to. Frequently this is all that is needed. Often, however, the tourists continue as if they had heard nothing. Perhaps they did not. Or perhaps they had developed the habit of not listening when Tunisians call out to them, thinking that it is just another attempt to sell something. Whatever the case, such a non-response elicits more direct action. Someone will jump up and actively pursue the errant group, shouting that they are not allowed in. The comparatively polite, informative tone is replaced with a more definitive statement. "You can't go in there." This monitoring is a general community responsibility. If the first person to call out is not that close, someone more nearby may leap up to confront the interlopers.

The goal of keeping the tourists out is not one of privacy, of keeping prayers secret from prying eyes. Those tourists who behave well will be directed, often with great care and politeness, to establishments with roofs that overlook the courtyard. The issue is not that tourists may not see worship, but that the crass tourists are themselves polluting, not because of their lack of faith, but because of their lack of sophistication. While the salesmen work to preserve and define the mosque's sacredness, it is clear that the tourists also play a role in defining the place and that this is both valuable and threatening to the salesmen. While the interest and engagement of tourists helps demonstrate Zeituna's importance, there is also the chance that tourists may cheapen the mosque. If the mosque becomes the preserve of poorly behaved tourists from marginal areas (Poles are held in particularly low regard by the salesmen) then it loses something of its allure, both in religious terms, but also as a marker of globally important cultural heritage. Given that the salesmen draw some of their identity from the mosque, a redefined mosque threatens their own identity, potentially cheapening them. There is then, a flip side to protecting the mosque from boorish tourists, which is encouraging appropriate ones. As noted above the salesmen will take careful pains to direct tourists to viewing areas from which to survey the mosque's courtyard.

Some Muslim visitors to Tunisia are offended by the exclusion of visitors to the mosques, arguing that this is not in keeping with the traditions of Islam. However, the community in the plaza defends the practice. A mosque official, sitting in the coffee house with me one evening brought up the topic and defended the rule, arguing that tourists should be excluded as they did not show proper reverence. That is, the tourists are the parochial locals who do not appreciate or understand a religion that is different from their own. They do not give it the respect they would accord a sacred place in their own community. The members of the plaza community, then, construct themselves as more cosmopolitan by contrast, navigating between their own culture and those of the various tourists, enacting their own understanding and appreciation of different groups. While the salesmen do not travel, and therefore do not have the chance to demonstrate respect of other people's sacred places, their claims of understanding and appreciation signal a belief in the importance of respecting the values of other cultures, and by extension, the places considered to be sacred in those cultures. Whether or not the salesmen would actually act with great respect is not clear, but the contrast they assert between themselves and the tourists makes the claim that the salesmen's behavior would be better. It is part of the identity they construct for themselves.

Absent the tourists who must be excluded from the mosque, the salesmen's relationship to the space is hardly one of profound respect or even interest. While the mosque draws worshippers from around the Muslim world, the salesmen rarely enter for any reason, and certainly do not pray. On their own, the salesmen can show far less respect to the place than the tourists. After all, my sin in talking about alcohol on the steps was not so much the subject matter of the conversation as the volume. The salesmen felt no compunction against talking about alcohol as long as they kept their voices down. One slow afternoon when the tourists had disappeared, an impromptu soccer game started up, using the exterior wall of the mosque as a backstop, with the ball frequently almost bouncing in. Eventually a passing police officer put an end to their games, and they were lectured for not respecting the mosque. When they needed to hang a makeshift awning in front of the shops because the tiled one collapsed, several of the younger salesmen swarmed the columns in the colonnade, stringing ropes across the plaza for pulling up the tarpaulin awning and treating it more like useful scaffolding than a revered place.

For the salesmen, the sacredness of the place becomes particularly salient in the context of interactions with outsiders, whether they be boorish tourists or potentially more appropriate anthropologists. Absent any outsiders, the place becomes far more mundane. This stands in marked contrast to those Tunisians who engage with it as a site of religious worship, for whom it is more consistently sacred. If sacredness is marked by a contrast with the profane, for the salesmen, this profanity is found in tourists, while for the religiously observant, the profanity is found in the non-religious realm, including the salesmen, who religiously minded Tunisians view as vulgar and unsophisticated.

Over time, even I was allowed to violate the mosque's purity. My missteps when discussing alcohol came early in my fieldwork. An incident that occurred later during on suggested that my status had changed. After Friday prayers one afternoon, I heard a bright conversation in the mosque colonnade above the steps where we were sitting. Two young women in *hijab* were looking out over the crowd, talking about the passing throng. They noticed me looking at them and a conversation developed which, at its beginning, seemed like one of the many conversations I have had regarding who I am and what my work in Tunisia addresses. This took an odd turn though, as it involved much giggling on their part and rather unusual questions, such as how old I was. To my mortification, I realized that the conversation seemed to have turned into a flirtation. However, in this instance, rather than begin shocked at my behavior, the young men who had censured me about alcohol were egging me on. It was not that flirtation was any less forbidden. A passing clerical official was outraged at the behavior. The difference was that, having become a quasi-member of the salesmen's community, I was permitted a certain amount of license.

When examining the exclusion of tourists from the mosque, it is tempting to see this as driven by an understanding of the mosque as a private space that stood in contrast to the obviously public character of the plaza. But of course, mosques in general are quintessential public spaces and members of the community treated it as such, sometimes lounging in its shaded colonnades to escape the heat. While on the face of it, this casualness might suggest a view of the place as non-sacred, but this lounging carries an element of separation and distinction. The salesmen can lounge there; they could come and go to the colonnade as they pleased. The tourists, however, did not have such a luxury. They had to purchase a ticket and were viewed as alien visitors. However, for all that it is a useful space for the salesmen, it is not a completely open public space. The salesmen men rest there on occasion, but they do not carry out their business there. It is also controlled by the state, and it is not a place for commerce. It is among the locations featured heavily in state television evocations of the nation and in many ways must be treated with care as a monument of the nation. In discussing the mosque, the salesmen draw on this nationalist component of its identity, depending on the context. For example when discussing the United States, many Tunisians, both in the plaza and beyond, referred to the relative youth of the United States as a nation, particularly compared to Tunisia. A couple of times salesmen in the plaza made the comparison physical, by referring to Zeituna, whose colonnade uses salvaged Roman columns. In such a comparison, the religious nature of the space is not nearly as important as its antiquity and links to the nation. At other times, they emphasized its spiritual importance, sometimes explicitly making connections beyond national boundaries. For example, when the mosque hosted the exams of students learning to recite the Qur'an (to be discussed further, below), the merchants described it to me with pride, drawing particular attention to the fact that examiners were an international panel of preeminent Qur'anic reciters. While this certainly emphasized Zeituna's importance beyond the immediate Tunisian nation, it did so in a specifically religious context that was distinct from, although not opposed to, its importance as a world heritage site, which chiefly focused on its historic and cultural importance.

Although there is a range of definitions of 'cosmopolitan' in both popular and academic discourse, the various understandings do share a sense of both secularism and modernity. The relativism of the globe trotting cosmopolitan seems to fit poorly with the normative demands of a bounded religion. And yet global religions, such as Islam, may invoke a cosmopolitan identity in which local variations are regarded as trivial in the face of much larger identifying attributes. The conception of a community of believers, the *umma*, invokes a cosmopolitanism quite at odds with the standard Western model. At some level the idea of the *umma* invokes an Andersonian imagined community (1991), insofar as it depends on the vision of a community that has never and can never meet or interact, but exists only to the extent that it is imagined by members of the group. But of course, the imagined *umma* predates Anderson's national print capitalists. Rather, this is the imagining of Durkhemian religious communities who experience collective effervescence in the execution of religious rituals (1995). While Durkheim (the seemingly uncited inspiration for Anderson's imaginings) would point out that religious rituals and sacred spaced tend to invoke the massive community of believers, some spaces do this more or less than others. There are, in the medina, many smaller neighborhood mosques that draw on a more specific, bounded community. While the actual rituals in such mosques create a connection to the global community of believers, the mosques themselves are more anchored in their specific neighborhoods. Zeituna, by contrast, always evokes larger associations. It is not a mosque of the neighborhood, but of the nation. On significant dates, important government officials will publicly pray there, and images of the mosque are frequently broadcast on national television. When describing to other Tunisians where I was doing my fieldwork, every one of them knew exactly where I was based. Beyond the national, however, a parade of distinguished and mundane international visitors come to the mosque to pray. The international religious prestige of the mosque is crucial to its national power and prestige.

This internationalism was, not coincidentally, highlighted during my own entrance to the mosque. The caretaker had previously allowed me free entry to the tourist areas. We had many conversations during the long, dull stretches of the day, and it was a companionable thing to do. But that was quite different from admission to the mosque proper. Several people, including the caretaker, said that I should visit the mosque, that I would get a lot out of it, but I understood this to be an indirect reference to a hoped for conversion. One week, however, the regular routine of the mosque was held in abeyance for the yearly examination of aspiring Qur'an reciters. An impressively distinguished panel of judges from around the Muslim world was assembled to test the students' memorization and recitational skills. Loudspeakers set up at the mosque's entrance broadcast the recitations, and while the salesmen did not actively listen to them, they expressed great pleasure at the event. In the afternoon, an official at the mosque with whom I drank coffee (indeed, the same one who defended the exclusion of tourists from the mosque) came out to find me and invite me into the mosque to listen to the exams in person. This might have been a simple gesture of friendship, like the caretaker's, but along the way he introduced me to more senior officials at the mosque, who were in turn quite welcoming of my presence. This was not mere friendship; this was an acknowledgement that I was not the sort of person who needed to be excluded from the mosque. Unlike the tourists, I had demonstrated the requisite cosmopolitan characteristics that would allow me to appreciate this place and activity.

When the oral exams had ended and I left the mosque, the salesmen in the plaza were eager to find out how I had enjoyed it and were quite pleased with my visit. And yet, none of them went themselves. While they deeply valued the mosque's existence, the mosque's religious values did not affect their existence. This was demonstrated clearly during Ramadan, when tourists who smoked or ate on the steps of the mosque were sometimes chastised for their lack of respect for the fasting Muslims around them. However the salesmen themselves sneaked cigarettes or cookies in the back of their stores. When I spotted them, they expressed no guilt or shame at having broken the fast, but only wry amusement at being caught. They readily defined themselves as non-practicing Muslims and felt no sense of spiritual or religious connection to the mosque.

Their encouraging me to enter the mosque, then, was not simply religious. Islam was the underpinning of its cultural (and hence capital) value, but its significance extended beyond religion. It was the defining element of both the physical space and the surrounding community. The salesmen invested in the place the values that they held to be important: a rooted connection to the region alongside an active engagement with the larger world, a respect for other cultures while still maintaining one's own values and beliefs. They ascribed characteristics to the place, but also drew their own identity from it. In the constant stream of outsiders passing through the plaza, it was the anchor that kept the community grounded. My admission to the mosque was not merely a matter of my good manners. Certainly there had been many other non-Muslims who had passed through who had displayed perfectly good behavior and a commitment to the cosmopolitan ideals exemplified by the mosque who were not invited in. It is not trivial that it was during my return trip to the plaza that I was invited in. By coming back after my first visit, I demonstrated a commitment to the plaza that distinguished me from the many visitors who spent time there, but never returned. Indeed, in addition to being invited into the mosque, I was introduced to other prominent members of the plaza community who had always been excluded from me during my first trip. My admission to the mosque was linked to this admission to more prominent social groups in the plaza; the group considered me to be importantly affiliated with the community. As such, to exclude me from the mosque would have run against the grain of the values of the community. This context emphasized its importance as a local institution, a key component of the surrounding community.

As should be clear, however, the community's self image is itself built on a cosmopolitan identity. While I was certainly not a 'real' member of the community, the community itself demonstrated an ideology of cosmopolitan inclusiveness that was at odds with broader Tunisian ideologies of linking one to region. For example, one afternoon a discussion broke out among the salesmen about where they were from. One of the group said that he was from Tunis. The others argued against this, asking where he was born. "Tunis," he replied. "Well sure," they said, "but where were your parents born?" "Tunis." "Oh. But what about your grandparents?" "Tunis." "Ah, well I guess you really are from Tunis." Only generations of habitation authenticated a claim to Tunis as a whole. However, at another times the group described itself as "sons of the medina," a far more specific claim. While they could not all claim identity with Tunis the city, they could with the medina, the heart of Tunis. For indeed, they had grown up there and were thoroughly integrated into it. To be a son of the medina, one did not have to be born into it, unlike the rest of Tunisia, where identity came from one's forbearers. With Zeituna at its heart, the medina embraces a cosmopolitanism into its identity. With the stream of diverse people moving through, and occasionally settling, to be a local is to be cosmopolitan and the cosmopolitan can become a local.

By creating the mosque as a cosmopolitan space, they created the possibility of their own community. While they might be outsiders to Tunis, forever pushed to the margins, a cosmopolitan Zeituna allowed them to occupy the center. Over the centuries, Zeituna has been deeply associated with the elite of Tunis and the state[3]. While the salesmen's particular construction of the mosque as a sacred place drew from the contemporary state's definition of the place and the nation as cosmopolitan and sophisticated, the salesmen's appropriation of these characteristics challenged the state's exclusion and erasure of undereducated underemployed men from rural regions. Further, the salesmen's strong connection to the mosque and inclusion of secular, nationalist components in defining its sacredness challenges the perspective of assertively devout Muslims who view its sacredness in purely religious terms. The contestation of what marks and defines the place as sacred is bound up in the varying social relations and encounters (Massey 1991).

The community took pride in its openness, and I was not the only outsider who was folded into the community. During the Ramadan evenings, other dis-

---

3   While historically it offered the chance for social mobility for educated young men from Tunisia's hinterland (Green 1978), the salesmen were far removed from such cultural capital. The mosque had not historically created prestige for men such as them before.

tinguished visitors were adopted into the group of coffee house regulars who held the prestigious and prominent corner table in the plaza. Ramadan was the time when the plaza was at its peak. The summer before, the salesmen had regaled me with tales of how the coffee house swelled to fill the plaza and people drank coffee and smoked *shisha* (waterpipe) all night long. If I wanted to know about the plaza, they told me, I had to come for Ramadan. The reality lived up to their descriptions. Ramadan was when the world came to the plaza, many to pray, but still more simply to spend time there[4]. It was the plaza at its most diverse, filled with Tunisians, but also visitors from many other countries. In particular though, this embraced the Muslim cosmopolitanism of the *umma*. It was a uniting of the Muslim global community, even if many of those present did not actively pray. This cosmopolitan *umma* intersected with the more classically secular cosmopolitanism, as various international non-Muslims were readily welcomed. Unlike the tourists, these other visitors distinguished themselves by a willingness to immerse themselves in Tunisian social life. In particular, those who came to the local coffee house after the breaking of the fast were viewed as participating in the social order and distinct from the tourists who might smoke or drink on the steps of the mosque during the day. Ramadan, then became the cosmopolitan height of plaza, and while protecting the mosque from tourists increased, it became generally more accessible to the non-Muslim cosmopolitans.

CONCLUSION

Zeituna's importance to the plaza community is as a symbol of their cultural patrimony, a symbol of the nation's identity and importance. Its importance also stems from its status as a nationally and internationally significant mosque. As a place, then, it is doubly sacred. While these different aspects may come into conflict for some groups – for example, assertively religious groups object to its use as a secular tourist attraction – for the salesmen in the plaza, these aspects are mutually reinforcing, marking it at a place unlike others. The fact that they readily market this sacred place in no way cheapens or demeans its status. Indeed, the marketing of it serves to mark its importance and international status. Their embrace of the selling of their cultural patrimony goes beyond the self-interest tied to the money that they make from the mosque's existence. When they happily

---

4   Those who did not pray were easy to note. When the post sunset call to prayer came, some coffee house clients rose to go to the mosque, but many more stayed where they were.

direct tourists to rooftop viewing stations where tourists can look down into the mosque's courtyard, they are actually sending the tourists to large stores that have constructed these panoramic vistas as a lure to customers. While the practice of kick-backs for directing tourists to stores is quite common in the medina, in this instance it does not come into play. Directing tourists to these overlooks is the community norm in the plaza. The guidance is not given grudgingly, but eagerly, despite the fact that tourists will end up in stores that are, in many ways, bitter rivals of the small shops in the plaza.

In short, marketing the mosque, marketing their cultural patrimony, becomes a symbol of pride. As the Comaroffs (2009) point out, regarding the broader practice of such marketing, it helps establish them as simultaneously global citizens and locals. The salesmen are very much aware of their existence in a global tourism market, discussing not only their broadly international clientele, but also how Tunisia is regarded globally and what kinds of tourists it attracts as a result. They see themselves as in competition with other vacation destinations around the world, such as Morocco and Egypt, but also Florida (in particular Disney World). As a key component of their cultural patrimony, Zeituna makes their participation in the global market possible. Their history is all that they can mobilize in response to the massive capital needed for luxurious tourist destinations. Interestingly they do not see themselves as in competition with, for example, the Island of Jerba, off the southern coast of Tunisia, which has luxury beach resorts and an international airport. They view the competition in nationalist terms, with the quality of the tourists reflecting Tunisia's standing on a global stage. What Tunisia, the medina, Zeituna, have that Disney, the United States, can never have is the physical connection to an ancient and revered history. Zeituna's physical embodiment of the national history, with columns salvaged from Roman ruins, in many ways overshadows its formal religious status in constructing it as a sacred place. The salesmen's participation as global citizens depends upon their assertion of elements of their national identity.

But is that local identity really so vulnerable that it needs to be protected? Is their patrolling of the mosque's boundaries really necessary? Indeed, the mosque has enough internal personnel to monitor its sanctity perfectly well. At some level, their efforts are protecting the tourists from the mosque – from the embarrassment of being formally asked to leave by mosque personnel – as much as protecting the mosque from the tourists. It seems odd that they should render as so dangerous and vulnerable something they seek to capitalize on. But of course, this threatening and threatened status is part of its exotic allure, part of its literal value to them. Turning people away makes it all the more valuable, both to those licensed to enter – certainly I was aware of the privilege I was granted in being invited inside – and those kept at a distance. Ultimately they are selling the chance to watch. The selling reinstantiates the distance. One can watch, but only from afar. They commodify the spectacle, but not the experience. Directing people to the panorama is not simply altruistic. The witnessing of the spectacle that cannot be purchased creates the desire for purchasing culture. One cannot buy admission to prayers, but one can buy a prayer rug. The commodification of culture here depends on this sacred and forbidden core that cannot itself be commodified.

What constitutes this identity and how it is solidified (or at least marketed) is mediated by various economic and cultural forces that themselves exist at both the local and global level. In the neo-liberal order described by the Comaroffs, ethnicity becomes one of the few commodities available to those without capital or natural resources. Of course, as they are quick to point out, not all groups even have access to a marketable ethnicity. While heritage sells, not all heritages sell equally, and groups must struggle to develop and define their particular brand. This branding occurs within the frame of global expectations of what marks authenticity and ethnicity. Wilk (1995) writes of working in Belize in the 1970's, and the absence of any sense of a Belizian identity or culture. Returning a few decades later he is surprised to discover an efflorescence of Belizian culture, marked by such clear commodities as food, clothing, and music. His argument is not so much that these markers of culture and tradition were recent inventions in the classic form (Hobsbawm and Ranger 1992), as that existed practices were reinterpreted to meet the need of Belizians for some form of national cultural marker. Forms of ethnic and cultural distinction become standardized into commodifiable entities, which among other things, makes cultural differences appear manageable and non-threatening. The value of cultural forms becomes directly quantifiable by the monetary value it represents. The money generated becomes a scorecard to compare cultural products and sacred places. In the logic of the plaza, if the global market does not recognize it, than a place cannot be truly considered sacred.

This simultaneous engagement with a local and cosmopolitan identity complicates traditional understandings of the sacred which rest on a dichotomy between the sacred local and the profane cosmopolitan. While certainly pilgrimage sites drew people from far and wide and were thus, at a geographic level, not local, the pilgrims nonetheless shared religious beliefs and found the pilgrimage experience to be unifying. This is a far cry from the experience of the cosmopolitan traveler who expects to encounter profound difference and not share in the system of beliefs that holds the site to be sacred. What makes the place sacred to the local is not, in this classic framework, what makes it valuable to the cosmopolitan, and visa-versa. In this instance, however, the two are mutually reinforc-ing. The cosmopolitan and local components cannot be untangled. The sales-men's very identity comes through this interaction. They construct their cosmo-politanism through the performance of localness. There is, of course, nothing ter-ribly unusual about the blending of spiritualism with commerce and making money from worshippers visiting from afar. Pilgrimage sites have long made money from the faithful flowing through. What makes this example different from the pilgrimage model is that in the plaza, neither the salesmen nor most of the tourists are faithful. While its spiritual religious nature is a crucial part of Zeituna's importance, most of those involved in the buying and selling around it make no pretense at being particularly affiliated with that component. The tour-ists come not to worship, but to be broadened, to bear witness to an exotic alien culture. To fulfill this goal, the salesmen consciously play up the role of the ex-otic, selling themselves as much as their wares (Hawkins 2009).

And yet, the mosque is not merely something to be packaged and sold. They both protect the mosque and direct tourists to viewing points, even when there is no immediate economic benefit o them. It is an object of pride to them. The very influx of tourists around the mosque reinforces their sense of its – and therefore their – importance, even if those tourists ultimately must be excluded from the mosque. Protecting the mosque creates a sense of affiliation with, and connec-tion to, it. It inverts the relationship with tourists, in which, rather than beseech-ing the passing foreigners to make a purchase, they can correct and direct the tourists. If Zeituna is strongly linked to the nation, then in defending the mosque they are defending the nation and ultimately defending themselves.

REFERENCES

Anderson, Benedict (1991): Imagined Communities. Reflections on the Origin and Spread of Nationalism, New York: Verso.

Appiah, Kwame Anthony (2006): Cosmopolitanism. Ethics in a World of Strangers, New York: W. W. Norton and Company.

Comaroff, Jean, and Comaroff, John (2009): Ethnicity, Inc, Chicago: University of Chicago Press.

Chidester, David and Linenthal, Edward (1995): "Introduction", in: David Chidester and Edward Linenthal (Eds.), American Sacred Space, Blooming-ton: Indiana University Press, pp.1-42.

Diouf, Mamadou (2000): "The Senegalese Murid Trade Diaspora and the Mak-ing of a Vernacular Cosmopolitanism", in: Public Culture 12:3, pp. 679-702.

Durkheim, Emile (1995): The Elementary Forms of the Religious Life, New York: Simon & Schuster.

Evans, Matthew (2003): "The Sacred. Differentiating, Clarifying and Extending Concepts.", in: Review of Religious Research 45:1, pp. 32-47.

Ferguson, James (1999): Expectations of Modernity. Myths and Meanings of Urban Life on the Zambian Copperbelt, Berkeley: University of California Press.

Frohlick, Sucan (2007): "Fluid Exchanges. The Negotiation of Intimacy between Tourist Women and Local Men in a Transnational Town in Caribbean Costa Rica", in: City & Society 19:1, pp. 139-168.

Gaonkar, Dilip Parameshwar (2001): "On Alternative Modernities", in: Dilip Parameshwar Gaonkar (Ed.), Alternative Modernities, Durham, North Carolina: Duke University Press.

Geertz, Clifford (1972): "Deep Play. Notes on the Balinese Cockfight", in: Daedalus, Journal of the American Academy of Arts and Sciences 101:1, pp. 1-38.

Green, Arnold (1978): The Tunisian Ulama: 1873-1915, Leiden: E.J. Brill.

Hannerz, Ulf (1990): "Cosmopolitans and Locals in World Culture", in: Mike Featherstone (Ed.), Global Culture. Nationalism, Globalization and Modernity, London: Sage, pp. 237-252.

(2004): "Cosmopolitan", in: David Nugent and Joan Vincent (Eds.), A Companion to the Anthropology of Politics, Oxford: Blackwell Publishing, pp. 69-85.

Hawkins, Simon (2011): "Who Wears *Hijab* with the President. Constructing a Modern Islam in Tunisia", in: Journal of Religion in Africa 41, pp. 35-58.

(2009): "Cosmpolitan Hagglers or Haggling Locals? Salesmen, Tourists, and Cosmopolitan Discourses in Tunis", in: City & Society 21:2, pp. 319-344.

Hobsbawm, Eric, and Ranger, Terence (1992): The Invention of Tradition, Cambridge: Cambridge University Press.

Massey, Doreen (1991): "A Global Sense of Place", in: Marxism Today 5:6, pp. 24-29.

Mignolo, Walter (2000): "The Many Faces of Cosmo-polis. Border Thinking and Critical Cosmopolitanism", in: Public Culture 12:3, pp. 721-748.

Nussbaum, Martha (1994): "Patriotism and Cosmopolitanism", in: Boston Review 19:5, pp. 3-34.

Pinto, Paulo (2007): "Pilgrimage, Commodities, and Religious Objectification. The Making of Transnational Shiism between Iran and Syria", in: Comparative Studies of South Asia, Africa, and the Middle East 27:1, pp. 109-125.

Tsing, Anna (2005): Friction. An Ethnography of Global Connection, Princeton: Princeton University Press.

Weiss, Brad (2002): "Thug Realism. Inhabiting Fantasy in Urban Tanzania", in: Cultural Anthropology 17:1, pp. 93-124.

Werbner, Pnina (2006): "Vernacular Cosmopolitanism", in: Theory, Culture, and Society 23:2-3, pp. 496-498.

Wilk, Richard (1995): "Learning to be Local in Belize. Global Systems of Common Difference", in: Daniel Miller (Ed.), Worlds Apart, London: Routledge, pp. 110-133.

Ahmad al-Tijani and his Neighbors

The Inhabitants of Fez and their Perceptions of the *Zawiya*

JOHARA BERRIANE

It is 5 p.m. The *'asr* prayer[1] has just finished and the streets are crowded with people. Parents with their children and groups of young people are shopping in the different stores selling clothes, spices and perfumes. Passers-by are stopped by young men selling nougat and sweets from carts. Today the city is crowded. It is the evening before the *mawlid*[2] in the old town of Fez.

Walking through the Attarine street known as the street of spice sellers, and approaching the district of Blida, the streets are becoming more crowded and a new kind of passer-by appears. Among the mass of local residents, shoppers from Fez, other visiting Moroccans – often from the countryside, who have come to visit the tomb of the patron saint – and tourists following their guides in organized queues, another type of traveler stands out because of their colorful, dazzling clothing. These are visitors from sub-Saharan Africa. Every year, during the celebration of the *mawlid*, the number of sub-Saharan visitors increases in the city. They are members of the Tijaniyya brotherhood and have come to Fez to visit the tomb of the founder of their Sufi order, who is buried in the old centre.

The Tijaniyya was founded in an Algerian oasis by Ahmad al-Tijani in 1781/82 and it was later based in the city of Fez. Today, this brotherhood has more members in sub-Saharan Africa than in the Maghreb (Triaud 2000: 10-11).

---

1 The prayer performed in the afternoon.

2 The birthday of the prophet Muhammad, which occurs in the third month of the Islamic calendar.

Since Ahmad al-Tijani was buried in the center of his *zawiya*[3] in Fez where he spent the last years of his life, this place has become a sanctuary attracting Tijani pilgrims from everywhere, especially from West Africa. Since the spreading of the Tijani teachings in the sub-Saharan regions, the spiritual leaders of the Tijaniyya have been visiting Fez in order to maintain and intensify their ties with Ahmad al-Tijani's descendants, who are in charge of the *zawiya* (Kane 1994: 2). During the colonial period, despite the vigilance of the colonial authorities in French Sudan and North Africa, relations between Fez and the Tijani community of West Africa continued and intensified after the Second World War. Since then, many pilgrims have stopped in Oran or Casablanca on their way to Mecca in order to visit the tomb of Ahmad al-Tijani (Kane 1994: 6). The first pilgrims who traveled to Fez belonged exclusively to the political and religious elites. After their countries won their independence, the social strata of the pilgrims diversified as traders and craftsmen began to visit the tomb as well (El Adnani 2005: 28).

Although Tijani disciples are present in many African countries, the Tijanis from Mauritania and Senegal visit the *zawiya* of Fez more frequently (Marfaing 2004: 238) and combine their sacred journey to Morocco with economic activities. Senegalese women in particular use the sacred image of Morocco as a pilgrimage country in order to trade between Morocco and Senegal. The pilgrimage to Fez has even contributed to the development of commercial activities between Morocco and Senegal. But the pilgrimage has also been used as an alibi by Senegalese people who wished to escape their country, because until 1981 they were not permitted to leave Senegal without authorization. Travelling to Fez for religious reasons was an excuse for leaving the country temporarily. Today, the pilgrimage to Fez is part of every Tijani's journey to Morocco. Many of them refer to visiting the tomb of Ahmad al-Tijani in Fez as the "little pilgrimage" – the pilgrimage to Mecca being the "great" one (Ibid.).

The research of Abdoullaye Kane has shown that through the pilgrimage to Fez, strong social ties have been built between the visitors. The pilgrimage to Fez is seen as an opportunity to meet other Tijanis from the same region and/or religious branch. Kane describes how the Gounassianke community[4] uses the

---

3   A *zawiya* is a place in which Sufi disciples meet in order to be initiated and instructed by a *shaykh*, to practice litanies and invocations and to commemorate God. In some cases – as for instance in the *zawiya* of Ahmad al-Tijani – it is also a place in which the founding *shaykh* is buried.

4   There are many Tijani branches. The Gounassianke, who belong mostly to the Haalpulaar ethnic group, are disciples of the Tijani branch of Thierno Mansour Barro. Their spiritual centre is Madina Gounass.

pilgrimage to Fez to stay in touch. Living in Senegal or in the diaspora, the disciples of the Tijani branch of Madina Gounass use Fez as a meeting place to maintain and consolidate their ties (Kane 2007: 188). The pilgrimage to Fez has also contributed to the development of social relations between people from different cultural backgrounds. Social ties have been built between foreign Tijanis and native ones. For instance, Moroccan Tijanis have joined the Tijani branch of Madina Gounass (Ibid.).

Marfaing and Kane focus on the perspective of foreign pilgrims, described as transnational agents, circulating between Morocco, Senegal and sometimes Europe, and who, on their way, stopover at Fez. While focusing on Senegalese pilgrims and observing the phenomenon as an aspect of transnational circulation, these studies are not concerned with the local impacts of the *zawiya* and the practice of pilgrimage. For example, they do not explicitly take into account what the *zawiya* and the pilgrimage mean to the political and economic agents of Fez and its local inhabitants.

Privileging an ethnographic approach, this paper attempts to give a first insight into the perceptions of the *zawiya* from the perspective of local authorities, local entrepreneurs and the inhabitants of Fez who live near this shrine and/or visit the place regularly. How do locals behave at this sanctuary and what role does this place play in their daily lives? What impact does the presence of black African pilgrims at this place have on their perceptions of the *zawiya*? What meanings do local authorities assign to the *zawiya* and the practice of pilgrimage?

I will begin by describing the different practices of Moroccans visiting the *zawiya*. These descriptions are based on the data I collected during my first stay in Fez in 2009. While in Fez, every morning I sat on the edge of a fountain not far from the main entrance of the *zawiya*. From this spot I was able to observe the street life and all the people entering and leaving the shrine. Sometimes I chatted with women passing by. In the afternoons, I entered the *zawiya* and took part in the daily rituals. Additionally, I had numerous discussions with local inhabitants and with my host family, their friends and a few shop owners in the street in front of the *zawiya*. Because women and men are separated inside the *zawiya*, I mainly met women there. Thus, my description will first focus on the practices of Moroccan women in the shrine and on the many functions this place has for local female visitors. I will then broaden my perspective and describe the inhabitants' perceptions of the *zawiya* based on my observations and on the informal discussions I had with locals (men as well as women).

Through these descriptions, I will try to show that due to the international reputation of the *zawiya* in Western Africa, local inhabitants of Fez have a mixed opinion of this shrine and an ambivalent relationship to it. On the one hand, they are proud to live in the neighborhood of the tomb of a well-known man whom most venerate and perceive as being a saint. On the other hand, they consider the *zawiya* and its saint as alien components that belong to foreigners, especially Black Africans. With this in mind, I now describe how a day passes in the *zawiya*.

PRACTICES OF MOROCCAN WOMEN IN THE *ZAWIYA*

After taking off their shoes and entering through the main door, female visitors to the Tijani *zawiya* cross a courtyard used for ablutions in order to get to their designated place at the back end of the building. At the main door two caretakers take turns in keeping an eye on the visitors who enter the *zawiya*, making sure that all have taken off their shoes and that women have covered their hair.

Like in mosques and many shrines, there are separate spaces for men and women in the *zawiya*. The place reserved for women is surrounded by a wooden fence. The tomb of Ahmad al-Tijani is located in the centre of the building and is surrounded by a golden railing. There are compartments for foreign pilgrims who need a place to rest and sleep during their stay in Fez located behind this golden barrier.

The barrier surrounding the tomb has a golden door, which faces the side of the *zawiya* reserved for men. Sometimes this door is open and worshippers sit and pray around the tomb and touch it. During my first stay in Fez, the worshippers who had access to the tomb were mostly foreign pilgrims (men and women), who entered in groups and prayed together. Sometimes I also saw Moroccan men there but I never met a Moroccan woman who had entered the golden door.[5] From their place, Moroccan women could see the tomb. They could touch the golden railing but could not gain access to the sepulcher. Although Moroccan women are not allowed the same access to the saint as men and foreign visitors, the *zawiya* is a place visited regularly by women living in Fez.

One Shrine, Many Practices

Most of the female visitors I met explained to me that they come to the *zawiya* in order to visit Ahmad al-Tijani's shrine. But 'visiting' Ahmad al-Tijani may

---

5   Since I made these observations (in March 2009) the access to the shrine was further restricted: no more visitors are allowed to enter the golden door.

mean different things and includes a variety of activities. Some visitors position themselves in front of the tomb, touching the railing and murmuring prayers, while others sit on the floor in front of the tomb. For some of the women the *zawiya* is a place to meet or to take naps in one of the corners. Some of them do not seem to be interested in visiting the saint at all. Instead of going to the tomb, they sit or lie down and chat with other visitors while their children run around and play. Others seem to be just there out of curiosity. They are particularly attracted by what is happening behind the fence, where the Moroccan men and foreign visitors are. Whenever foreigners are present, their eyes remain fixed on the other side of the fence, observing the scenes. During prayer times, the number of female visitors increases considerably. Some of them enter to pray, turning towards the *qibla*[6] and ignoring the tomb. They leave just after their prayer. Others wait until the collective prayer starts before starting to pray. Some of them stay on for a little while after.

The *zawiya* is visited for many different reasons and practices. Whereas some of the female visitors focus on the tomb, others perceive the *zawiya* as a place where they can have a rest, relax and meet their friends. A third group uses the place as a mosque to pray without paying attention to the tomb. But the *zawiya* is also a meeting place for the female Tijani community of Fez. Among the Moroccan female visitors, there are also Tijani disciples who meet regularly during the rituals to practice their litanies and invocations and to commemorate God together. The daily *wazifa,* a prayer that Tijani disciples have to say every day, is performed in the *zawiya*[7]. Some of the female Tijanis meet every evening in order to pray together.

After the collective *'asr* prayer, the women sit cross-legged in a small circle. Every woman takes out her rosary and waits until a man's voice announces the beginning of the *wazifa* from the speakers. They then start to recite the different prayers together. During this time, an older woman monitors the behavior of all the others, summoning those for instance who stretch their legs. On Friday evenings, the ritual is longer than on the other days because the *hadra* – that should be performed collectively – takes place after the *wazifa* in the evening.

During Sufi rituals, not all women who are present seem to be Tijani disciples. While the group of regulars gather in a small circle, occasional spectators sit everywhere around them. During collective rituals, women also enter and leave continuously, sometimes disturbing the devotees. Walking into the *zawiya* during rituals does not seem to be forbidden.

---

6   The direction that should be faced when a Muslim prays.

7   The *wazifa* can be performed in the morning or in the evening.

Not all visitors give a religious reason for their practices and participation in the rituals that take place in the *zawiya*. I spoke to many of the occasional visitors and they told me that they just came to listen to the prayers because they liked to listen to litanies. They found it relaxing and they enjoyed the atmosphere inside the *zawiya* during the rituals. A few of them insisted that they were not Tijanis and considered listening to the *wazifa* and *hadra* as spare-time activity.[8]

The fact that female visitors of sanctuaries use these places for various activities and do not exclusively come to spend some time at Ahmad al-Tijani's gravesite is not unusual in the Moroccan context. The *zawiya* of Ahmad al-Tijani has the same functions as other Moroccan shrines. Female visitors come to worship the saint and/or ask him for help or healing but they also use the shrine as a meeting point, to have a rest or to listen to prayers. As in other Muslim countries, shrines are seen as religious places for women, whereas mosques are considered religious places for men (Mayeur-Jaouen 2000: 137).[9] In contrast to the street, the women who visit the *zawiya* of Ahmad al-Tijani seem to behave as if they were at home. It is a place where women seem to feel free to stay because they feel protected. This part of the *zawiya* is a place for women, where they can escape their daily life activities and the noise of the street and have a moment of rest.

A Strict Discipline

However, unlike the other shrines in the city, the discipline that prevails in the *zawiya* is very strict. It seems that the caretakers of the place try to impose certain rules that contrast with the popular practices commonly linked to saint veneration in Morocco. Thus, if women are too loud inside the *zawiya*, the caretakers summon them to be silent and occasionally ask them to leave. As mentioned before, women have no direct access to the tomb, whereas they do in most other Moroccan shrines.[10] Furthermore, they are not allowed to light candles as they do in other sanctuaries.

These restrictions contrast, for example, with the atmosphere that prevails in the mausoleum of Mulay Idris. Located close to the *zawiya*, this shrine contains

---

8   My informants used the word *hiwaya* to explain their motivation for being there. I would translate it as hobby.

9   Many authors emphasise the social function of shrines for women (Mernissi 1977; Reysoo 1988; Tebaa 2002).

10 In her study on Moroccan shrines, Ouidad Tebaa insists on the importance for women venerating saints to touch or to kiss the tomb and she emphasises the joyful atmosphere in these sanctuaries (Tebaa 2002).

the tomb of the city's most important and popular saint. Mulay Idris is the patron saint of Fez. He founded the city 1200 years ago and is considered to be the second sultan of Morocco. Although Mulay Idris was not the founder of any specific Sufi order, many Sufi scholars who lived in Fez consider him as an important saint (Skali 2001: 27). His influence extends far beyond the city. Besides the citizens of Fez, people from distant regions visit his mausoleum (LeTourneau 1965: 286).

Thus, its visitors are greater in number and, unlike in the *zawiya*, they are not expected to be quiet. People talk and laugh, children run and play. All visitors (men as well as women) have access to the saint's tomb. Although distinct spots are allocated to men and women inside the mausoleum, these places are not separated. For instance, in order to enter the tomb, female worshippers have to cross the area reserved for men. In this mausoleum, many visitors enter with candles which they light and set down near the tomb.

One might assume that Mulay Idriss' popularity and the atmosphere that prevails in his mausoleum would lower the *zawiya*'s attractiveness amongst locals. But although Ahmad al-Tijani's shrine is located in the same neighborhood as Mulay Idriss', the *zawiya* still receives a regular amount of local visitors.

Some of these visitors even try, by different means, to bend the rules and boundaries that are imposed by the caretakers. Thus, although it is not allowed to light candles in the *zawiya*, local worshipers buy candles and put them near the tomb. Although it is not allowed to sleep in the *zawiya*, female visitors stay there until the caretakers throw them out. Although it is forbidden to speak loudly inside the *zawiya*, Moroccan women use the shrine as a meeting place and discuss loudly. All these attempts illustrate how diverse understandings of saint veneration and varied practices can prevail inside one single shrine (Eade and Sallnow, 1991). It shows that although local women are not allowed to venerate Ahmad al-Tijani the way they would like to, they try to impose their own practices. This attempt to impose their understanding of saint veneration is all the more striking since the city of Fez has numerous shrines in which visitors have more freedom to do as they please.

Paradoxically, it is the more rigorous etiquette imposed by the caretakers of the *zawiya* that seems to partly explain why some locals prefer visiting Ahmad al-Tijani instead of other local saints. The strict rules that prevail in the *zawiya*, for instance, guarantee women more protection from men. The contrast between the space outside and the space inside the *zawiya*, being more distinct in terms of rules and tolerated behavior, makes the place seem more respectful, emphasizing its sacred character. Even though most of my female informants tried to bend the rules inside the *zawiya*, they still insisted on the correctness of the etiquette imposed to visitors in the *zawiya*.

The *Zawiya* in Times of the *Mawlid* Celebration

During some particular periods of the year – the celebration of the *mawlid* and the month of Ramadan for instance – the *zawiya* changes considerably and attracts a significant number of visitors, foreigners as well as Moroccans. In the week before and after the celebration of the *mawlid*, many pilgrims come to Fez to spend the night before the festivities in the *zawiya*. According to local inhabitants, the number of foreign pilgrims also increases before and after this feast. The season of pilgrimage starts during the *mawlid* festivities and stops after Ramadan. Most of the pilgrims arrive on the birthday of the prophet or on the 27th night of Ramadan (commonly believed to be the holiest night for many Muslims[11]). During the period of *hajj*, many pilgrims also stop in Fez on their way to or from Mecca.

The *mawlid* is also an important time for locals who visit the *zawiya*. During the night that precedes the *mawlid*, the *zawiya* of Ahmad al-Tijani attracts numerous local women and during the festivities the place changes considerably. The fences are taken down and all visitors (women as well as men, locals as well as foreign worshippers) are allowed to move freely in the *zawiya*. During the *mawlid* night that I attended, the *zawiya* was crowded. Five hundred people, both Moroccan and foreign, were gathered in the place. All spent the night praying, listening to religious poems and eating together. The family in charge of the *zawiya* and a few wealthy families from Fez donated food to the visitors. Plates of couscous, glasses of milk and dates were distributed amongst the visitors.

On this occasion, different groups met at the shrine. The first Moroccan visitors were Berber women from the surrounding countryside. They arrived in the afternoon and settled down in the *zawiya* for the night. Later, after dinner time, local families came to spend a part of the night there too. Also present were sub-Saharan Africans who had come to celebrate the *mawlid* in Fez. But although the fences were taken away for the night, these different groups still sat in separate places, not mixing with each other. Most Moroccan women and their children stayed apart, in spaces that are usually reserved for them. When the place started to get too crowded, they moved away to the courtyard, while foreigners and men took over their places. Thus, the celebration of the *mawlid* is not seen as an op-

---

11 It is the anniversary of the night Muslims believe the first verses of the Qu'ran were revealed to the Islamic prophet Muhammad.

portunity to meet and to exchange a few words with other visitors. It is rather a time when more devotees appear, however they maintain their separate ways.

The *zawiya* of Ahmad al-Tijani is a place visited by several different groups. However, apart from celebrations like those of the *mawlid*, the people in charge of the shrine do not endeavor to make the shrine an attractive place for Moroccan women. Although some women argue that the rules inside the zawiya add to its respectful character, the discipline in this place and the spatial arrangements that prevail make it a space where Moroccan women do not have the same freedom of movement as in other sanctuaries. I would say that whereas other sanctuaries in Morocco are seen as religious places that belong – more than anything – to women, and in which female visitors can find rest and comfort, the *zawiya* is a place where they are merely tolerated as guests. The prevalence of foreign pilgrims reinforces this impression: the shrine being mainly perceived as 'the place of Others'.

THE 'AFRICAN' SAINT OF FEZ

On my second day in Fez, while I was sitting on the edge of the fountain outside the *zawiya*, I met a girl who stood in front of the main door. She looked very bored, so I decided to talk to her. I asked her who she was waiting for and she told me that her mother was inside the *zawiya*. She was very angry and said, talking about her mother:

"I don't know what she is doing inside. I mean, we all know today that there are no saints and that we should only venerate God. But my mother still visits saints, although they are only human beings like us. We don't know if the man who is buried in here is now in heaven or in hell. If he was Moroccan, it might have been understandable – but he is a Senegalese. Why does my mother venerate a Senegalese person?"

This statement is a lively reflection of the representations I encountered during this first fieldwork. For that reason, I will use this case in order to illustrate the different perceptions that locals have of saint veneration in general and Ahmad al-Tijani in particular.

Is the Younger Generation Rejecting Saint Veneration?

The comment of the girl exemplifies, first of all, different opinions about saint veneration and Sufism[12] encountered in the Moroccan context, as well as the discussions between mothers and their children over the topic. According to some recent works on religious practices in Morocco, saint veneration is increasingly becoming obsolete and is widely contested (El Ayadi 2000; Rachik 2007). One reason for the growing rejection of this religious practice can be found partly in formal education. While studying the religious values of Moroccan students, El Ayadi compares the values transmitted in different school books with the opinions of students and wonders whether these books influence the students' opinion about saint veneration. More than half of his interviewees did not visit saints and many of them had even tried to convince their mothers to stop. This decline in saint veneration has been linked to the reformist ideas promoted by Moroccan schools, in which they insist on the unity of God and reject saint veneration as "popular Islam" (El Ayadi 2000: 94-95).

The introductory statement of the girl I met, above, clearly reflects this trend. But in the *zawiya* I encountered women of different age groups – young women who were accompanying their mothers or aunts as well as groups of teenagers, sitting and chatting with each other. The same observation applies to the mausoleum of Mulay Idris: it attracts visitors from different generations. When I visited this mausoleum the evening of the *mawlid* day, it was crowded. Many teenagers were present. They seemed to be having a lot of fun sitting and chatting together. Therefore saint veneration might be contested in public discourses but mausoleums and *zawiya* still attract visitors from different generations. Beyond the question of veneration, shrines, so it seems, are part of the lived space of inhabitants of the old town of Fez.

The *Zawiya's* Alien Character

Going back to my encounter with the girl in front of the *zawiya*, another observation can be made. The girl quoted above did not only reject Ahmad al-Tijani because she does not believe in saints. What was more important to her was the fact that Ahmad al-Tijani was not Moroccan but Senegalese. This statement not only reflects the debate on saint veneration, it also shows that the *zawiya* and its

---

12 Sufism and saint veneration are phenomena that are intermingled. However, some authors writing on saint veneration and 'popular Islam' in Morocco make explicit distinctions between Sufism and saint veneration (Kerrou 1991; M'Halla 1998).

saint are seen by some local inhabitants as something that belongs to foreigners; a place for strangers. For most of the female interviewees I met inside the *zawiya*, Ahmad al-Tijani was a Senegalese person. Besides the few female disciples who came every day to participate in the Sufi rituals and who were aware of the origins of their saint, many women believe that Ahmad al-Tijani was the ancestor of the Senegalese people. Some of them did not know what the word 'Senegalese' meant and asked me if it was a tribe. Moreover, most of them explained to me that many 'Senegalese' people visit the shrine in order to venerate their ancestors. Therefore, if he is venerated by them, Ahmad al-Tijani must be Senegalese.

This explanation of the pilgrimage of foreigners to the *zawiya* also reflects the way black Africans are perceived by my informants. The Moroccan women I spoke to tended to identify all black Africans as Senegalese. Since the beginning of the 20th century, different groups of Senegalese people have stayed in Morocco and added to the confusion between Senegalese people in particular and other black Africans in general. During the French Protectorate for instance, colonial rulers employed Senegalese soldiers in Morocco to control the country. Moroccans called them *saligan* (Aouad-Badoual 2004: 353). Other Senegalese people – traders, students and pilgrims – have also been travelling to Morocco since the beginning of the 20th century (Fall 2004: 282-285), contributing to the historical ties between the two countries.

The representations of the *zawiya* by Moroccan locals show to what extent the *zawiya* is linked to its black African visitors. It seems that the possibility to come across foreigners (in this case black Africans) is one of the incentives that attract Moroccan women into the *zawiya*. Female black African pilgrims in particular attract the attention of local women. They often wear dresses of shiny white or bright colors and golden jewellery. During the *mawlid*, many Moroccan women told me how the dresses and the beauty of the black African women fascinated them.

During my fieldwork inside the *zawiya*, I met several Moroccan women who not only believe that Ahmad al-Tijani is a Senegalese person, but also that his foreign descendants own the place. They consider the people in charge of the *zawiya*, especially the Moroccan caretaker whom the women meet regularly and who supervises their conduct there, as employees of those same foreigners. The women believe that the Senegalese people give a lot of money to the persons in charge of the *zawiya* and that they are therefore the ones who control the place. They seem to ignore the fact that Moroccan descendants of Ahmad al-Tijani live in Fez and that they are the ones in charge of the *zawiya*. But unlike the girl I spoke to, who might be skeptical about saint veneration in general and the veneration of a foreigner in particular, others do not seem to find it contradictory to venerate a saint considered to be Senegalese. And even though Ahmad al-Tijani is perceived as a foreigner, local entrepreneurs and local authorities in Fez discovered the economic potential of the *zawiya* a few years ago and have since been trying to reclaim the *zawiya* as part of the cultural heritage of Fez.

SPIRITUAL TOURISM AND PATRIMONIALIZATION OF THE *ZAWIYA*

Although the main objective of my first stay in Fez was not to study the economic aspects of the Tijani pilgrimage, I did notice several economic activities around the *zawiya* which were linked to foreign Tijani pilgrims. Local institutions and authorities have discovered the economic potential of the *zawiya.* These activities affect both the type of visitors coming to the *zawiya,* as well as the perceptions that locals and authorities have of the foreign Tijani guests.

The shops outside the *zawiya* do not stock the typical products that are sold around other shrines. There are no sweet shops and no candle or perfume shops. Rather, products on offer are more similar to products targeted for tourists. A restaurant called 'Tijani restaurant' in the street offers Moroccan food. A little bit further on, a 'Tijani Hotel' opened its doors ten months before my first visit. The commodities Tijani pilgrims are looking for are quite different from those that tourists – mostly Europeans – buy in Morocco. In many discussions, local interviewees explained to me how important Moroccan fabrics are to foreign Tijanis. Especially the *djellaba* – a long hooded coat worn by men and women – and Moroccan slippers are highly appreciated by West African pilgrims. It is common for Senegalese to wear Moroccan clothes on Fridays for the visit to the mosque. Because the *zawiya* is located close to the commercial streets of the old city of Fez, many pilgrims use their visit to the city to buy such commodities. As Laurence Marfaing shows in her study on Senegalese traders in Morocco, the journey to Fez is also often an opportunity to bring back Moroccan commodities to the traders' home countries and sometimes the pilgrimage is financed through trade activities (Marfaing 2004).

Apart from the commercial activities that have developed as a by-product of the pilgrimage to Fez and some recent initiatives to establish services like hotel accommodation and restaurants for wealthier Tijani travelers, NGOs and the municipal authorities have also discovered the impact that the *zawiya* can have on the local economy as well as on the development of tourist activities in the city. In order to attract more tourists to Fez, the city has developed new tourism options related to projects that are linked to the practice of pilgrimage to Fez.

The main NGO working for the development of new tourist activities is the Conseil Régional du Tourisme[13] (CRT). This council, which has been created in every Moroccan region to develop local tourism projects, works closely with the national ministry of tourism. In Fez, the CRT operates an advertising campaign in sub-Saharan Africa offering specialized trips from West Africa to Fez (Al Bayane, Dec.7, 2009). Package tours of eight days – labeled *Ziyara Tijaniyya* – are offered to disciples starting from Dakar and Bamako. This way, pilgrims can visit different Moroccan cities and finally travel to Fez to spend some time at Ahmad al-Tijani's gravesite (l'Économiste, Jan. 29, 2009).

The municipality of Fez also organizes cultural days in different African capitals in order to promote the customs and traditions of Fez. It is a novelty that a Moroccan city is promoting its cultural and tourist attractions in sub-Saharan countries. It is probably no coincidence that these cultural weeks take place in regions where many Tijani disciples live. According to the CRT, the *zawiya* of Ahmad al-Tijani possesses a great potential that the city should make use of (l'Économiste, Oct. 17, 2008). Cultural days have already been organized in Bamako, Yaoundé, Dakar and Kano (l'Économiste, Jan. 1, 2009). Their objective is to enrich the spiritual image of Morocco with a cultural dimension and to inform potential tourists about Fez (l'Économiste, Oct. 17, 2008).

The CRT has also developed a special accommodation package called *Ziyarat Fez*[14] (these accommodations are best described as 'Bed and Breakfasts'). This project is aimed at enabling poor families living in the old town of Fez to find a well-paid activity as hosts and thus to encourage them to stay in the old town. This project is designed to appeal to western tourists who would like to stay in an ancient house and discover the everyday life of people of Fez as well as local customs. This program also caters to Tijani pilgrims and was tested during the 2006 International Forum of the Tijaniyya in Fez.

During this International Forum, initiated by the Moroccan king, foreign Tijanis were hosted by local families who had been chosen by local authorities as suitable for the program. The family I stayed with during my last visit to Fez was one of those families. For them, the forum was the first time that they received foreign visitors in their house. After the conference, they continued to host sub-Saharan pilgrims, which provided them with a new income. It has become common for pilgrims to knock on their door and ask for lodging for one or two

---

13 The Regional Council for Tourism.

14 The Arabic word *ziyara* means 'visit' in general and can be used specifically to refer to the visit and pilgrimage to a tomb or shrine.

nights. My host family, for example, told me that one summer day, a bus with pilgrims arrived from Casablanca. Although they had planned to spend the night in the *zawiya*, a group of women did not find the accommodation suitable. When they got out onto the street they asked around for a place to spend the night and consequently found my host's home.

In the past, pilgrims who wanted to lodge not far from the *zawiya* were accommodated in the *zawiya* or by their acquaintances in Fez (Kane 2007: 193). Since 2000, a Senegalese person living in Fez could work as an intermediary between pilgrims and local families willing to host foreigners. Although it is not a novelty for the inhabitants of Fez to rent out their rooms to Tijani pilgrims, it was for my hosts. It means that through the new program, more local families than ever before are coming into closer contact with sub-Saharan Africans.

Within the framework of the renovation of the old town of Fez, which has been a World Heritage site since the 1970s, other agents have contributed indirectly to the reconditioning of the *zawiya*. The Agence de Dédensification et de Réhabilitation de la Médina de Fès (ADER) has existed since 1989. As part of the Ministry of Domestic Affairs, its main function is to help to safeguard the old town of Fez and to adapt it to the demographic, economic and touristic evolution of the city. The ADER has helped to reconstruct the city walls of the old town and has also devised six recommended walks, directing tourists in their discovery of the old town; this brings added value to the *zawiya*. While the *zawiya* did not formerly appear in tourist guides of Fez, today it is part of these tourist routes.

Today, the *zawiya* is also mentioned more often in official documents and discourses as one angle of the "historical triangle" of the old city of Fez (Program de Développement Régional Touristique de Fès 2015: 63). Older literature about Fez (Fejjal 1993; Escher and Wirth 1992; Idrissi Janati 2001) only names the mausoleum of Mulay Idris and the mosque of the medieval al-Qarawiyin University as main historical monuments. One study on the young inhabitants of Fez in 2000 indicated that the *zawiya* had no place on their mental maps. The mosque of al-Qarawiyin and the mausoleum, on the other hand, were considered the most important monuments of the local patrimony (Idrissi Janati 2001: 254). The *zawiya* was not mentioned at all in this study. It could be part of a new trend to view the *zawiya* as part of the historical triangle. The projects that now give new value to the *zawiya* of Ahmad al-Tijani are well known by my informants and affect their representation of their city. For example, my host family proudly told me that they not only live close to Ahmad al-Tijani, but also in the historical triangle of Fez.

It can thus be concluded that the tourism activities, as well as the renovation of the old town of Fez, have resulted in a revaluation of the *zawiya* and contributed to its increased visibility. This value can also be linked to the economic opportunities that the *zawiya* provides for local families. But the discussions I had with my host family, their neighbors and friends, demonstrated above all that local inhabitants discovered the *zawiya* through their foreign visitors. Very often the foreign Tijanis inform their hosts about the saint, contributing to the (re)discovery of Ahmad al-Tijani by locals. Locals did not only discover the economic benefits that the *zawiya* provided and become aware of its historical value, they also became convinced of the supernatural power of Ahmad al-Tijani who had blessed their houses with new wealth and importance.

AHMAD AL-TIJANI (RE)DISCOVERED BY LOCALS?

What was very interesting during the discussions I had with the family I lived with is the fact that since they started to host Tijani pilgrims, they seem to have rediscovered the *zawiya* and given a new meaning to the saint Ahmad al-Tijani. Previous studies argue that social ties are woven between local inhabitants and foreign guests through pilgrimage. Kane argues that these relations are established through the *zawiya*, which is a privileged place of sociability (Kane 2007: 193-194). Through the city's new programs, that promote the Tijani pilgrimage, a new group of people from Fez encounter foreign pilgrims. It is through the interactions they have with their guests that Moroccan families seem to be (re)discovering the *zawiya*.

My host family, for example, had not had any contact with the Tijaniyya before they started to accommodate pilgrims. My landlord was born in the same house where the family still lives now and which is located in the same street as the *zawiya*, only one hundred meters from there. Formerly though, he had never been interested in this place, because in his eyes it was a shrine like any other. He did not have any knowledge about the saint either. His roots, the teachings and the rituals of the Tijaniyya order were of no interest to him. Things started to change a year before my stay, after he met a guest who had come from Senegal with his young wife to spend their honeymoon in Fez. The couple spent two weeks with the family. During their stay, the Senegalese couple explained to their Moroccan hosts why Ahmad al-Tijani was so important to them and why they considered their hosts so very lucky to live close to his tomb. The man told me that he still does not believe in the teachings of the Tijaniyya although he is now convinced that the man buried in the *zawiya* is a saint.

I also noticed that his wife Lamia[15], with whom I spent more time, had started to develop new impressions of the *zawiya,* despite the fact that sometimes she contradicted herself in her statements. On the one hand, she often insisted that she was against Sufism and saint veneration because of her monotheism. On the other hand, and probably due to the fact that she frequently met pilgrims who came a fair distance to Fez just to visit the saint's tomb, she could not completely ignore the virtues of this saint, buried not far from her house and who, in a way, added new value to her home. She also told me of many occasions in her house which she considered were miracles performed by the saint.

In fact, Lamia attributed the new source of revenue, which the family now receives by accommodating pilgrims, to the 'blessing' of the saint. She gave me an account of a dream she had had before the family started to host pilgrims. In this dream, an old man, who – as she explained – could only have been Ahmad al-Tijani, appeared to her and advised her not to sell the house. She further related to me stories of pilgrims who came to Fez to be healed by the saint, insisting on the fact that they were indeed successfully cured.

What might also factor in this newly gained interest for the *zawiya* is that most African visitors to the shrine belong to a certain elite in their country. Lamia insisted that her guests were mostly entrepreneurs, politicians and the like, which led her to conclude that the saint had to be very important. Thus, paradoxically, while saint veneration is highly criticized by certain urban Moroccan elites today, foreign elites are the ones who contribute in legitimating the Tijani shrine. In addition to their elite status, their guests were also very religious people, practicing the same Islam as people in Morocco. They therefore demonstrated that Sufism and the 'orthodox' conceptions of Islam can be intermingled and are not contradictory.

I also spoke to other people offering accommodation to Senegalese pilgrims and they showed a similar admiration for their guests. Zineb[16], for example, emphasized how she recently discovered a part of her culture through these foreigners. She told me that she had never paid attention to saints and Sufism before. To her, these were utterly foreign concepts although she did not live far from a Sufi shrine. When she met the Senegalese pilgrims she discovered the meaning of the *zawiya.* Before these encounters, she had never given any thought to the important religious place she was living in such close proximity to. "See," she said to me, "we had to meet black Africans in order for us to discover the meanings of a place located in our own neighborhood!"

---

15 This is a fictional name chosen in order to preserve the anonymity of the person.
16 Fictional name.

Even if the local people offering accommodation have a positive opinion of the saint and sometimes believe in his *baraka*, they do not enter the *zawiya* very often. For them, the *zawiya* and the Tijaniyya are linked to their visitors. None of my informants decided to become Tijani disciples after meeting and hosting Tijani pilgrims. The local families discovered the *zawiya* through their visitors but they still considered it a place for foreigners and saw Ahmad al-Tijani as the saint of the others.

It is striking to see that the *zawiya* of Ahmad al-Tijani is part of the mental map of the families living in the neighborhood and that they believe that the *baraka* of the saint is radiating around and blessing their homes. But the families who live in their neighborhood do not really know who Ahmad al-Tijani was. According to them, the real keepers of the memory of the place are foreigners. Africans know who he is and cultivate the pilgrimage to his grave. One may assume that despite the few Moroccan Tijanis I met, inhabitants of Fez conceive of the *zawiya* as part of their lived space like other shrines and buildings in their neighborhood but not as an important place for local cultural memory. According to them, foreign pilgrims are the main agents who put meaning into the *zawiya* and keep the memory of the shrine alive. In other words, foreigners are making the *zawiya* a place whereas local inhabitants and local authorities have only (re)discovered its significance as a place through its international reputation.

CONCLUSION

The *zawiya* of Ahmad al-Tijani has a variety of meanings and has numerous functions for locals: historical monument and cultural heritage of the city, exotic shrine belonging to the Senegalese people, a saint with supernatural powers who has blessed the neighborhood in which he is buried, a protected area with a strict etiquette. Everyone might have his own perception of the *zawiya* and his own relationship to it and even one single person might have contradictory understandings of this place and its saint. This shows the variety of understandings of the sacred. Like other pilgrimage sites, the *zawiya* of Ahmad al-Tijani is "an arena for the interplay of a variety of imported perceptions and understandings" (Eade and Sallnow 1991: 10). However how locals have understood this shrine has also been changing because of their interactions with African pilgrims.

Although the *zawiya* is part of the lived space of locals who visit it and know where it is, it may not have played an important role for them as a place before. Although the *zawiya* is visited by locals, it has only become a place of importance in their eyes through the interactions they had with foreign pilgrims.

Thus, the integration of the *zawiya* into the local cultural heritage is intimately linked to its international reputation. This might explain why the *zawiya* is perceived as an alien place that belongs to black African people. In other words, the *zawiya* and its saint seem to have been 'africanized' by locals: although the *zawiya* and its saint play a role for local inhabitants, the representations of the *zawiya* are always related to its African visitors.

REFERENCES

Aouad-Badoual, Rita (2004): "'Esclavage' et situation des 'noirs' au Maroc dans la première moitié du XXe siècle", in: Laurence Marfaing and Steffen Wippel (Eds.), Les relations transsahariennes à l'époque contemporaine. Un espace en constante mutation, Paris: Karthala – ZMO, pp. 337-361.

Eade, John and Sallnow, Michael J. (1991): "Introduction", in: John Eade and Michael J. Sallnow (Eds.), Contesting the Sacred. The Anthropology of Christian Pilgrimage, London, New York: Routledge, pp. 1-27.

Fall, Papa Demba (2004): "Les Sénégalais au Maroc. Histoire et anthropologie d'un espace migratoire", in: Laurence Marfaing and Steffen Wippel (Eds.), Les relations transsahariennes à l'époque contemporaine. Un espace en constante mutation, Paris: Karthala – ZMO, pp. 277-293.

El Adnani, Jillali (2005): "Entre visite et pèlerinage. Le cas des pèlerins ouest africains à la zawiya Tijaniyya de Fès", in: Al-Maghrib al-Ifriqi: Revue spécialisée dans le patrimoine et les études africaines 6, pp. 7-37.

El Ayadi, Mohamed (2000): "La jeunesse et l'Islam, tentative d'analyse d'un habitus religieux cultivé", in: Bourqia, Rahma; El Ayadi, Mohamed; El Harras; Mokhtar and Rachik, Hassan (Eds.): Les jeunes et les valeurs religieuses, Casablanca: Eddif, pp. 87-167.

Escher, Anton and Wirth, Eugen (1992): Die Medina von Fes. Geographische Beiträge zu Persistenz und Dynamik, Verfall und Erneuerung einer traditionellen islamischen Stadt in handlungstheoretischer Sicht, Erlangen: Selbstverlag der Fränkischen Geographischen Gesellschaft in Komission bei Palm & Enke.

Fejjal, Ali (1993): Fès. Héritages et dynamiques urbaines actuelles 1, Ph.D. Thesis: Tours.

Idrissi Janati, M'hammed (2001): Les jeunes des quartiers populaires de Fès (Maroc). Représentations sociales et territorialités urbaines. Ph.D. Thesis: Tours.

Kane, Abdoullaye (2007): "Les pèlerins sénégalais au Maroc. La sociabilité autour de la Tijâniyyain", in: Elisabeth Boesen and Laurence Marfaing (Eds.): Les nouveaux urbains dans l'espace Sahara-Sahel, Paris: Karthala – ZMO, pp. 187-209.

Kane, Oumar (1994): Les relations entre la communauté Tijane du Sénégal et la zawiya de Fèz. Annales de la faculté des lettres et sciences humaines, 24. www.tekrur-urad.refer.sn/IMG/pdf/annales_24_OKane_VI.pdf.

Kerrou, Mohamed (1991): "Le temps maraboutique", in: IBLA 54:167, pp. 63-72.

Le Tourneau, Roger (1965): La vie quotidienne à Fès en 1900, Paris: Hachette.

Marfaing, Laurence (2004): "Von der Pilgerschaft nach Fès zum Handel in Marokko: Senegalesische Händler und Händlerinnen in Casablanca", in: Steffen Wippel (Ed.): Wirtschaft im Vorderen Orient. Interdisziplinäre Perspektiven, Berlin: Klaus Schwarz Verlag, pp. 235-260.

Mayeur-Jaouen, Catherine (2000): "Tombeau, mosquée et zawiya. La polarité des lieux saints musulmans", in: A. Vauchez (Ed.), Lieux sacrés, lieux de culte, Sanctuaires. Approches terminologiques, méthodologiques, historiques et monographiques, Paris and Rome: Collection de l'ecole française de Rome, pp. 133-170.

Mernissi, Fatima (1977): "Women, Saints and Sanctuaries", in: Signs: Journal of Women in Culture and Society 3:1, pp. 101-112.

M'Halla, Moncef (1998): "Culte des saints et culte extatique en Islam Maghrébin", in: M. Kerrou (Ed.), L'autorité des saints. Perspectives historiques et socio-anthropologiques en Méditerranée occidentale, Paris: IRMC, pp. 121-131

Rachik, Hassan (2007): "Pratiques rituelles et croyances religieuses", in: El Ayadi, Mohammed; Rachik, Hassan and Tozy, Mohamed (Eds.), L'Islam au quotidien. Enquête sur les valeurs et les pratiques religieuses au Maroc. Rabat: Editions Prologues, pp. 43-96.

Reysoo, Fenneke (1988): Des moussems du Maroc. Une approche anthropologique de fêtes patronales, Den Haag: Cip-Gegevens Koninklijke Bibliotheek.

Skali, Faouzi (2001): Saints et sanctuaires de Fès, Rabat: Marsam.

Triaud, J.-L. (2000): "La Tijaniyya. Une confrérie pas comme les autres?", in: J.-L.Triaud and David Robinson (Eds.), La Tijaniyya. Une confrérie musulmane à la conquête de l'Afrique, Paris: Karthala, pp. 9-17.

Tebaa, Ouidad (2005): "Les femmes et l'espace du sacré. Le culte des saints au Maroc", in: Collette Dumas and Nathalie Bertrand (Eds.), Rencontres Orient-Occident. Actes du colloque. Femmes d'Orient – Femmes d'Occident. Espaces, mythes et symboles. Toulon: L'Harmattan, pp. 99-102.

Zawiya, Zikr and the Authority of Shaykh 'Al-Pepsi'

The Social in Sacred Place-making in Omdurman, Sudan

KARIN WILLEMSE

When I returned to Khartoum in 2006 after a five-year absence, during the first weeks I walked around the city in a constant state of wonder.[1] Khartoum had changed rapidly after the exploitation of the oilfields provided a reliable source of revenue for the state, as well as for the oil companies and other associated businesses that had flocked to Khartoum. In particular, after the signing of the first peace agreement at Machakos in 2002,[2] which would end the off-and-on half-century of civil war between North and South Sudan, many companies have opened branches in Khartoum. Some of the many dusty streets have now been turned into tarmac roads and are filled with cars, taxis, *amjad*s (the newly intro-

1   I conducted anthropological research in Khartoum, in 2006-7 for about 4,5 months and again in 2007-8 for 4 months. I hereby thank the NWO, the Netherlands National Endowment for academic research, for funding my research as part of the multi-country research project 'Islam in Africa. Globalization and Moving Frontiers' as part of the NWO program 'The Future of the Religious Past'. I thank the NIAS (Netherlands Institute for advanced studies in the humanities and social sciences) for their research grant 2006-7 and 2008. I also thank the Erasumus School for History, Culture and Communication for material and immaterial support that allowed me to take leave from teaching responsibilities in the same period.
2   The Machakos agreements would lead up to the Comprehensive Peace Agreement between North and South Sudan in 2005 (Rogier 2005). Designing an integrated strategy for peace, security and development in post-Agreement Sudan (The Hague: Netherlands Institute of International Relations 'Clingendael').

duced small taxi buses), and *riksja*s: in 2007 about 500 new car licenses were issued every day, most of which would be used in Khartoum.[3] Flats, newly designed skyscrapers, large office buildings, and walled compounds with large villas now line the newly constructed highways between the heart of the city and the outlying areas that quickly become wards in Khartoum. A shopping mall provides air-conditioned spaces for cafes serving cappuccinos, a food court with Chinese, Philippine, Italian and Mediterranean restaurants, boutiques selling wedding dresses, jewelry, perfume, lingerie and shoes: all luxury items that formerly were bought abroad by family members who were able to travel, in order to dress the bride and her closest female relatives, to assemble in suitcases the bride price that is to be offered and to entertain the wedding guests – at least so long as the family had money enough to observe these wedding obligations. Apart from these luxury shops, the mall hosts a huge supermarket selling all kinds of food items that previously were hard to obtain and available only at certain select supermarkets run by foreign families. In short, foreign products are now routinely offered in the many supermarkets, restaurants and cafes that have proliferated – and some of them even boast terraces and WIFI zones.

What was most surprising to me was the large number of Sudanese who frequented these places, which I had assumed were meant to cater for the ever-growing community of foreign aid workers and embassy staff. Apparently, the signing of the peace agreement and the booming oil industry attracted many Sudanese migrants back home, some of them quite affluent businessmen, academics or artists, while others had been less fortunate. These returnees, especially the nouveau riche, as well as male and female students who aspire to a different lifestyle from that of their parents, have become important consumers as regular customers at these new leisure places.

It was while I was drinking cappuccino in the company of a group of these young Sudanese on one such terrace that the name of a young Sufi shaykh came up. One of the young men said, "*Huwaaru chicksi, wa mihayatu Bebsi*": "His followers [lit. young camels] are good-looking youngsters, and his (healing, curing) potion is Pepsi". The words drew much laughter, *chicksi* referring to both women and men, like 'yuppies'. The remark in fact summed up the opinion of those who were critical of the popular young Shaykh al-Amin and his small Sufi order of Mikashfiyya[4]. He and his order were highly controversial, and many non-followers considered him an imposter, a fake *shaykh*, referring to him as 'Shaykh al-Pepsi'. At the same time, he was attracting a growing following of

---

3   Information from a government official.
4   Spelled in different ways: Mokashfiy(y)a, Mukashfiy(y)a.

mainly young men and women, the so-called *chicksi*, as his name and fame spread rapidly over town.

Given *uthat* the Sufi order of the Mikashfiyya is only a small branch of the large Qadiriyya Sufi order, the interest he elicited is remarkable in view of the long history of the many Sufi orders in this part of the Sudan and their influence on Sudanese society. In the context of this article I cannot offer a detailed history of the diverse Sufi orders: generally speaking, the Sudanese, especially those living in the Nile Valley, where the capital is also located, consider their culture to be based on Sufi orders coming from the North, the West and in particular the Arabian Peninsula. The Sufi orders that functioned as mass supra-tribal organizations were introduced to Sudan in the late 18th and early 19th centuries (O'Fahey 1992: ix-x). Apart from the Qadiriyya and Shadhiliyya orders, which were already present in the Nile Valley, the popularity of the 'new' orders of Sammaniya, Khatmiyya, Rashidiyya and others were "to lead to profound changes in the lives of most Sudanese Muslims" (O'Fahey 1992: x). The spread of Sufi orders has had an inclusive effect, since the Sufi, broadly speaking, preach peace, love, kindness, hospitality, understanding and compassion towards strangers. But the influence of Sufi orders has also had an exclusive aspect, partly because the orders are often related to certain families and localities, and partly because they have been instrumental in Sudanese politics. Previously, and certainly after Independence in 1956, the political field had been dominated by two major parties founded by two religious families: the Democratic Union Party of the Khatmiyya Sufi order of the Mirghani family in East Sudan, and the UMMA party of the Ansar of the Mahdi family, heading a Sammaniya Sufi branch, whose headquarters are located on Aba Island in the Nile.[5]

When the Islamist Sudanese government came to power in 1989 as a result of a military coup, it banned all kinds of organizations, including Sufi orders, as their practices were considered to be backward, traditional and even un-Islamic. The new Islamist NIF party put itself forward as the modern alternative to the domination of public and political life by the competing Sufi orders.[6]

---

5 The Ansar is the label given to the followers of the Mahdi, the founder of the Islamist state of the Sudan (1885-98). It is now used to refer to the followers of the politico-religious UMMA party that is headed by the great-grandson of the Mahdi, al-Sadiq al-Mahdi (Warburg 1985: 100-113; Warburg 2003: 125-127).

6 Despite the coalition with the UMMA and DUP it participated in after the elections of 1985, the NIF of al-Turabi, formerly the Muslim Brothers, allied itself with the military government that came to power in 1989 after having ousted the same democratic regime in which the NIF had participated (See Ibrahim 1999: 195-223; Warburg 1985: 400-413, 1995: 219-236).

However, since the 1990s the Sufi orders have revived, in particular in the city of Khartoum, focusing on communal experience and the enactment of a religious identity. As these orders have officially renounced any political aspirations, they are condoned by the Sudanese government. During my eight-month stay in Khartoum between 2006 and 2008, the reputation of Shaykh al-Amin became increasingly discussed: he attracted as many followers and fans as critics, who referred to him with disdain and even scorn. What was clear was that he triggered a sometimes heated debate. Of interest, then, is the question of what caused this debate and what the attraction of this particular *shaykh* was to those who, despite the ridicule and negative comments about his capacities as a *shaykh*, chose to become his disciple[7], following his Sufi order of the Mikashfiyya.

In this article I want to take a closer look at the popularity of Shaykh al-Amein and his Mikashfiyya Sufi order and his contested authority, focusing on one of the main questions that is central to this volume, namely, 'what makes a place a sacred Muslim place?' The role of sacred place-making by the *shaykh* is related to the performance of certain religious practices that establish and reconfirm his capacities as a *shaykh* and attract followers. This enactment of the Sufi identity by the *shaykh* and his followers revolves around two related aspects: the *zawiya*, literally 'corner', the place where the *shaykh* and his Sufi followers (and their audience) assemble during religious practices; and the *dhikr*, most commonly spelled *zikr*, a communal meditative ritual meant to commemorate 'god'[8], practiced by the Sufi 'brothers' guided by their *shaykh*. If the *zawiya* is the 'what' of the sacred place-making, the place that is made sacred, it is these religious rituals, of which the *zikr* is the most tangible and distinguishing practice, that form the 'how'. As is elaborated upon below, the *zawiya* is not so much an existing building or place, bounded by easily distinguishable landmarks; it exists by virtue of the religious practices that are important to the performance of Sufi identity. This means that it is during the performance of the *zikr* that the *zawiya*

---

7   Categories of followers can be distinguished, like the adepts and lay-affiliates. The adepts are formally initiated into the order and may fulfill all kinds of positions within the hierarchy of the order (Osman 1985: 107-108). In the context of this article I will not distinguish between these and refer to those who frequent the *zawiya* of the *shaykh* as his 'followers'.

8   The ritual is meant to fill the mind and heart with the notion of 'god' by reciting his name and rhythmically moving the body, with or without music to guide the rhythm, in order to fall into a trance. The Sufi believe that it is in this meditative, trance-like state that closeness to god is achieved and thus a process of physical, mental and moral purification takes place. See below for further details of this process.

is transformed into a sacred place. To address the question of how a *shaykh* performs this 'sacred place-making' by looking at the *zikr* performed in the *zawiya* means to understand this capacity of the *shaykh* as a process that needs to be re-enacted continuously in order to establish his status and reputation as a *shaykh*.

It is also during these ritual meetings that Sufi followers, *murid* or *huwaar* (lit. young camels), openly practice an important Sufi ritual in which the open communal commemoration of god not only marks them as Sufi brothers but also facilitates the socializing of a group of followers. It is precisely in this interface between the sacred and profane, the religious and the social, that the authority of Shaykh al-Amein over certain groups of Sudanese is to be found. I will, however, first look at the *zawiya* as a religious place for the Mikashfiyya order.

THE ZAWIYA: A 'SACRALIZED' PLACE

On YouTube[9] one of the many references to Shaykh Al Amin[10] features a black four-wheel-drive Volkswagen at the centre of a group of new and expensive-looking cars that are speeding along the tarmac roads of Khartoum, accompanied by a motorized police officer sounding his siren. The video, recorded by a person in one of the accompanying cars, shows, in fragments, the journey from the airport in Khartoum via the old bridge across the Nile to one of the smaller shopping streets in 'medieval' Omdurman. At the end of the video we see the cars turning into a sandy alley leading to an open square, where they are welcomed by a crowd consisting mainly of men, mostly clad in green *jellabiyas,* long male robes, with a red sash. The green garments mark them out as followers of the Qadiriyya Sufi order; the sash is reminiscent of the waistband and belt worn by policemen. As Shaykh al-Amin gets out of his car some followers lift him on to their shoulders, and he waves at the crowd that is chanting *la illa illa'llah.* After greeting the crowd with *as-salamu 'alaykum* through a microphone that has been handed to him, he almost immediately starts the *zikr.*

This brief video footage is of interest for two reasons. It shows the *shaykh* being rushed through Khartoum to the 'twin city' of Omdurman in the way a celebrity or high-ranking foreign visitor would be, with police escort, sirens and flashy cars. At the same time, the cars end their journey at a small dusty square

---

9   http://www.youtube.com/watch?v=FCtpgloWckA&feature=related, (last accessed September 25, 2011, uploaded by agab 132 on September 12, 2007, 3.59 minutes).

10 Spelled in different ways: Shaykh/shaykh El/Al Amein, El/Al Amien, El/Al Ameen, but mostly Sheikh El Amin.

where the *shaykh* gets out and which is only just visible on the video: the *zawiya* of Shaykh al-Amin. This is the place where Sufi adherents and followers meet their *shaykh* during the biweekly *zikr*, the commemoration of Allah.

Zawiya literally means 'corner' and referred originally to the location in a cell of a Christian monk used for private worship. It was adopted by Muslims to refer to a Sufi *tariqa* (brotherhood) centre where prayers and other religious practices could be performed. A *zawiya* is often a space near the lodge of the Sufi *shaykh*, but it can also be a room, a series of buildings, or a courtyard within the compound of the *shaykh* (Karrar 1992: 141). It is the place where devotees meet and perform Sufi rituals and religious practices. The *zawiya* is organized around a local *shaykh*, nominated by the leading spiritual leader, the main *shaykh* or *khalifa*, of the order (Osman 1985: 111).

The Mikashfiyya *zawiya* of Shaykh al-Amin is located in Wad al-Banna, a quarter in Omdurman. This location is significant as Omdurman is often referred to as the old or 'medieval' capital representing the diversity of the Sudanese population. This belies the fact that Omdurman was founded only in 1884, by the Islamic leader Mohammed al-Mahdi, who used the village Umm Durman for his siege of Khartoum, the then capital of the Turkiyya, Turkish or Ottoman Sudan. Khartoum had already been established in 1821 as a garrison town for the Egyptian army by Ibrahim Pasha, the son of Egypt's ruler, Muhammad Ali Pasha. It was located about 15 miles north of the Soba, the then capital of the Funj Sultanate. The settlement grew quickly as a regional administrative centre, and now has more than 5 million inhabitants. Omdurman lies opposite Khartoum, on the western bank of the Nile. With a population of 2.4 million in 2008, it is the second largest city in Sudan and is the national centre of commerce. Along with Khartoum and Khartoum North or Bahri, it forms the tripartite metropolis and cultural and industrial heart of the nation.

The location is significant not only because of its dense living quarters and the fact that many Sudanese consider Omdurman to be the unofficial national capital of Sudan, since it hosts many 'national' institutions such as the National Theatre, Alwataniya Cinema, the Sudan TV and radio studios and the Higher Institute for Music. It is important also because it boasts the renowned Sufi performance on Fridays at sunset, when green-robed 'dervishes' (as the tourist guide calls Sufi followers) gather to chant and pray at the tomb and mosque of Shaykh Hamid al-Nil,[11] a 19th-century leader of the Qadiriyya Sufi order.[12]

---

11 See for example Kurcz (2004) who compares the zikr at Hamid al-Nil with a zikr in Old Dongola in Northern Sudan.

12 Who is again seen to be related to the 11th-century Baghdadi saint Abd al-Qadir al-Jailani. The *silsila*, or chain of spiritual descent of forebears, goes further back, how-

Although Sufi orders are located in all of the three cities of the capital, Omdurman has a special significance since, as an elderly Omdurmani Sufi follower, an engineer, explained to me, "the Nile is rife with malign spirits, like *jinns*, who may attack you when you cross the river. We need the guidance of a Sufi *shaykh* to fight them". The journey shown on YouTube therefore also has a symbolic meaning: it shows the transportation of the *shaykh* from Khartoum, the place of luxury and decadence and of most of the business and government offices, to the place of 'tradition' and 'authenticity', of which the Sufi order is one of the most outstanding manifestations.

Shaykh al-Amin of the Mikashfiyya, a branch of the same Qadirlyya Sufi order as Hamid al-Nil's, is one of the *shaykhs* who reside at Omdurman, where he attracts Sufi followers who wish to be guided on the Sufi path. Although not as famous as Hamid al-Nil, the *zawiya* is increasingly visited by aspirant Mikashfiyya Sufi, followers of other Sufi orders, as well as those interested in the Sufi order, such as journalists, tourists, and the occasional anthropologist. The *zawiya* constitutes a central place of a Sufi order; it is different from other important Sufi places, such as the *khalwa* (a place of retreat for a Sufi *shaykh* which in Sudan generally denotes a Qur'an school[13]), a *masid* or *masjid* (a mosque) or a *qubba* (the shrine of a saint or founder of a Sufi order) (Karrar 992: 137-144).[14] Although in Sudan there is considerable overlap between these functions, the *zawiya* is the place where the *zikr* is practiced.

The *zawiya* of Shaykh al-Amin is not located near a shrine or a mosque, but consists of the empty sandy square that lies literally on the western side of Shaykh al-Amin's house. It is bordered by high walls which actually constitute the outer boundaries of the compound of the *shaykh's* house and neighboring houses, some of which are still under construction. Several small dirt roads lead to the *zawiya*, one of them leading from the main tarmac road on to which many

---

ever, via the prophet Mohammed, the angel Gibriel (Gabriel) to Allah (Osman 1985: 145).

13 *Madrassa*, used elsewhere in the Islamic world for this purpose, are in Sudan used as schools for formal non-religious education.

14 *Khalwa* originally denoted the place of retreat for a Sufi *shaykh*, but in Sudan it also means a place for teaching Islamic sciences and the Qur'an (*'ilm*), which caused it to be generally used to denote a Qur'an school. A *khalwa* could also be used as a place of refuge or sanctuary, of hospitality, or for settling disputes, hearing complaints, and issuing *fatwas* (legal opinions), and as a medical centre. The *masid*, a dialectical variant of the classical Arabic *masjid*, mosque, refers to a centre of learning where *'ilm* is taught; and *qubba* means the shrine often of a saint or founder of a Sufi order, a place of refuge, sanctuary and even safe keeping (Karrar 1996: 137-144).

small shops open and which carries a lot of traffic. On ordinary weekdays, the square looks like any other open sandy square one can find in Omdurman, perhaps somewhat cleaner than most. In any case it is hard to discern that the area plays such an important role for this Sufi order.

When the place is used for religious practice, it is adorned with small lights and bunting, mostly green and red but also some white, with larger banners (*raya*) in green and red along the sides. Carpets are rolled out on the edges of the square, a microphone is set up connected to huge amplifying boxes, and strong lights on light poles illuminate the *zawiya* as in a football stadium. Rows of chairs are placed on the eastern side of the square and in the alley in front of the *shaykh's* house, especially for women, who sit around the *shaykh's* wife and/or mother, both referred to as *Umm al Huwaar*, mother of the followers, watching the Sufi brothers performing the *zikr* under the guidance of the *shaykh*, while also practicing a less visible *zikr* to the rhythm of the music. Although the colors of the flags and banners and the location of the square next to the *shaykh's* house signify the relation with the Sufi order of the Qadiriyya, to the innocent visitor the decoration may also be related to weddings or to other festive occasions with more private connotations. It is only when a religious practice, such as the *zikr*, is performed here that the square becomes a *zawiya*.

The *zawiya* is thus characterized by its temporary nature and can 'be' a religious place only when people make use of it with that intention. In addition, the place itself constructs a person as a follower of the brotherhood, especially when wearing the green and red *jellabiya* that signals one's status as a follower of this particular Sufi order. A *zawiya* is therefore different from a mosque, a Qur'an school, or even a shrine of a saint, even though it may have similar functions (Karrar 1992: 137-144; Osman 1985: 111-115). Although the *zawiya* has a fixed location to the initiated, it has no recognizable existence as a sacred place in and of itself. Only by practicing religious acts and rituals do the *shaykh* and his followers construct the place as sacred.

The *zawiya*, as the religious centre where followers of a Sufi order meet, is thus the focal point of the activities of a Sufi brotherhood: it forms the location where one's religious identity is enacted, while this enactment at the same time constitutes the *zawiya* as a 'sacralized' place. The terms 'sacralized' and 'sacralizing' (Werbner 1996: 309-338) emphasize the continuous process of sacred place-making that is related to the notion of *zawiya*. The view expressed in the introduction to this volume, that "sacred places are the result of a specific mode of place-making; they are the product of people's investments and practices that endow physical space with diverse, religious connotations" (Desplat in this volume), is particularly true for the *zikr* in sacralizing the *zawiya*.

PRACTICING THE SACRED, SACRALIZING SPACE: THE ZIKR AS PROCESS OF SACRED PLACE-MAKING

Religious rituals performed by Sufi followers and guided by the *shaykh* constitute the enactment of the sacred whereby the *zawiya* becomes, however temporarily, a sacred place. It is the place where the *shaykh* organizes and guides religious rituals and other public meetings. One such ritual, the *zikr*, referring to the remembrance of god, is by far the most important religious practice that constitutes the *zawiya* as a sacred space and its practitioners as Sufi followers. Most of the other religious practices, like *durus*, religious lessons, private consultations and religious, medical or social advice, take place after or between *zikr*s.

The silent *zikr* (*khafi*), also referred to as *zikr* of the time (*al-waqt*), is performed after the five prayers which a Sufi follower should attempt to perform daily, mostly in the privacy of the home.[15] Here I focus on the loud *zikr* (*jali*), also referred to as *zikr* of the circle (*al-halqa*). This most important commemorative practice brings together the *shaykh*, his disciples, lay adherents, and affiliated and non-affiliated visitors in one place, at one and the same time. The Mikashfiyya *zikr* is a biweekly event and takes place on Friday afternoons after sunset prayers (*'asha*) and Sunday evenings after the last prayer of the day (*'isha*).[16]

Sufi followers can practice *zikr* in one of two formations. They can be part of the outer circle, which is one of the formations and which bounds the area where the *shaykh* and musicians guide the movements of another group of followers. Followers standing in this outer circle move the whole of their upper body and hands. In the inner circle stands the man who, with the help of a microphone and accompanied by musicians, recites the name of Allah during the *zikr* and who on occasion sings religious songs of praise (*madih*). Together they develop a rhythm that the *shaykh* follows while leading the movements of those inside the circle, the second formation. The Sufi followers are grouped on one side of the inner circle and move around following the *shaykh* while imitating his movements, which he guides with a long stick. Followers may move from one for-

---

15 Several practices are meant to be performed after the daily prayers, often after the last one of the day. However, the *zikr* is ideally performed continuously in order to 'commemorate' god as a basic aspect of (daily) life.

16 In addition, *zikr*s are held on special religious days like 'Id al-Adha but also on anniversaries of the deaths of *shaykhs* and famous members of their families (Karrar 1992: 161).

mation to the other during the *zikr*.[17] Women, seated or standing on the far eastern side of the *zawiya*, form an audience watching the male followers practicing the *zikr*. They practice the *zikr* by using only their raised forefinger with slight movements of the upper body.[18]

During the *zikr* a participant may fall into trance and make the inward journey as a Sufi. Even if the trance is not achieved, it is the aim of every Sufi to overcome the self. In Sufi belief, the relationship between body and soul is a complex one whereby knowledge is considered to be gained through practice and experience, and divine knowledge is acquired via the heart. The *zikr* can conquer the 'wild' passions and emotions of the material body. The ultimate goal is to attain self-purification by transforming the *nafs*, the vital self or spirit, by transcending carnal desires and needs. Complete self-denial through the disregard or denial of the 'natural', 'animal' or 'wild' inclinations and passions of the body means that this self dies and leaves the *ruh*, the eternal soul, the immaterial aspect of a person, to merge in stages with the sublime (Osman 1985: 116–119; Werbner 1996: 321).

For an aspirant Sufi, the first movement of purification and 'deanimalization' (Osman 1985: 116) of a human being concerns the transformation of the body via enactment of the religious ritual such as the *zikr* in a sacred space. Both *zikr* and *zawiya* thus form part of the journey of a Sufi: adherence to a Sufi order is therefore referred to as choosing or following the Sufi 'way'.

The space of the *zawiya* thus constitutes at one and the same time both the starting point and the end point of a spiritual journey that Sufi adherents may undertake. At the same time as the *zawiya* constitutes the place whereby the bodily movements of followers constitute a *zikr*, the *zikr* constitutes the dusty open square beside the *shaykh's* house as a sacred space: *zikr* and *zawiya*, movement and place, constitute and thereby transform each other into internal and external sacred spaces. As this is a potentially dangerous journey, one requires spiritual guidance by a Sufi *shaykh* who has himself undertaken this journey (Karrar 1992: 151-167; Osman 1985: 116-119, 130-135; Werbner 1996: 310, 322-323; 2003: 22-85). The reputation of a *shaykh* depends precisely on the kind of guidance he can provide, not only in religious but also in socio-economical terms.

---

17 In many publications, women are relegated to the role of 'audience' (Osman: 1985; Karrar: 1996). This is, however, not completely true. As onlookers of the *zikr* practice performed by men as 'Sufi brothers', women also engage in movements of the body and thus themselves partake of the *zikr*.

18 Some of these *zikr* movements can be seen on YouTube by using the key words *zikir/zikr* and el-Amin Omdurman. For example: http://www.youtube.com/watch?v-=bEdS08O_o0w, (last accessed Oct. 4, 2011).

THE *SHAYKH* AND HIS FOLLOWERS: CONQUERING THE WILD AND UNRULY

The role of the *shaykh* is important to understanding the transcendence of the *zawiya* as a sacred place. A *shaykh* and his *zawiya* often attract followers because he is the representative of a renowned Sufi order: his reputation reflects the kind of guidance and protection he is able to offer. This is expressed not only in the amount of *baraka* (beneficent force of divine origin) he wields but also in the *karamat* (miracles) he has performed and the kind of protection he can offer his disciples, both through his in-depth knowledge of the Qur'an and the *ahadith* and through the religious knowledge that he can convey on oneness with God (*tawhid*), on the curing of illness and on protection against the devil or black magic (Karrar 1992: 187; Osman 1985: 117-121). As the mocking rhyme about 'Shaykh Al-Pepsi' suggested, the reputation of Shaykh al-Amin is problematic, as his critics consider that he fails on all these counts.

To start with *baraka*, there are several ways that a *shaykh* can receive it. One is through seclusion in a *khalwa* in order to attain spiritual and moral purity. As his wife told me, Shaykh al-Amin lived nine months with no food and hardly any water in order to attain this purity. However, as *baraka* is thought to be hereditary, for followers the most tangible proof of the Shaykh's religious authority is his *silsila,* or chain of spiritual descent, "which links the founder through a number of well-known Sufis of the mother *tariqa* to the Prophet Mohammed, to the Angel Gabriel and ultimately to god. This can be called the genealogy of Sufi knowledge or *sir* (the secret of truth), which every successor inherits from his direct spiritual patron" (Osman 1985: 104). To many, this means that a *shaykh* has to come from a family of *shaykhs*: in the case of the Mikashfiyya the genealogy is traced to the founder of the Qadiriyya, Shaykh Abd al-Qadir al-Jilani, who "is the most popular and universal saint in the Islamic world", according to Osman (1985: 101), which can be read from the name of the Sufi order "al-Tariqa al-Mikashfiyya al-Qadriyya (the Mikashfi Qadiri brotherhood)" (Osman 1985: 105).

Shaykh al-Amin is no relation of the founding family, while the Mikashfiyya were renowned for bestowing the title of *shaykh* on descendants of the main *shaykh* (Karrar 1992: 128; Osman 1985: 105-107). Shaykh al-Amin is therefore considered less authoritative than those who are related to the Mikashfi family.

This is probably why much attention is paid on his website to the way that 'Shaykh al-Amin Umar al-Amin', to give him his full name, became a Sufi.[19]

To summarize, after having met Abdulla Yousif Qorashi Mikashfi, he took the Sufi oath (*bay'a*) and was adopted as a godson by Al-Shaykh Abdulla, a cousin of the leading *shaykh* of the Mikashfiyya order. The website then relates the story of how this shaykh was ordered to wander with a fellow *shaykh* into 'the wilderness of western Sudan' where they founded the *zawiya* al-Manarah near al-Rahad in Kordofan.[20]

The centre of the Mikashfiyya order, however, is a small village in White Nile province, Shikaynayba,[21] near the town of Manaqil. This centre was founded by Shaykh Abd al-Baqi al-Miskashfi in the first half of the 20th century. The founder died in 1960, and his tomb now constitutes the central point in the village where commemorative rituals and pilgrimage take place (Osman 1985: 102-106).

What is interesting is the fact that, on the birthday of prophet Mohammed (*mawlid an-nabi*), the followers of Shaykh al-Amin visit the centre in al-Manarah in western Sudan and not the Shikaynayba *zawiya*, which is the headquarters of the Sufi order and is located closer to Khartoum. This is understandable since he has been adopted by this particular Shaykh Abdulla, and he therefore has none of the connections with any of the *shaykhs* in Shikanayba that other shaykhs related to the family would have. In addition, in popular opinion western Sudan is synonymous with uncivilized wilderness, and by choosing to pay paying allegiance to the founder of the Mikashfiyya branch there, Shaykh al-Amin made the taming of the wilderness part of his achievement.

This aspect is important as *shaykhs* who are revered as founders of Sufi orders are renowned for embarking on a physical journey as well as a spiritual one. In conquering the 'wild' by travelling to alien places, pacifying them and thus constructing sacred places, Sufi orders could spread over a wide area; and this enhanced the authority of the *shaykh* and his order. Shaykh al-Amin established the Omdurman *zawiya* in 1992. Osman (1985), who published his account of the Mikashfiyya *shaykh* and his family in Shikanayba in 1985, did not refer to any branch having been established in a town, let alone in the capital of the Sudan. Shaykh al-Amin is thus the first of the Mikashfiyya *tariqa* to have conquered the wilderness or jungle of the city, "a cityscape", and inscribed it, in Werbner's

---

19 http://www.shelamin.com/en/view/section/about/elzawya/community, (last accessed Oct. 2, 2011).

20 http://www.sh-elamin.com/en/view/section/maseed/elmokashfy/overview, (last accessed Oct. 20, 2011).

21 Also spelled Shikayneiba, Shikeiniba.

words, with "a new moral and cultural surface". Werbner goes on, "the moral conquest of alien space is a test of charismatic authenticity that legitimizes the rise of new 'living saints'" (Werbner 1996: 309-310). On this view, Shaykh al-Amin is such a 'new living saint' and his *zawiya* forms part of a segmental network of hierarchically organized sacred centers and sub-centres which, having been founded by *shaykhs* in 'wild places', are linked via the *zawiya*s as sacred places. The biweekly loud *zikr* that takes place in Omdurman under the guidance of Shaykh al-Amin thus connects all Sufi members of the brotherhood of the Mikashfiyya by performing the same ritual with similar features at the same moment every week. The practice of the *zikr* connects Shaykh al-Amin's followers to a network of sacralized places, which not only unite Sufi members in an imagined community of fellow believers (Anderson 1991) but also tie this sacred universe to one's own journey as a Sufi. In other words, while the performance of the *zikr* reconfirms the connectedness of the *zawiya*s belonging to the same order, it also constitutes a reconfirmation of the Sufi identity and its connection to other Sufi members. The *zawiya*s in fact form knots in a network of sacralized places constituting a common sacred space that is expanding, in both the seen and the unseen worlds. Thus, the religious authority of the *tariqa* also extents to the branch of Shaykh al-Amin.

As for *karamat*, a follower of a different *shaykh* urged me: "Let me bring you to a real Sufi *shaykh* who can perform miracles, for he can be at two places at one and the same moment." This notion of being simultaneously in more places than one is, however, a common thread in the narratives of the followers of Shaykh al-Amin. One of his followers, when he was studying in Egypt, saw the *shaykh* in a dream telling him to go home; he claimed he had never met the *shaykh* before. Others point at the miracles the *shaykh* has performed with his healing powers. Some point out they do not need to witness any miracles in order to acknowledge the capacities of 'their' *shaykh*. I will come back to this issue below.

Concerning the proper knowledge of Qur'anic texts and principles – which is in Sudan an important part of the status of a Sufi *shaykh* – is considered by his critics to be a major fallacy, since al-Amin uses colloquial Sudanese Arabic in his sermons and *durus* lessons. In addition, as one of the commentators on a five-minute clip of Shaykh al-Amin's *zikr* on YouTube, entitled 'irshad' and posted by 'mubrmij', wrote:

"In Islam you follow a shaikh for reasons of education and guidance, to get closer to Allah. For God's sake, for what reason is this guy being followed? NO knowledge whatsoever. Even the verses he recited were not read correctly. Please, people of Islam seek knowledge." (wadkeyree 9 months ago)[22]

Those who consider Shaykh al-Amin to be an imposter expressed doubts not only about his *baraka* and his capacity to perform *karamat* (miracles) or his ability to read and explain the Qur'an and other religious texts. They also believe that he is too young; that he owns several businesses and thus is too busy with 'worldly' issues that distract him from a truly religious life; and that he and his followers look too smart, and do not hide their wealth, even during rituals, which is supposed to be contrary to the principle of soberness that a Sufi follower should observe.

As it turned out, it is not despite, but because of, precisely these aspects that seem to disqualify him as a 'real' Sufi *shaykh* that he has gathered a growing band of followers in the last decade, especially among educated youths and richer families in the capital. They do not doubt his authority; they emphasize his stature as a 'modern' Sufi *shaykh* and consider him to be better placed than the 'traditional' shaykhs to guide his followers in the current age of rapid change and modernization. In other words, it is not so much his religious stature but his socio-economic background and thus his capacity to understand the challenges that his followers face in their daily lives that have conferred on him popularity among his followers. So in order to understand Shaykh al-Amin's authority as a *shaykh*, the question that needs to be answered is: what is the relation between the *shaykh's* religious reputation and his relevance for the socio-economic context of the lives of his followers?

Socializing and Sacralizing: Finding a Vantage Point and a Way to Belong

As indicated above, the respect and authority of the Mikashfiyya Sufi order is extended to the *zawiya* of Shaykh al-Amin. However, this cannot in itself account for his popularity among his growing number of followers. Even when the *silsila* is traced to one of the longest-established Sufi orders in Sudan, it concerns a little-known small and localized branch. Therefore, the success of the *shaykh* cannot in the first place be the result of the reputation of his Sufi order, but is to

---

22 http://www.youtube.com/watch?v=x816P5NdQqc&feature=related (last accessed Oct. 20, 2011).

be sought in the more personal influence that he has exerted on his branch and subsequently on his followers.

The importance of the personal aspect of the Sufi cult can be observed from the name of his website, which is not that of the Mikashfiyya in Omdurman or any other indication of the genealogy of the Sufi order. Instead, his website carries his own name (http://www.sh-elamin.com), and he himself is in fact the main subject of the texts and images that are featured on it. It is clear that the reverence and devotion of the followers are directed to their *shaykh*. The text emphasizes not only his standing as a pious and God-fearing man, but also recommends his worldly experience and involvements.

The *shaykh* told me in an interview that his main goal is to present to young people an alternative to the attractions of fundamentalist Islam on the one hand and a life of drinking, smoking and other kinds of morally despicable acts on the other. This is clear from the link 'Role in the community':

"Early youth (14-23 years of age) has always been a critical age in the lives of members of the community... In this day and age youth have the tendency to wallow in materialistic pleasures and are disinclined to explore matters of worship and religion hence depriving themselves from spiritual growth and the gratifying religious experiences. The Mokashfiya *zawiya* is a model example of how influential the implementation of the teachings of Islam are in reforming the society by way of encouraging the spiritual growth of its youth, the building blocks of the society."

In this process the *shaykh* is central since "purifying the soul is not a straightforward uninvolved task, but is in itself a science. And like all sciences, a teacher is needed to guide and lead the way."[23]

This moral message is interesting, not only for its propagandist style but also because it explicitly connects social issues to the potential 'guiding' powers of the *shaykh*. The text seems addressed not so much to the young people themselves, since it constructs them as social problems because of their 'bad' behavior. Rather, the *shaykh* seems to address himself to those who would agree with him on this 'problem of youth'.

To understand better both the strategic aspect of addressing people other than the youth that constitute the majority of his followers and his attraction for affluent youth, the mocking rhyme I quoted at the beginning of this article requires a closer look: *Huwaaru Chicksi, wa Mihayatu Bebsi*, 'His followers are the good-looking young urban professionals, and his (curing) potion is Pepsi'. The term

---

23 http://www.sh-elamin.com/en/view/section/about/elzawya/ethics-of-sufism, (last accessed 20 Oct. 20, 2011).

chicksi clearly refers, as I pointed out, to those who are young, possibly just out of college, have often studied or worked abroad, have high-paying jobs and affluent urban lifestyles, and are considered to flaunt their wealth. The image of a modern Western middle-class life-style is sharpened by the reference to *mihaya*, a curing drink, like Pepsi. The drink consists of liquid that is 'blessed' by texts from the Qur'an[24] and that a religious leader like a Sufi *shaykh* may prescribe for physical and mental ailments and illnesses, while Pepsi is an icon of the modern, Western luxury goods that only the affluent can afford to buy.

The rhyme thus considers a direct relation between the religious identity of the *chicksi* as followers of a Sufi order and their socio-economic status as a rising modern elite that profits from the recent upsurge in businesses and companies setting up in Khartoum since the oil boom began. In the last decade, this boom has prompted many Sudanese who had emigrated for study, work or political asylum to return with their families to Khartoum to make a living there. They are looked upon warily and with ambiguous feelings by many of those who did not have a chance to emigrate. After all, they left when life in Sudan was tough; and now that political and economic circumstances have eased, they have returned to continue living in Sudan the good lifestyle they enjoyed abroad. Although the issue is economic, since most returnees are supposed to have more money to spend than most Sudanese who remained at home, it is also social: the changes in the capital take place so fast that especially the elderly, but also the less fortunate young Sudanese, fear that not only are their culture, traditions, norms and values at stake, but so in particular are their chances to make a (better) living.

Even within families that have a long history as city dwellers there is a sense of loss when family members return from abroad with their children, who turn out to be 'westernized' in their tastes in food, clothes and leisure; who prove to have a poor command of standard Arabic and a lack of knowledge of their religion, even though they have been raised as Muslims; and who show an indiffer-

---

24 Sometimes by speaking the text into the liquid or having the liquid stand in the middle of the circle during meditative ritual meetings like the *zikr*: sometimes by literally mixing water with the ink of the written Qur'an text, or the ashes from burnt paper that contained the written text. The potion may be used for washing certain parts of the body or for drinking, or both. I have witnessed the blessings by the Sufi *shaykh*, while details of the other ways of mixing the potion have been conveyed to me by followers of the *shaykh* who are treated in this way; and it is consistent with my own experience of being treated by a *faqi* (religious leader) during my research in Darfur in 1990-1992 (see Willemse 2007a).

ence to keeping up family traditions of hospitality and socializing that are so central to Sudanese culture.

These returnees, however, find it hard to adjust to the hospitable and sharing ways that family life in Sudan upholds: material wealth and personal assistance are shared widely among family members, and visiting relations in order to maintain these ties takes up a lot of time and energy. These re-migrants and their children come into the transformed place that the city of Khartoum is, while at the same time they return 'back home' and feel that their stay abroad has turned them into persons who no longer 'fit' easily into the existing networks of family and former friends. Some complain that they have become strangers in their own country and do not understand their families, while others try to keep family members at a distance while climbing the social ladder. There is little room for privacy or personal achievements, let alone personal entertainment, outside the family circle. In other words, it is hard to satisfy the habits and needs they have acquired abroad.

It is therefore perhaps not surprising that members of the nouveau riche in particular, and the recently re-migrated educated young men and women, sometimes whole families[25], look for a place of belonging that is outside the tightly-knit family network. The same is true for youngsters who come from families that did not emigrate, but who by virtue of their education or professional position are searching for new venues to enact their new, 'modern' identities. In the town many of the newly opened cafés and restaurants are frequented by these returnees. However, at night the Islamist perspective on proper gender behavior still rules. For example, the café at the roundabout where the best cappuccinos, croissants, ice creams and smoothies can be found closes on Thursday evening, which is in fact the busiest evening of the week as Friday is a day off. This is because the religious police have threatened to close the café on the grounds that its owners are disturbing the public peace (fitna) by allowing young men and women (who have not in fact not always consumed much) to mix on its terraces and on the adjoining pavement.

It seems, therefore, that the zawiya of Shaykh al-Amin is a place that offers these young men and women an opportunity to mix with like-minded others, with whom they can share their religious aspirations as well as socialize. This is even acknowledged on the home page of the website of Shaykh al-Amin (http://www.sh-elamin.com/en/view/section/home), where the zawiya is described as "a place of worship, gain [sic] of religious knowledge, and a hub of socializing of the ikhwan within [sic] themselves and members of the communi-

---

25 One of the main importers of soft drinks, like Pepsi Cola, attends the zikr with his family.

ty". Clearly socializing goes hand in hand with the sacralizing of places. The socializing aspect may even be of major importance to those who feel they do not readily 'fit' in the huge conglomerate of the tripartite town of Khartoum/Omdurman/Bahri. They yearn for new urban niches that allow them to construct an identity that fits their transformed sense of self. The *zawiya* constitutes such a place where like-minded and like-spirited persons, with comparable aims, desires, experiences and socio-economic backgrounds meet. The *zawiya* thus offers a vantage point from which to 'walk in the city', and at the same time it serves as a place of belonging: "'Space is existential' and 'existence is spatial'" (de Certeau 1988: 117).

The brotherhood constitutes for these people a new family, with the *shaykh* as the religious and moral father, and their fellow Sufi followers their 'brothers' (*ikhwan*) and 'sisters' (*ikhwat*). Here their newly acquired wealth and/or status and their 'modern' identity are accepted and even emphasized. At the same time, while their search for spiritual fulfillment may be genuine, Sufi orders offer a relatively unproblematic alternative since they are considered to be at the core of 'Sudanese' cultural identity. Shaykh al-Amin's *zawiya* connects the 'traditional' and the 'modern': young people in particular can reinvent themselves without being criticized for 'betraying' Sudanese culture; even if their families do not belong to one of the many Sufi branches in Sudan they are considered to be part of Sudanese culture and history.

THE *SHAYKH* AS AN INTERMEDIARY BETWEEN THE SOCIAL, THE MORAL AND THE RELIGIOUS IN AN URBAN CONTEXT

Taking into account the socio-economic background of the followers thus identifies the attraction of Shaykh al-Amin to this particular group of urbanites. It is not only the demeanor of the *shaykh* in the sense that he is not judgmental about their lifestyle, aspirations and ambitions: the background of the *shaykh* himself facilitates this sense of belonging. Shaykh al-Amin has a BA in business administration from King Abul Aziz University in Saudi Arabia. His website tells us that it was Abouna as-Shaykh Abdullah, the godfather of Shaykh al-Amin, who facilitated his enrolment in the university, emphasizing the religious consent that this acquisition of worldly knowledge had from the start. The *shaykh* now has several successful businesses in which he can occasionally even place some of his followers when they are in need of a job. In this way, while helping out some of his followers, he can abstain from worldly dealings and practices. For the same reason, he is one of the few *shaykh*s to expect no donations in either money or kind for his services.[26]

While his followers often mention his fasting and his long stretches of contemplation at his *khalwa*, and while there is the notion that the *shaykh* never sleeps and hardly eats, emphasizing his piety and sober lifestyle, his attraction seems to lie precisely in those qualities that his critics claim disqualify him as a 'good' (in other words orthodox) *shaykh*. Rather, his position in the worldly domain validates his religious status as a *shaykh*: his background as a university graduate who runs successful businesses all over Sudan makes him a role model in both the religious and the worldly realms. Followers with similar aspirations are not considered 'out of place' by trying to attain worldly wealth, while they can simultaneously participate in religious practices.

In addition, Shaykh al-Amin's use of the vernacular is attractive to his followers, especially most of the returnees, since they often lack knowledge of standard Arabic. His achieved rather than ascribed status as a *shaykh* adds to rather than detracts from his *baraka*, which is taken to be especially effective in blessing business deals, examinations and applications for study grants abroad. These powers are considered part of his *karamat*. His aptness in including urban events in his religious speeches gives him the authority of a religious *shaykh* for precisely those who experience the burdens of city life on a daily basis.[27]

Interestingly, he is known to attract a large number of young women, who come to the *zawiya* on their own account and not necessarily as a relation of a male follower, as is usually the case. Many of the young women appear in *ibaya*, the black caftan-like outer garment that has recently been imported from Dubai, the preferred shopping centre for affluent Sudanese. Some wear jewelry and others even make-up when attending religious practices. When I asked them why they attached themselves to this particular Sufi order, female followers, after mentioning his religious qualities as a *shaykh*, would comment on his well-groomed appearance with his clean, new and well-tailored *jellabiyas* in green, red and black. As a female follower put it: "We do not need to walk around in dirty and torn clothes to be pious, we can dress nicely and be clean, which is im-

---

26 He does, however, get a lot of presents like air tickets, the use of cars, luxury goods, like watches. But these are often not given in exchange of a concrete 'service' by the *shaykh*.

27 The *zikr* may result in a state of trance among some of the participants with two possible results: the *jedbha shaitaniyya* (attraction by the devil) and the *jedbha rahmaniyya* (attraction by the compassionate) (Osman 1985: 133-134). As I have never witnessed people fall into a trance nor heard any reflections by followers nor non-followers, this may testify to the abilities of the *shaykh* to prevent this kind of captivity.

portant for all Muslims, and still be a good *huwaar.*" This is clearly a reference to other Sufi orders, such as that of Hamid al-Nil, whose followers are sometimes dressed in old and patched *jellebiya*s (sometimes even in new garments with false 'mending spots') and may roll on the ground dirtying their garments and their skins.

The *shaykh's* light skin and regular features made some of his female followers ask me whether I didn't think their *shaykh* was handsome. Other aspects that make the *shaykh* attractive, according to his female followers in particular, are his quiet demeanor, his friendliness and openness, his care for his followers, and the opportunities he creates to talk to him about all kinds of personal problems. He receives all those who seek his advice, old and young alike. Moreover, most of his followers would stress that he is tolerant not only of wealth but also of young people interested in finding a marriage partner, of foreigners from all kinds of religious backgrounds, and even of homosexuality, although that was a topic that could hardly be discussed openly.

It is clear that, for the majority of the young people that assemble at the *zawiya* of Shaykh al-Amin, the socializing aspect plays a major role in their decision to become a follower of this religious leader at this particular religious place. The social even dominates the religious when young laypersons first find their way to the Mikashfiyya *zawiya*. This is not to say that the *shaykh* does not cater for spiritual needs; but it is their social needs, their desire to belong and to construct a meaningful self in the huge city of their families, that they feel most urgently.[28]

To return to the rhyme about 'Shaykh al-Pepsi', the relation between *mihaya* and Pepsi may have a twist. In the event of illness 'modern' yuppies would certainly go to hospital and not rely on drinks that were supposed to cure them because of the power of Qur'an texts. Thus, the line can be taken to be quite literally: the only drink available is Pepsi. Indeed, while one of the main importers of Pepsi-Cola has become a follower with his own family, religious lessons and occasionally the *zikr* on Sunday night are often concluded by handing around soft drinks along with small pieces of food, like falafel or apples. However, the *shaykh* does prescribe *baghra*, the burning of incense and paper with Qur'an texts and *mihaya*, potions that are also invested with religious texts for certain ailments. Therefore, the connection between 'potion' and Pepsi may be read in the sense that drinking Pepsi-Cola is like taking a potion and thus bringing people under the influence of the *shaykh*, even in worldly matters.

---

28 See for an anthropological reflection on the social in a Sufi order in Aleppo, Syria: Pinto (2010: 464-478).

It is therefore not surprising that one of the female followers of Shaykh al-Amin proudly told me: "He even marries people." Although this sounded patronizing to me, it was apparently considered a virtue. It proved to fulfill a deeply felt desire among most women and men who follow Shaykh al-Amin: finding a suitable marriage partner is one of the main problems that young people who aspire a modern lifestyle face when living in Khartoum. For women the problem is to find a suitable man who is willing to allow her the space to work, to receive her friends and to go out if she wants to and to not burden her too much with the demands of (extended) family life.[29] For men the first challenge is to find a woman who shares his ambitions and lifestyle; and if he meets one, often the sister of one of his friends or male colleagues, he has to ascertain whether his family considers his choice of a wife to be suitable. The bride price and wedding costs are often too high for the bridegroom to afford on his own, even those of the modest weddings of less affluent *chicksis*. So in order to have a wedding that suits the status of both families and then to provide his bride with a house that is well-furnished and private enough to start a family of their own, he depends on his family members to pool resources.[30]

The *shaykh* is reported to have intervened both in introducing potential marriage partners to each other and in negotiating the decision of one or both followers with either family should it be resistant to this particular marriage partner. The *shaykh* intermediates more often in cases where his young followers have a disagreement with their parents that they feel they cannot resolve, over matters like career or study choice, permission to travel abroad, or, indeed, marriage partner. He actually visits the house of the family of the particular follower and discusses the matter with them as if it concerned his own child.

In addition, the *shaykh* may turn up at his followers' weddings with a number of his followers in attendance, well-groomed and dressed in neat dark suits with expensive shirts and shoes. They take a seat in a specially reserved part of the room, mostly a couch or sofa.[31] The *shaykh* mostly does not stay longer than half an hour, leaving again with his followers at his heels. The wedding couple feels extremely proud when their party is thus honored by their revered *shaykh*,

---

29 I have written earlier about this plight of educated men and women (see Willemse 2007a and b).

30 See Willemse (2007a) for a similar position that educated men in towns in Darfur found themselves in.

31 The *shaykh's* mother, wife and female followers are often present during the whole evening, and they are given the best table in the wedding hall. It is the table near the podium on which the wedded couple sits in between dances and which is mostly reserved for female relations of the bride.

even though family members sometimes feel that too much attention is paid to this event.

So in effect, just as the 'traditional' merges with the modern and the social invades sacred places, such as the *zawiya*, the opposite is also true: the sacred intersects with the profane as the *shaykh* ventures outside the *zawiya* in his capacity as a *shaykh* with followers in attendance. The boundaries between the two 'worlds' thereby become fluid and permeable. It is precisely the capacity of the *shaykh* to intermediate and intervene between these worlds that attract a particular part of the growing urban population of Khartoum to the Sufi order of this particular Shaykh al-Amin. The acknowledgment of his role as an intermediary on behalf of young people, in the sense of offering them a place of worship, religious knowledge, and a hub of socializing is thus addressed to those who may have doubts about the intersecting of the social and the sacred, of men and women, out of (their) sight. The message seems to mean to reassure those whose youngsters frequent his *zawiya* by pointing out that both social and religious aspects are important in order for the *shaykh* to take care of and to guide young people on the correct path.

As noted above, *shaykhs* who are revered as founders of Sufi orders are renowned for embarking on a physical journey as well as a spiritual one. In conquering the 'wild' by travelling to alien places, pacifying them and thus constructing sacred places, Sufi orders could spread over a wide area; and this enhanced the authority of the *shaykh*. Shaykh al-Amin has conquered the jungle of the city and has become to some extent a new 'living saint' (Werbner 1996: 309-310); and in this capacity he has conquered other alien spaces.

CONQUERING THE WILD AND THE UNKNOWN: FROM CITYSCAPE TO TRANSNATIONAL PLACES

Shaykh al-Amin's willingness to attend wedding parties and to defend his followers extends across the boundaries of Sudan. The purifying of the body through *zikr* is also a 'sacralizing of space', also on foreign soil, in the words of Pnina Werbner:

"Sufi Islam is not only a journey within the body and person, conceived of as a journey toward God. It is also a journey in space. The sacralizing of space is not [...] simply a coincidental feature of Sufi cultic practices. It is a central, essential aspect of Sufi cosmology and of Sufism as a missionizing, purificatory cult. Beyond the transformation of the person, Sufism is a movement in space that Islamizes the universe and transforms it into the space of Allah. The journey, the *hijra* empowers a saint as it empowers the space through which he travels and the place where he establishes his lodge." (1996: 322-323)

The wild of the jungle or the desert has thereby been replaced by the wild of the alien space of the *kufar*, the unbelievers, in the 'West'; a dangerous journey that endows the *shaykh* with charisma. What is interesting is that in this case the *shaykh* has followed his (potential) followers who travelled abroad when some of the migrated Sudanese invited him to their new homes. In thus sacralizing alien places, the *shaykh* facilitates his Sufi followers to ground their identities as Muslims in a new locality and thus embed this moral space 'in' this new place.[32] At the same time they connect themselves through the link with the *shaykh* to the brotherhood back home, thus creating a new road along which followers of the *shaykh* can travel abroad, as stated on the website:

"When the individual growth of a *fageer* (Sufi follower, KW) is stunted in Sudan, Sidi Al Shaykh Al Amin encourages travel abroad. The blessing and benefit in this is two-fold. First the *mureed* will seek individual growth in attaining knowledge, or developing professionally. On the other hand, Islam has yet another representative in the non-Muslim world. A sound individual that will spread the teachings of Islam and may be a guide to some lost souls. The biggest congregations of followers of Sidi Al Shaykh Al Amin's in the western world are in Chicago and Amsterdam."

And for those who, for whatever reason, cannot attend, there is the internet. In this virtual space they can share the experiences that are recorded, mostly on mobile phones and occasionally with small cameras, by the followers themselves as they actually participate in the *zikr* while turning the *zawiya* into a sacred place. They can watch their *shaykh* and their companions perform the *zikr* in the *zawiya* they know so well, or join him in Amsterdam, Chicago, Brussels, London. While abroad, he connects his followers to his *zawiya* in Omdurman; and when in Omdurman he connects the followers to their brothers elsewhere in the world, often by literally referring to those places as part of one extended sacred space. In this way their *shaykh* is not in just two, but in multiple, sites at one and the same time.

---

32 Werbner refers to Sufi cults as 'chaordic' and point out that migrants engage in sacred place-making as is used in this volume to extend the boundaries of their religious identities (2002: 119-133).

TO CONCLUDE:
CONTINGENT SACRED PLACES AND THE ENACTMENT
OF IDENTITIES

It is in this way that the *zawiya* and *zikr* construct and reconstruct a chain of sacred and sacralized spaces through the performance of both the *shaykh* and his
followers at specific places that relate the individual to the communal, the worldly to the otherworldly or esoteric, the local to the transnational, and the corporal
to the virtual: in the end, it reconnects the sacred spaces of the Sufi as a brotherhood to practiced sacred places of the *zawiya* at particular locations. It is the fact
that the *shaykh* intermediates between diverse worlds, that of the religious and
the social, the sacred and profane, the Dar al-Islam and 'alien' places, that makes
his role in the 'Sufi way' of such importance. As I have shown, it is not only his
'religious' capacities that are of importance in making him a successful intermediary between those different worlds which Sufi followers have to cope with. To
some, Shaykh al-Amin's socio-economic background counts as most relevant for
the experience of modern, urban daily life, while to others it is precisely this that
casts him as an imposter.

The *shaykh* and his followers form the contingent foundation of the *zawiya*
as a sacred place. The *zawiya* is considered to be the place that connects a particular Sufi *shaykh* to his followers, a connection that needs continuous reconfirmation by performing the *zikr*. A Sufi *shaykh's* authority as a religious leader
is directly connected to his capacity to attract followers to his *zawiya*, to get as
many Sufi adherents as possible to attend and practice the *zikr* he presides over,
and thus extend the influence of his Sufi order. In the making of the *zawiya* as a
sacred place, however temporarily, the Sufi *shaykh* plays a pivotal role; and by
performing this role he is intrinsically bound to his followers in order to enact
the sacred that, in turn, sacralizes the place where the ritual takes place. It is in
the way he leads his followers and attends to their needs in the periods between
zikrs, when followers are dealing with the challenges of their social lives, that a
shaykh establishes his authority and attracts followers. This agrees with the notion of a place as 'a process, a site on which multiple identities and histories are
inscribed' (Massey 1991 cited in Desplat in this volume).

By choosing to perform the *zikr* guided by this particular *shaykh* at his particular *zawiya*, his followers, both men and women, engage not only in the
movement of the body in order to purify the soul, but also in a chain of interlocking sacred places, both corporeal and virtual, both worldly and spiritually: from
inside to outside the body, from public space to private places, and from the local 'known' religious brotherhood to outside 'imagined' religious communities,

via the heart and the soul, by travel or internet. In this way the *shaykh* and his followers are in the end creating a community, not only of believers, but of people who are similar in lifestyle, background, class. The *shaykh* thus 'connects' the spaces and places he moves in and out of: he marks them as sacred while these sacralized places constitute him as a *shaykh* Thereby, this connectedness of local and transnational sacred places, and of embodied (*zikr*) and virtual (internet) enactments of the sacred, mark his order, his *zawiya* and his followers as modern.

Alternatively, by attending events which are not seen as religious, like the wedding party, the *shaykh* and his followers transform them into additional, alternative (because outside the *zawiya*) places in which to expose and perform this common religious identity as a group. As a result, the community of believers constitutes a community of belonging, moving from religious to worldly places, connecting and intersecting each other. The sacred place-making by a Sufi *shaykh* and the enactment of social and religious identities by his followers thus constitute each other, transforming both in the process.

REFERENCES

Anderson, Benedict (1991): Imagined Communities. Reflections on the Origin and Spread of Nationalism, London: Verso.

de Certeau, Michel (1988): The Practice of Everyday Life, Berkeley: University of California Press.

Ibrahim, Abdullahi Ali (1999): "A Theology of Modernity. Hassan al-Turabi and Islamic Renewal in Sudan", in: Africa Today 46:3/4, pp. 196-222.

Kurcz, Maciej (2004): "The Contemporary *dhikr*. Different Aspects of the Sudanese Religious Expression" in: Africana Bulletin 52, pp. 67-83.

Karrar, Ali S. (1992): Sufi Brotherhoods in the Sudan, London: Hurst & Company.

Massey, Doreen (1991): "A Global Sense of Place", in: Marxism Today 35:6, pp. 24-29.

O'Fahey, Sean (1992): "Foreword", in: Ali S. Karrar (Ed.), Sufi Brotherhoods in the Sudan, London: Hurst & Company, pp. ix-xi.

Osman, Abdullahi Mohamed (1985): "The Mikashfiyya. A Sufi Tariqa in the Modern Sudan", in: M. Daly (Ed.), Al Majdhubiyya and Al Mikashfiyya. Two Sufi Tariqas in the Sudan, Khartoum: University of Khartoum, Graduate College Publications 13, pp. 101-146

Pinto, Paulo (2010): "The Anthropologist and the Initiated. Reflections on the Ethnography of Mystical Experience among the Sufis of Aleppo, Syria", in: Social Compas 57:4, pp. 464-478.

Rogier, Emeric (2005): Designing an Integrated Strategy for Peace, Security and Development in Post-Agreement Sudan, The Hague: Netherlands Institute of International Relations 'Clingendael'.

Warburg, Gabriel (1985): "Islam and State in Numayri's Sudan", in: Africa 55:4, pp. 400-413.

Warburg, Gabriel (2003): Islam, Sectarianism, and Politics in Sudan Since the Mahdiyya, London: Hurst & Madison: pp. 125-127.

(1995): "Mahdism and Islamism in Sudan", in: IJMES 27, pp. 219-236.

Werbner, Pnina (2003): Pilgrims of Love. The Anthropology of a Global Sufi cult, London: Hurst & Company.

(2002): "The Place which is Diaspora. Citizenship, Religion and Gender in the Making of Chaordic Transnationalism", in: Journal of Ethnic and Migration Studies 28:1, pp. 119-133.

(1996): "Stamping the Earth with the Name of Allah. Zikr and the Sacralising of Space Among British Muslims", in: Cultural Anthropology 11:3, pp. 309-338.

Willemse, Karin (2007a): One Foot in Heaven. Narratives on Gender and Islam in Darfur, West-Sudan, Leiden: Brill.

(2007b): "'In my Father's House'. Gender, Islam and the Construction of a Gendered Public Sphere in Darfur, Sudan", in: Journal for Islamic Studies 27, pp. 73-115.

A Complete Life

The World of *Mawlids* in Egypt. Photo Essay

SAMULI SCHIELKE

Pilgrimages and festivals are like temporary cities made up of wood, cloth, and electric wire. They rise in a matter of days, stand lofty and crowded with people for a day or two, and afterwards disappear in a matter of hours. Temporary as these structures are, the bits and pieces that make them up are very durable. The buildings of the festival are modular, designed to be taken apart, transported, and put together again. Wrapped together and loaded on trucks they are taken to other festivals where they come together in new formations. Covered with scratches and kept from falling apart with countless minor repairs, they show the traces of long travels through the country. Like the crowds who after the festival disperse to go home and maybe come back next year, these structures return year by year giving the temporary city of festival a magic permanence.

Mawlids, Egyptian festivals in honor of Muslim and Christian saints, are festivals of the extraordinary. Once a year they transform a city or a village into a world of celebration marked by its striking contrast to everyday life. At the festival, the everyday order of things is suspended for a few nights by a utopian celebration of a joyful world open for everybody. This world of festivity is characteristically transient. After a few nights it is packed up, and people return to their daily affairs. Yet for many among its visitors, the festival appears as somehow more real, more intense and significant than the daily life it interrupts.

This permanence-in-transience of the festival, its ephemeral yet somehow independent reality, is something that I have tried to explore with these black and white photographs taken at the *mawlid* of as-Sayyid al-Badawi (Mayeur-Jaouen 2004) in Tanta, Egypt in 2006 and 2010. These images are part of a research on the contestation and transformations of *mawlids* in contemporary Egypt (Schielke 2006, 2008), yet in this photo essay I leave the issues of modernity, habitus, and Islamic reform aside. Instead, I focus on the question of the reality of the festive world.

Part of an underlying consensus of the modern age is a kind of common-sense functionalism, the implicit assumption that social life is an ordered whole, in which some parts are central and essential, others marginal and accidental. Festivals, our modernist common sense suggests, belong to the marginal and accidental part. But why is this so? And does it need to be so? In cultural and social anthropology, the old functionalist view of festivity as an instrument of social cohesion has become credibly contested by a view that shows festive culture as essentially dynamic and contested, productive of social order rather than merely reproducing and mirroring it. It is in this sense that David Guss, working on festive traditions in Venezuela, argues that

"[...] festive traditions, despite claims to the contrary, are in a constant state of flux. Such plasticity often reflects the changing social order in which these events are realized. But they are not simply mirrors, for it they reflect, they also create, and the festive state is one in which new realities are also constituted. Whose reality, however, remains a question, for the flexibility of these forms is derived, in no small measure, from their agonistic and contested nature. [...] To those involved, the stakes are high. For, as participants well know, festivals, for all they joy and color, are also battlegrounds where identities are fought over and communities made." (Guss 2000: 170)

With Guss, one could argue that *mawlids* are a site through which conflicting views on progressive modernity, correct Islam, and the habituated virtues and attitudes of citizens and believers are articulated. But this is not entirely satisfactory. Would this not be slipping back to the functionalist reduction of the festive to the maintenance of social order, only in a more sophisticated version that highlights contestation over cohesion? If I say that the contested nature of *mawlids* is a key to something outside *mawlids*, something which the whole issue is 'really' about, am I not ignoring my own point about *mawlids* being essentially about festivity for its own sake, a time in its own right, not reducible to an external purpose?

What if, instead, we viewed festive culture as having inherent social significance in itself? Samuel Martínez argues on the case of the rara festival in the Dominican Republic that the excessive and intense 'heat' of the festival is its main aim: "It is a celebration of excess and, more particularly, of humanity's unique capacity for desiring beyond utility and imagining beyond the reality of our senses" (Martínez 2007: 194). In this sense, festive experience appears not merely as a battleground of social dynamics, but as a social dynamic in itself. A festivity creates a temporary reality – a reality which, for a transient moment, can be just as solid and real as the everyday. During this moment, everyday life, too, may come to appear as exotic and transient.

Which one, then, is the real, original one? Is a festival there to provide a rest from daily work, or is daily work there to gather money and resources to celebrate a festival? I do not think that a definite answer can be given, but the question itself is worth contemplating about, because it offers us a clue to the contested nature of festivity. And in the course of that contemplation, partial answers can be given. One is offered by Italo Calvino in his novel Invisible Cities:

"The city of Sophronia is made up of two half-cities. In one there is the great roller coaster with its steep humps, the carousel with its chain spokes, the Ferris wheel of spinning cages, the death-ride with crouching motorcyclists, the big top with the clump of trapezes hanging in the middle. The other half-city is of stone and marble and cement, with the bank, the factories, the palaces, the slaughterhouse, the school, and all the rest. One of the half-cities is permanent, the other temporary, and when the period of sojourn is over, they uproot it, dismantle it, and take it off, transplanting it to the vacant lots of another half-city.

And so every year the day comes when the workmen remove the marble pediments, lower the stone walls, the cement pylons, take down the Ministry, the monument, the docks, the petroleum refinery, the hospital, load them on trailers, to follow from stand to stand their annual itinerary. Here remains the half-Sophronia of the shooting-galleries and the carousels, the shout suspended from the cart of the headlong roller coaster, and it begins to count the months, the days it must wait before the caravan returns and a complete life can begin again" (1974: 63).

Inverting the story of the fairground and the city, inviting us to think about the fair as permanent and the urban infrastructure as temporary, Calvino offers us a key to the problem of festivity. It is about the question as to what makes up a complete life. The question about festive culture and the everyday is, in essence, a question about the human condition. The celebration of a festival is an expression – and an experience – of a particular sense of being human, magnified by the transient and extraordinary momentum of festivity.

IMAGES AND CAPTIONS

Figure 1, Tanta 2010

Schielke

Figure 2, Tanta 2006

Schielke

Figure 3, Tanta 2006

Schielke

Figure 4, Tanta 2010

Schielke

Figure 5, Tanta 2006

Schielke

Figure 6, Tanta 2010

Schielke

Figure 7, Tanta 2010

Schielke

Figure 8, Tanta 2006

Schielke

REFERENCES

Calvino, Italo (1974): Invisible Cities, New York: Harcourt Brace Jovanovich.

Guss, David M. (2000): The Festive State. Race, Ethnicity, and Nationalism as a Cultural Performance, Berkley etc.: University of California Press.

Martínez, Samuel (2007): Decency and Excess. Global Aspirations and Material Deprivation on a Caribbean Sugar Plantation, Boulder and London: Paradigm Publishers.

Mayeur-Jaouen, Catherine (2004): Histoire d'un pèlerinage légendaire en Islam. Le mouled de Tantâ du XIIIe siècle a nos jours, Paris: Aubier.

Schielke, Samuli (2006): "On Snacks and Saints. When Discourses of Order and Rationality Enter the Egyptian Mawlid", in: Archives de Sciences Sociales des Religions, 135, pp. 117-140.

Schielke, Samuli (2008): "Policing Ambiguity. Muslim Saints-day Festivals and the Moral Geography of Public Space in Egypt" in: American Ethnologist 35:4, pp. 539-552.

PART II Contested Meanings and Places

The Case of the Jaipur Jami Mosque

Prayer and Politics Disruptive

CATHERINE B. ASHER

On an early afternoon in April I stopped for a cup of tea in a small courtyard of Istanbul's historic district near major transport lines to the rest of the city. Much to my delight, I was seated between the newly restored Yeni Camii and its famous spice bazaar. Enjoying the sunshine and moderate weather, I suddenly realized it was Friday as I watched scores of men stand in line for their turn at ablutions as the *adhan* (call to prayer) was heard throughout the city. I thought: where one goes to pray in the city such as Istanbul is a non-issue, but this is not necessarily the case in an Indian city such as Jaipur, even though it is a city known for its tolerance and multi-cultural population.

The original core of Jaipur is a walled city founded in the early 18th century by a monarch, Maharaja Sawai Jai Singh (1686-1743) as a replacement for the older capital, Amber, about 10 kilometers to the south. Sawai Jai Singh was a Maharaja who exercised authority over his own ancestral lands, yet at the same time he served as a high ranking officer in the Mughal military system.[1] While many popularly believe that Sawai Jai Singh of Jaipur, founding ruler, established his city as a Hindu enclave, in fact, the city embraced multiple ethnic and religious groups.[2] With some exceptions, the largely ecumenical spirit with which Jaipur was founded remains the status quo today. While most Jaipurians will insist the city is one of communal harmony, individual incidents do not so much disrupt this image but rather provide nuance to a picture that is otherwise painted in too solid and certain of a hue.

---

1 For Sawai Jai Singh see V.S. Bhatnagar (1974).

2 Joan Erdman, *Patrons and Performers in Rajasthan. The Subtle Tradition* (1985) and her, *Jaipur. City Planning in 18th Century India* (1989) are notable exceptions.

Let's start with the position of Muslims in Jaipur. At least since the 16th century, if not earlier, Muslims had served in important military positions in the State's previous capital Amber, and this continued after Jaipur's establishment in 1727 (Gupta and Kangarat 1994: 145-147; Nath and Jodha 1993: 163; Roy 1978: 181-182; Erdmann 1989: 212-233). As the city flourished and grew, Muslim families with skills in trades such as textiles, music, paper making and more were invited to move to Jaipur. While it is impossible to know the size of Jaipur's Muslim population in the 18th and 19th centuries, today it is between 20 and 25% of the population, a figure which may well reflect historical realities.

Today many proud residents of the areas surrounding Jaipur's prestigious Johari Bazaar, then the equivalent of Paris' Champs-Élysées, refer to the Jami Mosque [Figure 1] as the oldest in the city. Others in Jaipur seemed to agree, suggesting a date perhaps as early as the founding of the city itself in 1727.[3] Yet I discovered in field work first in 1996 and then on subsequent trips that the mosque records themselves indicate that the idea for establishing the Jami mosque started only to 1867 when prominent Jaipur resident, Roshni Begum, left 22,000 rupees from her estate to acquire land for its construction.[4] Her heirs purchased a block of shops not far from the Maharaja's palace and later acquired two small two-storied houses above the shops that they used as a mosque; however, their goal was to build a mosque anew it this same location. Throughout the later 19th and into the 20th century, the Jaipur government objected to the mosque's location arguing it was zoned for commercial purposes only. It was not until 1924 that these same two houses, sitting atop ground floor shops, unambiguously gained the legal status of a mosque. How is it that this site created a perception of its history so radically different from what the historical record itself indicates? The key to this apparent discrepancy lies in repeated requests to the government and their subsequent denials to widen the notoriously narrow staircase to the mosque. The controversy surrounding the long legal struggle over the staircase became a focal point symbolizing the aspirations of the Muslim community in Jaipur and ultimately the community's visions of its role first in the

---

3   For the older view of the Jami mosque's history, see Catherine B. Asher (2000: 132, 146).

4   This section on the mosque's history and early appearance is drawn from three independent sources, Nairang (1939: 2-3); JMJ (1956); Shameem (1996). Shameem had access to the 1956 history of the Jami mosque but not to the Nairang document; it is unlikely that the author of JMJ had access to the Nairang document. I have since given Shameem copies of all the documents about the mosque's history that I was able to procure including the Nairang report as well as newspaper accounts, so he can write his own history of the mosque.

city and eventually in the nation.[5] The eventual rebuilding of the mosque under-scores its centrality to the idea of a Muslim community unified by congregation-al prayer in Jaipur.

The Jami mosque as it stood until the 1980s resembled a house, the original function of the top stories. An area behind the shops on the ground floor housed washing facilities, latrines and storage. Prayers were offered on the visible two floors above the shops that were originally houses. In keeping with the shops, temples and houses of Johari Bazaar and other localities in the walled city of Jaipur, the approach to the upper floors was by a narrow flight of stairs about two and a half feet wide located beside the shops under the mosque. The stair-case was only wide enough for a single person to enter the mosque at a time. Such an arrangement was not a problem for temples, where worship is an indi-vidual event, or for houses where only a few people come and go at any one time. But the narrow staircase caused many problems for the Muslims attending congregational Friday prayer, especially on the last Friday before 'Id, when the entire community gathers. Photographs of a recent gathering for Id prayers [Fig-ure 2] give an idea of the thousands of people involved. Even realizing India's population has increased dramatically over the last century, the numbers of peo-ple attempting to enter the mosque via the narrow staircase would have been overwhelming.

Applications made to authorities since the late-19th century to build a new wider staircase remained stymied until 1939. Requests before 1924 were denied since the mosque's status was not official. The rejection of later petitions appears to be grounded in fears of communal reprisals (*HT* March 19, 1939: 3). With the triumph of 1924, a Jami Masjid Committee was formed to oversee the mosque's governance and activities. Initially the Committee submitted a detailed ap-plication to the appropriate authorities to build a wider staircase. However, after being refused permission, the Committee became moribund. Many of Jaipur's Muslims became so distressed by nearly a decade of inaction on the part of the Committee to widen the stair that they decided to take matters into their own hands. On November 17th, 1938, the few days before the last Friday before '*Id al-Fitr* (the last day of the month of Ramadan, the month of fasting), they pro-vided a makeshift ladder-like entrance from the ground to the second story. It

---

5   Jaipur's Muslim population is virtually unstudied. An exception is Joan L. Erdmann (1985), whose work concerns dancers and musicians in Jaipur many of whom were Muslims. In spite of the dearth of studies on Jaipur Muslims, differences in economic and occupational status indicate there is no single community. My personal interaction with a number of Jaipur's Muslims who belong to disparate economic and profession-al communities further underscores this impression.

was still narrow and did not allow many people access to the mosque at any one time.

That same evening speeches critical of the current Committee's inaction were delivered at the Chishti *dargah* (shrine) of Maulana Zia al-Din, the most important Sufi shrine of the city. Humiliated, the entire Committee resigned, and a new Committee was formed with Nasiruddin Hyder as one of the new members. Young and zealous, Hyder recently had been dismissed from service in the Jaipur State Army on account of his outspoken religious views. Taking advantage of his military training, he became the local leader of the Khaksars, a Muslim independence movement modeled on military lines. Hyder's enthusiasm to widen the mosque approach made him a popular known in Jaipur State figure with Jaipur's Muslim population. Protest against authorities was already, for during this same time events associated with the Praja Mandal, a movement of the Congress Party demanding independence from Britain, were transpiring in Jaipur. My guess is that, in part, the well-publicized activities of the banned Praja Mandal in Jaipur, of which Hyder was a member,[6] empowered members of the Muslim community to participate in the subsequent events of 1939. On Friday, January 20th, 1939, the last Friday before 'Id, Hyder was able to amass a large following, many of whom belonged to the Khaksar movement. Wearing white turbans they marched in procession from Jaipur's most important Sufi shrine, at one end of the walled city, to the Johari Bazaar Jami mosque to demand permission to relocate and widen the mosque's approach staircase. They wished to do so by constructing a staircase under the mosque adding to the original narrow stairwell the adjacent space of a shop owned by a Muslim who was willing to donate it for this purpose. A photograph preserved by a local Muslim family records this event, for most people in this large crowd showing the difficulty of entering the prayer chamber on the narrow hastily rigged ladder are wearing white turbans.[7] [Figure 3] I showed this photograph to a number of Jaipur residents without first telling them what it was; they commented that it must document an unusual event, since normally Jaipur's Muslims do not wear white turbans. In fact, white turbans are a symbol of mourning in Jaipur. The ones worn for this protest march specifically were called *kafans*, meaning both coffin and shroud, by the marchers indicating the Muslims' despair resulting from the State's failure to sanction their simple request to widen the mosque's staircase. When Hyder led the procession to protest the state of the stairs there was no reason to believe that this would result in violence as it did a week later. As Freitag (1989),

---

6   IOLJ, Letter written by C.L. Corfield, Apr. 10, 1939.

7   I am grateful to Mr. Inamul Haq for providing me with this unpublished photograph. See, Asher (2007: fig. 20).

Masselos (1982), Kakar (1996: 46-47) and others have convincingly argued, the public sphere, and the importance of gathering and processing in public spaces, is essential to understanding how communities define and express themselves. Jaipur, with its wide and spacious avenues, specifically laid out to accommodate royal and religious processions, captures the centrality of the public sphere (Erdman 1989: 226-247). For Muslims in Jaipur, the space is used in analogous ways including community prayer in the open streets in Johari Bazaar on the Friday before 'Id. Thus when Hyder led a procession to protest the state of the stairs the wearing of white turbans, a symbol of despair, was a public statement, but not one of violence toward others. Since this incident is not mentioned in any political document from or about Jaipur State there is no reason to believe that during this march any misbehavior occurred. Moreover, the site of the procession's commencement was the *dargah* of Maulana Zia al-Din Sahib, which I was told explicitly by several Muslims of Jaipur, is one of Jaipur's four major shrines, each one marking a corner of the city, thus imbuing the city with an aura of peace. The *baraka*, that is, the spiritual essence of the four major *dargahs,* flows into the city, thus encapsulating it; by extension all Jaipur's Muslims, including the procession traversing it in January 1939, were protected. The Muslims of Jaipur had claimed Johari Bazaar's urban space as their own and as a result their own centrality in it. That belief was to be challenged.

Upon reaching the mosque, Hyder announced that if the State did not grant permission by Friday, January 27th, that is, within a week, the Muslims themselves would commence the project.[8] The State authorities, including F.S. Young, Jaipur's Inspector General of Police, met with some prominent local Muslims and a leading Muslim from Delhi, Khwaja Hasan Nizami, giving oral permission, but nothing in writing. However, the authorities assured it was forthcoming. On the evening of Thursday, January 26th, again at the *dargah* of Maulana Zia al-Din Sahib, Khwaja Hasan Nizami implored all present which included Hyder, to wait patiently for formal permission to widen the stairs and not act impulsively. Hyder agreed. The following day, Friday, November 27th, several leaders, including Khwaja Hasan Nizami, reiterating his message of the previous day, spoke in the Jami mosque during the congregational prayer. While Khwaja Hasan Nizami was speaking those in the overflow group of Muslims who could not enter the mosque began making considerable noise, and the Khwaja asked Hyder to defuse the situation. Upon Hyder's return, two men, Lallu and Azim Jamadar, termed by Syed Ghulam Bhik Nairang in his 1939 Report on this incident as "bad character[s] and notorious tool[s] of the police," commenced dis-

---

8   This account of the events leading to and including the firing on the mosque is drawn from Shameem (1996); JMJ (1956) and especially Nairang (1939: 3-13).

mantling the mosque's railing on the balcony and immediately others joined in the demolition (1939: 4). Hyder's role was never clear, although he had received a telegram from the head of the Khaksar movement, Allama Mashriqi, telling him to hold off on the stair widening project (Ibid; *SM* Jan. 31, 1939: 10). While Nairang in his report was reluctant to claim any police complicity in this event, it is telling that by the time Lallu and Azim Jamadar commenced tearing down the railing, over 200 police, armed with rifles and *lathis* (police sticks), had gathered on roof tops and on the ground around the mosque. The Inspector General of the Jaipur police, F.S. Young, ordered his men to start firing into the mosque and even chased people into the surrounding streets, shooting and killing people there as well as in the mosque. In the end, at least 22 people were killed with more than 84 wounded. Hyder and all those involved were arrested.

The firing was reported in the 1939 press and was roundly condemned (*NH* Jan. 28: 1; *APB* Jan. 28: 6; *SM* Jan. 28. 14; *BC* Feb. 2: 1). Some papers expressed confusion, for, as they pointed out, it was Muslims who were pulling down their own wall; this was not a communal action (*HT* Jan. 29: 6). The writer for the January 29th issue of the *Hindustan Times* suggested that Jaipur's officials were attempting to "set up the Muslims in Jaipur against the [pro-independence] Praja Mandal (1939: 6)", then actively trying to gain sympathy in Jaipur State; reports issued by the Resident's office in Jaipur feared the incident was instigated by Congress Muslims residing outside of Jaipur to gain support for the independence movement (IOLR Jan. 1, 1939, Feb. 2, 1939). Jawaharlal Nehru, active in the Congress Party and India's future first Prime Minister, sent several delegates to investigate the matter and the full text of his conclusions, dated March 4th, 1939, calling for a formal inquiry into the firing was published in the papers (*APB* March 5: 13; *NH* March 5: 8). A few days after Nehru's text was circulated, a complete *hartal*, that is, a strike, in Jaipur city was observed by Hindus and Muslims alike in support of the Muslim community (*HT* March 8: 3). Syed Ghulam Bhik Nairang of the Muslim League also went to Jaipur and wrote a detailed report which analyzed every piece of evidence, from blood stains to spent bullets, placing full blame on the police and the State (Nairang 1939: 1-13).

It does not appear that the full text of his printed 13 page report was ever made public, but the *Hindustan Times*, and perhaps other papers, did publish Nairang's conclusions:

"The firing was absolutely unjustified and unjustifiable, a piece of high-handedness which could only be indulged in a State ruled on medieval lines, wanton in nature and ruthless in manner. The demolition of the balcony railing of the mosque was at the worst only a violation of municipal law, and was evidently not a criminal offence, cognizable or non-cognizable. The sequel has amply proved that there was no apprehension whatsoever of a breach of the peace over this demolition. Whatever disturbance took place was created by the police themselves when they indulged in the admitted *lathi* charge which was rightly resisted by the crowd in self-defence. By poking their nose into a matter which did not come within their cognizance, the police put themselves in the wrong from the beginning and are solely responsible for what followed. The number of rounds fired must have been more than 170 as shown by bullet marks on the spot and the list of casualties. The number of casualties so far ascertained is 22 killed and 84 wounded. More casualties remain to be ascertained. The manner of firing was all the more indefensible in view of the fact that people practically locked up in the mosque with a notoriously narrow staircase which was also blocked, were fired upon, and the crowd when fleeing was pursued and fired upon in places very far from the mosque. As the Jaipur Government admit only 32 rounds having been fired which cannot be accepted in view of the number of rounds disclosed by the condition of the spot and list of the casualties, our demand for an independent and impartial enquiry is completely justified and even the Jaipur Government should be anxious to institute such an inquiry in the interests of its own good name." (Nairang 1939: 8-9; *HT* March 17: 4)

On the 18th of March, the following day after this portion of the report was published in the newspaper, the Prime Minister of Jaipur, Beauchamp St. John, informed the Resident of Rajputana that 10 newspapers with either Congress or Muslim leanings would be banned from Jaipur State. He wrote, "Certain articles [...] are seditious and tend to bring the Jaipur government into contempt" (NAI). As of March 24th the Rajputana Resident saw no reason to take Nairang's report seriously (NAI), but by April 8th the Muslim League had passed an official resolution expressing sympathy for all the victims of the Jaipur mosque incident (Pirzada 1990: 296). The text was reproduced in a number of papers and within three days the Resident's office had prepared a blow by blow defense of the firing dated April 11th should Nairang's full report become public (IOLJ). It never appears to have been fully released, but all the same the cavalier tone of the defense was telling. For example, Nairang's report included a two page appendix listing all those killed. Numbers 21 and 22 were beggars: "the Resident's draft ended, the two beggars are pure myth. They never existed" (IOLJ).

Toward the end of March in that same year, 1939, the Jaipur Government did officially what the Resident was in the process of doing behind the scenes. The Jaipur Prime Minster, Beauchamp St. John, issued a statement announcing that after careful consideration of the evidence Maharaja Man Singh II, the ruler of Jaipur, had decided that the Muslims, not the police, were guilty in the mosque firing (*JGE*). However, in the following paragraphs he agreed to compensate those innocent Muslims injured or their heirs. Full consideration would be given to the widening of the mosque stairs. Then Beauchamp St. John noted that the Maharaja had agreed to build a new larger mosque at State expense providing that the congregation not use the streets of Johari Bazaar as an overflow area for prayer (*JGE*). Hoping to appease Muslim sentiments with this offer, Beauchamp St. John and the Maharaja were surprised when the offer was not accepted. They failed to see that new stairs, monetary compensation or even an entire new mosque were inadequate reward for the anger felt at the refusal to properly investigate the events surrounding the shooting. The firing had rendered the Johari Bazaar location more important than ever, for here was a specific demarcated space where Jaipur's Muslims had spilled their blood and became martyrs. Jaipur's Muslims claimed the firing and resulting martyrdom was a second Kanpur, alluding to the danger meted out to their community by the British-controlled police in 1913 and 1931 (JMJ 1956; Freitag 1989: 197, 210-216). Jaipur's Muslim communities on some level now saw themselves as a single unified community, ultimately becoming part of the larger Indian one who defied British tyranny, here in the guise of Jaipur's British appointed officials, for independence and for their own identity free from oppression.

From then on, the issue changes; it shifts from that of widening the mosque's stairs in order to facilitate community prayer to one of pride. At the urging of men associated with various socially and politically active Muslim movements outside of Jaipur, such as the Ahrar and the Jamiyyat ul-'Ulama' who were largely distrustful of the educated British-oriented Muslim League, a number of Jaipur's Muslims migrated to Delhi. As those migrating said to the Resident's secretary, they would never feel safe in Jaipur unless an inquiry were made.[9] In a follow-up letter dated April 1st, these Muslims stated, "[we] are loyal to the Darbar but with the refusal of demands [we] need to seek the benign protection of the British Government and abandon Jaipur (IOLJ)".[10]

On April 4th, 1939 those intending to migrate and about 3000 supporters walked in procession carrying black flags to the train station. There a special train with an engine and seven cars was provided for those migrating to Delhi.[11] The train was covered with black placards bearing slogans in Urdu (unfortunately no source reports the text) and black flags, probably the same ones carried in

9   IOLJ Report from the Secretary to the Resident, Apr. 1, 1939.
10   Darbar here refers to the princely State of Jaipur headed by Maharaja Man Singh II (1912-70).
11   It is not clear who arranged for the train, but very probably it was politically active Muslim groups including the Ahrar and Jamiyyat ul-Ulema; the Muslim League did not support the migration (IOLJ April 1, 1939; June 15, 1939).

procession, including one over the engine's funnel (*HT* April 5: 4; *NH* April 6: 8). Black also were the clouds of smoke and soot belched from the engine trailing behind the train. Earlier these same Muslims had worn white turbans as symbols of despair, a visual gesture which was immediately understood in Jaipur. Now, however, that red blood had been spilled, and they were leaving Jaipur, it was no longer appropriate to use an iconography unique to Jaipur, already known as the Pink City. Instead they choose the color black, the complete opposite of the white of Jaipur's turbans of despair. The black shrouded train, moving away from Jaipur, syr.bolized the Muslims' feelings of utter rejection and the loss of their larger community, Jaipur State. Shrouding the train in black foreshadows events of 1987 when in protesting communal riots where a number of Muslims were killed, Delhi's Jami mosque was covered with black cloth.

Black as a color choice to symbolize the migrating Muslims' sense of betrayal may have been more appropriate than they had imagined, since from April through September of 1939, matters for those migrants became increasingly grim. Impoverished and powerless, they were criticized widely by the Muslim League, including its head, Muhammad Ali Jinnah, and the National Congress Party for leaving Jaipur (*APB* April 11: 7, 15; *HT* April 20: 4). Even the Ahrars, who initially had encouraged the Jaipur Muslims to migrate, advised them to return and find a leader (*HT* April 20: 4). The Imam Shahi of Delhi who early on attempted to help the migrants, abandoned his efforts, although in a letter of August 24th he did suggest that the Darbar pay for their return home (IOLJ). While the Imam Shahi was told this was not possible, on September 4th the Resident of Rajputana privately wrote the Viceroy's Political Advisor, Bertrand Glancy, suggesting this would be one way to get the Muslims back in Jaipur where they belong and away from subversive outside forces (IOLJ). In the end it is not known which private source subsidized the cost of providing the trucks that brought the Muslims back to Jaipur between August and September (IOLJ; *HT* July 9: 6). Neither Jaipur State nor the British claimed responsibility.

In early April, the officials of Jaipur State in an attempt to whitewash their own image began a campaign to discredit the Muslim community involved in the migration to Delhi, claiming that all respectable Muslims have lost control. In the Resident's report of an April 1st meeting with several Muslims representing the migrants he declared them lowlife; one was a gambler, another tailor, the third a dentist and the fourth a commission agent (IOLJ). The Rajputana Agency's Fortnightly Report of April 29th reflected a similar view stating,

"Muslims of Jaipur are for the most part butchers and tonga drivers [...] They are a very rough and ignorant crowd. But for outside influence they are not difficult to control, but once out of hand capable of any atrocity. The better class of Muslims of Jaipur live in Sheikhwati and are [...] fine people [...] [who are] [...] not taking part in this agitation which is confined to city Muslims." (IOLR)[12]

This attack on the unworthy character of Jaipur's Muslims, I believe, did much to stimulate the mosque's revival just several decades ago.

The migration lasted from April until September of 1939, while in Jaipur itself outside Muslim groups were sending in batches of protestors to commit *satyagraha* (nonviolent resistance) (*HT* June 22: 14; June 25: 16; June 29: 5; June 30: 12; Aug 11: 3). The whole matter was so embarrassing to the Jaipur Government that H.J. Todd, the new Prime Minister of Jaipur State, suggested on June 23rd to the Rajputana Resident that releasing those involved rather than arresting them, would at least get them to leave Jaipur (IOLR). On August 25th, 1939 the same police officer, F.S. Young, responsible for ordering the firing on the mosque in January, wrote a letter to the local Muslim representative, Mir Ahsen Ali, indicating all prisoners taken in conjunction with the firing would be released, those injured and dependants of those killed would be compensated, and stated that orders for the widening of the mosque stairs had been given (IOLR). This rather abrupt about face was, on one hand, an effort to get pro-independence parties out of Jaipur, and on the other, an attempt to counter the press which increasingly was critical of the Jaipur State government, not only for its handling of the mosque incident, but also for its dealings with the Praja Mandal (*NH* April 11: 6; *HT* June 8: 8; *APB* Feb 2, 10; *HT* Feb 8: 11; March 19: 4; March 24: 4) Letters to the editor published in the English language press indicate that the maharaja was seen as weak and controlled by the British and his British-appointed Prime Ministers, police officers, and the Residents. Young was specifically named as one of the worst offenders. The vernacular presses which must have been even more critical were banned and destroyed (*HT* June 8: 8; NAI).[13]

Although small numbers of migrants had been trickling back to Jaipur since at least June, large numbers returned after Young's letter of August 25th indicating the prisoners would be freed, compensation for the firing victims was guaranteed, and that mosque stairs would be widened. The somber mood and visual iconography of their departure was reversed. The returning migrants carried white placards of peace (not to be confused with white turbans of mourning) as

---

12 A *tonga* is a horse-driven cart for passengers.

13 Records in the National Archives of India indicate these include the *Hindustan, Vir Arjun, Sainaik, Qaumi Gazette, Azad, Hurriat, Pesh, Tegh.* The ban lasted through November 1939 and perhaps beyond.

opposed to the black ones of betrayal carried on the departure. Johari Bazaar as well as the homes of many Muslims was decorated. (*HT* Aug 30: 14; Sept. 14: 14: *SM* Aug. 31: 5). Their mood was ebullient, and speeches congratulating the Maharaja were offered.

These celebrations mark a genuine shift in how many members of Jaipur's Muslim communities began to perceive their ruler, Man Singh II.[14] In fact, a number of Muslims told me it was Maharaja Man Singh himself who begged the migrants to return (Shameem 1996), although preserved documents do not suggest this is so. But it does appear that the Maharaja was beginning to take the affairs of his State seriously. After the firing incident, Sir Bertrand Glancy, the Political Adviser to the Viceroy, in a secret memo of February 3rd, had complained, "The Maharaja of Jaipur seems hardly to have the political acumen necessary to deal with a difficult internal situation," since, Glancy noted, playing polo in Delhi, visiting London and taking a third wife were the Maharaja's prime concerns (IOLR). By 1942 Man Singh was able to manipulate the British backing them into a position where his own choice for his next Prime Minister, Mirza Ismail, was appointed (Stein 1988: 272-273).

It seems that a genuine concern for his State started around the end of 1939, as the young Man Singh began to mature and also began realizing that what was good for the British was not necessarily the same for him. He became a hero for the Muslim community, and his British Prime Ministers, police officers, and the Residents were seen as adversarial forces. Many times I was told in considerable detail how in 1947 this same Maharaja came to each Muslim *mahalla*, that is, neighborhood, and asked the residents not to leave Jaipur for Pakistan. Very few repeated a migration that seemed so appealing in 1939. In recent discussions with some of Jaipur's Muslims, as fears about repression under a Hindutva-run nation are rampant, there is an increased nostalgia for Jaipur's raj.[15] One well-educated Muslim, who both runs a successful engineering firm and is the *sajjada nishin* (heritory custodian) of one a Jaipur's major *dargahs*, said recently when speaking of Man Singh II's famous third wife, who died in 2009, "Gayatri Devi is our princess." Emphasizing the word, our, he was alluding to an imagined unified Muslim community whose interests, memory now tells him, were better served first under Man Singh II and then, after the dissolution of Jaipur State, under Gayatri Devi, a Member of Parliament representing the right wing Swan-

---

14 I use the term 'communities' intentionally for some documentation exists to suggest tension existed between those Muslims who had migrated to Delhi and those who had not. (IOLR, Jul. 31, 1939).

15 Hindutva was a term coined in the 1920s meaning Hinduness with a sense of Hindu nationalism.

tantra party, than by the much further right BJP Indian government that was in control during the time of this conversation (Brass 1990: 76; Crewe 1985: 210-211).[16]

In the end, the Maharaja bore the expense of the new wide staircase which was completed in November of the same year, 1939.[17] That staircase then became a symbol of the very pride which had triggered the migration to Delhi. One eloquent gentleman, Shameem Sahib, who was the force behind the mosque's refurbishment in the 1980s, with great hyperbole, informed me that 100s of innocent Muslims were killed by the police for the sake of these stairs. In the handwritten history he provided for me about the mosque, Shameem stated: "These stairs have made history and even today when Muslims go up keeping their feet on these stones they remember those martyrs and pay their homage to those persons who actually sacrificed their lives for this noble cause" (1996). It was not 100s, remember, but 22 who died. For Shameem and the Jami Masjid Committee these stairs took on monumental significance, one that is even more meaningful than they consciously may realize. Shameem's own words indicate that the stairs are a tribute to the individual martyrs who now represent an imagined cohesive community which shares a common sanctified space. While the pre-independence Jami mosque was a symbol of Jaipur's Muslim community initially wronged by the State, but with the reconstruction of its stairs, it became a symbol of corrective action on the part of the Maharaja, who to their eyes was insuring their ability to pray together as a community.

In our discussion of the events of 1939 it might be useful to recall that some of the most important commenced with speeches or decisions made at the *dargah* of Maulana Zia al-Din. This information comes from Nairang's Muslim League report which is dated March 12, 1939. No comparable information based on interviews with Muslims present at the *dargah* when key decisions transpired, including the march and reactions to the firing, exists for subsequent events, but it would seem that the venue for the decision to immigrate and other key moments would have been taken at the *dargah* as well. The significance of this venue as well as the general belief, addressed earlier, that Jaipur's *dargahs* protect the city and Jaipur's Muslim subjects, suggests that religious and even Sufic imagery played a role in the meaning the rebuilt stairs held for the community.[18]

---

16 For a recent discussion of group or collective memory is South Asia, see Peter Gottschalk (2000, especially chapters two and three).

17 IOLJ Sept. 13, Corfield to Thompson; Sept. 17, Thompson to Corfield; Sept. 21 Thompson to Corfield; IOLR, documents of Oct. 26th, Nov. 9th, Nov 12th; Nov 23rd, 1939.

18 I am grateful to the late Aditya Bhel for this suggestion.

The first and most obvious concerns the *shahid*, that is, the martyr who died for the cause of those steps, and is guaranteed a place in paradise. These stairs thus are the threshold to God for those martyrs and hold the promise of attaining paradise for surviving Muslims as they climb those steps in memory. The imagery of the stairs as an *astana*, that is, a door to God, is common in *qawwali*, devotional songs, that are sung each Thursday evening and on important occasions at *dargahs* including that of Maulana Zia al-Din Sahib. To suggest such imagery as part of the stair's iconography is thus not farfetched.

After the dramatic events of 1939, little out of the ordinary appears to be associated with the Jami mosque, although it remained the locus of community prayer, until the late 1970s. By then there was an increasing desire to have the mosque appear as a clearly Muslim place of worship, not like a house. Although no photograph of the mosque seems to exist between 1939 and its reconstruction, I was assured by a number of well-informed people old enough to remember the earlier mosque that the top floors were exactly as seen in the 1939 photograph. The new stairs were the same ones provided in 1939.[19] What was the vision of Jami Masjid Committee headed by Abdul Hai Shameem, in charge of its reconstruction for the mosque's refurbishment?

Abdul Hai Shameem is an educated man who has traveled to a number of Islamic countries. By the 1970s he was aware that outside of India, new beautiful mosques were being built in great numbers. Even in Jaipur by now many new mosques had been built both in the walled city and outside the walls, but the Jami mosque as Shameem (1996) stated had no 'symbolic marks' to identify it as a mosque. Additionally, it was at this very time that preparations to build the large white marble Lakshmi Narayana temple provided by the industrial magnet, B.M. Birla, outside the walled city were underway (Taknet 1996: 67; Hardgrove 2004: 122-123).[20] The construction of this new temple whose doors opened in 1985, addressing the increasingly flush Hindu middle class, clearly caught the interest of Jaipur's Muslims who in general lagged behind economically Jaipur's non-Muslim communities. These Muslims too wanted a visual symbol of their community.

---

19 I am grateful to Mr. Shameem for providing me with an original blue print of the mosque's façade dated 1979. Mr. N. Ravi of the American Institute of Indian Studies' Center for Art and Archaeology has drawn an elevation based on the original blue print which is in the archives of the Center for Art and Archaeology, American Institute of Indian Studies, Gurgaon.

20 (Asher 2007: fig. 21). The temple's image is easily found on the web, for example, http://rajasthanindiapicture.blogspot.com/ (last accessed Oct. 23, 2010).

It is the perception of those Muslims with whom I spoke that procuring permission to build a temple is easy, but gaining permission for a mosque is difficult. The accuracy of this perception is unclear, but because of the charged history of the Jami mosque gaining permission to rebuild it was no doubt problematic. In 1979 a contact with well-oiled political connections arranged for Shameem to meet with the then Chief Minister of Rajasthan, Mr. Bhairon Singh Shekhawat, on very short notice. Shameem wished to bring a large delegation with him in his request to rebuild the mosque, and in the account he wrote for me in 1996, claimed that he met the Chief Minister with a delegation of 500 prominent Muslims. But a decade later he told me a slightly different version, stating that he had only a few hours between the time he learned of his impending meeting and its scheduled time. So he went to Johari Bazaar and requested Muslim street vendors and shop keepers to join him at the meeting. Regardless of the details, the point here is a remembered solidarity of Jaipur's Muslims who together worked for a rebuilt mosque.

After some resistance, for the Minister feared communal repercussions, permission was granted. According to Shameem, he pointed out to the Chief Minister that under "British rule [...] there was a trend of conflict created between Hindus and Muslims; but now the situation is quite different. Today Hindus and Muslims are living together with a keen sense of brotherhood" (1996). While he wrote this for me in 1996, in several meetings of 1999, Shameem repeated these words. In spite of an increased sense of Hindutva throughout India, Shameem, here representing the view of Jaipur's larger Muslim community, remains firm in his belief that the unsavory aspects of government under the Jaipur Raj were the fault of the British and should be differentiated from those positive ones which he associates with Maharaja Man Singh and Gayatri Devi. Shameem is extremely proud that the Muslim community gained the permission by peaceful means; this is a sort of negotiation of power by the marginalized in South Asia which needs to be more fully explored. By January 1st, 1980 the city planning office had signed papers approving the mosque's plan and design, although the mosque was not completed until about 1985 (CTP 1979; NP 1980).

Before I discuss the reconstructed mosque, a consideration of location is relevant. In 1939 the Maharaja had offered to build a completely new and spacious mosque "at State expense on a free site to be provided by the Darbar (IOLJ)."[21] According to Shameem (1996) two sites were considered. One location offered was just outside the city walls where today Jaipur's Gem Cinema Hall and the Ram Lila grounds are located. It only would have been a 10 minute walk from

---

21 In IOLJ this appears as a typed noted under the printed press release of March 22, 1939, the *JGE*.

the Johari Bazaar where the Jami mosque is situated. The other location was inside the city walls, today the site of the Ramganj Police Station. It is less than a 10 minute walk from the mosque. So far I have suggested that the main reason for turning down a new mosque was anger at the State's refusal to hold an inquiry into the firing. But there may have been another reason, that is, the potential locations' orientations. While both sites offered were not far from Johari Bazaar, neither had an east facing one that would allow the mosque to be easily and effectively oriented toward Mecca, a requirement in Islam. Both those sites were south-facing ones. Of course designers are capable of angling interiors for proper orientation, but by and large in India mosques are most easily built if the facade faces east and the interior *qibla*, that is, prayer wall, west. Such is the case with the Johari Bazaar Jami mosque.

Since the mosque is relatively small, I asked Shameem why not relocate the Jami Mosque in a more spacious venue where the entire Muslim community could gather. He responded that perhaps the Maharaja's offer of a new mosque in a new locale should have been taken, but he made it very clear that the location of Johari Bazaar in the heart of old and prestigious Jaipur, held a great deal of meaning for the community. This location, near the palace, the wealthy business community of Jaipur's jewelers as well as its oldest temples, elevated the status of a community so maligned by the State and Resident in 1939. The term 'prestige point' was used by a number of people for the Johari Bazaar location. Even if only about 3000 people can pray inside the mosque on the Friday before 'Id, I was told, there is no more beautiful a sight than 'Id prayers when the devout gather along Johari Bazaar and all the surrounding streets and chowks (street intersections). Just as all the shopkeepers of Jaipur observed hartal in 1939 to protest the firing (*BC* Feb 27: 7; *HT* March 8: 3; March 24: 14), so, too, on the occasion of 'Id, all the shopkeepers of Johari Bazaar and vicinity, many of them Hindu and Jain, allow their doorsteps, streets and stairs to be used for the offering of prayers. This underscores the Muslim community's sense of belonging to the city not just to their own community. I was told by many people, non-Muslims included, that communal problems in Jaipur are minimal.[22] Even before I knew anything about the Jami mosque and its history, in March 1995, three years after the destruction of the Babri Masjid in 1992 and subsequent riots, I had seen thousands of Muslims during 'Id prayers praying in the streets includ-

---

22 This is not entirely true, for violence in 1993 after the demolition of the so-called Babri Masjid in December 1992 resulted in curfews. However, is comparison to many other cities communal violence in Jaipur is relatively uncommon.

ing on the steps of temples.[23] At the time I was amazed, for the atmosphere was completely peaceful. In maintaining the Johari Bazaar location, the Muslim community claimed a legitimate place in this centrally located urban space. Here, the community felt protected from the increasing encroachment of Hindutva in the larger nation state of India.

As important as the location is the rebuilt mosque's appearance. A man who wishes to remain anonymous, whom I will call Ustad Mimar (Master Architect), designed the current mosque. While this was not his first architectural project, for he had redesigned the facade and added stories to the Mominan mosque built by his grandfather in A.H 1335/1916 C.E., his main occupation was his family's lucrative jewel business until his retirement. After he completed the Jami mosque, he later built a *dargah* over the grave of Adam Shah, one of Jaipur's important saints. Ustad Mimar is not a formally trained architect, but this not unusual, since most structures are built by traditional craftsmen.[24] As I noted at the outset of this paper, Ustad Mimar's only significant experience outside of Jaipur was in Mecca and Medina, his sources of inspiration are likely to be local. In fact, he has never even seen the Mughal architecture of Delhi, for I commented that he must have gone to Delhi to catch his plane to go on the Hajj. He replied, yes, but only to the airport. Ustad Mimar evidently learned his art from his grandfather who early in the 20th century had designed Jaipur's Mominan mosque located in *mahalla* Anserine near Ghat Darwaza. His grandfather's mosque, with its profusely painted interior, is considerably more elaborate than is Ustad Mimar's own Jami Mosque, but this is not surprising. While ten lakh rupees, that is about a million rupees, ultimately were raised by subscription for the project, Ustad Mimar repeatedly told me that this was a very tight budget in which to work. I asked him if he were happy with his Jami mosque. Yes, he said; its only flaw is the asymmetrical arrangement of the stairs.

The Hindu owners of the centrally placed shop beneath the mosque, the ideal location for the stairs, would not sell the shop, and the city planning office felt the 12 meter-wide staircase to its left, provided in 1939, was sufficient. But given the feelings about the stairs and their association with those martyrs who died for the sake of the Muslim community, I suspect that there was never any plan to change them on the part of the Jami Masjid Committee even if Ustad Mimar was driven by a desire for symmetry and balance. These stairs are a visual symbol of past events and memories that allowed Jaipur's Muslims to imagine themselves

---

23 The so-called Babri Masjid was torn down by Hindu fundamentalists on December 6, 1992 setting off massive riots across much of the subcontinent into 1993.

24 It appears that he designs these structures, leaving the technical and constructional aspects of the design to a contractor.

as a unified community. And it was the sense of a unified community living in harmony with Jaipur's majority Hindu and Jain communities, at least in Shameem's mind, that was successful in gaining permission to rebuild the mosque.

When asked how he decided on the final design, Ustad Mimar simply said that he listened to what the Committee wanted and then created a design to their liking. So what is it that the Committee wanted and what did Ustad Mimar use for his inspiration to translate a Committee's vision into structure?

I will start briefly with the interior, for this is the space actually used for prayer. Three of the interior four stories serve as a place of prayer, but here I will only examine the main floor since the others are not yet fully completed. Following the layout of most 18th and 19th century mosques in Jaipur, the prayer chamber is divided into multiple aisles by pillars supporting cusped arches. Dados with painted floral motifs found inside the Jaipur Jami mosque are similar to those seen on many 18th-century buildings, including mosques, of Jaipur.[25] Examples for these features include the interiors of the mosque at *dargah* Maulana Zia al-Din, the Mominan Mosque and Masjid Pannigaran (Asher 1999: plate 7, 2000: plate 5.7). The interior thus is typical of older local mosques.

The facade, however, is quite different from most other older mosques in Jaipur which is interesting, since, as indicated near the beginning of this paper, the Jami mosque is recognized by many as Jaipur's oldest mosque. Typical 18th and 19th-century mosques in the city tend to have large arched entrances surmounted by domes, following a mosque type standardized under the Mughals, for example, another mosque known as the mosque of Maulana Zia al-Din, this one in *mahalla* Hadipura (Asher 1999: plate 6, 2000: plate 5.6). Other domed mosques have been built on Jaipur's main streets, for example, Masjid Sambhariyan, dated 1913, in Kisanpole Bazaar just near the Agra Darwaza (Nath and Jodha 1993: 71). The presence of domes, usually accompanied by minarets as well, indicate a clear Muslim presence. In spite of the overwhelming precedence of domed mosques in Jaipur, it appears that from the outset no domes were planned for the reconstructed Jami mosque. This is interesting since Shameem's Committee was concerned with achieving an Islamic appearing building.

The approved elevation indicates a mosque with a three-storied prayer chamber above the ground level stairs and shops. Each story of the prayer chamber has nine arches of alternating sizes, reserving the largest one for the central bay of the mosque. It more resembles the three-storied pink stone arched facade that Ustad Mimar had placed on his grandfather's Mominan mosque than any

---

25 My visit in January 2008 indicates the painted floral panels are being replaced with slabs of Makrana marble carved with floral motifs.

other mosque in Jaipur. But that mosque is radically different in appearance from any other structure surrounding it, thus making it stand out. By contrast, the new Jami mosque, remembered as Jaipur's oldest mosque, blends in so well with its neighboring buildings that many people are not particularly aware even that it is a mosque. In fact, the mosque's appearance parallels that of 18^{th-} and 19^{th-}century Hindu and Jain temples in the walled city which are no different in appearance from the surrounding dwellings (Asher 1999: 127, 2000: 130-131, 2002: 201).

The question that comes to mind is did Shameem and his Committee really want an Islamic appearing building or did they want something else? After all there was no attempt to design a mosque that resembled most historic mosques in Jaipur or anywhere in South Asia, and thus, would be immediately understood as such. The only concession to marking an Islamic presence is the slender minarets on the north and south sides of its facade, which are decorated with chevron patterns. Ustad Mimar mentioned to me that the facade had a feeling of the mosque at Medina. Yet it is only the chevron patterns on the minarets that evoke similar minarets on the mosque at Medina, the second most sacred site in Islam, located on the spot of Muhammad's house. But that reference would only be known to members of the Muslim community who have either been on the Hajj or decorate their offices and homes with calendars or posters featuring the mosque. Moreover, the minarets are small and really only noticeable from a distance, since when looking down Johari Bazaar the eye does not tend to look that high. Just as the reference to Medina would only be understood by the Muslim community, so too the mosque's model, the Mominan mosque's new facade, even though it is in Jaipur, would only be known to a few. Not only is the Mominan mosque atypical of most mosques in Jaipur, but also it is tucked away in a remote part of the city rarely visited by anyone but the Muslims of that particular *mahalla*. It would hardly meet the criterion for an immediately recognizable Islamic presence.

To help understand this issue, let us examine the building permits and the Committee's interpretation of them. Of the two documents I was able to procure giving permission to proceed with the building plans, one from the Nagar Parishad, Jaipur (Municipal Council, Jaipur) dated January 1st, 1980 deals only with legal, technical matters and fees (NP 1980). But the other, from the Office of the Town Planner and Architectural Adviser, dated December 24th, 1979, makes minor changes to the initial plans using the word 'traditional' to dictate what those changes must be. One example reads, "The arch shaped openings should either have a traditional style railing or should [...] be closed with a traditional jali" (CTP 1979). A *jali* is a net like screen common on South Asian architecture and especially in Jaipur. Without getting into a discussion of the problematic term 'traditional', it seems clear that the city planners wanted a building that blended well with its surroundings.

It appears that Ustad Mimar, Shameem and the larger community had no problem with this either. When I asked whether they had to paint the mosque pink, I was told that there was no compulsion to do so, but that pink is Jaipur's color. In fact, there is a bylaw mandating that all structures of Johari Bazaar must be painted dark pink with white trim (Rewat and Verma 1966: 22), but Shameem and Ustad Mimar indicated, law or not, this conformist color was their own choice. They stated that the mosque would not look good if it did not correspond with the appearance of other structures in Jaipur. By painting the mosque pink, the color of conformity and homogeneity in Jaipur, the troubled iconography of color we have seen – white turbans of despair, the red blood of martyrs and the black flags of betrayal – is made right. In essence the mosque's current appearance and color underscores the Muslim communities' sense of rightfully belonging to Jaipur, a city whose uniform appearance is intended to recall its planned nature. Part of the planned nature of Jaipur was a conscious intent to create a universal secular city by inviting various communities, Muslims among them, to achieve this goal.

While Jaipur's Muslims may feel a close sense of belonging to the greater Jaipur community, in part due to the existence, location and appearance of the Jaipur Jami mosque, this sense was made all the more public a little more than a year and a half ago. On May 13th, 2008 over 60 people, both Hindus and Muslims, were killed and many more injured as a series of closely timed bomb blasts rocked the old walled city. Exactly who was responsible for this act and many of the other recent bombings in India remains unclear as does the target of these bombings. Many attribute the violence to outside forces that are trying to pit Hindus and Muslims against each other. But solidarity was most clearly shown on Friday, May 16th, 2008 when thousands of Jaipur's Muslims came together to offer a special *namaz* (prayer) in memory of the serial blast victims,[26] just as did Jaipur's other religious communities that day. In doing so, they once again sought integration with the greater Jaipur community.

---

26 http://ishare.rediff.com/video/news-politics/india-jaipur-bomb-blast-13th-may-2008/ 214811, and also http://timesofindia.indiatimes.com/Home/Terror-strikes-Jaipur/This-Friday-namaz-for-blast-victims/articleshow/3048116.cms (last accessed Oct. 22, 2010).

Figure 1, Jami Mosque, East façade 1980-1990

Asher

Figure 2, 'Id Gathering near the Jaipur Jami Mosque 2001

Asher

Figure 3, Photograph of protest movement in favor of widening the staircase of the Jaipur Jami Mosque, Jan. 20, 1939

Courtesy of Inamul Haq

In addition to the editors of this volume, I am grateful to Sandy Freitag, David Gilmartin, Barbara Metcalf, Janice Leoshko, Richard Davis, Jennifer Joffee, Thomas Asher and Rick Asher for reading and commenting on various drafts. I am deeply indebted to many people in Jaipur, in particular Inamul Haq and Abdul Hai Shameem, for their help and cooperation in learning about the pur Jami mosque.

ABBREVIATIONS

APB: Amrita Patrika Bazaar

BC: Bombay Chronicle

CTP 1979: Letter (N[?]PR 1624.02JP) from Government of Rajasthan, Office of the Chief Town Planner and Architectural Adviser, Jaipur approving building plans and proposed alterations of Johri Bazaar Jami mosque Dec. 24, 1979

HT: Hindustan Times

IOLJ: India Office Library. R/1/1/3306, file 6 (33). Muslim Agitation in the Jaipur State in conjunction with the Jaipur Juma Mosque (Johri Bazar) incident and Activities of Syed Bhik Nairang, MLA.

IOLR: India Office Library. Rajputana Reports.

JGE: Jaipur Gazette Extraordinary, LVI, 22 March, 1939, no 4845.

JMJ: ANONYMOUS. 1956/Shawwal 1375 A.H. Jama Masjid, Jaipur. Jaipur: Publisher unknown.

NAI: National Archives of India. Jaipur Residency Reports, 1926-47.

NH: National Herald

NP 1980: Letter from Nagar Parishad (Municipal Committee) to Abdul Hai, 1.1.80. This has been added p. 24

SM: Statesman

REFERENCES

Asher, Catherine B. (2007): "From *Rajadharma* to Indian Nationalism: Iconographies of Pre- and Post-Independence Jaipur" in: Richard H. Davis (Ed.), Picturing the Nation. Iconographies of Modern India, Mumbai: Orient Longman, pp. 117-143.

(1999): "North India's Urban Landscape. The Place of the Jain Temple," in: Islamic Culture LXXIII:3, pp. 109-50.

(2000): "Mapping Hindu-Muslim Identities Through the Architecture of Shahjahanabad and Jaipur", in: David Gilmartin and Bruce B. Lawrence (Eds.), Beyond Turk and Hindu. Rethinking Religious Identities in Islamicate South Asia, Gainesville: University Press of Florida, pp. 121-148.

(2002): "Piety, Religion and the Old Social Order in the Architecture of the Later Mughals and Their Contemporaries", in: Richard B. Barnett (Ed.), Rethinking Early Modern India, New Delhi: Manohar, pp. 193-230.

Bhatnagar, V.S. (1974): Life and Times of Sawai Jai Singh 1688-1743, Delhi: Impex India.

Brass, Paul (1990): The Politics of India Since Independence, Cambridge: Cambridge University Press.

Crewe, Quentin (1985): The Last Maharaja: A Biography of Sawai Man Singh II, Maharaja of Jaipur, London: Michael Joseph.

CTP 1979: Letter (N[?]PR 1624.02JP) from Government of Rajasthan, Office of the Chief Town Planner and Architectural Adviser, Jaipur approving building plans and proposed alterations of Johri Bazaar Jami mosque Dec. 24, 1979 (unpublished).

Erdmann, Joan L. (1985): Patrons and Performers in Rajasthan: The SubtleTradition, Delhi: Chanakya Publications.

(1989): "Jaipur. City Planning in 18th Century India", in: A.L. Dallapiccola and S. Zingel-Ave Lallemant (Eds.), Shastric Traditions in Indian Arts, Stuttgart: Steiner Verlag, pp. 219-133.

Freitag, Sandria B. (1989): Collective Action and Community. Public Arenas and the Emergence of Communalism in North India, Berkeley: University of California Press.

Gottschalk, Peter (2000): Beyond Hindu and Muslim. Multiple Identity in Narratives from Village India, New York: Oxford University Press.

Gupta, T.N. and Khangarot, R.S. (1994): Amber Jaipur. A Dream in the Desert, Jaipur: Classic Publishing House.

Hardgrove, Anne (2004): Community as Public Culture. The Marwaris in Calcutta, New Delhi and New York: Oxford University Press.

IOLJ: India Office Library. R/1/1/3306, file 6 (33). Muslim Agitation in the Jaipur State in conjunction with the Jaipur Juma Mosque (Johri Bazar) incident and Activities of Syed Bhik Nairang, MLA (unpublished).

IOLR: India Office Library. Rajputana Reports (unpublished).

JMJ (Anonymous) (1956): Shawwal 1375 A.H. Jama Masjid, Jaipur, Jaipur: Publisher unknown. [This volume was about the financial accounts of this mosque; I had access only to a photocopy of the 8 page introduction with no page numbers, concerning the mosque's history; I was unable to locate a complete copy so do not know the author, precise title or page numbers]

Kakar, Sudhir (1996): The Colors of Violence: Cultural Identities, Religion and Conflict, Chicago: University of Chicago Press.

Kahera, Akel Ismail (2002): Deconstructing the American Mosque: Space, Gender and Aesthetics, Austin: University of Texas Press.

Masselos, Jim (1982): "Change and Custom in the Format of the Bombay Moharram in the Nineteenth and Twentieth Centuries", in: South Asia 5:2, pp. 47-67.

NAI: National Archives of India. Jaipur Residency Reports, 1926-1947 (unpublished).

Nairang, Syed Ghulam Bhik. 1939. The Jaipur Juma Mosque Tragedy, Being a Report Submitted by the Muslim League Party of the Central Legislative Assembly. Delhi.

Nath, Aman and Jodha, Samar Singh (1993): Jaipur. The Last Destination, Bombay: India Book House.

NP 1980: Letter from Nagar Parishad (Municipal Committee) to Abdul Hai, Jan.1 1980 (unpublished).

Pirzada, Syed Sharifuddin (1990): Foundations of Pakistan. All India Muslim League Documents, 1906-1947, Vol. III, Karachi: Royal Book Company.

Roy, Ashimkumar (1978): History of the Jaipur City, Delhi: Manohar.

Stein, Robert W. (1988): The Cat and the Lion. Jaipur State in the British Raj, Leiden: E.J. Brill.

Shameem, Abdul Hai (1996) "Notes on Jama Masjid, Johri Bazaar, Jajpur" (unpublished).

Taknet, D.K. (1996): B.M. Birla, A Great Visionary, New Delhi: Indus.

Arenas of Contest?

Public Islamic Festivals in Interwar Dar es Salaam

KATHARINA ZÖLLER[1]

INTRODUCTION

Public time in Dar es Salaam, the colonial capital of Tanganyika Territory and an important port city, was marked by a festival calendar that reflected the religious and ethnic diversity of its inhabitants in the years between the two World Wars. The town's most widely attended religious celebrations were the Islamic festivals *Idi el Fitri*[2] (the feast of fast breaking), *Idi el Haji* (the feast of sacrifice) and *Maulidi ya Nabii* (the annual celebration of the Prophet's birthday). From 1926 on, a new location was chosen for the celebration of these main Islamic festivals in Dar es Salaam. For the first time in the town's history, all Muslims were invited to celebrate together. The location, today well-known as Mnazi Mmoja, was then part of the so-called 'open space' and became an important place for the town's Muslims in the late 1920s and 1930s. In analyzing the Islamic festivals, this chapter aims first to trace the transformation of abstract urban space through various social practices into a sacred place for Dar es Salaam's Muslims. Secondly, I will show how this act of place-making advanced the creation of a public arena in which the different Muslim communities debated about issues concerning Islam and the Muslim population in Dar es Salaam.

As Dar es Salaam is a comparably young city without the long history of Islamic networks enjoyed by other Swahili towns such as Mombasa or Zanzibar,

---

1   I wish to thank the editors, Patrick Desplat and Dorothea Schulz, as well as Jim Brennan for comments on earlier versions of this chapter.

2   I chose the common local spelling in Kiswahili for all Arabic-Islamic terms in this paper.

the role of Islam has been rather neglected in the town's historiography. Nevertheless, the emergent metropolis Dar es Salaam was historically a predominantly Muslim city. Since its foundation by the Sultan of Zanzibar in the 1860s, Dar es Salaam had attracted migrants from the Indian Ocean region and the African mainland. The number of inhabitants grew from 20,000 at the end of German colonial rule in 1916 to 26,000 inhabitants in 1938. During the interwar years, the capital of Tanganyika Territory (Mandate of the British Empire from 1919-1961) was marked by a heterogeneous, predominantly Muslim population. Despite the architectural visibility of Christianity with church buildings on the central waterfront, Christians played a numerically minor role during that period. The same was true for practitioners of Hinduism and other religions present in town. The Muslim population was composed of a wide range of Islamic branches and reflected the diverse origins of its inhabitants, including African and Hadrami Sunnis, Ibadis from Oman, as well as South Asian Shias and Sunnis. The Muslim community was divided not only by their origins, but also by their unequal economic and political influence. The whole range of Dar es Salaam's Muslims, members of different Islamic schools, Muslims from different regions of origin and various Sufi-brotherhoods assembled from 1926 onwards at Mnazi Mmoja to celebrate the *Id* festivals and, from 1930, also the *maulidi* together.

I describe the heterogeneous composition of Dar es Salaam's Muslim population to introduce my understanding of Mnazi Mmoja as a 'place' as opposed to a rather abstract notion of 'urban space'. Massey conceptualizes places "in terms of the social interactions which they tie together" (1991: 29). This is a fruitful basis for my analysis of the relation between festivals and place in the city. A place in her understanding is not something static, with clear-cut boundaries, but is constituted by the specific constellation of social relations which meet at the location in a given time, in my case during the festivals. The fact that the festivals merely took place on a public square and people met there is not sufficient to consider them as public arenas. Just as a place is made through interaction, the festivals as public arenas are constituted by "[s]ocial practices that are based on ideas of the common good and that contribute to shaping public Islam" (Salvatore and Eickelman 2004: xiii). This quotation by Salvatore and Eickelman on the notion of 'public' in Islamic discourses relates the 'public' with the idea of the common good. The same relation is emphasized by Eisenstadt in his definition of 'public sphere' as "a sphere where collective improvements, the common good, are at stake" (Eisenstadt 2002: 140). This sphere, located between the official and private spheres, "denotes the existence of arenas that are not only autonomous from the political order but are also public in the sense that they are accessible to different sectors of society" (Eisenstadt 2002: 140). It is in this sense that I understand the Islamic festivals at Mnazi Mmoja as 'public arenas' in which various actors from different sectors of the town's population discussed their understanding of the common good and articulated socio-political claims vis-à-vis other members of the Muslim community. Furthermore, discussion in these public arenas, including those about religious practice, did also have influence beyond the time and place of the Islamic festivals.

To set the festivals in their specific historical context, I will first trace the evolution of Islam in Dar es Salaam and describe the various actors involved in the arena of the festivals in the interwar years. I then discuss the 'timing' of the festivals, highlighting the difficulties which evolve out of the complex timescapes in a colonial city to synchronize the start of the Islamic celebrations. At the same time this introduces one highly contested topic which gave rise to numerous discussions in the public arena of print media. The following section on the placing of the festivals considers the spatial relationship between the celebrations and the city and examines the practices which led to the transformation of abstract urban space into a place for the town's Muslims and the groups and individuals involved in this process. Finally, I discuss the festivals as public arenas regarding the topics the actors raised during and after the festivals, the tensions which came to the fore on these occasions and the underlying and resulting social dynamics for the Muslim community of Dar es Salaam.

The main source for this historical analysis of Islamic festivals in Dar es Salaam was the newspaper *Mambo Leo*, which is Kiswahili for 'current affairs'. The paper was published monthly by the Education Department from 1923 on and had a print run of around 10,000 copies. As a governmental publication, it was subject to censorship and the editor stated several times that some articles and letters were not printed because they were discriminatory in treating *mambo ya dini* (religious affairs).[3] Furthermore, only a small part of the colony's population was educated in mission or governmental schools and thus literate in the Latin script. But, on the other hand, discussions from *baraza* gatherings in the colony and beyond were brought into the newspaper, especially through letters to the editor, issues were estimated to have been shared among ten readers on average, and the contents of the newspaper were orally communicated to a wider audience.[4] In this sense the newspaper was referred to as *baraza* by its readers[5]

---

3   See for example the *sanduku la posta* (letter box) in Mambo Leo 43 (July 1926), 44 (August 1926), 157 (January 1936).

4   See e.g. *Mambo Leo* 85 (January 1930): 15; *Mambo Leo* 93 (September 1930): 160; *Mambo Leo* 96 (December 1930): 218; see also Bromber (2000: 98); Geider (2002: 263-268); Sturmer (1999: 51-52); Suriano (2008: 97-98).

and did constitute a public arena in which various matters of interest including Islamic practice were discussed between Muslims from various places. In addition, the newspaper provided information for Muslims, for example on religious scholars or the dates of Islamic festivals. Thus, it has proved to be a valuable source for the analysis of Islamic festivals which took into account aspects ranging from organization, timing and preparation, restrictions and regulations, programs and speeches as well as debates evolving around the festivals.[6]

ISLAM IN INTERWAR DAR ES SALAAM

The years following World War I until the late 1930s are a particularly interesting period for the analysis of Islamic festivals in Dar es Salaam. Not only did the location of the main Islamic festivals change during these interwar years, but the city gained more and more influence as a religious centre for its hinterland. The growing presence of Sufi brotherhoods which attracted numerous new followers and an increasing internal organization of the town's Muslims were central for the organization and performance of Islamic festivals.

According to the historian John Iliffe, the colonial capital Dar es Salaam was "too big, too diverse, too shifting in composition, too secular and too eclectic in culture for religious leaders to dominate it", although "*shaykhs*, imams, and *waalimu* clearly enjoyed considerable prestige before and during the Second World War" (1979: 388). This point was also emphasized by missionary and theologian Reusch who visited the town in 1930. He described Dar es Salaam alongside Bagamoyo, where the mufti was based, as the main centre of Islam in

---

5   For example, see the article by Hector Nkonjera (1930: 15) where he represented a group of neighbours in Dar es Salaam who had decided to bring a contended issue from their discussion group into Mambo Leo's *baraza*. For the concept of *baraza*, see e.g. Loimeier (2007: 16-38).

6   This paper is based on parts of my master's thesis on Islamic festivals in colonial Dar es Salaam, in which I analysed the festivals from 1905 to 1938 on three levels: first, the Islamic festivals themselves regarding developments over time and borrowings between the various festivals in town; second the colonial authorities' "handling" of Islamic festivals and the alliances involved; and third, the social dynamics of the festivals for the town's predominantly Muslim population. I read *Mambo Leo* systematically from 1923 to 1938, and all articles and letters to the editor dealing with Islamic practices and various festivals, calendars, calculation of times and the town of Dar es Salaam were included in the analysis (see Zöller 2009).

the colony (1930: 297). Dar es Salaam, once founded by the Sultan of Zanzibar as his commercial empire's base on the African mainland in the early 1860s, had developed from a small outpost into the economic and political centre of German East Africa (later Tanganyika Territory), while Zanzibar, under British domination since 1890, gradually lost its hegemony. Zanzibar as a centre of Islamic scholarship in East Africa still exerted considerable religious influence on the mainland, however Dar es Salaam showed its first signs of religious emancipation in the interwar years: "The role of Islamic teachers and scholars from Dar es Salaam seems to have changed considerably from the subsidiary function they had fulfilled while in the shadow of Zanzibar" (Anthony 2002: 26-27).

One indication for the growing popularity of Islam in Dar es Salaam was the rising number of mosques and their location in town. Most of the various Islamic branches in Dar es Salaam had their own communal mosques which reflected the respective wealth of the communities and their status within the town's Muslim population. A German colonial street map from 1910, for example, showed five mosques: 'Ismaili' mosque, 'Mshihiri' mosque (the mosque of the Hadrami), 'Araber' (Arab) mosque (the mosque of the Omani who were Ibadi), 'Thenashiri' (Ithnasheri) mosque and 'Bohora' mosque, all located in the so-called 'Indian quarter' (Uhindini).[7] By 1930 the number of mosques in town had grown considerably. The eleven mosques in Uhindini were mostly built of limestone, the 'Ismaili' mosque being the biggest and wealthiest one (see Reusch 1930: 298-299; Iliffe 1979: 388). The wealth of the Ismaili community displayed by its community institutions hints at the considerable economic and political influence of the Ismaili and also other Indian Muslim communities in Dar es Salaam, despite their small numbers compared to the African population.[8] But also in the growing African quarters numerous smaller mosques and *madrasa* were built during the interwar period. In the central African quarter Kariakoo, for example, 17 mosques were counted in 1941 (Iliffe 1979: 388).

The flourishing of mosques and *madrasa* in the African quarters was accompanied by a growing presence of Sufi brotherhoods in town. They had a consid-

---

7   See "Stadtplan von Daressalam", *Deutsche Kolonialzeitung* (1910: 89). The number of mosques varied according to different sources. The missionary inspector of the Berlin Mission, Klamroth, for example, counted eight mosques in 1910 including the less prominent mud buildings (Klamroth 1910: 480-483).

8   In 1916, around 960 Ismaili were living in Dar es Salaam. This constituted two thirds of the Indian Muslim population. The number of Indian inhabitants grew steadily since the end of Word War I to around 9,000 in 1937. Dar es Salaam's population numbered around 26,000 in 1938 (see Anthony 2002: 33-34; Brennan and Burton 2007a: 34-37; Raimbault 2007: 241-244; Walji 1974: 29-32).

erable impact on the spread of Islam in Dar es Salaam, especially from the 1920s onwards. Various brotherhoods which had their roots at the Barawa Coast in present Somalia, in Hadramaut or on the Comoro Islands found their way to the Swahili Coast via Zanzibar at the beginning of the 20th century. Their most important religious praxis was *dhikri*, collective invocations of the names of God, which constituted an integral part of *Maulidi ya Nabii*. It was not only the specific religious practice which attracted Africans to the brotherhoods, but also the social dimension of these Islamic networks. This was the time of slave emancipation and shifting power relations in the region. These Sufi brotherhoods increasingly welcomed less privileged members of the population, such as former slaves, thus enabling their integration into the urban coastal society. Not origin and ancestry, but rather individual piety and devotion, defined one's social status within the brotherhood, facilitating upward social mobility (see Becker 2008: 180; El Zein 1974: 118-125; Martin 1976: 1-2, 165; Nimtz 1980: 70-71).

The growing number of African converts around the turn of the century challenged the Swahili patricians on the coast, for whom Islam and the concept of *ustaarabu*[9], 'civilization', had been an essential means to define themselves as local elites and to exclude newcomers from the town's major institutions (Glassman 2001). The access of African Muslims to the closely-knit East African *ulama*, the religious elite, was still limited in the beginning of the 20th century. Besides religious knowledge, ethnicity and ancestry were important elements for a *shaykh's* conferring of the *ijaza*, 'license', to a student, thus allowing him to lead a local branch of the brotherhood. As Martin noted, "the best qualification for becoming a learned man was to be the son of another learned man" (1971: 530).[10]

The most influential brotherhoods in Tanganyika and its capital during the interwar years were the Qadiriyya, the Shadiliyya, and from the 1940s onwards also the Ahmadiyya. The First World War, subsequent famines and the changes in political power led to a prolonged period of crisis and uncertainty in Dar es Salaam during which the Sufi brotherhoods gained more and more popularity among the African population. Particularly newcomers from the wider hinterland converted to Islam and joined the brotherhoods. Islamic scholars from Dar es Salaam like Shaykh Ali bin Mzee Comorian gained reputations and were, like

---

9   See Bromber (2006) for an analysis of the concept *ustaarabu* in *Mambo Leo*.

10 A notable exception to this exclusive pattern was Shaykh Ramiya: despite being of slave origin he became leader of the Qadiriyya brotherhood in Bagamoyo 1905. Brotherhoods contributed far more to the spread of Islam in Tanzania than in Kenya or Uganda (see Anthony 2002: 39-40, 234; Raimbault 2007: 414-419; Iliffe 1979: 211).

Shaykh Athman Muki, involved in conversions in the hinterland.[11] The foundation of the Askariyya brotherhood serves as an example to illuminate the growing importance of Dar es Salaam as a religious centre and the emancipation of African Muslims. The brotherhood was founded around 1930 in Dar es Salaam by Shaykh Idris bin Saad, a Makua (a south Tanzanian ethnic group). He was denied the *ijaza* by a famous Qadiri *shaykh* in Zanzibar, and therefore decided to set up another brotherhood on his own – not in Zanzibar, but in Dar es Salaam. The Askariyya was the only indigenous brotherhood on the East African mainland. Despite disdain from more established brotherhoods which also had far more members, the Askariyya flourished and opened branches in Morogoro, Kilosa, Mahenge and Songea (Martin 1971: 530; Nimtz 1980: 61; Lodhi and Westerlund 1997).[12]

Religious knowledge was not exclusively shared between scholars or within the brotherhoods. It was also increasingly provided and discussed in Islamic print media, including the government-controlled *Mambo Leo*, thereby integrating African Muslims from all over the colony in a kind of religious exchange. Letters to the editor, sometimes inspired by *baraza* discussions, were handed in from towns in Tanganyika and beyond, especially Zanzibar and Mombasa. These letters and reports in the newspaper's main sections written by individual Muslims, leaders of Muslim organizations or representatives of the *ulama* covered visits of *shaykhs* and *walimu*, funerals of prominent members of the *ulama*, the foundation of Muslim organizations or the main Islamic festivals in the region.[13] They were mostly of informative character, providing or asking for Islamic knowledge. Public condemnation of popular religious practice like in Zan-

---

11 The Qadiriyya was the first brotherhood in Tanganyika. Important *khalifa* were Shaykh Uways from Barawa coast, Shaykh Zahor bin Muhammed in Tabora and Shaykh Ramiya from Bagamoyo. Shaykh Athman Muki established the Qadiriyya in Dar es Salaam. The Shadiliyya came from the Comoro Islands and was established on the mainland by Shaykh Husein bin Mahmud in Kilwa, who instructed Shaykh Abdalkheri and Shaykh Ali Wafa from Dar es Salaam. The Ahmadiyya was brought to Dar es Salaam by Shaykh Ali bin Salih (see Nimtz 1980: 60; Iliffe 1979: 211-212, Ahmed and von Oppen 2004: 89, 93-97; Brennan 2002: 143; Anthony 2002: 39-40).

12 Evidence in *Mambo Leo* suggests that the Askariyya was also established in Dodoma in 1937 as the brotherhood took part in the *dhikri* performances on Id (see Ponda 1937a: 74).

13 For example for visits of scholars, see Kambi (1936: 45) and Salum (1934b: 130). For obituaries, see "Marehemu Seyid Ahmed bin Abubaker Sumeit", *Mambo Leo* 1925 (32): 175-176; bin Haji el Battawey (1929: 1098); Minjuma (1931: 154).

zibar, partly resulting from the cooperation between the religious establishment and colonial administration, were less pronounced.[14]

Islamic festivals in Dar es Salaam were increasingly covered in long articles, highlighting the town's growing importance as a centre for Islamic practice and scholarship (see e.g. Kidasi and Mambo 1926a: 375; Dahal 1931: 88; Bin Rashidi 1934: 146; Nasibu 1936: 159-160). Many of the Muslim organizations covered in *Mambo Leo* were founded in Dar es Salaam. Besides the spread of Islam in Dar es Salaam, largely due to the activity of the brotherhoods, the internal organization of the town's Muslim population was another factor, which played a major role in the organization of the town's social and festive life in the interwar years. The organization of the town's Muslim population into different sections was also in the colonial administration's interest. Besides the Arab *liwali*, an official appointed by the colonial administration and responsible for the 'native' court and the tax collection under the township authority, representatives of the various Muslim communities played an important role in administrative and judicial matters, and also on official occasions like colonial festivals or formal receptions on Islamic holidays (Zöller 2009). However, the colonial administration had difficulties to determine the "duly authorized representatives of all sections of the Sunni community of Dar es Salaam" as exemplified by the following court case in 1930 (Wilson 1930: 25). A Government Notice printed in *Mambo Leo* named representatives for the 'Punjabi', 'Kokni', 'Memon', 'Arabs' and 'Swahili' and invited them for a hearing. The uncertainty and the limited knowledge of the administration concerning the internal organization of the towns' Sunni community are revealed in the following request:

"Any section of the Sunni Community not named above should communicate with the Registrar of the High Court [...] giving a description of such section and the name of a responsible representative of that section. Similarly any of the sections named in this notice may elect any other person to represent them other than the person named in this notice." (Wilson 1930: 25)

---

14 In Zanzibar, for example, extensive funeral expenses were criticised by the *ulama*, the religious elite, as *bidaa* (innovation) and by the colonial administration as economic wastefulness. This resulted in regulations and prohibitions backed by the religious elite (see Loimeier 2006). The government-controlled *Mambo Leo* in Tanganyika Territory, where this collaboration was less articulate, was scarcely used for similar criticisms. Perhaps this was partly due to the fact that *Mambo Leo* was unlike the Islamic pamphlets that primarily meant to "educate the natives" and therefore was at least trying to refrain from debates on Islamic authority and contested religious issues.

The terms used in this notice raise further questions on the internal organization and its official representation: Was 'Arabs' a collective term meant to include Omani ('Ibadi') and Hadrami ('Shafi'), or did it refer to the community associated with a specific mosque, the 'Arab' mosque? Did 'Swahili' include all African Muslims of various ethnic affiliations and origins in Dar es Salaam or was it reserved for the local *wenyemji*, the 'owners of the town', leaving the growing numbers of immigrants without official representation?[15] And what about the various brotherhoods and their leaders? All these aspects, ethnic affiliation, association to a mosque, and brotherhood membership played a role in the internal organization of the Muslims in town. Newly founded Muslim associations added new dimensions to this internal organization in terms of their composition, their agenda concerning all Muslims in town, and the format of Islamic festivals.

In the 1930s the Muslim community of Dar es Salaam increasingly organized itself to foster education, welfare and the preparation of the main Islamic holidays. The first Muslim association was founded around 1926. The Anjuman Islamia was a Muslim welfare organization dominated by Indian Sunnis originating from Kachch and Punjab. The association aimed to provide education, the building of mosques and organizing Islamic festivals for the town's Muslim population of all races. Despite internal conflicts and the emergence of competing associations, the Anjuman Islamia under the leadership of M.O. Abbasi was the most influential Muslim association in interwar Dar es Salaam that lost its influence only in the mid-1930s (see Brennan 2002: 141-144; Iliffe 1979: 551; Kidasi and Mambo 1926: 37). In the early 1930s prominent African Muslims, amongst them Kleist Sykes and Mzee bin Sudi, founded another important Muslim organization, a branch of the Zanzibar-based Jamiatul Islamia. Its first president was the town's Arab *liwali*, the highest ranking non-European colonial officer in Dar es Salaam. The founders were concerned about the lack of appropriate education for African Muslim children and wanted to take part in the organization of Islamic festivals. Their ambition was "to safeguard and promote the interest of Muslims of all denominations inhabiting not only Dar es Salaam but the whole of Tanganyika Territory."[16]

The founding of the Jamiatul Islamia was also a sign for the growing opposition to Indian paternalism towards their African fellow Muslims. Racial relations

---

15 The question "who are the Swahili?" is not only debated in academia, but was also a topic for discussion in *Mambo Leo*. One author, for example, condemned the practice of hiding one's true identity in fear of being denigrated a *mshenzi*, and of calling oneself a Swahili as soon as one wears nice clothes and knows some Kiswahili (see Nganzi 1925: 179).

16 "Islamic Rally in Dar-es-Salaam", *Samachar* (1930: 4-5).

were worsening since the disastrous effects of the Indian shopkeepers' strike on the African population in 1923 and the ongoing Indian quest for equal treatment with Europeans (see Brennan 1999: 27-28, 2002: 139-144). But the efforts of pan-Islamic organization did not bring the expected results. As Brennan states: "Far from uniting Dar es Salaam's Muslims, inter-war projects of Islamic universalism became points of contention that revealed the major divisions among the town's *umma*." (2002: 139-140) Most communities had their own mosques and schools, which only highlighted the unequal distribution of wealth. Arab scholars saw themselves as the Muslim elite and made it difficult for African Muslims to gain access to the *ulama*. Brotherhoods competed for followers and challenged the established *ulama*. The local Zaramo and Shomvi saw themselves as the real *wenye mji* (owners of town) and drew a sharp line between themselves and African migrants such as the 'Zulu' Kleist Sykes, as they feared losing their influence in the town's Islamic institutions (Brennan 2002: 145-150).[17]

The issue of 'time' in relation to Islamic festivals, especially in a heterogeneous colonial city like Dar es Salaam, is illustrated in the following section.

THE TIMING OF THE FESTIVALS

Following Durkheim I understand festivals as periodical interruptions in the course of life. They arise out of the common understanding of time in a community, what Durkheim called 'social time'. The periodicity and the rhythm of these collective activities are fixed in calendars (Durkheim 1981: 27-29, 592-593). In colonial Dar es Salaam, various calendars existed side by side. This made a common understanding of time as a basis for the joint celebration of festivals more difficult and had effects on religious praxis. The city was marked by a complex 'timescape', referring to the competing notions and concepts of time in a locality.[18] Internal debates among East African Muslims about the exact beginning of the lunar months were complicated by the introduction of the Gregorian calendar and the establishment of an official holiday calendar by the colonial administration.

---

17 Kleist Sykes, whose ancestors came from South Africa, was born in Pangani in 1894. Patronized by his uncle Effendi Plantan, the highest ranking African officer in the German colonial army, Sykes became one of the most prominent inhabitants of Dar es Salaam in the 1930s (see Anthony 2002: 44-45; Said 1998: 29-49).

18 For the concept of 'timescape' in East Africa, see Loimeier and Mwakimako (2006).

The new Gregorian time regime, which disciplined at least the lives of those inhabitants who were working for the colonial administration,[19] was introduced and promoted in missionary calendars and Swahili newspapers.[20] The Education Department (that is, the editor of *Mambo Leo*) provided a free calendar in each January issue. However, the introduction of the Gregorian calendar did not exclude former common calculations of time in Tanganyika. This is also evident in *Mambo Leo*: additionally to the Gregorian calendar one finds an almanac in which each beginning of the months of the Islamic year is assigned to Gregorian dates.[21] In reports on Islamic festivals most authors used both calendars, *Kiislamu* (Islamic) and *Kikristo* (Christian), to describe a date (e.g. Nasibu 1936: 159-160). Another indication of the coexistence of calendars were the various New Year celebrations in Dar es Salaam, like the Gregorian New Year on January 1, the beginning of the Islamic year on first *Muharram*, the Swahili New Year called *mwaka* which marked the beginning of the Swahili solar year, and the Hindu New Year.[22]

Even if not all of the secular and religious festivals celebrated in town were part of Dar es Salaam's official holiday calendar, the calendar reflected the town's heterogeneity and also the status of different communities. The holiday calendar was not static but was constantly renegotiated, and thus the holidays included changed over the years. In particular, the official recognition of religious holidays altered during the interwar years. In a notice published in 1921, a list of Indian and Muslim holidays included *Idi el Fitri* and *Idi el Haji*, but did not name *maulidi*.[23] This is particularly significant, as a large number of Hindu and Sikh festivals were listed in that same Notice, although the Hindu and Sikh

---

19 For colonial subject building and the new colonial elite in Tanganyika, see Wirz (2003: 9-11 and 16-19).

20 This was also an important topic in German colonial times; for missionary calendars, see "*Mweleza Mwaka wa 1911 kwa wakristu weusi katika D.O. Afrika*". Katholische Mission, "Kalender 1912". Die evangelischen Missionen in Deutsch-Ostafrika. See for Swahili newspapers various articles in Kiongozi, e.g. Farjala (1912).

21 See e.g. "Almanak hii imetuwasiliya kwa hisani ya 'Zuhura binti Simba', ikapigwa chapa kwa mintaraf ya Waislamu", *Mambo Leo* 1927 (52): 614.

22 For a discussion on various New Year celebrations, see Muhsin (1923: 16).

23 The recitation of *Maulidi* texts and poems honouring the Prophet on festive occasions like weddings had a longer tradition in Dar es Salaam, as did the private celebration of the Prophet's birthday or various saints' birthdays. This paper focuses on the 'public *Maulidi*', usually organised by a village, quarter or the state, and exclusively celebrated in the honour of the prophet's birthday on a public square. For a categorisation of *Maulidi* in East Africa and the Comoros (see Ahmed 1999: 83-89).

communities were clearly outnumbered by Muslims celebrating *maulidi*. This imbalance in the listing of festivals by the colonial administration could be explained by the fact that Indians ranked higher up in the colonial hierarchy. The Government Notice did not specify whether these festivals were treated as public holidays like Empire Day or Easter, when banks and offices were closed (Hollis 1921 (2): 28).[24] However, colonial administrators in interwar Dar es Salaam also attended the main Islamic festivals themselves or invited – like their German predecessors – representatives of the various Muslim communities in honor of the Idi celebration to a formal reception.[25] In doing so, the colonial administration gave public recognition to these representatives as important in Dar es Salaam and at the same time confirmed the Islamic festivals as part of the official holiday calendar. The calendars printed in *Mambo Leo* in the 1920s and 1930s seemed to be more closely oriented to the actual praxis of religious celebration in the colony than the Government Notice which was published in 1921, shortly after the takeover of the former German colony by the British government. The *Mambo Leo* calendar of 1938 *Sikukuu za serikali za wakristo na za waislamu* (holidays of the government, the Christians and the Muslims), included, for example, also *maulidi*, which was not mentioned in the Government Notice.[26]

Dar es Salaam's heterogeneous timescape and the official recognition of religious holidays as public time were not the only factors which influenced and complicated Islamic festivals in the colonial city. There were, like elsewhere in the Islamic world, also internal debates about determining the beginning of the lunar months. Especially contentious was the start of *Idi el Fitri* on the first of *Shawal* or *mfunguo mosi* (the first breaking of the fast); this is still discussed today throughout the antecedent month of *Ramadan*. The holiday coincides with the beginning of the Swahili lunar year and is for East African Muslims more important than the *Idi el Haji* (see El Zein 1974: 324; Loimeier and Mwakimako 2006; van de Bruinhorst 2007: 167-168, 174-176).[27] The beginning of *maulidi* was not a main topic of debate.[28]

24 Ongoing debates in Mambo Leo about religious holidays and work suggest that the decision to give employees a day off on religious holidays so that they were able to fulfill their religious duties was up to employers. See *"Majibu kwa Waandikaji. B.H.S. Maloki, Kondoa-Irangi"*, Mambo Leo 1936 (162): 96, Bin Sansa 1923: 1114, 1937a: 142; 1937b: 177.

25 See "Idi-El-Fitr. Dar es Salaam", Mambo Leo 1925 (30): 125-126, "Islamic Rally in Dar-es-Salaam", Samachar, 1930: 4.

26 See *"Sikukuu za serikali za wakristo na za waislamu"*, Mambo Leo 1938 (2).

27 The local names for the festivals are misleading: *Idi el Haji*, called *Idi kubwa*, the 'big festival', is less important than the *Idi ndogo* or 'small festival'. The Islamic lunar

The traditional method for fixing the beginning of the lunar month is the sighting of the crescent moon in a given locality. That results in the Islamic festivals starting on different dates in different towns around the globe and also within certain regions, thus hindering the *ummas'* synchronous start of the celebrations. In Dar es Salaam, like in other parts of the Islamic world, great emphasis was laid on a collective start of the *Idi* celebrations.[29] Shaykh al-Amin bin Ali al-Mazrui, *khadi* (Islamic judge) in Mombasa, for example, stated in 1934 that the sighting of the new moon in a region within a radius of 560 miles was binding for a month to start in the whole region (see Frankl and Omar 1996: 419-420). Responding to massive protests by those communities who had not seen the crescent locally but were nevertheless obliged to start the celebrations, the following order was given: "If the crescent is seen in Mombasa, and the news is carried to Lamu (by telephone or radio), then the people of Lamu have to fast, even if they are unable to see the crescent in Lamu." (El Zein 1974: 8) Dissent about the means of reaching a collective date to begin the festivals was also common in Tanganyika, as the following discussions in *Mambo Leo* illustrate (see Kidasi and Mambo 1926a: 375, 1926b: 445-446; Ponda 1937: 23).

The *Idi el Fitri* in 1926 for example, started one day later in Dar es Salaam than in other towns in the region. This asynchronous start was commented upon by two authors. In the Muslim community in Lindi, a small coastal town further south on the Swahili Coast, the crescent moon was sighted after 29 days which occasioned the community to start with the celebration. They had informed the community in Dar es Salaam about the sighting too late, causing Dar es Salaam's Muslims to have to fast for one more day. The Dar es Salaam-based authors of the article, however, were sure that they had started on the right date in their city, namely *kwa hesabu kamili* (with the exact calculation) (Kidasi and Mambo 1926a: 375). They relied on the astronomical calculation, which was scheduled in the Gregorian calendar, and condemned other calculations as *mpungufu* (foolishness). The traditional sighting of the crescent seemed to be less important for them as compared to Muslims in Lamu. The same argument was repeated at the beginning of *Idi el Haji* later that year (Kidasi and Mambo 1926b: 445-446). It was not a new phenomenon – already during German colo-

---

year starts with the month of *Muharram* and not with *Shawal* like on the Swahili Coast.

28 Nowadays debates surround the question of whether or not *Maulidi* should be celebrated at all, since reformers disapprove of it as *bidaa*, undue innovation (see Kresse 2006: 209-210).

29 See e.g. van de Bruinhorst (2007: 165-195) on Idd el-Hajj and the contest of calendars in 20th century Tanzania.

nial times a schoolteacher proposed, "let's use the calendar which is clear, the one of the Europeans"[30] (Farjala 1912) to avoid uncertainty about the beginning of Islamic festivals. Like both authors from *Mambo Leo*, he was working for the colonial administration, which may have been one reason for his strong support of the Gregorian calendar.[31]

The timescapes of Islamic festivals had thus been influenced by the fact that Dar es Salaam was a colonial city and a new calendar system had been added to the existing ones. Modern communication also played a role in appointing the start of Islamic festivals, as cable and telephone were increasingly accessible to the African population in the major towns of the colony.[32] In 1936, for example, a teacher from Dodoma described that the Muslim community in Dodoma could not see the crescent because of the cloudy sky. Unsure whether to start the celebration or not, they sent a cable via Indian middlemen to a *shaykh* in Dar es Salaam who affirmed that the crescent had been seen there. At the end of his article the teacher proposed that officials and religious scholars in the bigger towns should regularly send cables to smaller towns when they have seen the crescent at the beginning and the end of *Ramadan* to secure a joint start and end of the fasting (Ponda 1937: 23). Like religious leaders in Mombasa, he suggested to amend the traditional method of sighting the moon instead of relying on astronomical calculations. He rather advocated using modern communication technology to guarantee a collective beginning of Islamic holidays in the region.

The discussion about competing calendars, the problems of ascertaining the exact beginning of the celebrations, and the various means of solving these problems show that the collective start of the *Idi* celebrations in the region was central for the city's Muslims. The timing of the festivals and their official recognition was, as elsewhere in the Islamic world, an important topic, not only within the *ulama* but also in the broader Muslim community. It was dealt with in the

---

30 *"Sisi tushike kalendari iliyo safi ni ya kizungu."*
31 Zibe Kidasi and Akida Mambo had already been working as typesetter at the German Government Printing Press and were part of the towns' "intellectual aristocrats" (Iliffe 1979: 408). See Mambo (1909); Ranger (1975: 94-95); Iliffe (1979: 407-408); Tsuruta (2003: 220).
32 Whereas Emily Ruete describes how messengers were sent in 19th century Zanzibar to distribute information on the sighting, in 20th century East Africa the telephone gained more and more prominence. It was not only praised for communication with relatives like in Ali Abbas' poem, but was also increasingly used to communicate about the start of the Islamic months (see Ruete 1989: 165; Abbas 1927: 674; Omari Libajuni 1934: 66).

newspaper as one arena for public debates on religious issues in 20th century
Tanganyika.

THE PLACING OF THE FESTIVALS

To understand the interrelations between Islamic festivals and the city in a specific historical setting, it is crucial to examine both the temporal dimension of
festivals – be it contestation of their timing or the tracing of changes in the long
durée – and their spatial dimensions. In her volume *Fêtes Urbaines en Afrique.
Espaces, Identités et Pouvoirs*, historian Odile Goerg identifies two relations between festivals and urban space. The structure of urban space has implications
for the festive practice and the appropriation of space during festival times reveals the relation of the participants to the urban space. This relationship differs
according to social categories, regional or ethnic origin and thus mirrors existing
power structures (see Goerg 1999: 5-8). In the context of interwar Dar es Salaam, colonial visions of order were also inscribed in the urban space, which was
relevant for the placing of the celebrations. The placing of the festivals was thus
influenced by the structure of Dar es Salaam's urban space. But placing a festival goes beyond the choice of an appropriate location for the festivals. The practice of "appropriation" in Goerg's terms is crucial here, or, in Massey's understanding, how the place was "constructed out of a particular constellation of social relations, meeting and weaving together at a particular locus" (Massey 1991:
28).

Combining Goerg's approach to urban festivals with Massey's concept of
place, the transformation of urban space by Dar es Salaam's Muslims through
the celebrations will be seen as a form of place-making. Arguing that the new location for the Islamic festivals in interwar Dar es Salaam became an important
place for the town's Muslims and therefore advanced the creation of a public
arena, I examine the following questions: What were the changes regarding the
locations of the Islamic festivals in Dar es Salaam from before World War I to
the late 1930s? What practices led to the transformation of abstract urban space
into a place for the city's Muslims at these articulated moments in time? And
which groups and individuals interacted during the festivals and therefore constituted the place as an intersection of relations reaching beyond that place?

The spatial dimension of the Islamic festivals was particularly interesting in
interwar Dar es Salaam. The *Id* had so far usually been celebrated by the various
Muslim communities in different locations all over town. On the eve of the festivals, the town's Muslims assembled on top of their festive decorated houses for

the sighting of the new moon. The prayers were performed in the Friday mosque, feasts were organized in the respective communal mosques or in private homes, the official representatives of the different Muslim communities were received by the colonial administration in the governor's house, and *ngoma* (dance performances) took place at various locations in the periphery of town. As one writer in *Mambo Leo* stated "a holiday is a holiday and everybody enjoyed the day in his own way".[33]

From 1926 onwards the spatial dimension of the main Islamic holidays in Dar es Salaam changed considerably as the ceremony was centralized. It was the Indian-dominated Anjuman Islamia which invited all Muslims in Dar es Salaam for the first time to celebrate the *Idi el Fitri* together. The festival was located in a vast area in front of the organization's headquarters on the corner of Kichwele Street and Sultan Street. At this central square the prayers were said, speeches were delivered by representatives of the different branches, brotherhoods performed *dhikri*, the feast was held, and sport games, dances, cinema and small sales stalls entertained the festive crowd.

The square, later colloquially called Mnazi Mmoja (One Coconut Tree) by the inhabitants, was appropriated by the town's Muslim community as a festival place from 1926 on and gradually developed into Dar es Salaam's most important public square. The location was soon well-established as Islamic festival ground, as this description of *maulidi* in 1936 suggests: "The *shaykhs* and *sharifu*, the town elders and all Muslims assembled at Mnazi Mmoja square, as was the rule every year" (Nasibu 1936: 159-160)[34] Called 'open space' or 'neutral zone' in colonial town planning vocabulary, it was conceived of by the British colonial administration to separate the Indian and African quarters of the town.[35] Paradoxically, Dar es Salaam's Muslims chose exactly that area, which was the

---

33 *"Siku kuu ni siku kuu, na killa mmoja alipata furaha ya siku kuu kwa njia yake"*, "Idi-El-Fitr. Dar es Salaam", *Mambo Leo* 1925 (30): 125-126. See further "Die Festtage unserer mohammedanischen Bevölkerung", *DOAZ* 1902 (4), "Ramadhan", *OAZ* 1908 (10), "Daressalam. 15. Januar", *Kiongozi* 1908 (33); Jagina (1910); Raimbault (2007: 168); Zöller (2009: 74-83).

34 " [...] *walikusanyika Mashehe na Masharifu na wazee wa mji pamoja na Waislamu wote katika kiwanja cha Mnazi I kilicho kanuni kwa kila mwaka.*"

35 The German building code from 1914 envisaged a *cordon sanitaire* – a plan that the British colonial administration implemented in the 1920th. It was forbidden to build new houses in the 'open space' or repair existing ones. The last remaining houses were destroyed in 1930 and their inhabitants resettled (see Becher 1997: 46-49; Brennan and Burton 2007: 19-29).

embodiment of colonial visions of spatial order, to celebrate together and to overcome the racial segregations envisaged by the colonial power.

That 'profane' location, the 'open space', was transformed into a place with a religious meaning in times of the Islamic festivals through different practices, preparation and decoration, performance and prayer, and the naming of the place. In the advent of the Islamic festivals the location was especially prepared for its religious task. It was decorated with flags, flowers and colorful light bulbs. A separate prayer place was arranged for the *Id* prayers. Tents were erected for the sales stalls and separate areas for games and dances were prepared. On the occasion of the annual *maulidi,* pulpits were erected from where the *maulidi* texts were recited and speeches were held in various languages like Arabic, Swahili, English, Urdu and Gujarati. Additional stages were built up for *madrasa* students who sang *qasida* (Islamic poetry); and chairs and floor mats were provided for the guests. Invitation letters were sent and the festival program was announced beforehand, e.g. in newspapers. Movements in the form of journeys of believers from all over the town and its hinterland and parades by brotherhoods from their *madrasa* to the location contributed to the place-making. Thousands assembled at the square on these occasions. Approximately 8000 people, for example, attended in Dar es Salaam in 1930, a town which was at most inhabited by 25,000 people.[36]

However, not only did the square become the most important location for Islamic festivals in Dar es Salaam. Mnazi Mmoja turned out to be the central public place of the city. Colonial festivals like the 25th crown jubilee of King George V were also celebrated there, as were sport competitions. In the late 1930s, recreation grounds and community centers like the Arnautoglu Centre were built. With the rise of the independence movement after World War II, public meetings were held there and still today official national celebrations take place at Mnazi Mmoja.[37]

---

36 For *Idi el-Fitri* in Dar es Salaam, see "Idi-El-Fitr. Dar es Salaam", *Mambo Leo* 1925 (30): 125-126, Kidasi and Mambo 1926a: 375, 1926b: 445-446, 1929: 1064; Kayamba 1933: 66; Salum 1934a: 81, "*Ukifika kwa Kanga nawe jigeuze Kanga*", *Mambo Leo* 1936 (160): 55. For *Maulidi* in Dar es Salaam, see "Islamic Rally in Dar-es-Salaam"; *Samachar* 1930: 4-5; Dahal 1931: 88; bin Isa and bin Ahmadi Kombo 1933: 209; bin Rashidi 1934: 146; Nasibu 1936: 159-160; Madenge 1938: 112-113.

37 See "Islamic Rally in Dar-es-Salaam", *Samachar* 1930: 4; "*Taratibu za Shangwe ya Mei 6*", *Mambo Leo* 1935 (149): 69; Burton 2001: 206; Brennan and Burton 2007: 48; Geiger 1998: 61; Ricard 1998: 16–17; *Maulidi ya Kiserikali* 2008, see also http: //charaz.blogspot.com/2008/03/maulidi-njemaaa.html.

The question whether the place was temporarily, during the times of the Islamic festivals, or even generally conceived of as a 'sacred space' by the Muslims in the late 1920s and 30s is by now difficult to answer and would require further investigation. The name of the square, 'Mnazi Mmoja', 'One coconut tree', suggests, however, that Islamic practice was decisive for the naming of the place: it was adopted from a square in Zanzibar where the first public *maulidi* on the island took place (see Brennan and Burton 2007: 31, 69).[38] For the festival location in Dar es Salaam, the name was first mentioned in *Mambo Leo* in 1929 (see Kidasi and Mambo 1929: 1064). A few years later, the same name was adopted for the squares in Dodoma and Ujiji, where the Islamic festivals took place (see Selemani 1936: 163; Ponda, 1937b: 74). The fact that this name was first given to the place by the population of Dar es Salaam and only later on officially adopted by the colonial government is a further means of appropriation of the place, not only through the preparation of the location and the festive praxis, but also through the naming.

It is the constitution of the place through the process of interaction of individuals and groups which links the place-making with the aspect of its public dimension. First of all, Mnazi Mmoja was a public square open to all inhabitants of town. Every Muslim community had the possibility to present itself on the occasion of the festivals and to confirm its existence in front of the attendees (see Raimbault 2007: 168). It was thus a local stage where Muslims with different backgrounds came together, ranging from scholars, intellectuals, official representatives, members of Sufi orders, and students, to ordinary Muslim inhabitants of the town. Men and women, who rather seldom met in their everyday lives due to racial segregation or differing economic and occupational situations, for example, and who were affiliated with different social networks like mutual help or dance associations, interacted at these specific moments. But not only Muslims of various branches, origins and communities came together at the festival grounds. Non-Muslims also joined the festive crowd on these occasions.[39] Various colonial administrators were explicitly invited to join as guests and to give speeches (see Kidasi and Mambo 1926a: 375). The police force was also present and responsible for maintaining order because of the large crowd of participants

---

38 The square in Zanzibar got its name from the fact that only one coconut tree survived the disastrous cyclone in 1872 (see Ricard 1998: 16). According to Farsy (1972: 64) it was the Punjabi Sayyid Muhammad Hasan who started the public *maulidi* at Mnazi Mmoja in Zanzibar.

39 For processes of transcultural appropriation in the context of festivals in colonial Dar es Salaam (see Zöller 2009: 55-83).

– 'control' always being an important topic in colonial urban space, especially in times of festivals.[40]

The fact that the festivals merely took place on a public square is not sufficient to consider them as public arenas. The notion of 'public' has a strong communicative aspect, in addition to the physical dimension, in this case the presence of the diverse actors at Mnazi Mmoja (see Salvatore and Eickelman 2004: xii). This communicative aspect is particularly relevant for seeing the Islamic festivals in interwar Dar es Salaam and the related discussions as a public arena. Not only diverse views on religious practice but also differing ideas about the common good for the Muslim community in Dar es Salaam were directly articulated and debated by various actors during the festivals and also in the print media. The notion of the common good is, according to Eickelmann and Salvatore (2004: xii), central for the shaping of public Islam and it is in this sense that the festivals as social practice can be seen as a public arena for Dar es Salaam's Muslim population. The subject matters and claims which were raised by individuals and groups in this context and the underlying and resulting social dynamics are discussed in the next section.

THE SOCIAL DYNAMICS OF THE ISLAMIC FESTIVALS

The role of Mnazi Mmoja as a place constituted by the Muslim population of Dar es Salaam has to be seen from two angles. Existing relations, hierarchies or tensions between the festival participants and their visions of the festival and related issues were brought in and had an influence on festive practice. At the same time, the public festivals at Mnazi Mmoja had an influence on these relations beyond the actual time of the festivals.

In his pioneering study *Feasts and Riot* on the late 19th century Swahili coast, Jonathan Glassman sees festivals primarily as a "stage for some of the town's most divisive conflicts" (Glassman 2001: 221). In his opinion it is important to

---

40 The "Rules for the Township of Dar es Salaam" restricted not only worldly leisure activities but also Islamic practice: "No public entertainment, drumming, ngoma dancing, 'Thik', '*Maulidi*' or mourning '*matanga*' shall be held in town without the permission of the District Political Officer in writing, or at any place or time than that mentioned in such permit, and any person obtaining such permission shall be held responsible for maintenance of order thereat, unless he shall prove that any disturbances was occasioned by causes beyond his control." See "Notice. Rules for the Township of Dar es Salaam. Government Notice No. 6, 15.10.1919".

separate the ideal of the *umma* from the reality, because otherwise an interpretation of festivals could wrongly result in a narrative of unity. Therefore, one should not overlook that existing relationships were not merely reproduced in the arena of ritual, but were continually contested in a discursive struggle over ritual (Ibid. 1995: 22-24).[41] In his analysis of *maulidi* in Lamu, El Zein draws a similar conclusion: "Rather than being a unifying device of a primary sort, ritual is a language through which certain structural tensions or contradictions are unconsciously expressed and communicated." (El Zein 1974: xxi) Looking at these underlying tensions which were articulated in the public arena of the festivals, three examples will serve to illustrate the complexity of the social dynamics connected with and stimulated by the public Islamic festivals in interwar Dar es Salaam.

ENTERTAINMENT AND ISLAMIC FESTIVALS

"There is no moulid without a fraternity, just as there is no moulid without a fairground, attractions and trade stalls." (Madoeuf 2005: 72) What Madoef states for contemporary Cairo was also true for Zanzibar at the beginning of the 20th century: the *Id* celebrations were associated with a fair with stalls, riding schools, swings and dance floors.[42] The *Idi* were joyful celebrations and *ngoma* dances were an integral part to praise God and to express ones' joy, especially after the end of *Ramadan*, as one author in *Mambo Leo* explained. The popular performance of *ngoma* for purely competitive reasons, though, was condemned by the same author with the words *Vita tena, si goma!*, "That's war, not dance!" (Bin Mwalim 1923: 7-9) In fact, the competitive *beni ngoma* were, according to Ranger, still flourishing in smaller coastal towns. Also Dar es Salaam and especially Ujiji saw a strong rivalry and enmity between the different dance companies in the interwar years (see Ranger, 1975: 98-105). Debates about the competitive character of Islamic practices like *maulidi* performances and the extravagance on occasions such as Islamic weddings were more numerous and more pointed than debates about the main Islamic festivals.[43] However, the fairground

---

41 Pouwels, for example, stated that community-wide rituals in East Africa first and foremost strengthened solidarity and integrated outsiders as existing tensions were channeled through ritual rivalries (1987: 33-34, 63-64).

42 See *Das Kurbahn-Fest in Zanzibar. Zweiter Teil*, in: *DOAZ* 1907 (9).

43 This was not only true for Tanganyika Territory, but also for Zanzibar and they often involved alliances between Islamic scholars and colonial administrators (see Bin Hemedi El-Buhuriy 1935, 40-42, "*Maombezi ya Warabu katika Mombasa*", *Mambo*

character of the *Idi* in Dar es Salaam also raised criticism. Especially two articles written by Zibe Kidasi and Akida Mambo, who often reported on Dar es Salaam, criticized that the fairground with all its entertainment went overboard. Their initial enthusiasm for the first centrally organized *Idi el Fitri* at Mnazi Mmoja in 1926, with its games and stalls, was short-lived (Kidasi and Mambo 1926a: 375). Later that year they addressed the town's religious authorities in an article entitled "Salaam Aleikum Ma*shaykh*! Idi Mbaraka!" to tell them that "the Idi el Fitri had been better than this Idi el Haj, because there was not that much amusement, just a little. And I think a little like that is enough." (Ibid. 1926b: 445-446)[44] Three years later they lamented again that there was too much turbulence during *Idi* and also a tense atmosphere on the fairground (Ibid. 1929: 1064). Possibly, this critique was also directed to the organizers, as the Indian-dominated Anjuman Islamia gave African Muslims little chance to participate in the planning of the celebrations.[45] We do not know how far this critique of the entertainment character of the festivals was shared by other Muslims in Dar es Salaam and in particular by the *shaykhs*.[46] However, as these articles in *Mambo Leo* show, there was dissent among East African Muslims about the 'right' course of the festivals and the question of who had the authority to decide over it, and these questions were articulated in public.

SOLIDARITY AND FUND-RAISING ON *MAULIDI*

In the festival speeches which were printed in the newspapers, the narrative of unity and fraternalism played a major role. That was especially the case for *maulidi*. An Indian speaker, for example, highlighted in 1930 that "the great gospel of brotherhood preached by the founder of Islam had no room for any prejudice of caste, color or creed; black, brown, white, yellow, red, all were equal in the

---

Leo 1927 (52): 608; Farsy 1972: 14-15; Askew 2002: 162-169; Glassman 2001: 221-225; Loimeier 2006: 113-116).

44 "*Id-el-fitr ilikuwa bora kuliko Idi hii ya el-hadji, haikuwa tafrija nyingi ila kiasi tu. Nami naona inatosha kwa kiasi kami hicho.*"

45 Another reaction to this exclusion and Indian paternalism was the foundation of the *Jamiatul Islamia* in the early 1930th, as mentioned earlier.

46 This would require further investigation and field research, as the scope for criticism on religious issues in *Mambo Leo* was limited by censorship. Furthermore, harsh criticism on Islamic festivals was contrary to the ideal of unity and therefore rather unlikely to be explicitly stated in a newspaper.

eyes of Islam".[47] He called on his fellow Muslims to pursue that doctrine of equality. In 1936 Dar es Salaam's *liwali* invited the attendant crowd with *"tu-fanye umoja ndugu zangu"*, "let's unite brothers and sisters", to donate for the well-being of all Muslims in the city (Nasibu 1936: 159-160). Fund-raising was an especially important topic in the speeches. It is in this respect that the notion of the common good for the Muslim population in Dar es Salaam was brought up in the public arena of the festivals. On the one hand, donations were used on the festivals themselves, to feed and entertain the participants. At *Idi el Fitri* in 1926 for example, the Anjuman Islamia sponsored a huge feast and cinema by means of charitable donations (Kidasi and Mambo 1926a: 375). On the other hand, and with more repercussion beyond the festivals, strong emphasis was laid on fund raising for education, especially by African speakers.[48] Good schools were an urgent need particularly for the African children, as government expenditures for schooling had dropped dramatically due to the Great Depression.[49] The Islamic festivals therefore constituted an important occasion to call upon Muslim solidarity and during *maulidi* 1931, for example, around 1,800 *Shilingi*[50] were donated as stated by the secretary of the Islamic Society (see Dahal 1931: 88).

The Islamic festivals occasioned public claims to solidarity among Muslims, thus propagating the ideal of the *umma*. But to achieve this solidarity as a sign of unity and fraternity, it was at the same time necessary to highlight the existing unequal distribution of wealth and the segregation within Dar es Salaam's Muslim community in everyday life. The diverse participants and their respective social networks were called upon to strengthen the common good of all Muslims in town beyond the specific moments of the festivals as meeting place.

THE ORGANIZATION OF *MAULIDI*

The organization of Islamic festivals was a prestigious affair and underlined the high social rank of the organizers in the Muslim community. The celebration of the Prophets' birthday became the most popular festival for East African Muslims in the 1930s. Not surprisingly, then, its organization was a field of contesta-

---

47 See "Islamic Rally in Dar-es-Salaam", *Samachar* 1930: 4.

48 See "Islamic Rally in Dar-es-Salaam", *Samachar* 1930: 4-5.

49 The annual expenditures for education in the colony had fallen from 123,000 pounds in 1931 to 98,000 pounds in 1938 (see Iliffe 1979: 354).

50 For comparison, a *kanga* (the traditional garment for women) cost 2 or 3 *Shilingi* in Dar es Salaam in 1931 (see Iliffe 1979: 353).

tion among the various individuals and associations aiming to prove their rank in town. The social contestation was not the sole and certainly not the proclaimed function of the religious festivities; they first and foremost conveyed a strong, positive, spiritual and emotional meaning to the participants. But the existence of social tensions during festivities and their impact on the wider community as described by Glassman for the pre-colonial Swahili coast cannot be overlooked in the case of *maulidi* organization in interwar Dar es Salaam.

This was exemplified in a poem by a disappointed Muslim in Kilwa, a town further south on the Swahili coast. Due to tensions between different Muslim groups, the *maulidi* was celebrated in three different locations at the same time, forcing the wider community to divide among the competing parties (see Hashil 1937: 164).[51] In interwar Dar es Salaam there were mainly three organizations involved in the preparation of the annual celebration of the Prophet's Birthday: the Indian dominated Anjuman Islamia, the Maulidi Committee, which comprised the notables of the town, and the African dominated Jamiatul Islamia. However, diverging data in the research literature, as well as the multitude of established and new actors like the Mahfal-Mustarshidina[52] and finally, competing factions within the associations make it difficult to trace the roles of individual organizers of specific *maulidi* celebrations in Dar es Salaam.

The *maulidi* in 1938 will serve as an example to show how complex underlying tensions within the Muslim community came to the fore on the occasion of Islamic festivals. The *maulidi* in this case became a public arena contesting religious practice as well as power relations between different factions within Dar es Salaam's Muslim community. The Jamiatul Islamia, supported by donations and a major contribution by the Aga Khan, had opened a school for Muslim children in 1936, where religious as well as secular knowledge was taught. The school was involved in the organization of the *maulidi* 1938 and school children, divided into groups of boys and girls, sang *qasida* from separated stages (see Brennan 2002: 145-148; Madenge 1938: 112-113).

---

51 He asked the three competing groups in Kilwa, which each organised their own *Maulidi*, to settle the dispute and come to an arrangement. Otherwise he would rather stay at home the following year. A similar conflict about who was to have the most prominent part in the celebration took place in Ujiji where, besides arbitrators from Dar es Salaam, also the District Officer and police intervened (see Nimtz 1980: 80).

52 1933 and 1934 Madrasa students around Shaykh Mzee bin Ali Comorian performed their own *maulidi* two days after the public *Maulidi* (see bin Isa and bin Ahmadi Kombo 133: 209; bin Rashidi 1934: 146). For a similar practice in Tanga where various brotherhoods were competing after the main *Maulidi*, see van de Bruinhorst (2007: 174).

The comment in *Mambo Leo* reads as follows:

"Although joy was great, many were astonished to see a stage where girls were singing *qasida*. This astonishment left some grumbling behind. They were alarmed that this year, the Maulidi was conducted in that special way. That showed the people, that everybody who wants to present himself at a suitable place in order to express the joy of his heart can do so without any difficulties" (Madenge 1938: 112-113).[53]

Grumbling was a discreet term for the storm of protest that followed the girls' public performance at *maulidi* as described by Brennan and Said, who had access to further sources (Brennan 2002: 145-148; Said 1998: 46-47).[54] The *liwali* of Dar es Salaam, spokespersons of the Zaramo and the Shomvi, and some parents saw this as an affront against their religious feelings and caused the closure of the school. Two factions of African Muslims were involved in that conflict: "One faction comprised what were considered 'foreigners'. These were Manyemas, Nubis and a few Zulus. The other group was made up of locals; the Zaramo, Ndengerenko, Rufiji and others." (Said 1998: 47) The locals, who called themselves *wenye mji* (owners of the town), tried to push back the growing influence of the 'foreigners' or *watu wa kuja* (the people who came), who formed the Jamiatul Islamias' progressive leadership.

Conflicts between migrants and the local elite about the control of Islamic institutions have a long history on the Swahili Coast (see Glassman 2001: 211-214; El Zein 1974: 13-17). Dar es Salaam's colonial context further expanded the conflict between the two factions within the Jamiatul Islamia: each faction sought help from different colonial administrators. The faction which I will call the 'locals' caused the District Officer to close the school because of the scandal surrounding the girls' performance, but also because they did not want to succumb to the progressive leadership's refusal to accept the *liwali* instead of Shaykh Ali Saleh as the Jamiatul Islamia's new president. The other faction, the leadership of the Jamiatul, approached the Provincial Commissioner via an Indian lawyer and the school was reopened again. However, the conflict was too deep to reconcile the factions of the association. One faction thus dissociated it-

---

53 *"Ingawa furaha ilikuwa kubwa, wengi walistaajabu kwa kuona jukwaa la watoto wa kike ambao walikuwa wakisoma Qassida. Maajabu hayo yaliacha miguno hapa. Walishtuka kuwa, Maulidi ya mwaka huu yameendeshwa namna ya peke yake. Hiwi imewadhihirikia jamaa kuwa, Ye yote [sic] ampendaye wake haoni vigumu kujidhihirisha mahali panapostahili kumtolea furaha za moyo wake."*

54 Said dates the conflict to 1940, but evidence in *Mambo Leo* suggests that *Maulidi* 1938 was the starting point of the conflict.

self from the organization and opened its own school (see Brennan 2002: 145-148; Said 1998: 46-47).

The initial debate about religious orthodoxy on *maulidi* illustrated different religious attitudes between *wenye mji* and *watu wa kuja*. It evolved into a fundamental political conflict about the control over the Jamiatul Islamia, the central association of the town's African Muslims. The progressive leadership let the girls sing to raise funds without regarding the sentiments of some of the locals. These locals took the public performance of *qasidas* by schoolgirls as a provocation serious enough to close the school and thus push back the progressive leadership's influence. The existing tensions within the African Muslim community were thus articulated in the public arena of the Islamic festival and the media and affected the relations between the factions even in the aftermath of the festival.

CONCLUSION

Let us return to the question raised in the title of this paper: In how far did Islamic festivals in interwar Dar es Salaam constitute a contested public arena?

The new location for the Islamic festivals at Mnazi Mmoja became an important place for the Muslim population in interwar Dar es Salaam. This was the prerequisite for the emergence of a public arena, seen as a forum of interaction between the different actors involved. In this arena issues concerning the religious practice and the common good of the Muslims in town were raised. Dar es Salaam's Muslims literally stepped out of their various community-based mosques and assembled at Mnazi Mmoja, presenting themselves as one group in public. They appropriated the city's 'open space' during the times of the festivals with permission and control by the colonial administration through various practices of place-making. The town's Muslims performed their prayers at Mnazi Mmoja and interacted with each other, either individually or community-wise, through religious practices like *dhikri*, through *ngoma* dances, the feast, or speeches that were held on the occasion of the festivals. The public arena of the Islamic festivals did not exclude non-Muslims. Guests were welcome and especially colonial state officials were addressed in the speeches. *Mambo Leo*, the newspaper edited by the Education Department, can be seen as another arena for contest. By bringing issues related with the Islamic festivals from the realm of private discussions into the media, East African Muslims developed a new forum for exchange on debates about Islamic festivals and the Muslim community in Dar es Salaam and beyond.

The communicative aspect of the public Islamic festivals stressed the vision of the *umma*, which brought Muslims of various branches, origins and ranks during the times of the festivals together at Mnazi Mmoja and revealed at the same time diverging ideas on religious praxis and existing tensions between the festival participants. To perform the ideal of the unity of the *Umma*, a synchronous beginning of the Islamic festivals in the region was considered essential. However, there was dissent about who used the correct means and had the authority to determine the exact date of the beginning of the celebrations. Socio-political claims were articulated in the festive speeches, e.g. in respect to education. The funds, which were subsequently raised during the festivals, e.g. to provide for education for less privileged children, were a sign of solidarity among the town's Muslims. But to address a sense of solidarity among the listeners, the speakers had to point to the underlying racial and economic divisions of Dar es Salaam's Muslims in urban everyday life. The invitations to colonial administrators to the fairground as well as the invitations to representatives of the various Muslim communities to the governor's house on the occasion of the *Idi* were an affirmation of the existing social and political order. However, in times of contest, e.g. following the girls' performance on *maulidi* in 1938, even the colonial administrators had to take sides in the struggle for authority over Dar es Salaam's Islamic institutions between various factions of Muslims. The public arena at Mnazi Mmoja was not only constituted at the times of the festivals by the interaction of the various actors and their existing relations to each other. It was further supported by discussions in the media and also had an influence on the relations between Dar es Salaam's Muslims and their visions of the common good beyond the times of the festivals.

The pivotal point of this historical analysis is the place of Mnazi Mmoja in the centre of Dar es Salaam. It is a place that was transformed by Dar es Salaam's Muslim population in the 1930s from an 'open space' into their most important meeting place. In times of the main Islamic festivals the believers transformed it through their religious practice into a 'sacred place'. Mnazi Mmoja is a public square with diverse functions and meanings which were changing over the course of time. The imagination of the place as 'sacred', therefore, was only one perception of the place. The same location was seen in the interwar years as a rather abstract, controllable area, important in terms of urban development; as former home by those who were forcibly removed in order to establish this 'open space'; as meeting place and sacred place for Muslims from the town and beyond at the most important times in their religious calendar. Mnazi Mmoja became also a festival ground for diverse colonial celebrations, a recreation ground and finally, a symbol for the success of the independence movement, as the Uhuru torch monument, located at the southern end of the nowadays partly fenced park interrupted by streets, buildings and a parking space, still reminds us. These diverging visions of a place in its specific historical context, which are far from complete, illustrate Massey's understanding that places do not have single identities and that their uniqueness arises inter alia out of the various layers of different sets of relations to a place throughout its history (see Massey 1991: 24-29).

REFERENCES

Abbas, Ali (1927): "Shairi la Telefoni", in: Mambo Leo 55 (July 1927), p. 674.

Abdallah Saleh Farsy (1972): Baadhi ya wanavyuoni wa kishafi wa mashariki ya Afrika, Mombasa.

Ahmed, A. Chanfi (1999): "La passion pour le prophète aux Comores et en Afrique de l'est ou l'épopée du Maulid al-Barzandji", in: Islam et sociétés au sud du Sahara 13, pp. 65-89.

Ahmed, A. Chanfi and von Oppen, Achim (2004): "Saba Ishirini. A Commemoration Ceremony as the Performance of Translocality around the South Swahili Coast", in: Stauth, Georg (Ed.), On Archaeology of Sainthood and Local Spirituality in Islam. Past and Present Crossroads of Events and Ideas (Yearbook of the Sociology of Islam 5), Bielefeld: Transcript, pp. 89-103.

Anthony, David Henry (2002): "Islam in Dar es Salaam, Tanzania", in: Studies in Contemporary Islam 4:2, pp. 23-47.

Askew, Kelly Michelle (2002): Performing the Nation. Swahili Music and Cultural Politics in Tanzania, Chicago: University of Chicago Press.

Becher, Jürgen (1997): Dar-es-Salaam, Tanga und Tabora. Stadtentwicklung in Tansania unter deutscher Kolonialherrschaft (1885-1914), Stuttgart: Steiner.

Becker, Felicitas (2008): Becoming Muslim in Mainland Tanzania. 1890-2000, Oxford: Oxford University Press (A British Academy Postdoctoral Fellowship Monograph).

Bin Haji el Battawey, Zaharani (1929): "Unguja. Sheikh Salim bin Maka", in: Mambo Leo 78 (June), p. 1098.

Bin Hemedi El-Buhuriy, Ali (1935), "Habari za Mrima", in: Mambo Leo 147 (March), pp. 40-42.

Bin Isa Ramadhani, Hasan and Sefu bin Ahmadi Kombo (1933): "Dar es Salaam. Maulidi", in: Mambo Leo 129 (September 1933), p. 209.

Bin Mwalim, Karani (1923): "Nawaweke maduka, yataishia ngomani", in: Mambo Leo 6 (June 1923), pp. 7-9.

Bin Rashidi, Ali Musa (1934): "Dar es Salaam. Maulidi cha Chama kipya 'Mahfal-Murstarshidina'", in: Mambo Leo 140 (August), p. 146.

Bin Saidi, Ali (1931): "Shukarani za African Association, Dar es Salaam", in: Mambo Leo 107 (November), p. 197.

Bin Sansa, Komagi (1923): "Idi El-Haji", in: Mambo Leo 79 (July), p. 1114.

Bin Sansa, Komagi (1937a): "Majibu kwa Waandikaji. Abdallah Sudi, Iringa", in: Mambo Leo 9 (September), p. 142.

Bin Sansa, Komagi (1937b) "Majibu kwa Waandikaji. Abdallah Sudi, Iringa", Mambo Leo 11 (November), p. 177.

Brace, Catherine; Bailey, Adrian R., and Harvey, David C. (2006): "Religion, Place and Space. A Framework for Investigating Historical Geographies of Religious Identities and Communities", in: Progress in Human Geography 30:1, pp. 28-43.

Brennan, James R., and Burton, Andrew (2007): "The Emerging Metropolis. A History of Dar es Salaam, circa 1862-2000", in: James Brennan, Andrew Burton and Yusuf Lawi (Eds.): Dar es Salaam. Histories from an Emerging African Metropolis, Dar es Salaam: Mkuki Na Nyota, pp. 13-75.

Brennan, James R. (2002): Nation, Race and Urbanization in Dar es Salaam, Tanzania, 1916-1976. Ph.D. Thesis: Evanston.

(1999): "South Asian Nationalism in an East African Context: The Case of Tanganyika, 1914-1956", in: Comparative Studies of South Asia, Africa and the Middle East 2, pp. 24-39.

Bromber, Katrin (2006): "Ustaarabu. A Conceptual Change in Tanganyikan Newspaper Discourse in the 1920s", in: Loimeier, Roman and Rüdiger Seesemann (Eds.), The Global Worlds of the Swahili. Interfaces of Islam, Identity and Space in 19th and 20th Century East Africa (Beiträge zur Afrikaforschung, Band 26), Berlin: Lit, pp. 67-81.

(2000): "Biashara nzuri – biashara mbaya. Eine textanalytische Untersuchung zum Abgrenzungsdiskurs in der kolonialen tansanischen Presse (Mambo Leo, 1923)", in: Swahili Forum 7, pp. 97-125.

Burton, Andrew (2001): "Urchins, Loafers and the Cult of the Cowboy. Urbanization and Delinquency in Dar es Salaam, 1919-1961", in: Journal of African History 42:2, pp. 199-216.

Dahal, Ibrahim (1931): "Dar es Salaam. Maadhimisho ya Maulidi ya Mungo sita", in: Mambo Leo 101 (May), p. 88.

Durkheim, Emile (1981): Die elementaren Formen des religiösen Lebens, Frankfurt am Main: Suhrkamp.

Eisenstadt, Shmuel Noah (2002): "Concluding Remarks. Public Sphere, Civil Society, and Political Dynamics in Islamic Societies", in: Miriam Hoexter,

Shmuel Noah Eisenstadt and Nehemia Levtzion (Eds.): The Public Sphere in Muslim Societies, Albany: State University of New York Press, pp. 139-162.

El Zein, Abdul Hamid M. (1974): The Sacred Meadows. A Structural Analysis of Religious Symbolism in an East African Town. Evanston: Northwestern University Press.

Frankl, P. J. L. and Yahya Ali Omar (1996): "The Observance of Ramadan in Swahili-Land (with Special Reference to Mombasa)", in: Journal of Religion in Africa 26:4, pp. 416-434.

Farjala, Sawedi (1912): "Shauri njema. Kalendari", in: Kiongozi 83 (April).

Geider, Thomas (2002): "The Paper Memory of East Africa. Ethnohistories and Biographies Written in Swahili", in: Axel Harneit-Sievers (Ed.): A Place in the World. New Local Historiographies from Africa and South Asia, Leiden: Brill, pp. 255-288.

Geiger, Susan (1998): TANU Women. Gender and Culture in the Making of Tanganyikan Nationalism, 1955-1965, Portsmouth, NH: Heinemann.

Glassman, Jonathon (2001): "Stolen Knowledge. Struggles for Popular Islam on the Swahili Coast, 1870-1963", in: Scarcia Amoretti, Biancamaria (Ed.): Islam in East Africa. New Sources, Roma: Herder, pp. 209-225.

(1995): Feasts and Riot. Revelry, Rebellion, and Popular Consciousness on the Swahili Coast, 1856-1888. Portsmouth, NH: Heinemann.

Goerg, Odile (1999): "Introduction", in: Odile Goerg (Ed.): Fêtes urbaines en Afrique. Espaces identités et pouvoirs, Paris: Karthala, pp. 5-16.

Hashil, Seif (1937): "Maulidi Jumuiya ya Kilwa Mfungo Sita", in: Mambo Leo 10 (October), p. 164.

Hollis, A. C. (1921): "Notice. Indian Holidays. Government Notice No. 15", in: The Tanganyika Territory. Official Gazette 2, p. 28.

Iliffe, John (1979): A Modern History of Tanganyika. Cambridge, New York: Cambridge University Press.

Jagina, Shaha (1910): "Kumuwajihi Herr Gouverneur", in: Kiongozi 56 (Januar).

Kambi, F.D. Yussuf (1936): "Kikombo, Nzinge, Dodoma. Kuwasiliwa na Sheikh Idrisa wa Dar es Salaam", in: Mambo Leo 159 (March), p. 45.

Kayamba, H.T.M. (1933): "Dar es Salaam. Habari za Mji", in: Mambo Leo 123, (March), p. 66.

Kidasi, Zibe, and Mambo, Akida (1926a): "Siku kuu ya Idi-el-Fitri, katika Dar es Salaam", in: Mambo Leo 41 (May), p. 375.

(1926b): "Salaam Aleikum Masheikh! Idi Mbaraka", in: Mambo Leo 44 (August), pp. 445-446.

(1929): "Idi El-Fitri", in: Mambo Leo 76 (April), p. 1064.

Klamroth, Martin (1910): "Ostafrikanischer Islam", in: Allgemeine Missionszeitschrift 37, pp. 477-493, 536-546.

Kresse, Kai (2006): "Debating Maulidi. Ambiguities and Transformations of Muslim Identity along the Kenyan Swahili Coast", in: Roman Loimeier and Rüdiger Seesemann (Eds.): The Global Worlds of the Swahili. Interfaces of Islam, Identity and Space in 19th and 20th Century East Africa, Berlin: Lit, pp. 209-228.

Lodhi, Abdulaziz Y. and Westerlund, David (1997): African Islam in Tanzania. See http://www.islamfortoday.com/tanzania.htm.

Loimeier, Roman (2007): Sit Local, Think Global. The Baraza in Zanzibar, in: Journal for Islamic Studies 27, pp. 16-38.

(2006): "Coming to Terms with 'Popular Culture'. The 'Ulama' and the State in Zanzibar." In: Roman Loimeier and Rüdiger Seesemann (Eds.): The Global Worlds of the Swahili. Interfaces of Islam, Identity and Space in 19th and 20th Century East Africa, Berlin: Lit, pp. 111-129.

Loimeier, Roman and Mwakimako, Hassan (2006): Plurale Konzeptionen von Zeit in (trans)lokalen Kontexten. Zentrum Moderner Orient. See http://www-.zmo.de/forschung/projekte_2006/zeit.html

Madenge, B.M.S. (1938): "Dar es Salaam. Maadhimisho ya Maulidi, 11 Abu Awal", in: Mambo Leo 7 (July), pp. 112-113.

Madoeuf, Anna (2005): "Feats. Panoramas in Town – the Space and Times of the Moulids of Cairo." In: Simone AbdouMaliq and Abdelghani Abouhani (Eds.): Urban Africa. Changing Contours of Survival in the City, Dakar: Codesria Books, pp. 68-95.

Mambo, Akida (1909): "Daressalam. Taa za stimu", in: Kiongozi 47 (April).

Massey, Doreen (1991): "A Global Sense of Place", in: Marxism Today (June), pp. 24-29.

Martin, B.G. (1976): Muslim Brotherhoods in 19th Century Africa. London: Cambridge University Press.

(1971): "Notes on Some Members of the Learned Classes of Zanzibar and East Africa in the 19th Century", in: African Historical Studies 4:3, pp. 525-545.

Minjuma, Mshenzi (1931): "Bagamoyo. Sheikh Ramiya bin Abdallah", in: Mambo Leo 104 (August), p. 154.

Muhsin, Hassen Mohamed (1923): "Kwa Editor, Mambo Leo, Dar es Salaam", in: Mambo Leo 11 (November), p. 16.

Nasibu, S. Juma (1936): "Dar es Salaam. Ziara", in: Mambo Leo 166 (October), pp. 159-160.

Nganzi, Jiriwa (1925): "Ujinga wa kuficha Makabila yenu wacheni!", in: Mambo Leo 32 (August), p. 179.

Nimtz, August H. (1980): Islam and Politics in East Africa. The Sufi Order in Tanzania, Minneapolis: University of Minnesota Press.

Nkonjera, Hektor (1930): in: Mambo Leo 85 (January), p. 15.

Omari Libajuni, Th. M. (1934): "Moshi. Idi Mbaraka", in: Mambo Leo 136 (April), p. 66.

Ponda, Ali Mwl (1937a): "Dodoma. Idi el Fitri", in: Mambo Leo 2 (February), p. 23.

Ponda, Ali Mwl (1937b): "Dodoma. Idi el-Haji", in: Mambo Leo 5 (May), p. 74.

Pouwels, Randall L. (1987): Horn and Crescent. Cultural Change and Traditional Islam on the East African Coast, 800-1900, Cambridge: Cambridge University Press.

Raimbault, Franck (2007): Dar-es-Salaam. Histoire d' une Société Urbaine Coloniale en Afrique Orientale Allemande (1891-1914). Two Volumes. Dissertation, Paris.

Ranger, Terence Osborn (1975): Dance and Society in Eastern Africa 1890-1970. The Beni Ngoma, London: Heinemann.

Reusch, Richard (1930): Der Islam in Ost-Afrika mit besonderer Berücksichtigung der muhammedanischen Geheim-Orden, Leipzig: Adolf Klein.

Ricard, Alain (1998): Ebrahim Hussein. Théâtre Swahili et Nationalisme Tanzanien, Paris: Karthala.

Ruete, Emilie (1989): Leben im Sultanspalast. Memoiren aus dem 19. Jahrhundert. Edited by Annegret Nippa, Frankfurt am Main: Athenäum.

Said, Mohammed (1998): The Life and Times of Abdulwahid Sykes (1924-1968). The Untold Story of the Muslim Struggle against British Colonialism in Tanganyika, London: Minerva Press.

Salum, A. Idi (1934a): "Dar es Salaam", in: Mambo Leo 137 (May), p. 81.

(1934b): "Ilala. Sifa njema juu ya mtaa wetu", in: Mambo Leo 140 (August), p. 130.

Salvatore, Armando and Eickelman, Dale F. (2004): Public Islam and the Common Good (Social, Economic and Political Studies of the Middle East, Volume 95), Leiden: Brill.

Selemani, Yusufu (1936): "Ujiji. Jumuia el Islam", in: Mambo Leo 166 (October 1936), p. 163.

Sturmer, Martin (1999): The Media History of Tanzania, Ndanda: Ndanda Mission Press.

Suriano, Maria (2008): "Clothing and the Changing Identities of Tanganyikan Urban Youths, 1920s-1950s", in: Journal of African Cultural Studies 20:1, pp. 95-115.

Tsuruta, Tadasu (2003): "Popular Music, Sports, and Politics. A Development of Urban Cultural Movements in Dar es Salaam, 1930s-1960s", in: African Study Monographs 24:3, pp. 195-222.

van de Bruinhorst, Gerard Cornelis (2007): 'Raise your Voices and Kill your Animals'. Islamic Discourses on the Idd el-Hajj and Sacrifices in Tanga (Tanzania). Authoritative Texts, Ritual Practices and Social Identities Dissertation, ISIM, Amsterdam University Press: Leiden.

Walji, Shirin Remtulla (1974): A History of the Ismaili Community in Tanzania. Dissertation, University of Wisconsin-Madison.

Wilson, W.A. (1930): "Notice. In his Majesty's High Court of Tanganyika at Dar es Salaam", in: Mambo Leo 86 (February), p. 25.

Wirz, Albert (2003): "Einleitung: Körper, Raum und Zeit der Herrschaft", in: Albert Wirtz, Andreas Eckert and Katrin Bromber (Eds.): Alles unter Kontrolle. Disziplinierungsprozesse im kolonialen Tansania (1850-1960), Köln: Köppe, pp. 5-34.

Zöller, Katharina (2009): Islamische Feste im kolonialen Dar es Salaam, 1905-1938. Master Thesis: Berlin.

FURTHER REFERENCES

"Almanak hii imetuwasiliya kwa hisani ya 'Zuhura binti Simba', ikapigwa chapa kwa mintaraf ya Waislamu", in: Mambo Leo 52 (April 1927), p. 614.

"Das Kurbahn-Fest in Zanzibar. Zweiter Teil", in: DOAZ 9 (43), 21.08.1907.

"Daressalam. 15. Januar", in Kiongozi 33, February 1908.

"Die Festtage unserer mohammedanischen Bevölkerung", in: DOAZ 4 (3), 18.01.1902.

"Idi-El-Fitr. Dar es Salaam", in: Mambo Leo 30 (June 1925), pp. 125-126,

"Islamic Rally in Dar-es-Salaam", in: Samachar, 14.09.1930, p. 4.

"Kalender 1912", Die evangelischen Missionen in Deutsch-Ostafrika. Tanga: Schuldruckerei.

"Majibu kwa Waandikaji. B.H.S. Maloki, Kondoa-Irangi", in: Mambo Leo 162 (June 1936), p. 96.

"Maombezi ya Warabu katika Mombasa", in: Mambo Leo 52 (April 1927), p. 608.

"Marehemu Seyid Ahmed bin Abubaker Sumeit" in: Mambo Leo 32 (August 1925), pp. 175-176.

"Maulidi ya Kiserikali" (2008), See: http://charaz.blogspot.com/2008/03/-maulidi-njemaaa.html.

"Mweleza Mwaka wa 1911 kwa wakristu weusi katika D.O. Afrika". Katholische Mission. Dar es Salaam: Druckerei des Rafiki Yangu.

"Notice. Rules for the Township of Dar es Salaam" (1919), in: The Tanganyika Territory. Official Gazette, Government Notice 6 (1), 15.10.1919, pp. 50-54.

"Ramadhan", in: DOAZ 10 (76), 03.10.1908.

"Siku kuu za serikali za wakristo na za waislamu", Mambo Leo 2 (February 1938).

"Stadtplan von Daressalam" (1910), in: Deutsche Kolonialzeitung, 05.02.1910, p. 89.

"Taratibu za Shangwe ya Mei 6", in: Mambo Leo 149 (May 1935), p. 69.

Competing Spaces, Contested Places

Muslim Struggles for Place, Space, and Recognition at a German University

Jörn Thielmann

A university in Southwest Germany. Since its establishment, the university hosts important faculties of sciences and of medicine. Therefore, it does not surprise that as early as in the 1960s Muslim students are enrolled. On February 17 and 18, 1962, the first Muslim student congress in Germany even took place here (cf. Meining 2011: 140). Out of this Muslim student community two Muslim associations with mosques emerged in 1989 and 1998.

Scene 1. On campus, in the basement of one of the older buildings, is a Catholic chapel, ignored by most of the university's faculty and students. In the early 2000s, however, this place became heavily contested between the Catholic university chaplain and Christian groups on the one side, and Muslim students on the other. In the late 1990s, some Muslim students asked the then Catholic chaplain if they could use the chapel for ritual prayers, especially on Fridays. So far, they had used the staircase just in front of the chapel's entrance, or other corners in various buildings. During that time, the chapel was always open and accessible. Holy Mass was celebrated on Wednesday. The other services took place in the parochial centre of the University Parish, off campus, where a proper church is found. For the chaplain the parallel use of the chapel by Muslims posed no general problem and there was mutual acceptance. During prayers, the Muslim worshippers covered the statues and tableaux with cloths, arranged for carpets, and became over time the only regular and by far the most important group of users, men and women alike.

Scene 2. Some years later, some years into the new millennium. It is the same place, but there is now a new Catholic chaplain and two new Christian student groups, one of which is a 'Rosary Prayer Group'. Of course, from time to time there has been some tension around these Muslim prayer groups of men and women, but mostly with the next institute on the ground floor, due to the use and abuse of toilets for ritual cleansings and ablutions – a wet business, irritating for non-Muslims. But now, the situation changed dramatically. The weekly Holy Mass moved to Friday at midday, at exactly the same time as the usual time for the most important – and the only obligatory – Muslim prayer. And when on one Friday two Muslims entered the chapel during mass, they raised their voices and prayed 'against' the Christians. The Catholic chaplain was very upset and seized the occasion to terminate the inter-religious dual use of the chapel. Muslim prayers in the chapel were forbidden. The door to the chapel shut. Thus, for the first time the chapel was closed to everybody. However, the chaplain offered an alternative space for Muslim prayers in the parochial centre off campus, relatively nearby, perhaps 5 minutes' walk away.

Scene 3. The situation escalates during an exchange of letters. The university president involuntarily enters the scene. He was addressed by the Muslim student group. The head of the president's office was officially charged to negotiate and to calm the situation. Other religious groups came in. The university's ombudsman for foreign students was brought in. However, until today Muslims remain banned and their prayers take place just in front of the chapel's door, in the staircase of the basement, like before.

Following the Austrian-Ottoman wars, some Muslims have been living here and there in what is today Germany, without forming any Muslim community. In the late 19th century, Ottoman and Arab diplomats, army officers, upper-class voyagers or students were quite common visitors. The 1920s then saw the establishment of the first mosque and the flourishing of Muslim bourgeois clubs in Berlin (cf. Motadel 2009).[1] Islam remained an elite phenomenon until the mass immigration of workers, the so-called *Gastarbeiter* (guest workers), in the 1960s. Now, Turkish Muslims with a rural background in most cases formed the German perception of Islam. Islam as a religion was unknown, but posed no threat. However, it was perceived as being a backward religion and as such an obstacle for integration. Nevertheless, across Germany, the first collective prayers of Muslims at the occasion of the Islamic feasts were quite often celebrated in Catholic churches, even in the Cologne cathedral.

The recruitment stop in 1973 led to families reuniting, permanent settlement, and the emergence of several religious organizations up to the early 1980s. The

---

1 Generally, on the history of Muslims in Germany, see Abdullah (1981). For a research survey, see also Thielmann (2008 and 2010).

three major ones among them, also in this university town, are – not surprising in view of the Turkish majority – Turkish, namely the religio-nationalistic Islamic Community Millî Görüş (Islamische Gemeinschaft Millî Görüş, IGMG), the Sufi-oriented VIKZ (the association of Islamic cultural centers – Verband der Islamischen Kulturzentren), and the Diyanet İşleri Türk İslam Birligi (DİTİB), the Turkish-Islamic Union of the Office for Religious Affairs – Türkisch-Islamische Union der Anstalt für Religion, by which the Turkish state tried to get hold of its (former) citizens in Germany and to control the religious scene among the Turks (cf. Seufert 1999; Rosenow 2010).[2] Since the early 1990s, supra-national mosque associations emerged, formed around a common understanding of Islam by Muslims of diverse ethnic, linguistic and cultural background, including German converts to Islam. Here, German is often used as the common language. In this university town, there are two mosques of this type grown out of Muslim student circles.

The Islamic Revolution in Iran in 1979 and the Soviet invasion of Afghanistan in the same year with the armed resistance of the *mudjahidin* brought the issue of political Islam, fundamentalism and radicalization to the fore. The terrorist attacks in the USA on 9/11 intensified this perception of Islam and placed it in the political and public debates in Germany. Besides intensified research on Muslims in Germany, this also led to suspicion and fear, especially towards young Muslim men of Middle Eastern background. The university authorities as well as other public actors, like the churches, are of course also affected by this.

For practicing believers of religious minorities, place, space and visibility through rituals are always of importance and a central issue. The old-established faiths in a country must literally give way to the religious newcomers and accept that other rituals or other religious configurations of space become visible in the public sphere. Across Europe, conflicts over the construction of mosques – with or without minarets – have their roots in this (cf. Schmitt 2003). Nevertheless, universities as arenas for such conflicts are surprising, because they are secular, if maintained by the state. In our present case, however, the situation is more complex. For historical reasons the chapel belongs to the local Catholic diocese

---

2 The legal framework for Muslim life in Germany is until today subject to debate among Muslims and German jurists and politicians alike (cf. Rohe 2008). So far, they are organised as registered associations (*eingetragener Verein*, e.V.) or as foundations (*Stiftung*). Since the late 1970s all associations have sought to obtain the status of a publicly recognised corporation (*Körperschaft des öffentlichen Rechts*), which would grant them the same status and rights (e.g. collection of church taxes by the state on behalf of them, teaching in schools) like the Christian churches or the Jewish community.

and is under the control and responsibility of the bishop, delegated to the university chaplain. The university has no say, even if the actual room in question lies in the midst of its buildings. The overwhelming majority of the faculty and student body has no idea about that and even ignores the very existence of such a chapel on campus. Muslim students are perhaps the only ones aware of the place. It is noteworthy, then, that it took them so long to dare ask for permission to use it for their ritual prayers, because there had been Muslim students already some decades before and the chapel has been at the same place since 1945/46.

In any case, Muslims need space and a place for prayer five times a day, and especially for the obligatory collective Friday prayer. Nevertheless, that requires little: a clean and proper ground, provided for by carpets or even newspapers placed on the floor; an orientation towards Mecca, the *qibla*; the ritual cleansing through ablutions by water, which means that they need access to water nearby to minimize the risk of becoming ritually unclean again on the way to prayer (cf. Schimmel 1995: 76-98, esp. 80-82).[3] Of course, the afore-mentioned staircase was – and is – not a very pleasant place to fulfill religious duties and to pray, and nor is it very spacious. The Muslim students are simply a bit hidden from sudden passersby and partially protected from curious looks, because it is dead-end, leading to some cellars with an ethnological collection. So, the nearly unused chapel was, and still is, an attractive place for prayer for Muslim students.

At stake in this conflict, however, is no sacred space as such, at least not from the perspective of the Muslim side. Instead, we observe processes of place-making in a very local and concrete sense, but also of space-making in the sense that the Muslim students are struggling for spaces of recognition and of action as religious activists amidst or against other religious – and non-religious – activists. For the competing Catholic groups, nevertheless, the place is of course sacred, as being consecrated, and naturally in their understanding it belongs to them as Catholics. Here, the prevailing sentiment might well be one of being an 'endangered species' so to speak, as Catholics. Their space is therefore now more and more under threat by strong believing Muslim groups growing.

In the following article, I examine the letters exchanged about the matter of using the chapel space for prayer. I start with the initial letter from January 26, 2006, written by the spokesperson of the Muslim student group (*Muslimischer Studentenausschuss*).[4] He is a German of Pakistani origin, born in Germany and

---

3   On ritual cleansing and ablutions, see Schimmel (1995: 128-133).

4   I was asked by one party to intervene as a mediator in this conflict and therefore had access to the complete correspondence. Due to the fact that the parties involved never gathered around a table to discuss the issues at stake face-to-face, the letters and e-mail exchanges are the central arena for this conflict and the object of my study.

raised here. I will call him Ahmad. As a former spokesperson of his fellows at his German *Gymnasium* and after already spending some years at the university, Ahmad knows the German rules and customs of public discourse well. His letter begins with a statement that

"for several years the university chapel has served Muslims and Christians as a space for inter-religious encounters [*interreligiöser Begegnungsraum*]. Thus, it fulfills a very important function in the present time. The closure of the chapel for an indefinite time," he writes, "deprives Muslims of a place for prayer at the university."

He later continues:

"We are endlessly disappointed by the KHG [*Katholische Hochschulgemeinde*: Catholic university parish; J.T.] who neglected the need to inform the presidency of the university and the Muslim Students' Association before [banning Muslims from using the chapel; J.T.]. We perceive this as a break of trust by the KHG, because all agreements have been broken. The Muslim students of this university feel themselves excessively overlooked, ignored and affronted. We appeal to the reason of the KHG to reverse their inconsiderate step, because by such blindfolded measures emotions will unnecessarily be stirred up."

The author totally ignored the factual situation at this time. For him, the chapel is not a Catholic consecrated place under the authority of the church, but an inter-religious room with free access and use at any time for Muslims. He perceived of the university authorities and the Muslim students as being on equal footing. His wording is self-confident, as becomes visible in his five demands concluding the letter:

"1. We consider the use of the university chapel by Christians as well as by Muslims as an important societal contribution. We hope that through learning mutual tolerance some prejudices and hate will be overcome.
2. As elected representatives of the Muslim students at this university we wish to participate in any conversation between the university authorities and the KHG concerning the chapel, because the Muslim students are directly affected.
3. For us, a regular dialogue between the KHG, the Muslim students and the university authorities is necessary. We therefore suggest a round table [*runder Tisch,* in Germany a very positively loaded term due to the peaceful revolution in the former German Democratic Republic] to establish mutual understanding, trust, respect, and tolerance.
4. As a confidence-building measure, we ask for a declaration that in the future the chapel can be used by Muslims and Christians and that the doors of the KHG [meaning here the Catholic students' parish and all its premises as such; J.T.] remain open.

5. Should this not be granted to us, it would be a sign that Muslims are not welcome and not wanted in the chapel. Then, we would be forced to invest all our efforts to obtain our own rooms from the university. But hereby, the positive effect of the common use would be gone and the only people who would have won are those who have always spoken against living together as Muslims and Christians."

The letter is flabbergasting: in a tone which is more a demand than a petition, it sets the terms with some impudence even for the university authorities, trying to make the – understandable – needs of practicing Muslims an important aspect of campus life. The religious neutrality of the state or a state institution like this university played no role. Instead, the letter advocated that the university should become a place for inter-religious dialogue and practiced religious tolerance, with the university authorities as mediator between religious actors.

The answer from the chaplain came immediately the next day, on January 27, 2006, with a copy to the president's office. He opened directly:

"Dear Mr. Y, allow me at the beginning to clarify that the university chapel was at no time a 'space for inter-religious encounters'. Please realize that the university chapel is not a multi-religious room for prayers and encounters, but a Catholic ecclesiastic space consecrated by the bishop of X to which we have with pleasure granted access to the Muslim fellow students as guests. For years, we prayed calmly and peacefully side by side."

Here, the different meanings attached to bricks, the process of making spaces sacred, become visible. For the Muslim students, the chapel is a place for prayer, for Muslims and Christians alike, but with equal rights of access and use. The chaplain first stresses that the place is not an inter-religious space, but Catholic, ecclesiastic, and consecrated by the local bishop. Thus, it is a sacred space *per se*, in his view. The Muslims are guests, not equals. The relationship between hosts, i.e. the Catholics, and guests, i.e. the Muslims, demands mutual respect. This respect is apparently lacking more and more from the Muslims' side, according to the chaplain. "We are hurt in our religious feelings by the behavior of Muslim fellow students in our own chapel and see ourselves confronted with a ruthlessness which makes us dumbstruck." He mentioned how structures in the room were changed by Muslims, though in reality they may have been caused by the university's technicians, according to a letter by the Muslim students' spokesperson from January 30, 2006.

Then, the chaplain recounted the critical events of Friday, January 13. On this day, "some Muslim students massively disturbed the Catholic service, against clear instructions and a plea for thoughtfulness, so that we saw no other way to protect ourselves against these assaults than to close the chapel. After discussing with the president, Prof. Dr. X, we consider the experiment to grant rights of hospitality to the Muslim students according to our (the host's) conditions (it concerns a sacred place for Catholics, after all) as failed. Due to the afore-mentioned assaults and the lack of deference and respect of Muslim students, we are no longer willing to grant you hospitality in our rooms. We very much regret that such behavior, to which we re-act only now, may also do harm to liberal and tolerant Muslim students with whom we would have wished to worship the one God in mutual respect. In no case are we willing to accept a situation of competitive prayer (*Gegeneinanderbeten*)."

The perception of the events and the context are totally different. The chaplain considered the granting of access to Muslims an experiment, which now has failed due to the disrespectful behavior of some Muslim students. He made it quite clear that both groups involved were not on an equal footing. Again, he stressed that the chapel is Catholic:

"Furthermore, you are in an error of judgment, if you believe that the university chapel is per se an inter-religious room for praying and getting together. Again, it is a consecrated Catholic chapel."

Finally the chaplain turned the story around and asked what the Muslims would do if Christians would begin to loudly celebrate their liturgy during the Muslim Friday prayer. He proposed to ask the university authorities for a multi-religious room for praying and getting together or for a Muslim prayer room, instead of harassing or coercing the Catholics to open their ecclesiastic place for fellow students who lacked respect and sensitivity. The chaplain felt his hospitality abused.

Ahmad reacted with a long letter to the university authorities (probably also sending a copy to the chaplain) on January 30, 2006. First, he mentioned that since 2002 the chapel was used by both groups for "praying side by side" and that mutual respect and tolerance can be learned. Then, he gave an interesting reading of the chapel as a sacred place:

"I can understand that it is important for university chaplain X. that the university chapel remains a sacred, ritual place. But personally, I am of the opinion that this chapel could be more than simply that. At the end, the KHG uses it only on Friday for its service. But if it would be used on the other days by Muslims and Christian groups who do not belong to the KHG, this chapel could be a sign of hope. So, this chapel would be at the same time a flagship of our university. [...] We – the Muslim student group – are not willing to give up our position that this prayer room must serve as an inter-religious place for encounters."

For the Catholic chaplain the consecratedness of the chapel is the essential aspect and this fixes the limits for the use of the place. For the Muslim student precisely these limits have to be overcome in order to give a "sign of hope". His understanding of the relationship between religion and university is much broader. Ahmad could not accept the historic fact that the chapel belongs to the Catholic diocese – and consequently ignored this in his arguments for considering it an inter-religious place. In the following, he again recounted the course of events. The first serious conflict emerged in his view with enlarging the circles of seats and thus reducing free space for Muslim prayers on the floor and with putting pictures on the wall in the direction of the *qibla*. This is indeed unacceptable for Muslims. So, some Muslim students put the pictures aside when praying. To solve this problem, Ahmad wanted to speak with the chaplain on the phone, but did not get through to him. Then, he contacted the university's ombudsman for foreign students who mentioned that the chaplain was still upset by changes in the chapel's structure (something to do with the coat-stand and a vestibule-like construction) which in fact were made by the university's technicians, it seems. Shortly afterwards, a plate was removed from the chapel's entrance which invited everybody to pray in the chapel. For Ahmad, this was the first sign of changing attitudes with regard to the common use of the chapel.

Ahmad recalled his first encounter with the chaplain in the chapel, stating that the chaplain was openly against Muslims praying in the chapel and against the university giving Muslims a prayer room. For the chaplain, in Ahmad's view, the Muslim students using the chapel hold fundamentalist opinions. The use of words like "occupation" or phrases like "[...] the chapel snatched by force" poisoned the climate.

A conflict with the Rosary Prayer Group arose involving loud prayers on both sides with the Catholics integrating passages in their prayers which offended the feelings of the Muslims. With the help of the university's ombudsman for foreign students brought in by the Muslims, such confrontations were solved by declarations to be considerate of each other. "Here, it becomes visible how useful this chapel could be for our co-existence, if it could be more than simply a sacred, ritual place". Once again, Ahmad insists on an opposition, calling the chapel "simply a sacred, ritual place" versus a place for interaction and inter-religious encounters. It becomes clear that for him a prayer room is not a sacred place *per se*, but that the common act of praying creates a special space for the participants, locally as well as temporarily. He further supported his argument by pointing at the positive social and political effects of sharing a religious room.

Reacting to the letter of the chaplain of January 27, 2006, he commented on the conflict with the Rosary Prayer Group, asking why this group was not excluded from using the chapel, when he informed the chaplain about the conflict. "Why does he [the chaplain] treat the same not equally?" So, for Ahmad both groups should have been excluded from using the chapel, if any. He continued by stressing that every story about the events could not but be subjective. He wrote of his own enquiries among Christian students after the service on Friday, 27 January 2006, on the events of Friday, 13 January, when the chaplain shut the chapel. He came to the conclusion that the chaplain exaggerated in his description of the situation. He nevertheless regretted the disturbance to the Christian service on that day. However, for him a pragmatic solution would be to hang a plate informing the public about the Christian service on Fridays. He informed readers that he himself put one on the door on Friday, 27 January.

At the end of his letter, he suggested that they have regular meetings at least twice during term time, attended by the university authorities, the KHG and the Muslim student group, and organized by the president's office. He used the term *runder Tisch*, round table, which is a highly loaded term in Germany since the breakdown of East Germany. He ended by stating that the image of the university is damaged by Muslim students praying in a noisy and cold basement staircase and that a lot of Muslim students are disappointed by this impression that the university does not care about them.

It seems that the president's office did not immediately react, because on February 14, 2006 Ahmad wrote a second e-mail to the president's office asking what the university authorities are planning to do about the affair this term (Winter Term 2005/2006). He attached some photographs of the staircase where they had to pray and emphasized the noise and coldness of the basement, concluding that this was not a dignified place for prayer for the Muslim students at this university.

The head of the president's office now reacted directly by e-mail on the same day, at first expressing regret in the name of the university authorities about the extent to which the situation developed. He asked for some patience because the president's office at that time was occupied in substantially preparing the content of a meeting among the various parties involved. For him, the aim of such a meeting should be, however, to re-establish the previous arrangement with the Catholic university parish.

On February 24, 2006, the university chaplain wrote an e-mail to Ahmad to inform him about a conversation he had with the bishop's vicar general the same day. Both chaplain and vicar general agreed to ask the university authorities for a prayer room especially for Muslim students. The chaplain reminded Ahmad that they were taking up a previous idea of the Muslim students. For him, this would help both Muslims and Christians to worship without interference or bad feelings. "I have the impression that other ways would demand too much of us," he wrote. In this letter, the chaplain carefully avoided the contested issues, referring instead to ideas of the Muslim student group and stressing his aim for the best for the Muslim students.

The next turn of events was a letter from the university president dated March 10, 2006 addressing Ahmad as the spokesperson of the Muslim student group and referring to the e-mail of the Catholic university chaplain from February 24, 2006 (which Ahmad had sent to the president's office) and to a letter from the bishop's vicar general, from March 3, 2006. The president informed the Muslim student group that he negotiated rooms for their use in the Catholic university parish just off campus across a big street. In his view the Muslim student group would be well advised to accept this generous offer by the Catholic Church, because it was the speediest solution to the problem. The university administration would nevertheless try to identify a possible prayer room, but the outcome was uncertain due to the limited capacities on campus.

If the president expected the situation to have finally cleared up, he was disappointed by an e-mail from Ahmad, written on April 11, 2006. After thanking the university authorities for their efforts – he did not address the president directly – he refused the offer of the KHG which he did not view as generous at all. The rooms offered were off campus, he argued, but since Muslims have to pray five times a day, the university chapel was better placed, so that after prayers everybody could be back to seminars and lectures in time. In my own view this argument does not hold, because the campus is quite extended and both the chapel and the parish buildings are on the same side of the campus at perhaps 500 meters distance from each other (the same argument was later used by the university president). The next sentence, however, makes the underlining reasons for the refusal quite clear: "At the same time, we won't allow ourselves to be prevented from practicing our religion in the university." Here, the visibility of practicing Muslims in the public space of a university on an equal footing with Christian groups was at stake. Hence the insistence on using the chapel for Islamic prayers. The goal was to make space for believing Muslims and to enable them to practice their faith on equal footing with Christians or any other religion. The offer to use rooms for Muslim prayers in the parish buildings was set against the interdiction to pray in the university chapel and the logic behind this interdiction was not understood. Furthermore, Ahmad did not understand why the KHG needs a chapel on campus when they have a parish centre and a church nearby, and why the KHG would after all allow Muslims to use the parish church for prayer without problems. In the letters exchanged, however, there was no mention of the parish church but of 'rooms' (*Räumlichkeiten*) in the KHG buildings. Ahmad considered it problematic that one religious community had privileges, like the chapel, on the university campus. Should the chapel be used only by the KHG in future, the Muslim students would insist on getting their own prayer room on campus. He took the argument further by pointing at the proportions of only 12 Christians using the chapel once in a week, but of more than 50 Muslim students using it constantly over the week. For him, it was unjust that the Catholics have two prayer rooms in or near the university, but the Muslims none. He expressed his disappointment that the impertinence of the KHG towards the Muslim student group had no consequences and declared that he would make use "of all democratic rights of freedom of expression concerning the KHG and its behavior".

The exchange of letters in this affair ended with a reaction from the university president the following day, 12 April 2006. The president regretted the refusal of the KHG's offer and refuted the argument that the rooms offered were off campus since the campus was extended and there were long distances that everyone had to cover all around. He then recounted the history of the chapel as being given to the Catholic Church by the allied military command in charge after the Second World War, stressing the fact that the university had no say in its use. The use of the chapel by other religious groups, he wrote, was always based on the hospitality of the Catholic university parish. The presidency had to accept any decision by the KHG concerning access to the chapel. The search for alternative places on campus was not successful due to the overuse of the buildings which was planned for only half of the actual university's body. The president explained that besides the Catholic chapel, no other religious place existed on campus and that no other religious community has asked for a prayer room, except the Muslims. He further stated that there is a general consensus of members of the university that the university is a secular space for research and education. He concluded, therefore, by again kindly asking the Muslim student group to accept the offer of the KHG as the best possible solution at the moment.

As already mentioned above, the situation has not changed since. Muslims pray regularly in the same staircase in the basement, just in front of the door of the university chapel which is still closed for everybody.

To sum up the central points of the affair: First, it is astounding that the spokesperson of the Muslim student group is unable to respond to letters and e-mails in a polite and respectful manner. Born, raised and educated in Germany, and active in politics since his school days, he nevertheless shows signs of what Devereux calls an "antagonistic acculturation" (1978: 204ff.). In our case, Ahmad took up cultural elements of the German legal order (religious freedom) and of German habits of conflict resolution (exchanging arguments by letter). But he nevertheless reacted to the statements of the chaplain as well as of the university authorities with a resistance to compromise which results from his inability to understand the meaning behind the sentences in their letters and to accept the historically grown particular and privileged relationship between the German state and the Christian churches. The basic conflict is between Muslims and non-Muslims, coupled with a very extensive and active understanding of religious freedom.

Thus, Ahmad struggles for place-making as understood by Thomas Gieryn (2000: 468), aiming at using the chapel for Muslim prayers and – even more importantly – declaring it a "place for inter-religious encounters". This aspect is more important than its being a sacred and ritual place for the Catholics. He tried to foster his argument by stressing the positive effects on the university's image and the social peace on and off campus. However, at least some Christian groups contend with the Muslim students through competitive praying and putting pictures in the direction of the *qibla*, thereby making claims to the chapel as a place. Here, boundaries are drawn through practices as performative acts, but also restricted by a general structuring order, namely the built environment of the chapel.

But Ahmad also struggles for space-making, fighting for recognition by both the university authorities and the Catholic chaplain as being equal and on the same footing. He will not be scared off from practicing his religion on campus, visible for the university community. For him, Muslim students have the right to practice their religion in a secular university and the university authorities have the duty to give space – and place – for that. So far, the contestation is not decided, but the struggle for place, space and recognition continues.

REFERENCES

Abdullah, Muhammad Salim (1981): Die Geschichte des Islams in Deutschland, Graz: Styria.

Devereux, Georges (1978): Ethnopsychoanalyse. Die komplementaristische Methode, Frankfurt am Main: Suhrkamp.

Gieryn, Thomas (2000): "A Space for Place in Sociology", in: Annual Review of Sociology 26, pp. 463-496.

Meining, Stefan (2011): Eine Moschee in Deutschland. Nazis, Geheimdienste und der Aufstieg des politischen Islam im Westen, München: C.H. Beck.

Motadel, David (2009): "Islamische Bürgerlichkeit. Das soziokulturelle Milieu der muslimischen Minderheit in Berlin 1918-1939", in: J. Brunner and Sh. Lavi (Eds.), Juden und Muslime in Deutschland. Recht, Religion, Identität, Göttingen: Wallstein, pp. 103-121.

Rohe, Mathias (2008): "Islamic Norms in Germany and Europe" in: A. Al-Hamarneh and J. Thielmann (Eds.), Islam and Muslims in Germany, Leiden and Boston: Brill, pp. 49-81.

Rosenow, Kerstin (2010): "Von der Konsolidierung zur Erneuerung. Eine organisationssoziologische Analyse der Türkisch Islamischen Union der Anstalt für Religion e.V. (DITIB)", in: L. Pries and Z. Sezgin (Eds.), Jenseits von 'Identität oder Integration'. Grenzen überspannende Migrantenorganisationen, Wiesbaden: VS Verlag, pp. 169-200.

Schimmel, Annemarie (1995): Die Zeichen Gottes. Die religiöse Welt des Islam, München: C.H. Beck.

Schmitt, Thomas (2003): Moscheen in Deutschland. Konflikte um ihre Errichtung und Nutzung, Flensburg: Deutsche Akademie für Landeskunde.

Seufert, Günter (1999): "Die Türkisch-Islamische Union der türkischen Religionsbehörde (DİTİB). Zwischen Integration und Isolation", in: G. Seufert and J. Waardenburg (Eds.), Turkish Islam and Europe/Türkischer Islam und Europa, Stuttgart: Steiner, pp. 261-293.

Thielmann, Jörn (2008): "Islam and Muslims in Germany. An Introductory Exploration", in: A. Al-Hamarneh and J. Thielmann (Eds.), Islam and Muslims in Germany. Leiden and Boston: Brill, pp. 1-29.

(2010): "The Turkish Bias and Some Blind Spots. Research on Muslims in Germany", in: A. Kreienbrink and M. Bodenstein (Eds.), Muslim Organisations and the State. European Perspectives, Nürnberg: Bundesamt für Migration und Flüchtlinge, pp. 169-195.

Confronting the Legacy of Antiquity

Pharaonism, Islam, and Archaeology – A Retrospective on
Local Islam and Modernity

GEORG STAUTH

Given the amount and the variety in historical depth as well as with respect to their current attraction, the study of saintly places in Egypt seems to be an endless undertaking. I have limited my beginning to certain 'exemplars' in the Nile Delta, 'Abdallah b. Salam near Mendes, the veneration of spoils and places in Fuwa and Sa al-Hagar (Sais) along the Western Rashidiyya branch of the Nile, and Abu al-Wafa' in the Lake of Manzala near Port Said (cf. Stauth 2000, see also Stauth 2005, 2006: 158-189, 2008, 2010). The perspective was set out by focusing on 'culture contact' in co-operation with a DFG-research program at the University of Mainz since 2000, we were looking to modes of social change due to tensions between 'local Islam' and 'Western Modernity' (see here the collection of studies in Bisang et al. 2004). However, questions of local modern order and search for cultural authenticity became of increasing importance, and specifically the 'Pharaoh' and the 'Prophet' are no 'dead' figures of history – as it has become obvious with many inherent conflicts in contemporary Egypt. Certainly this actualization has found a very vivid expression with and in the aftermath of the assassination of the former Egyptian president Anwar Sadat and in the title of a book on Egyptian fundamentalism (Kepel 1983).[1] Certainly, the effects of these conflicts and exchanges signify the overtures of any conventional culture con-

---

1 It should not be forgotten that before this event, Michel Foucault with his *reportages des idées* on the Islamic Revolution in Iran 1978/79 and specifically in *Corriere della Sera*, 22-10-1978 already had invoked the 'return of the prophet' in leading the struggle against a 'Western' influenced Shah (cf. Foucault 2003).

cept which was largely linked to unity of space and life interlocked within countries, landscapes and places.

It was, therefore, not by chance that I – the friend of the Piemontese and Valdostanian Alpes, – took up the famous study of Robert Hertz (1913) on St. Besse from Cogne which obviously is significant not only as an exceptional hagiography of a local saint, but also as a sort of 'heretic' study, signifying Hertz's emancipation from the methodological tradition of the Durkheim school. Hertz presented an in depth study on the 'European' effective history of a saint with a multi-dimensional approach. He did away with the ethnographic principles of Durkheim and his school, liberating himself from participant observation and the 'going native'-orthodoxy. In doing so, Hertz seemed to support my want for own methodological liberties, namely, to shift between oral and written sources, between observation and impression, between picture and language, between effects of interaction and contact with modern science and local rites, conflicting ideas and what could be local authenticity limits of set up by the stream of public affairs. All this certainly seems to be packed within a new dimension of antagonisms depending on the works of modern mass society and consumer culture. Certainly, the questions and problems could be traced in my studies in the Nile Delta, however, I am far from claiming that with the following paper I could give solutions and definite answers.

PEOPLE AND STONES: ARCHAEOLOGY AS CULTURE CONTACT

To start with a blunt remark, what Egyptian archaeologists call 'Delta-Archaeology', the archaeology in the Nile-Delta, is loaded with hard, detailed work and often rather 'small' results. There is nothing to belittle the immense efforts by these archaeologists to go further then what Biblical archaeology has brought to light in the late 19th century at places like Tanis, Tell al-Dabba, Quantir, Mendes, Buto, and Sais to mention a few and perhaps the most important ones. However, great findings are rare today and less spectacular, and the specific conditions of land, which was flooded annually over thousands of years until perennial irrigation gradually, and finally Nasser's High Dam stopped it, require a very disciplined work and extraordinary methods of excavation in swamps and flooded land. Manfred Bietak, the head leading the excavations at Tell el Daba, has given a most impressive report on these methods (Bietak 1975).

The few Egyptian-European teams with regular campaigns face all different problems at their places, however no one whom I met has failed to express his concerns about the interference of local administrative and police forces (often being directly emerged into the body of local workers and helpers) and, of course, they all made complaints about villagers entering the *kums* in search for the treasures of the site (*kanz*), for traditional fertilizers (*sebah*) or for new construction on cheep government land claimed by way of holding hand on it (*wada' al-yad*).

At first glance one feels always struck to see relations between the foreign crews and local dwellers governed by a certain underlying enmity: The struggle for life and today's needs seems to stand against the calling of preservation of authentic pieces at places of antiquity. As Alessandra Nibbi expressed the fear already in 1970, that the *kums* of the Delta might vanish with steady growth of population and accordingly expanding villages and towns (1992). However, the guarded and unguarded *kums*, that are often untouched by villagers and archaeologist still are many in the Delta, mounting as strange brown hills on top of green agrarian fields and speaking of an integrated presence of the past. On the other hand many of these places are still significant in the otherwise modern lives of the Egyptian peasants. Their graveyard placed on these hills (*tell*) often provide for a certain protection against devastation and also the *maqams* and *qubbas'* of local saint are placed here and signal similarly protection. This is specifically obvious at *kums* with recognized saints, as I have mentioned earlier for the 'great places' of Abdallah b. Salam at Thmuis and on the island of Tuna in Lake Manzala near Matariyya or the Abu Mandur Mosque and *maqam* at the Tell of Boulboutine near Rosetta (see Stauth 2005: 34-45, 51-60, 116-129, 146-159 and 163). Near Abu Mandur there exists a good example for such a graveyard which is not used hear by citizens of Rosetta (Rashid) but rather of a village across the Nile. The river here sets the border for two Provinces Bahariyya and Kafr al-Shaykh, a fact that lead to many administrative irritations. However, in general the graveyards and *qubbas* of the saints are an important component of integration of the red-brown and sometimes black hills in the modern life in rural Egypt. This is where, despite continuing destruction, the in-depth meaning of these places continues to exist among local people, and the quantity of pieces and symbols signifying the heritage from the past seems far from being exhausted by archaeological research.

In times of Biblical archaeology, the situation was much easier. William Mathew Flinders Petrie, for example, in his *Ten Year Digging in Egypt, 1881-1891*; demonstrates deep insights in the mentality and life of the Fellaheen, rarely seen among archaeologists. Petrie at his time was perhaps the only one, who maintained intrinsic contacts with the local population and who profited distinctly from his empathy for the Fellaheen (Petrie 1891). This is an attitude which today is rarely to be found among archaeologists and even at his time Petrie was perhaps the only one who cared for contact with the Fellaheen, spoke their language and was riding on the back of their donkeys. For Petrie this was also a method of great help in deciding about excavation places and deciphering the meaning of relics and spoils.

Today the situation of communication between the Fellaheen and archaeologists is a completely different and the situation more complicated. With the modern intensifications of culture contact, social recognition and human justice came largely dependent on new, reflexive forms and higher degrees of cultural authentication. This is where the local situation at places of antiquity and the treatment of spoils and ruins, among archaeologists, religious specialists and local dwellers became a very complex one.

WOMEN, FERTILITY, RITUAL INTEGRATION OF PHARAONIC RELICS

To come closer to this, I wish to present a short anecdote reported to me by Axel Krause, a German photographer in Cairo, a continuous companion to my own researches. He has been advised by Phillipe Brissaud, the head of the French team at Tanis, to take photos in the *kum* a few days after a group of women had secretly climbed on the statues and relics there to perform their fertility rites on the remains of the Ramesside period. The spontaneous idea in 2006 to have pictures of the monuments flooded with blood, derived from a certain helplessness of the archaeologists, to deal with the matter. The crisis came along with the concerns to preserve the monuments and with the spontaneous idea, probably, to draw the attention of Egyptian ethnologists to the rites and their damaging effects to the monuments.

Certainly, it is the task of the archaeologists to keep the monuments clean, and Brissaud's wish of unhindered preservation of the pieces, cannot be put in claim. However, considering the social pressure of non-fertile women in the Egyptian society in general, and in rural Egypt in specific, the pressure of interest of these – often very young and just married women, finding no other social response to their needs but the return to a suppressed tradition and rites – can likewise not be put in doubt.

I myself was confronted with the subject of women's fertility rites at Sais, Thumais and Mendes (for Sais, see Stauth 2008: 151-156).[2] However, to my regret, I declined to do active research on this in the field. However, I think that this example is shattering and intensive from the start. It shows that there prevails among the local population a specific mode of dealing with the past, which differs in form of experience and in degree of contact. Let me call this a mode of authentication, which connects the local women to the places. We know that after the rites they go to the shrine of the saint Yousuf near the *kum* for prayers. So that in addition to this figurative and symbolic contact to both, history and the everyday needs, in their rites, they also seek for religious purity.[3] This shows a dimension of intensive cultural experience of modern Egyptian women, a mode of authentication, which at first stands far beyond religion and archaeology, and at a second glance, integrates both.[4]

THE LONG HISTORY OF USURPATION, INVASION AND TRAVELERS

There is a further stage of trans-cultural interaction related to ancient places and modern cultural experience which relates to travel and literature. Perhaps Rilke's experience in 1911 is the most exceptional as it was decisive about the link to 'history' in his poetry. Rilke's symbolic citation of the 'pillar' of Egyptian antiquity perhaps would need today a more 'modernist' evaluation than a pure egyptological connotation.[5] However, in general the interplay of archaeology, in the

---

2   They form the core of survivals of Pharaonic imaginations and magic practices until today. In the 1920s Winifred Blackman has pointed to the modern importance of these rites (cf. 1926 and 2000).

3   On the regulative power of shame in modern civilising processes we may be able to trace some forthful descriptions by Norbert Elias *Scham- und Peinlichkeitsschwelle* as he calls it (1981: XI). However, it is often difficult to trace this in practice of old surviving rites. More than anything it was the modern 'Islamic' attire and the timing when men gathered in the mosque for Friday prayers that indicated such an underlying sublimation process (cf. Stauth 2008: 150-156).

4   For other such practices see also my *Ägyptische heilige Orte I* (Stauth 2005: 43f.).

5   The significance of Rilkes travel to Egypt for his work has been subject of a rich collection of material and egyptological interpretation by the German Alfred Herman (cf. Hermann 1966). As for travelling along the Western Nile see my *Passagen im westlichen Nildelta*, Kapitel II (Stauth 2008: 53-66).

broadest sense, religion and local people at places of antiquity, is specifically present in the history of Western descriptions and literary treatments.

European travelers often remarked the strange behavior and attitudes of local people moving around the ruins and remains. In European Renaissance art sometimes, ruins as such were positioned as part of transcendent images and figurative inventions (I remember Albrecht Altdorfer's and Albrecht Dürer's paintings of the *Heilige Nacht*). Goethe describes his nightly walks at the Forum Romano without worldly visions. Paintings of ruins of antiquity, nevertheless, show often illustrious scenes of everyday life of local contemporaries. Goethe, certainly, by drawing a sketch on *Landleute zwischen antiken Ruinen* is a great exception in making the ordinary people's leisurely use of the ruins a subject of dignity as he calls it.[6]

However, in view of how the relics were perceived by these locals, European travelers have rarely expressed any interest.

An uneasy relationship to locals dominates traveler's descriptions and reports of the sites. The impression that their local contemporaries brought a different life to the place and that their huts and shelves, their donkeys and sheep, would stroll around where once stood the temples and graves of Gods and Pharaohs or the festive halls of Caesars and kings, prevails.

In Egypt the complains of archaeologists about villagers raiding the Gebel or even settling on the *kum* are a standard topos, and *Sebacheen* is a standard term for Delta archaeologists to denounce over ages the peasants' activity of using mud-brick remains of antique cities for fertilizing their fields. As much as Alessandra Nibbi, in the 1970s expressed fears that possibly all *kums* in the delta will vanish with the expansion of villages and towns, and as much the destruction really happens, still we can observe today a considerable amount of *kums* relatively untouched from both archaeologists and villagers. Many places, however, remain significant to modern Egyptian life, by way of constructions of their grave yards and the shrines of Islamic saints at or near the *kum* and with it the local historical memory found continued and new cultic expressions, often integrated into modern religions styles.

While European travelers, specifically of the 19th century, perceived Islam as a strange and alien religion of the locals, they gave also notice to the *qubbas* of the Islamic saints in terms of enriching the exotic oriental atmosphere of the ruins and relics. In contrast, fundamentalist movements and government interference (often along with excavation projects) brought intense conflicts to the places and specifically in the 1990s raids of fundamentalists and police squads became frequent events.

---

6   "Country men between ruins of antiquity" (Goethe 1976: 539f.).

Places on the Western Nile, the Rosetta Branch, where well known to Europeans passing there on their way to Cairo and Upper Egypt. The famous French scientist Sonnini who passed there in the 1770s, and subsequently the English Mayer and Lane in the early 19th century, were giving critical designs and reports of the places and of local religion and the *qubbas*. Similarly, the qubba of Emir Abdallah on ruins of Thumai near Mendes ranked high in descriptions of European travelers and archaeologists as, de Meulenaire (1976: 43f.) gives us the sources and in this context it is interesting to see how the French 'revolutionary' expedition and reports, in the late 18th and early 19th century were setting the tone with words like 'superstition' and 'believe in pagan Talisman power' for conflicts that continued to take place even two hundred years later.

The irritating presence of the locals and their profane or pagan attitudes at the places, is one fact, the presence of spoils in mosques and shrines is another one and rarely noticed by Europeans. Trading with old Pharaonic spoils seems to have been historical practice since long, a current enterprise, not only among the Greek and Roman invaders. Destruction, reconstruction and re-use of temples and spoils reach back to early Dynastic times. Erik Hornung (1982) makes us aware, that the re-use of temples dates back to more than 3000 years, when symbols and inscriptions were replaced and then re-activated by later dynasties and used even for different cultic realities at different places. This is what Hornung called 'Usurpation', the re-use of temples and graves of the old dynasties and how spoils were integrated into different styles, eras, and for different religious and dynastic purposes (cf. Stauth 2008: 46ff.). So for Hornung, this was not just an event of the need of the day in search for cheap construction material or even blunt robbery, but it meant a sort of appropriation of a cultural good and an expression of the cultural attitude at the time. European esotericism is not my topic here, except briefly to note that Hornung and his students DuQuesne and Assmann take the symbolic situation of Pharaonic Egypt, as the very case of identifying the realm of spoils, and the magic, aesthetic and visionary expressions related to them, as a fundamental symbolic situation for Europe and the West.

As with respect to Islam, the spoils as much as the idea of the Pharaoh, remain as important, as much as the continued significance of the places does.

ALTERITY AND CLOSENESS OF THE PHARAO

In recent years, there was growing interest in 'classical' medieval Islamic scholarship and its attitudes towards Pharaonic Egypt. Following the footprints of Ali Mubarak Pasha (the Egyptian historian and explore of places in the late 19th century), the way how Arabs looked at historical sites became a subject of interest. Orientalists and recently the Egyptologists Gaballa Ali Gaballa (2004) and Okasha Al-Daly (2005) developed an interesting discussion on Egyptology and *Islamwissenschaft*, neglecting the achievements of classical Arab-Islamic scientific history on the ancients. This debate is far of being a closed subject.

The late Ulrich Haarmann, and Jean-Claude Garcin, both specialists of the literature of the Mamluk period were most outspoken on the medieval interest with the Pharaohs. Garcin's point raising the political issue, that the Mamluks positively re-evaluated the idea of the Pharaoh, easing an ambiguous acceptance of a split between secular power and religion in the Sufi circles of the period, is interesting to note. This idealization could help to understand the introduction of spoils in mosques and shrines at time, as I will discuss in greater detail later in the case of Fuwa.

Haarmann, however, gives us a more general picture. He stresses the monotheistic breakthroughs in late antiquity, and that "the adoption of Christianity first in the fourth century and then, three centuries later, by the Islamic conquest", made any feeling of continuity impossible (2001: 191). Furthermore, he identifies that medieval Islamic scholars were torn between the "exotism and weirdness of Egyptian antiquity", as well as admiring Ancient Egypt as "a land of technical ingenuity and scientific wisdom" – a double image that remains familiar to us until today (Ibid.).

Haarmann gave specific interest to attitudes of medieval Muslims at the places and their functioning with Pharaonic relicts:

"(1) they were target of pious iconoclasts who abominated the pictural pagan heritages (pictures being taboo in Islam)

(2) they attracted treasure hunters

(3) they provided cheap yet excellent building materials

(4) they have always been favorite areas of tourism" (2001: 193).

Haarmans's evaluations of Muslim attitudes were intensively criticized by Ursula Sezgin (1994 etc.) and Okashi El-Daly as neglecting the scientific concerns of Arab sources. However as much as one can trace a certain limitation in Haarmann's accounts, we may also wonder whether these attitudes and functioning are merely limited to Medieval Muslims. And also the incompatibility of certain egyptological and certain rival Islamic 'truths' about Pharaonic Egypt, may not just be a serious problem in Islamic fundamentalist quarters in the 1980s.

THE UNAVOIDABILITY OF CONTACT AT THE PLACE

Haarmann, however, understood, that the Islamic encounter of Pharonic Egypt and its relics – how prejudiced or unprejudiced it may be – entails more than scholarly or literary perceptions. So let me come back to practice.

I wish to draw attention, shortly, to two examples from the Western Nile Region south of Rosetta. This region is significant not only with respect to the richness of places of antiquity. It also bears major modern towns, Tanta and Disuq, which merely transformed from village to town through mass veneration of Islamic saints. But also there is a nearness to the West because it was a pass way for invaders and travelers from Greek, Roman, Medieval and early Modern times.

Looking to Fuwa[7], about 50 km south of Rosetta, tells us that attitudes towards Pharaonic and Ancient relics are more complex, than the pure juxtaposition of belief and Islamic law with pride and knowledge would allow for.

Fuwa has a great number of major mosques and sanctuaries build along the Nile front. It was once a flourishing major town of Egypt known for its trade to Istanbul and its crafts. The Mosques were built in the late Mamluk and early Ottoman periods 14th to 17th century and renovated many times after, recently in the 1990s. They all integrate pillars, thresholds and blocks of red Aswan granite displaying Pharaonic reliefs and hieroglyphic writing.

When we were finding these spoils in the mosques and shrines of Fuwa, Silvia Prell has registered them and worked on their Saiite background. In the grand mosque of Dairut, opposite of Fuwa on the Nile, we found a huge block of a perhaps very old period inearthed under the mosque's minaret. This is all published and I will not go on with further details here.[8]

I wish to register some points with respect to the extraordinary tolerant treatment of spoils and discuss some of the features of Islamic attitudes, here:

First of all, the way of setting and the building and positioning of spoils from the beginning in Mamluk times is intriguing basically because there are no signs of a casual filling them into the walls or foundations. They obviously were not used as cheap building material. There was a specifically positive cultural attitude involved at the start and the random setting of pillars and blocks shows signs of systematic use and style, and expressions of pride and scholarly treatment are clear.

---

7   See my chapter 5 of *Ägyptische heilige Orte II* (Stauth 2008: 67-116).

8   See further in Stauth (2008: 193-211).

Then we should note that the recent renovations of the places, which excluded so far until 2007 some, the more popular, and quarter-stile ones, took place in the heat of fundamentalist movements and concerns from 1992-1998 under the supervision of the Islamic Antiquities Department. Apart from some reported attempts of stealing, there was obviously no movement to prevent the repositioning and display of relics in the mosques.

In some mosques, legends and stories prevail about underground vaults (*sirdab*). In the Madrasa of Nasrallah, a scribe and highly estimated scholar and Sufi of the 15th century, which was then turned into a sanctuary, people claimed that they had seen themselves the *sirdab* – with hieroglyphic scripture. It was confirmed that during the renovation legends mounted about the treasures and miracles coming from below. Salafi-reformist-led groups entered. When finally the administration decided the refilling and complete of it with earth and bricks. Despite such interventions, Sufi-life continues in the town and so does the saint veneration at *qubbas* along the Nile. It was also interesting to note, that there was a sort of collective responsibility of the educated, professionals, scholars and Imams, to ease conflict. They helped to over-bridge a certain uneasiness to deal with legends and practices as *muta 'aqadat sha'bi,* the popular self-assurances of the believers. Orthodox terminology, here, was setting the framework for tolerance.

Fuwa in its historic quarters along the Nile has the flair of a small old metropolis with calmness and restraint of citizens in public appearance. There have been no excavations in its immediate vicinity, and although the belief that there is the 'town below the town' (*balad taht al-balad*), which until recently was assumed to be the fabulous Métélis (Bernand 1970) has triggered some uncertainties about its past with an influx of legends and beliefs. The cultural atmosphere of this small centre with no tourists or foreigners remained stable.

Sa el-Hagar[9], which is situated again about 30 km south of Fuwa, is my second example. It gives us a quite different picture. It is equal to Fuwa in size and population with about 30 000 inhabitants. It differs in all other characteristics completely. It was always a small village on the Nile close to the Tell of the old Saiis – the Egyptian capital of the late 26th dynastic period, a place of Neith the Nile goddess since early dynastic times. Starting with Petrie in the late 19th century, Sais became the subject of subsequent excavation campaigns, not to mention that since Herodot it remained a place of sojourn for visitors from the West. A symbolic place of Hellenism, and from Hermetism to Enlightenment it became a locus of Western literary importance. Just to note *Die Lehrlinge von Sais* of Novalis, in new times.

---

9   See my chapter 6 in *Ägyptische Heilige Orte II* (Stauth 2008: 117-156).

The village itself was always handled as a negligible appendix to the *kum* and for the campaigns of foreign scholars and Egyptian archaeological crews it always provided guides, guards and workforce for excavation. The village extended into the *kum* by mere increase of population. We witness the same peasant extension everywhere. The history of the *kum* is one of exploitation and, to use Hornung's word, of usurpation. The main attractions found in Saiis were removed and brought to Cairo or Europe, many are scattered in the region, in Fuwa, as described. A local open air 'Museum' of the Egyptian Administration of Antiquities is installed at the *kum*, it consists of scattered blocs and remains of statues, and most of them were removed from mosques and maqams in neighboring villages.

Islamic usurpation reflects the poverty of the village. In German we have a beautiful word of cardinal point and in each direction around the *kum* we find the Qubba of a peasant saint, including the one a female saint in the direction to the West, to the Nile. Dating back at least to the early 19th century, the 4 *qubbas* were all abandoned in the 1990s. Silent visits of women remained possible. There have been strong fights at these places and a number of killings took place. Since then all public expressions of venerating have been abolished with the exception a '*laila*', the night before the Prophet's birthday (*mawlid an-nabi*). The visit to the main mosque of the village, *al-masjidal-kabir*, leaves us with the taste of a suppressive atmosphere. Spurs are to be seen everywhere of a recent, awful Salafi-reformist-renovation witnessing the removal of all the old red Aswan granite pillars, which are to be found now limiting the space of the administered open-air 'Museum'.

The atmosphere of intolerance and suppression of popular 'survivals' on the one hand, and extreme neglect of relics of the past on the other hand, could be extended to surrounding places in this Nile area east and south of Disuq, the town which has no Pharaonic relics. However, this is a town of annual pilgrimage to the 'imperial' mosque and maqam of Ibrahim al-Disuqi, the great Saint of Egytian Islam and Sufism. The story of mass veneration of this famous saint seems to stand in reverse connection to the endless stories of destruction and renovation, finding and removing of stones and spoils, suppression of Sufi feasts and gatherings in public.

Despite all this archaeological research continues at the *kum* of Sais, and in the midst of everyday destruction, search for subsistence and satisfaction of needs, and of fundamentalist events around this *kum* of 'Great History', we found Penelope Wilson, a young archaeologist of Durham University, all on her own, living in a house with peasant women near the shrine of the abandoned woman saint. She has published a great report of her work recently and performs an extraordinary work supported by women networks from behind the public scene which is completely dominated by policemen and crews of guards (Wilson 2006).

EGYPTIAN SAINTLY PLACES IN CONTACT

This short sketch of two 'saintly places' from the perspective of practice shows the potentials of an accommodative and a suppressive approach in Islam. And although not directly dealing with Pharaonism, the work of two Egyptians, a sociologist and an ethnologists, which Samuli Schielke and I have published in a collection of articles recently, show again the different extreme poles in the ways of treatment of places of veneration. The stressing of an authentic continuity of Egyptian culture, folklore and history here (cf. Souzan El-Sayed Yousef Mosa 2008: 169-182), as against the discomfort that modernity has with it, in viewing the moments of retarding attitudes both psychologically and socially, there (Zayed 2008: 103-124). •

Certainly, this shows that 'Egypt and the Pharaoh' is not a matter of genius loci or of continuity. The question is, how modernity deals with it, and what difference does it make to those who live today with all, the Pharaonic, the Islamic and the modern realities.

I am avoiding attempting to work out the different models of treatment of spoils and places, in terms of distracting them away from their local and epochal bondage. However, let me conclude this some doubt that the types of contact and interaction could be explained with structural problems of perceived objective contradictions between different cultures: Pharaonism and Islam, here, and fundamentalist perversions of modernity there, female rites, male suppression etc. Perhaps contact and respective treatments, here, are defined by abstracted ideas of contact itself and the events of different cultural experiences and happenings of symbolic situations are more important than structural differences. With all structural contradictions behind, and despite all instrumental needs of the day, three attitudes prevail in front of the image of the Pharaoh today: the experience of the symbols and pictures in stone, first, facing the inner presence of the past and the value of things and the place, and often from all strands this is demonstrated with extreme portions of affection and love. Second, the experience of the symbol as fear, that the imagined pagan and diabolic character of the Pharaoh might return, a sentiment that stresses the esoteric and the out-worldly situation in front of the spoils and that creates the tensions of extra-everydayness and liminality, and also specifically with respect to the sort of crossing the borders which are set by the limits of the law and public religion. Third, there is this dimension of 'contact' which relates to the presence of the 'foreign', foreign Muslims, for example, like the Ottomans and Turks who gave Pharaonism a new blend of representation within Islam and re-emergent Sufism in Egypt. 'Foreigners' like the crews of archaeologists, which pass on their views of things and give a second interpretation to local experiences.

Pharaonism plays an extremely important role in public life in Egypt today and since the Mameluk and Ottoman periods it is part of all cultural and power politics of the 'Great' in the country. However, bearing Penelope Wilson's silent work in the back doors of Sais in mind – nevertheless 'Great' – the tone of a strange word of D.H. Lawrence, an archaeologist of his kind at Etruscan Places in Italy comes to my memory, when he asked about the importance of the Great Pyramid and compared it with the history of the nightingale. Lawrence, the cultural critic, meant this in terms of a given structural antagonism between archaeology and life.[10] This is where Wilson's archaeology at Sais, comes to me as an example, coinciding with women's presence at the place and the unfolding of everydayness, it shows something other than contradiction and difference: a coincidence of practical and symbolic experience. In these terms to study the culture contact at the ruins of the past could open up as a subject and a new dimension in intra-cultural research.

DIRECTIONS OF AUTHENTICITY

In the following, I shall be using the term 'authentication' in three different ways: First, in the sense of a scientific appropriation necessitated by the selective 'Museum of Modernity' (archaeology as part of it). Second, we have religion, Islam (I am not speaking of Coptic Christians who differ little in the type of experience). Islam sets perhaps even stronger the need for certain purifying perceptions of places and spoils. Third, there are ritual forms of celebrating and integrating places and spoils which surpass the limits of religious law and state regulation, which are emanating from traditional forms of everydayness and customary behavior.

First science: It was Karl Japers who spoke of 'Musealisierung' as a necessity of modernity. In 1945, in a situation of a European 'Ground Cero', Jaspers argued for a new selective scientifically grounded appropriation of history and

---

10 Cf. Lawrence (1932) passim. See also *In Search of Etruria: Science and the Imagina^tion* in the 1986 edition.

humanism as a tool of self-affirmation, not only of the individual human being, but also of nations, and even civilization. Certainly, the selectivity of this 'Museum of Modernity' is object of debate and struggle.[11] This is reserved, according to Jaspers, to the field of science, and of course, archaeology and history of religion were considered as the most important disciplines, and in this respect, most notably, Jaspers grounded his concept of *Verstehen* (understanding) on the historical fact of 'revelation'.

Second religion: Egypt is itself – with respect to the rise of monotheism – a place of the tenuous history of religion. Islam – as Ignaz Goldziher taught us – signifies a 'scientific', monotheistic break with anticipant history and despite its peculiar tolerance of saint veneration it otherwise depends on a sharp selectivity with respect to places and symbolic references.[12]

Third local life-worlds and historical memory: This is a realm of continuity of forms of veneration of places, relics and spoils in which people are turning to violate the limits set out by law or scientific understanding. In a lived-in-world of physical and psychological needs people do insist on communal or habitudinal 'law', and develop a continuity of traditional ritual integration.

Finally, it is important to concede that politics and modern attitudes of 'order' play a most important role in deciding about, how to solve the meeting and forms of contact of these diverse – as I would like to name them – moments of authenticity in local space and places of interaction.

REFERENCES

Al-Daly, Okasha (2005): Egyptology. The Missing Millenium. Ancient Egypt in Medieval Arab Writings, London: UCL Press. Cavendish Publishing Limited.

Arnason, Johann P.; Salvatore, Armando, and Stauth, Georg (Eds.) (2006): Islam in Process. Historical and Civilizational Perspectives. Yearbook of the Sociology of Islam, Band 7, Bielefeld: transcript.

---

11 Cf. Jasper's theory of 'Axial Age' as developed in *Vom Ursprung und Ziel der Geschichte,* specifically in his *Einleitung* (Jaspers 1952: 15-18); as for the European Museum see specifically his remarks in *Was ist Europa?* (Jaspers1986: 245-274, special reference: 268-274).

12 Beyond his famous studies on Hadîth, see for excample Goldziher's article on *Catholic Tendencies* (Goldziher 1913/14).

Assmann, Jan (2003 [1998]): Moses der Ägypter. Entzifferung einer Gedächtnisspur, Frankfurt am Main: Fischer Taschenbuch Verlag.

Bernand, André (1970): "Métélis", in: André Bernand (Ed.), Le Delta Égyptien d'après les Textes Greques, Cairo: Institut Francais d'Archéologie Orientale, pp. 443-489.

Bietak, Manfred (1975): Tell el Daba II: Der Fundort im Rahmen einer archäologisch-geographischen Untersuchung über das ägyptische Ostdelta. Denkschriften der Österreichischen Akademie der Wissenschaften, Band IV, Wien: Verlag der Österreichischen Akademie der Wissenschaften.

Bisang, Walter; Bierschenk, Thomas; Kreikenbom, Detlev and Verhoeven, Ursula (Eds.) (2004): Kultur, Sprache, Kontakt. Würzburg: Ergon Verlag.

Blackman, Winifred S. (1926): "Some Social and Religious Customs in Modern Egypt, with Special Reference to Survivals from Ancient Times", in: Bulletin de la Société Royale de Géographie d'Égypte 14, pp. 47-61.

(2000): The Fellahin of Upper Egypt, Cairo: American University Press.

De Meulenaire, Herman (1976): "Scholarly Exploration", in: Emma Swan Hall and Bernard v. Bothmer (Eds.), Herman de Meulenaire and Pierre Mackay, Mendes II, Warminster: Aris & Phillips Ltd., pp. 19-1969.

Elias, Norbert (1981): Über den Prozeß der Zivilisation. Soziogenetische und psychogenetische Untersuchungen, Band 1, Frankfurt am Main: Suhrkamp Verlag.

Foucault, Michel (2003): "Wovon träumen die Iraner", in: D. Defert und Fr. Ewald (Eds.), Michel Foucault. Dits et écrits. Schriften in vier Bänden, Band III, Frankfurt am Main: Suhrkamp, pp. 862-870.

Garcin, Jean-Claude (1987): Le sultan et pharaon. Le politique et la religion dans l'Egypte medieval, London: Variorum Reprints, pp. 261-272.

Goethe, Johann Wolfgang von (1976): Italienische Reise, Frankfurt: Insel Verlag.

Goldziher, Ignaz (1913/14): "Katholische Tendenzen und Partikularismus im Islam", in: Beiträge zur Religionswissenschaft 1:2, pp. 115-142.

Haarmann, Ulrich (2001): "Islam and Ancient Egypt", in: D. Redford (Ed.), Oxford Encyclopedia of Ancient Egypt, 3 Volume Set, Oxford: Oxford University Press, Vol. 2, pp. 191-194.

Hermann, Alfred (1966): Rilkes ägyptische Gesichte. Ein Versuch wechselseitiger Erhellung von Dichtung und Altkultur, Darmstadt: Wissenschaftliche Buchgesellschaft. (Aus dem Symposion 24, IV, 1955, pp. 371-461).

Hertz, Robert (1913): "Saint Besse. Étude d'un culte alpestre", in: Revue de l'histoire des religions 67, pp. 115-180.

Hornung, Erik (1982): Zum altägyptischen Geschichtsbewußtsein, in: Hermann Müller-Karpe (Ed.), Ärchäologie und Geschichtsbewußtsein, München: Verlag C.H. Beck, pp. 13-30.

Jaspers, Karl (1952): Vom Ursprung und Ziel der Geschichte, München: Piper. (1986): "Europa der Gegenwart", in: K. Jaspers (Ed.), Erneuerung der Universität. Reden und Schriften, Heidelberg: Verlag Lambert Schneider, pp. 243-274.

Kepel, Giles (1983): Le prophète et le pharao. Les mouvements Islamistes dans l'Égypte contemporaine, Paris: Éditions du Seuil.

Lawrence, D. H. (1932): Etrascuan Places. London: Secker. (1986 edition, Siena: nuova imagine editrice. Foreward "In Search of Etruria. Science and Imagination" by Massimo Palottino, pp. 9-27.)

Mosa, Suzan El-Sayed Yousef Mosa (2008): "Beliefs about Muslim Saints in the History of Towns in Egypt", in: Georg Stauth and Samuli Schielke (Eds.), Dimesions of Locality. Muslim Saints, their Place and Space (Yearbook of the Sociology of Islam, Vol. 8), Bielefeld: transcript, pp. 169-182.

Nibbi, Alessandra (1992): Some Geographical Notes on Ancient Egypt. A Selection of Published Papers (Discussions of Egyptology, Special Volume 4), Oxford: DE Publ.

Petrie, W. M. Flinders (1891): Ten Years Digging in Egypt. 1881-1891. London: Religious Tract Society.

Ritter, Karl Bernhard (1941): Fahrt zum Bosporus. Ein Reisetagebuch. Leipzig: Hegner.

Sezgin, Ursula (1994ff.): "Pharaonische Wunderwerke bei Ibn Wasîf as-Sâbî und al-Mas´ûdî. Einige Reminiszenzen an Ägyptens vergangene Größe und an Meisterwerke der Alexandrinischen Gelehrten in arabischen Texten des 10. Jahrhunderts n. Chr. (Teil I)", in: Zeitschrift für Geschichte der Arabisch-Islamischen Wissenschaften 9, pp. 229-291. Teil II, Ibid., (1997) 11, pp. 189-249. Teil III, Ibid., (2001) 14, pp. 217-256. Teil IV, Ibid., (2002-3) 15, pp. 281-311.

Stauth, Georg (2000): "Der 'entgrenzte' Islam als soziologischer Forschungsgegenstand", in Georg Stauth (Ed.), Islamische Kultur und moderne Gesellschaft. Gesammelte Aufsätze zur Soziologie des Islams, Bielefeld: transcript, pp. 253-266.

(2005): Ägyptische Heilige Orte I. Konstruktionen, Inszenierungen und Landschaften der Heiligen im Nildelta: Abdallah b. Salam, Bielefeld: transcript.

(2008): Ägyptische Heilige Orte II. Zwischen den Steinen des Pharao und islamischer Moderne. Konstruktionen, Inszenierungen und Landschaften der Heiligen im Nildelta. Fuwa – Sa al-Hagar (Sais), Bielefeld: transcript.

(2010): Ägyptische Heilige Orte III. Der Manzala-See bei Port Said und der Heilige der Fischer. Konstruktionen, Inszenierungen und Landschaften der Heiligen im Nildelta. Abû al-Wafâ`, Bielefeld: transcript.

Wilson, Penelope (2006): The Survey of Sais (Sa al-Hagar) 1997-2002. London: Egypt Exploration Society.

Zayed, Ahmad A. (2008): "Saints (awliyâ'). Public Places and Modernity in Egypt", in: Georg Stauth and Samuli Schielke (Eds.), Dimesions of Locality. Muslim Saints, their Place and Space (Yearbook of the Sociology of Islam, Vol. 8), Bielefeld: transcript, pp. 103-124.

PART III Everyday Prayer and Urban Topography

Building Community

Configuring Authority and Identity on the Public Squares of Contemporary Senegalese Sufi Centers

Eric Ross

INTRODUCTION

The urban spaces created by the Murid Sufi order,[1] beginning with its holy city of Touba and including the subsidiary shrine centers and enumerable villages in its orbit, consistently display an identical set of design principles. Succinctly, at the center of the settlement, whatever its size or importance, is a quadrangular public square (*pénc* in Wolof)[2] harboring the mosque. Streets enter the square at the corners. The large compound of the settlement's founder, a Murid *shaykh*, occupies the west side of the square. This is typically the largest compound in the settlement. Housing allotments are ordered around this nucleus according to

---

1 The Murid order (often spelled 'Mouride' and sometimes 'Muridiyya') was established by Shaykh Ahmadu Bamba Mbacké (1853-1927) in the 1880s. It is one of the most studied Sufi orders in the contemporary world. Especially since the late 1960s there have been numerous published studies, in French and in English, about the Muridiyya.

2 The Wolof term *pénc* designates a public square. It is also used more broadly to designate a place of public assembly. The first meaning of *pénc* is "palaver tree," the trees beneath which village assemblies are held (Fal et al. 1990: 168). Such trees are often to be found on the public squares of villages. For a discussion of the relationship between Senegal's historic palaver trees and its contemporary public squares see Ross 2008.

an orthogonal grid. Streets are wide and straight and cross at right angles. Often, both the *pénc* and the street grid are oriented toward to *qibla*.

This study aims to elucidate the origins and significance of the '*pénc* and grid' configuration characteristic not just of Murid settlements but of those of Senegal's other contemporary Sufi orders: the Tijaniyya, the Qadiriyya and the Layènes.[3] First, it will be demonstrated that this model is not an exclusively Murid one. While the Murid *tariqa* has developed the orthogonal design centered on the *pénc* and has diffused it widely, to some degree this configuration also characterizes the settlements of the other Sufi orders. Secondly, it will be argued that the orthogonal *pénc* and grid plan constitutes a distinctly Senegalese model of urban design, that the Sufi orders adopted and diffused a model that had previously characterized certain elite types of settlement, such as royal capitals and clerical towns. The *pénc* and grid model is both the expression and the vector of a larger political culture. What is being configured through this design is not just a physical settlement, it is a community structured by authority, that of the *shaykh* and his lineage.

The second part of the study explores the multiple layers of meaning and practice fixed to the central public squares of Senegal's Sufi settlements. It will be shown how these places, whether or not they constitute shrines, are paragons of community-building which both generate and represent order, authority and identity. Importantly, these are always represented as separate from the state; no symbols or references to the state or its agencies are to be found in these civic spaces.

When the argument about the historic pedigree of the contemporary *pénc* and grid model was first presented (Ross 2002), it was based on the descriptions of historic settlements provided in bibliographic sources and on the analysis of archival and recent maps of some of Senegal's major Sufi towns obtained from government agencies. Since then, the availability of high resolution satellite imagery of large parts of Senegal has permitted the substantiation of the argument through the accurate mapping of many more of the country's historic and contemporary settlements. While four high resolution (63-70 cm) Quickbird satellite images were purchased (at great cost) by the researcher in 2003,[4] in 2007 Google Earth (a free on-line digital globe collated from satellite imagery) began uploading numerous relatively high resolution images of the most populated regions of

---

3   On the emergence and development of Senegal's contemporary Sufi orders see Mbacké (2005).

4   The following Quickbird images were purchased: Tivaouane-Ndiassane (image dated Dec. 31, 2002), Touba-Mbacké (Jan. 26, 2003), Darou Mousty (April, 6, 2003) and Kaolack-Kahone (March, 31, 2005).

Senegal. This has permitted the mapping of many of the towns, neighborhoods and villages established by Sufi orders in the late 19th and early 20th centuries. It has also permitted the mapping of Senegal's historic capitals and of some of the pre-colonial Muslim centers referred to in the bibliographic sources. Analysis of the spatial configurations of these historic and contemporary settlements confirms the argument that the *pénc* and grid plans observed in contemporary Senegalese Sufi settlements are the product of an indigenous urban design practice and are not a colonial-era import.

The site plans which form the basis of the analysis in the first section of the present study aim to depict the overall layout and built fabric of towns, neighborhoods and villages. In particular, they show streets and squares, the location and configuration of religious structures (mosques, mausolea, and cemeteries), urban amenities (markets, wells, water towers, and schools), elite residential compounds as well as generic housing allotments. Much of this information was verified by direct observation in the field over the course of several years of study.[5]

PÉNC AND GRID DESIGN IN CONTEMPORARY SUFI SETTLEMENTS

The Murids are famous for having built a major holy city, Touba [fig. 1], now Senegal's second largest urban agglomeration, (Guèye 2002; Ross 2006). But the order has also created a number of ancillary shrine centers such as Darou Mousty [fig. 2], Darou Marnane Mbacol, Porokhane, and Boukhatoul Moubaraka neighborhood in Diourbel [fig. 3], and numerous other, mostly rural, settlements.[6] These places are considered by Murids to be holy or sacred for one of

---

5   Field investigation of Senegal's Sufi settlements began in 1988. Subsequent sessions of field work were conducted in 1994, 2000, 2001-02, 2004-05, 2006-07 and 2007-08.

6   Touba was founded in 1887 by Shaykh Ahmadou Bamba Mbacké (1853-1927). Construction of the city only really got underway in 1958. Darou Mousty was founded in 1912 by Shaykh Ahmadou Bamba's brother, Mame Tierno Birahim Mbacké (1866-1943). Prokhane is where Shaykh Ahmadou Bamba's mother, Mame Diarra Bousso (d. 1866), is buried. Construction of the town began in the 1950s. The neighborhood of Boukhatoul Moubaraka was created in 1912 to house Shaykh Ahmadou Bamba and his family and entourage after he was assigned to house arrest in Diourbel by the colonial authorities. The village of Ndindi Abdou was created by Shaykh Ahmadou Bamba's second eldest son, Sëriñ Falilou Mbacké (Caliph General of the Mourides

two reasons. In some cases the site is considered holy because the founding *shaykh*, a Sufi mystic, experienced a spiritually significant 'state' (*hal* in Arabic), such as a mystic vision or a divinely inspired revelation or else attained one or another of the elated 'stations' (*maqam*) of consciousness along the path to God. This is the case of the central shrine complex in Touba and of some of that city's central wards (Darou Khoudoss, Darou Minam) as well as of Darou Mousty, reputed the 'second city' of the Muridiyya. In other cases the sanctity of the site derives from the pious intention of the founding *shaykh*. Such settlements were set up in order to promote a higher religious purpose, that of establishing a proper religious community. The pious activities of the founder (praying, fasting, and teaching) established the sanctity of the site at its inception. This is the case of Darou Marnane in Mbacol, and of Ndindi Abdou and Darou Karim near Touba, among many others. All the shrines in the first category (site of mystic communion) also share the sacred attributes of the second (generated by pious acts and intent). Yet the latter type of sacredness also extends to some extent to the great number of rural Murid settlements (*daaras*, religious schools which doubled as agricultural estates) such as Tindody, Touba Bagdad, Taïf [fig. 4] and Touba Bélel, established in the 'heroic' era of internal colonization (1880s-1940s).[7]

Nearly all Murid settlements, great or small, more or less sacred, are organized according to the orthogonal *pénc* and grid model described in the introductory paragraph. While this model has proven congenial to modern urbanization, in fact, it was first manifest in the order's rural settlements and was first discussed by scholars studying the agricultural practices of the Murids. Their research took them into the Murid heartland, the areas of eastern Baol and the Ferlo which Shaykh Ahmadu Bamba had opened to agricultural colonization beginning in 1912. Sy (1969), Copans, Couty, Roch & Rocheteau (1972), Copans

---

1945-1968), ca. 1915. It is now a suburb of Touba. The village of Touba Bélel was created by Sëriñ Abdoul Ahad Mbacké (Caliph General 1968-1989) in the 1960s. These latter two villages were used as country retreats by the respective Caliph Generals, who otherwise resided in Touba.

7   Murid agricultural activities across Senegal's Peanut Basin have been well studied. The Peanut Basin refers to an agricultural region which stretches from 100 to 200 km inland from the Atlantic coast. Peanut production was introduced to Senegal in the 1840s and became the main cash crop of the colonial period, when vast 'new lands' were opened up to peanut cultivation. The Murid order was an important agent in the expansion of peanut cultivation and a prime recipient of new agricultural land. Dozens of villages were established in the process.

(1980) and Dubois (1975) all reported favorably on the neatness and orderliness of the villages they studied:

"The arrangement of compounds, or concessions – *keur* in Wolof, is one of the peculiar characteristics of Murid villages when compared to the traditional villages of Kayor. The basic principle is that of a large rectangular public square, *mpentye* [sic], around which are arranged the various compounds. The *keur* of the marabout is always on the west side of the square, facing east [...]. Thus, for Murids, the geometric organization of space prevails [...]. All streets meet at right angles [...]. Murid villages 'look good' and we were often touched by the charm of a well ordered *mpentye*, shaded by one or two trees. The center of this square is usually occupied by the mosque." (Copans 1980: 70-71)

"The outer appearance of the village [of Darou-Rahmane II] is clean and pleasant; houses are arranged around a large square (*mpentye*), covered in sand and shaded by trees. The compound of the marabout occupies the greater part of the western side of the square. In the center are a small mosque and the *secco* [the cooperative peanut warehouse]." (Copans et al. 1972: 96)

"Murid villages are usually well laid out: straight streets, a well or a pump in the village center, neatly fenced-in houses. Present here is a conscious will to modernize housing." (Sy 1969: 179)

The 'modernity' attributed to these settlements, manifest in cleanliness, order and straight streets, was in keeping with the larger narrative of the Murid order as a transformative social force within rural society.

The *pénc* and grid settlement type described by these observers is by no means the preserve of the Murid order alone. Settlements established by Senegal's other Sufi orders are often similarly configured. Like the Murids, the various branches of the Tijaniyya have built shrine towns, such as Tiénaba, Taïba Niassène [fig. 5] and Fass in Mbacol (all established in the late 19th century), and agricultural villages such as Fass in Saniokhor.[8] These places are all characterized by a central public square harboring a mosque. As with the Murid villages

---

8   Tiénaba was founded in 1882 by Amary Ndack Seck (1830-1899) and is home to the 'Mahdiya' branch of the Tijaniyya. Taïba Niassène was established by Al-Hajj Abdoulaye Niass (1844-1922) possibly as early as the 1860s. Fass in Mbacol was established by Sëriñ Tit Touré in 1894. The village of Fass in Saniokhor is used as a country retreat by the caliphs of the Sy branch of the Tijaniyya, centered in nearby Tivaouane.

described above, Tijani villages such as Tabakali (established in 1957) are neat, orderly and orthogonal:

"The village [of Tabakali] is laid out at the center of the agricultural estate. Though the founders were Tijanis, it resembles villages produced through Murid agricultural coloniza- tion. The large central square is determined by the rigorous alignment of compounds. It is open at the corners, has a make-shift mosque in its center and is kept scrupulously clean [...]. The founders created the plan. When newcomers arrive, they conform to it." (Dubois 1975: 103)

Significantly, this observer designates the *pénc* and grid plan observed in the Ti- jani settlement as characteristically 'Murid'.

The Qadiriyya order, though much smaller in size as compared to the Tijani and Murid *tariqas*, was also deeply involved in the cash crop colonization of the Senegal's Peanut Basin. The Qadiriyya has built up one major shrine center, Ndiassane [fig. 6] established near Tivaouane in 1884, as well as villages such as Ngourane.[9] All these places are centered on a *pénc* containing a mosque and the founding *shaykh's* compound to its west, and they too exhibit elements of a grid street plan. The Qadiriyya has also been particularly active in the lower and cen- tral parts of the Casamance region, establishing numerous small Sufi centers such as Daroul Khaïra, Bagadadji, Kerevan and Banguère. This latter settlement was described early in the 20th century as "a large village with regular, clean streets running perpendicular to the main thoroughfare. Its compounds are well aligned." (Marty 1915-16: 473)

Another, even smaller Sufi order, located on the Cape Vert peninsula, has built two shrine towns: Yoff Layène and Cambérène [fig. 7], both now com- pletely engulfed by Dakar's urban sprawl.[10] These small settlements too are or- ganized around a central square consisting of the mosque and the *shaykh's* com- pound to the west. While building the settlement of Cambérène, Seydina Issa Rohou Laye (Caliph of the Layènes 1909-49) is reputed to have personally over- seen the erection of houses in order to make sure that they were all properly

---

9   Ndiassane was created by Shaykh Bou Kounta (1844-1914) in 1884 and continues to serve as base for his branch of the Qadiriya order.

10   The Layène shrine-neighborhood in Yoff (called Yoff Layène) was established by Seydina Mouhamadou Limamou Laye (1844-1909) in 1884 to house his growing en- tourage of disciples. In 1914 his son and successor, Seydina Issa Rohou Laye (1876- 1949) established Cambérène on a similar beach front site five kilometers east of Yoff. Both shrines are central to the Layène order.

aligned.[11] In 1948 a French observer, by chance, was able to view Cambérène from the air as his plane landed at Dakar's airport. He was struck by its neat orthogonal plan and attributed its neatness to the diffusion of modern (french) urban principles from Dakar (Duchemin 1948: 17-18).

As will be demonstrated below, the grid plan observed in Senegal's contemporary Sufi settlements is not the product of the diffusion of Western urban planning principles during the colonial era. Had the orthogonal plan and the central square diffused as modern European urban planning principles, these principles would have effected secular settlements rather than Sufi communities like Touba, Taïba Niassène and Cambérène. Yet the layouts of secular villages – villages with no special religious rationale or Sufi affiliation – show none of these supposed Western characteristics while Senegal's Sufi establishments, which were far more resistant than secular ones to the penetration of European principles, are precisely the ones which exhibit the orthogonal street layouts.

PÉNC AND GRID DESIGN IN PRE-COLONIAL SETTLEMENTS

There are indications in the historical record (consisting of oral histories transcribed over the course of the 20th century) that the *pénc* and grid design characterized certain types of elite settlement prior to the colonial era. The capitals of many Senegambian kingdoms were configured in an orthogonal manner and were centered on a palace compound facing a public square. Maka, for example, was a new capital laid out at the beginning of the 18th century to serve the united kingdoms of Kayor and Baol:

"Established on sandy soil on the border between the two countries, Maka was a village of about one hundred houses arranged like the allotted *escales* of today, with its public square and the royal residence in the center. It had wide streets where the rowdy mounted escorts of the nobles could circulate freely. [...] It was a political village especially created for the government of the two countries, a royal village, a village of princes and princesses who did no manual labor." (Fall 1974: 117)

The author of this passage, Tanor Latsoukabé Fall, was a member of the royal Fall lineage of Kayor and Baol. He wrote this description in 1955. His comparison of the 18th century capital to the *escales* of the colonial period is revealing.

---

11   *Nurul Mahdi*, http://www.layene.sn, semi-official multilingual web site of the Layène Sufi order (last accessed Sept. 2, 2005).

Escales[12] were trading settlements established along Senegal's railways from the 1880s to the 1920s. They were configured as grids of straight streets that crossed at right angles. The street grids were aligned with the rail right of way. The orthogonal configuration of Maka pre-dates these colonial establishments. Moreover, while an *escale* is always centered on the train station and a market place, Maka was centered on its *pénc*, consisting of public square and royal residence.[13]

The urban ensemble of palace compound and central square appears to have characterized the capitals of the Empire of Mali (13th-15th centuries) and of its western successor state in Senegambia, the Empire of Gabu (16th-19th centuries). According to oral traditions, Dakajalan, the first capital of Mali (established c. 1222) was built around a palace-square complex. The square was the scene of major political events, such as the coronation of Mansa Sunjata, and it harbored in its midst the royal throne podium from which the *mansa* administered justice (Cissé & Kamissoko 1991: 51-53). The empire's second capital (called 'Mali' in contemporary sources) was likewise centered on a large public square which the Moroccan scholar Ibn Battuta, who visited the city ca. 1350, called a *mashwar*, a term which leaves no doubt that this was a fundamentally political space.[14] According to Ibn Battuta, the *mansa's* throne podium stood in the center of the square, under a large shade tree. (Charles-Dominique 1995: 1033) In Kansala, the capital of the Mandinka Empire of Gabu, the public square extended east of the palace compound. In the middle of the square was a tree, the *tabadjou*. (Niang 1989: 64) It was on this central square, beneath the tree, that young princes would congregate with their retinues for raucous drinking parties and amusement. In Soumacounda, a provincial capital of Gabu, the central square was also shaded by a great tree. The royal family would meet beneath it, amid much drinking of palm wine and millet beer, to settle accounts and resolve dis-

---

12 The French term *escale* literally means 'landing'. The first *escales* were landing sites set up along the Senegal River in order to conduct trade by river boat. The railway *escales* of the late 19th and early 20th century, established at regular intervals along Senegal's railroads, were given this name by analogy to the river trade.

13 Maka is no longer an extant settlement and there is no published archeological investigation of the site.

14 The Arabic term *mashwar* designates a place of assembly (possibly for 'consultation', *shura*). In Moroccan urban tradition the *mashwar* is a large walled court adjacent to the royal palace. Historically, it was where the sultan reviewed his cavalry, received ambassadors, etc. It was not a public square (*sahah*, or *maydan*) in the civic sense, a place where citizens might meet and interact, nor was it a market square. It was a space specifically created for public displays of authority and it was directly connected to the palace.

putes. (Niang 1989: 44) Ostentatious public displays of drunkenness and dueling were a hallmark of the warrior elites (*gelwaar* in Mandinka, *ceddo* in Wolof). The central squares of these various capitals of Gabu were effectively 'stages' upon which these political performances were conducted in public.

The capitals of Mali and Gabu were centered on a nucleus consisting of a public square with a royal compound on its west side. Like much else in Malian political culture, this trait was adopted by Senegambian states. Even in the acephalous societies neighboring Gabu along the Atlantic coast we find a similar configuration of a chief's compound facing a public square. This is how one French observer, de la Courbe, described the king's compound at Bolole in 1685: "The house of the king is one of the prettiest I have seen in this country; there was a large square (*grande place*) with an avenue neatly planted with two rows of trees" (cited in Mark 1995: 322). According to Mark, this type of 'grande place' for public gatherings, i.e. the Wolof *pénc*, characterized the layout of villages and wards throughout the lower Casamance region.

Across Senegambia generally, the central public square was a feature of virtually every settlement. Each village had its own *pénc*, and when a village or town was big enough to have several distinct wards, each of these had a *pénc* as well. The centrality of the *pénc* was both spatial and socio-political, as the square was always sited directly in front of the compound of the settlement's premier lineage. What distinguished certain politically important settlements, such as royal or provincial capitals, from 'civil' settlements was not so much the existence of a *pénc* as the grid plan of the streets which surrounded it, as in the case of Maka.

Contemporary satellite imagery confirms the *pénc* and grid configuration of royal capitals and other centers of power. The orthogonal regularity of the street grid and the public square is particularly evident in the cases of Diakhao and Lambaye. Diakhao [fig. 8] was the capital of the Sereer kingdom of Sine from the 16th to the 19th century. It still retains its original grid plan today. The royal compound and the *pénc* lay at the center of the town. The *pénc* is still used for official ceremonies (on national holidays for example). The mausoleum of the last king of Sine (d. 1969) lies in the first courtyard of the palace compound, which is still inhabited by members of the former royal lineage.[15] Of all of Senegambia's pre-colonial kingdoms, Sine was unarguably the most resistant to the adoption of Islam. Islamic practices had no place in court life or official culture. Today, Diakhao's Muslims live in a distinct neighborhood on the northern outskirts, a neighborhood distinguished by a mosque.

---

15 Diakhao was visited in 5 January 2003. Interview with Hadi Diouf, daughter of the last Bour Sine.

Lambaye [fig. 9] was capital of the kingdom of Baol from the 16th to the 19th century. In its case, both the central settlement and various outlying wards (Koul, Mbotal, Dakhar, etc.) are configured as orthogonal grids centered on a square *pénc*. The masonry mosques which grace most of these squares today are a recent (20th century) development.

In Senegambia an orthogonal street plan was conjoined to the palace and square complex to produce a distinctive *pénc* and grid plan. By the 17th century, this model of capital city design characterized the layout of many royal and provincial capitals. It represented a conception of royal power and promoted the exercise of political privilege perfectly in tune with the *ceddo* culture which came to dominate these ancient régime polities in the 18th and 19th centuries (see Diouf 1990). Muslim clerics (*sëriñ* in Wolof, *karamokho* in Mandinka, *cerno* in Pular) constituted a form of contre-pouvoir to the rule of the *ceddo*. They were integral to court politics, and to the wider public sphere represented by the *pénc*. Some served the courts as jurists, chancellors, diplomats and scribe. Others were attached to specific noble families. Indeed some even served the *ceddo* warriors, who protected themselves with the amulets the clerics made for them. Clerics were active in the operations and politics of the state alongside numerous other political clients. Islam was thus present in the political and public spheres, but it had to share a space dominated by the *ceddo* and their culture. Consequently, the clerics, acting in this space, became familiar with, if not imbibed by, its articulations of power.

In the 17th century, certain clerics who were either members of royal or aristocratic lineages or attached to a court began establishing their own agricultural settlements, marking the emergence of this new elite in the landscape. The Islamic studies centers they established had substantial legal and fiscal autonomy from the states in which they were embedded. Authority in them was vested in the founder and his descendants. The best known cases of such autonomous Muslim centers are Pire and Koki. Not only did both these centers achieve great renown for scholarship in the 18th century, each was also effectively administering an entire province. The fiscal autonomy of the clerical center applied to these lands as well. Because they had considerable political, administrative and legal autonomy, the clerical settlements were places of power as well as of religion; one 18th century French traveler, Père Labat, called those of Bundu "marabout republics" (Sanneh 1989: 51).

Some of the clerical centers appear to have been configured according to the orthogonal *pénc* and grid model of the royal capitals. This is the case of Ngalik [fig. 10], established in the 17th century by the Khouma lineage, (Diop 1966: 495-496) and of Ndanq [fig. 11], established early in the 19th century by Shaykh

Bounama Kounta (father of Shaykh Bou Kounta, founder of the Qadiri center of Ndiassane) (Fall 1974: 127). The founders of both of these clerical centers were closely attached to the court of the Kingdom of Kayor. This might explain why they implemented a courtly practice such as the *pénc* and grid configuration in their religious settlements. Their *pénc* and grid layout was primarily an indicator of the ambient political culture – authority residing in the leader's compound and displayed on the public square – not of religious practice or affiliation. Yet it proved congenial to the social life of the community.

Clerical communities of the *ceddo* era were structured by genealogy (the *shaykh's* extended family with all its matrimonial links, the *kër*, which often extended across Senegambia), master-student relations (the *taalibe* was also an agricultural laborer), client relations with artisans (*ñeeño*), and slave ownership. Much of the religious and social life of this community took place in the *shaykh's* compound. This included teaching, as well as daily prayers. Friday prayer might be held on the *pénc*, in a clearly demarcated space. Proper Muslim conduct was the norm in both public and private affairs. This was in sharp contrast to the *ceddo* culture that reigned in other centers of power. Furthermore, these marabout republics were closely networked with each other, through kinship and master-student ties. There thus emerged a national-scale network of actors, some more autonomous from the state then others, which linked up with similar networks of Islamic scholarship in Saharan and Malian countries. The public sphere in clerical settlements was thus far from parochial. By the 19th century there were influential Wolof clerics in Saint-Louis who were well acquainted with the workings of French colonial administration (Robinson 2000). While these *Dommu Ndar* clerics were actors in Saint-Louis' urban political and social life, the colonial administration valued them principally because of their personal and professional connections to clerics in the Wolof states of the interior.

In the late 19th century the founding *shaykhs* of Senegal's contemporary Sufi orders built their institutions upon the foundations of this highly personally structured *ancient régime* network of Islamic scholarship. Several of the Sufi founders, including Ahmadu Bamba, were members of old established clerical lineages.[16] Others had studied in the main pre-colonial clerical centers and, through erudition or pilgrimage, had become key figures within the network. The Sufi tariqa version of the master-disciple relationship which they implemented

---

16 Shaykh Ahmadou Bamba Mbacké's great grandfather, Mame Maram al-Khayri (d. 1802) had been a jurist at the court of Baol and had established the clerical settlement of Mbacké ca. 1796. Shaykh Bou Kounta, who established Ndiassane in 1884, was the son of Shaykh Bounama Kounta, who had established the clerical settlement of Ndanq earlier in the century.

reinforced the older version which had long structure interpersonal relations across space and generations. The great *shaykhs* also harnessed the other structures of community: kinship and clientelism, in order to build mass movements in both rural and urban milieux.

This explains the continuity between the spatial practices of both secular and Islamic elites in the pre-colonial era and those of the *tariqa*-led colonization of the colonial era. The *tariqas* were structured conduits for decisions and their implementation. The skill sets they inherited from the ancient régime 'order' were diverse and plentiful. The Murids recruited former *ceddo* with their organizational know-how – especially leadership in field – alongside former peanut estate slaves and peasants with all their agricultural know-how. The Tijaniyya recruited among the new urban classes: the Senegalese employees of the administrations, the teachers, the traders, *ñeeño* craftsmen attracted to the colonial cities. Among other groups, the Qadiris recruited migrant railway workers from Mali. The Sufi orders became mass movements whose principal social purpose was to instill Islamic decorum in public and private life. The creation of towns, villages and neighborhoods was a means to this end. The urban planning principles employed were those inherited from the ancient régime. This means that, while French colonialism undoubtedly had a major impact on urbanization and settlement configuration, urban places of the colonial era were also marked by indigenous conceptions of power and place, and by the agency of Senegalese institutions.

URBAN PRACTICES: BUILDING SETTLEMENTS AND COMMUNITIES

The grid plan can be found in a wide variety of geographical and historical contexts: ancient Egypt, Greece and Rome, Imperial China and Japan, Medieval Europe, colonial and post-colonial America, etc. It is highly versatile, adaptable to a great variety of city types, and applied at a gamut of scales ranging from imperial to peasant. In modern times the grid plan has been conducive to rational provisioning of public amenities (drinking water, sewage, electricity, civic addressing & postal service) and to the mass production of allotments. It is also well suited to motor vehicle traffic.

Undoubtedly, the mass application of the grid plan in Senegal's Sufi settlements mirrored French colonial practices of the time, and especially the rail *escales*. Often, civil engineers sent by the administration lent expertise to such tariqa endeavors. Nonetheless, the *pénc* and grid plans reproduced in tariqa settlements were the product of an autochthonous conceptual and practical tool kit.

Beyond its field-tested practicality, the model helped implement the proper religious and social decorum within the settlement. The *pénc* and grid plan was deemed to be most congenial to creating a 'well ordered' community. It set the community on the correct path. Moreover, the spatial ordering reflected the community's social and political order, with the *shaykh* and his *kër* occupying the center.

The initial acts of laying out and allocating space in the nascent settlement were decided and implemented by the *shaykhs* themselves, and then by their successors after their deaths. First, the *pénc* and the *shaykh's* compound had to be demarcated. The principle of alignment to the *qibla* was usually applied, but not always. The lots around the *shaykh's* compound and the *pénc* would be apportioned first, and then others further out as needed. Water had to be supplied and, eventually, space for a market place would have to be determined. Only then could the basic needs of the inhabitants be met. Touba is the best example of an entire city being laid out this way, but there are cases of *shaykhs* taking the lead in laying out Sufi neighborhoods in secular cities as well (notably Al Hajj Ibrahima Niass' settlement of Madina Baye ward in Kaolack in the 1930s).

The *pénc* in a Sufi settlement is primarily a religious space. It harbors the community's main mosque (often a Friday Mosque, where the *khutbah* is given), but religiousness extends well beyond the mosque building. In fact, the entire square is considered as an extension of the mosque and it is treated accordingly. A *pénc* is always kept scrupulously clean. It is usually covered over in sand or compacted earth which is swept regularly. While refuse or sewerage may accumulate on surrounding streets, this is never allowed on the *pénc*. In some instances, people heading for prayer will remove their footwear upon entering the *pénc*, long before they reach the mosque. Moreover, in many cases the mosques are often too small to accommodate all the worshippers who assemble for midday prayer on Fridays. For these occasions the entire *pénc*, or that portion of it lying before the *mihrab*, serves as an outdoor prayer space. This is also the case for the special mid-morning prayers held on the two main annual holy days: *'Id al-Adha (Tabaski* in Wolof) and *'Id al-Fitr (Korité)*.

The mosque-as-building is a relatively recent phenomenon in Senegambia. Small mosques built of adobe, similar in construction to the larger 'Sudanic' type mosques of Mali, were erected in the Fouta Tooro (middle valley of the Senegal River) beginning in the 17th century (Boulègue 1972). Elsewhere across Senegambia however, mosques were usually not buildings; they consisted of clean open-air prayer spaces. Such spaces were to be found on the *pénc* of villages or else in the courtyards of the homes of notables. They were fenced off to maintain their cleanliness. In some cases a small structure was also erected. These first structures were built in the local vernacular architecture, of wattle, reeds, earth and thatch. They were tiny, able to accommodate only a handful of worshippers; most people prayed in the open, on the clean space in front of the edifice. These tiny mosques were more symbolic (functioning as a *mihrab* to mark the *qibla*) than functional (accommodation of worshippers).

Large masonry mosques only emerged slowly in the course of the second half of the 19th century and the initial impetus for their construction came from the French colonial authorities. It was the colonial authorities who convinced the Muslim civic elite of Saint Louis, the capital of the colony, to erect a Friday Mosque. A masonry mosque large enough to accommodate an entire congregation of worshippers, the first of its kind in Senegal, was built in the city's north ward in 1838-47 (Aïdara 2005: 117). Until that time, as elsewhere, the Saint Louis Muslims had been praying in an open space set aside for this purpose. Mosque construction was also promoted by King Lat Dior during his second period of rule over Kayor (1871-83) as part of a policy to Islamize society. He is reported to have toured provinces in order to personally oversee the legalization of marriages according to Muslim rite, the setting up of Qur'anic schools and the building of mosques in villages and towns (Diop 1966: 518). These tiny mosques were of the vernacular type described above. Most worshippers continued to pray out of doors as before. What is significant in both cases is that the mosque-as-building was seen as an architectural representation of religiosity in the public sphere, a physical and spatial marker of a community's religious identity. Until then the actual practice of praying had been quite adequately accommodated without the need for a building. Given the tiny dimension of built mosques, they were primarily symbolic rather than utilitarian structures.

This was the situation that pertained when the country's contemporary Sufi orders began to organize communities and establish their own settlements. Their priority in most cases was the provisioning of new settlements with drinking water and maintaining a Qur'anic school (understood as an institution rather than a building), not the construction of mosques. For the most part, as in the past, clean open air spaces, occasionally augmented with a small makeshift mosque built of perishable materials, served for prayer in the new Sufi settlements. Of Senegal's various Sufi orders, the Tijaniyya were the first to pursue a policy of erecting masonry mosques large enough to hold congregations. Al Hajj Malick Sy opened the first Tijani *zawiya* in Saint Louis' northern ward in 1895.[17] After

---

17 The *zawiya* (equivalent to the terms *khanaqa*, *tekke* and *dargah* used elsewhere in the Muslim world) is a place of prayer distinctive to Sufi institutions. Though not usually used for Friday *khutba* prayers, *zawiyas* are used for a range of religious activities and practices. *Zawiyas* may also contain the tombs of important *shaykhs*.

he settled in Tivaouane he had a *zawiya* constructed there as well (completed in 1907). Another Tijani *shaykh*, Momar Talla Seck (1868-1946), erected a masonry mosque in Tiénaba in 1908 (Diop 2003: 66). Tijani *zawiyas* were thereafter erected in the cities of Dakar (1912) and Kaolack as well (Marone 1970). The *zawiyas* and mosques of this generation marked Muslim identity in the urban public sphere. They also symbolized the specific identities, and the growing strength, of the Sufi orders which erected them. They represented the first investment of surplus after the basic needs of the inhabitants had been met. This is especially evident in the case of the Diourbel Mosque. During WWI Shaykh Ahmadou Bamba Mbacké, though confined to house arrest, erected a very large mosque on the *pénc* in front of his compound [Fig. 3]. This mosque was built despite the financial constraints and labor shortage occasioned by the war.

A second generation of major mosques, much larger is size than those of the first, was erected toward the end of the colonial era; the Khalifa Ababakar Sy Mosque in Tivaouane (1957), the greatly expanded Madina Baye Mosque in Kaolack (completed in 1958), Touba's Great Mosque (inaugurated in 1963) and Dakar's new Great Mosque (1966). All were built of reinforced concrete. Following independence the colonial-era restrictions on the construction of mosques and religious schools were eased, and mosque construction has proceeded ceaselessly since.

The construction of the first masonry mosque in any community is always seen as constituting a significant milestone in its development. The building of Touba's Great Mosque took over 30 years, and the city of Touba only really began to grow after the mosque's completion. Most of the smaller Sufi settlements studied here were only endowed with congregational masonry mosques following independence in 1960. The decision to build the mosque, and any move to enlarge it or embellish it, comes from the *shaykh*. The mosque is the most tangible manifestation of his public role in the community. Yet mosque construction is a collective activity which mobilizes much of the community's resources, energy and imagination. This activity can take years, even decades to complete – for example, construction of Tivaouane's new Friday Mosque got under way in 1984 and is not yet finished – as the pace of construction is largely dependent on the availability of funding. In the case of Touba's Great Mosque, the determination of Murids to see the construction project through to completion helped the *tariqa* survive two very acrimonious succession disputes (1927 and 1945). The construction may even have been instrumental in preventing the Murid order from fracturing, as happened to several other Senegalese orders in similar situations.

The construction of the mosque reinforces the bonds which unite the community. Once built, the mosque provides the community with a strong focus and reinforces its identity, primarily through its central location and its architectural dominance. This applies as much to villages such as Touba Bélel, Ndindi Abdou and Fass, as it does to the major Sufi shrines. The situation of the mosque at the center of a *pénc*, which itself lies at the center of a settlement, serves the purpose of situating a community in and within Islam. The mosque is often the only architecturally substantial building in the settlement and its minarets are always the settlement's tallest structures. The mosque is intended to be, and effectively serves as, the main point of reference in the geography of the settlement.

Few activities other than religious ones take place on the *pénc*. Schools (in any case linked to religion) and health clinics (much less so) may be found there. Such institutions enhance the 'noble' or 'sacred' nature of the place. Often, one or more permanent open sheds (called *mbaar* in Wolof) are erected on the *pénc*. These covered spaces shield people from the heat and the sun. They can be used for informal gatherings or for assemblies, such as for sama' (group recitation of *dhikr*, panegyric poems, etc.). They can harbor *daaras* (classes where children are instructed in the Qur'an). *Shaykhs* will erect an *mbar* near the gate of their compounds, which means the shady structures also serve as antechambers to these elite residences.

Historic trees and sacred wells can also be found on the *pénc*, though they can just as often be located elsewhere in the settlement. The wells are important because, in the dry lands in which new settlements were established, the provisioning of drinking water was the first constraint to be overcome. In local lore the community's first well is often considered the outcome of a miraculous discovery, or else it was a divine reward for pious acts.[18] Even if they no longer produce drinking water today, the 'sacred' status of such wells remains and they survive in the urban landscape. Similarly, in the wooded savanna landscape trees are natural 'buildings' of sorts. They may have provided shelter for the settlement's saintly founder before any structure was built on the site. Thus certain of these trees are associated with the pious acts or mystic insights that occurred beneath them (Ross 2008). Like the wells, the trees too have acquired sacred status. Some have been replaced by mosques, but many others continue to stand on the *pénc* and they are integral to the overall public 'architecture' of these places.[19]

---

18 This is the case of Touba's Ainou Rahmati (the 'Well of Mercy') and of wells in Porokhane, Darou Mousty, Yoff-Layene, etc.

19 Venerable trees of this sort abound in Touba and can be found in Darou Mousty, Porokhane, Mbacké Kayor Boundao, Darou Khadim, etc.

Significantly, the *pénc* hardly ever harbors a market. Markets in these communities are always located at least a few streets away, a location that often marks the spatial limit of the initial settlement.[20] The only commerce that may be found directly on the *pénc*, and only in the largest shrine towns, is the selling of pious literature and religious paraphernalia in kiosks and book stalls. This of course emphasizes the 'sacred' nature of these places. Also, in cases where the Sufi settlement has acquired an administrative function as the seat of local state authority (as in Darou Mousty and Ndame), these administrative buildings are located some distance from the *pénc*. Whatever their effective administrative status may be, on the symbolic level of representation on the *pénc* these communities maintain their autonomy from the state and its structures.

The sacred nature of the *pénc* is more acutely evident in full fledged shrines. The shrine function of these places is manifest primarily through the presence of the tombs of the community's saintly founder and of his descendants. Such tombs may be located in cemeteries – always located to the east (*qiblah* axis) of the *pénc* – or else they can take the form of mausolea located on the *pénc* itself, either free-standing or integrated with the mosque to form a mosque-mausoleum complex. In some cases the *pénc* also harbors special memorials marking specific places where some important event occurred in the early, 'heroic' period of the settlement's establishment. These *lieux de mémoire* can take the form of small built structures (*maqam* or pavilions), but the historic wells and trees described above are more likely to serve this purpose.

The religious and temporal authority of the *shaykh* over the community is inscribed onto the *pénc*, not just by building and patronizing the mosque, but by inhabiting the large compound where the community's founder had lived. These compounds, usually located on the west side of the *pénc*, consist of a succession of courtyards which progress from more-or-less public areas, closest to the front gate leading to the *pénc*, to secluded family quarters at the compound's rear. The largest of them may even incorporate internal streets.

During the community's foundational years, the compound of the *shaykh* was not just the place of residence of the *shaykh* and his family; it was the central institution of the entire nascent community. To begin with, it often contained the community's first (and for a long time only) mosque. The mosques within these compounds were not built structures. As in earlier eras they consisted of a clean space set aside within the compound's first courtyard, enclosed by a fence. Eventually, a small masonry mosque could be erected in the courtyard. Yet even these were only large enough to accommodate the *shaykh* and a dozen or so wor-

---

20 Darou Mousty is the exception here. Darou Mousty's market place is located on the east side of its pénc [Fig. 3].

shippers. Most people prayed in the courtyard outside. The *shaykh's* compound could also harbor a school, a library, granaries and, in the earliest years, the equivalent of a 'treasury' (*bayt al-mal*) where the community's movable assets (money, cloth) were stored. The great compounds of the founding *shaykhs* were thus public spaces which harbored many diverse collective activities of great social and religious importance to the community. From this perspective, the *pénc* outside the gate served more as a forecourt to the *shaykh's* compound than as a public square in its own right.

So long as they were inhabited by the founding *shaykh* these compounds remained the living heart of the community, harboring numerous religious and social activities in addition to their residential function. After the deaths of the founders however, most of these activities were moved elsewhere and the compounds acquired increasingly symbolic functions as sacred 'memory places'. In some cases descendents of the founding *shaykh* and of his retainers continue to reside within the compound and many still harbor *daaras*. For the most part though, the successive caliphs (the founder's sons and grandsons who have had jurisdiction over these communities since the founder's death) have lived elsewhere, in large compounds of their own on adjacent streets. The founder's great compound nonetheless continues to mark the locus of power and authority in the community. This is because, even if the current caliph does not actually live there, he will use the compound to receive high-level visits, conduct audiences, receive pilgrims, etc.

Today, the founder's compounds are designated either as *kër gu-mak* ('house of the great one' in Wolof, as in Boukhatoul Moubaraka, Tiénaba, Yoff Layène and Cambérène), or else as *baïti* ('my abode' in Arabic, as in Darou Mousty and in Touba's Darou Khoudoss neighborhood). In some Murid settlements (Darou Marnane and Ndame) they are called Kër Sëriñ Touba ('House of the Shaykh of Touba'). They are now *lieux de mémoire* where the founder's overall legacy and specific events from the community's early years are literally enshrined. The high perimeter walls and the main gate of these compounds have been monumentalized, built of 'hard' materials (concrete masonry) as opposed to the original adobe, wattle and planks. Inside, masonry mosques and kiosks have been erected on select spots of symbolic significance. These historic compounds are used on official occasions by the current caliphs of the community. They are also the object of pious visits by pilgrims.

Most often, the other residential compounds which face the square also belong to imminent lineages, descendants of the founder's sons and disciples, which may constitute distinct constituencies within the Sufi order. Consequently, these too may evolve into similar places for the exercise and representation of authority based on lineage.

In the case of shrine towns, sense of community is strengthened through the organization of annual pilgrimages (there are a variety of types: *siyaare*, *gàmmu*, *màggal*, *mawlid*, etc. The *mawlid* commemorates the birthday of the prophet Muhammad and is celebrated by many Muslims the world over whereas the other gatherings are specific to a given *tariqa*).[21] The regular commemoration of religious events, and especially those events linked to the community's history, helps maintaining its identity. This identity operates at three different scales. First of all, there is an overarching Islamic identity. It is expressed through daily and weekly prayer in the mosque, as well as through the main holy day celebrations common to all Muslims. Spatially, it is manifest in the universal alignment to the *qibla* which the grids of Sufi settlements tend to adopt. There is also a specific *tariqa* identity: Muride, Tijani, Qadiri, etc. During *tariqa*-specific events, this identity is expressed through the presence of the *tariqa*'s main *shaykhs*, by regular references (including through visual media, displays and recitations) to the high spiritual status of the *tariqa*'s founder and to his continuing relevance. Identities at these scales ('global' Islamic and 'national' *tariqa*) correspond to Benedict Anderson's 'imagined' communities (1991). Communities of this scale can only exist if sufficient effort is put into manufacturing ideological bonds and affiliations between individuals who have no real contact with or knowledge of each other. Like nationalism, organized religion provides a plethora of such tools with which to forge such bonds. In the case of the places under study here, the commemorations and physical memorials are important vectors and agents of construction and maintenance of these 'large-scale' global and national identities. Touba's *Grand Màggal* and Tivaoune's *Gàmmu* are attended by millions of faithful and mobilize resources on a national scale.

There are however local identities embedded within these larger ones which are based on regular social interactions between the individuals actually living in these communities, and which therefore are not nearly as 'imagined' as Anderson's larger communities. In communities of this scale everyone knows every-

---

21 Touba's 'Grand Màggal' occurs annually on the 18th of the month of Saffar. It commemorates the day in 1895 when Shaykh Ahmadou Bamba Mbacké was sentenced to exile by the colonial authorities, an act understood by Murids to mark his status as 'friend' of God and 'servant' of the prophet Muhammad. The main Tijani pilgrimage to Tivaouane occurs on the *mawlid* (12th of Rabi 'al-Away). Each of these events attract well upwards of a million pilgrims. Other important annual pilgrimages include the *ngénte gàmmu* in Ndiassane (20th of Rabi 'al-Awwal) and the *daaka* retreat outside the Tijani city of Médina Gounass.

one else, and the same families have been neighbors for generations. Neighborly relationships are maintained on a daily basis, through multiple face-to-face interactions. Moreover, nearly all individuals in these local communities are linked somehow the *shaykh's kër* through kinship and master-*taalibe* ties. The spiritual and temporal authority of the *shaykh's* lineage thus penetrates deeply into the settlement's social life. There is also a strong identification with 'heroic' era of the settlements foundation and early development. The oldest of these communities are only a few generations old, so the foundation era still thrives in living memory.[22]

Community construction is an ongoing affair. In Murid settlements in particular, the *pénc* and grid model is still being applied. Touba's 1993 Master Plan for instance called for the *ex nihilo* creation of 26 new *pénc* distributed across the length and breadth of the city's expanding ring of suburbs (Guèye 2002: 337). It is still the *shaykh*, through his entourage, who is responsible for urban planning. The streets and lots are surveyed under his authority and quite often water is piped in at his bidding. The grids of urban infrastructure – streets, mains and lots – are effectively emanations of the *shaykh's* authority. The surveyors and water engineers may be civil servants, but the agency of the state is subordinate to the decisions of the *shaykhs*. This is clearly the case in Touba (which has a *de jure* autonomous status) but numerous other Sufi settlements exhibit a similar primacy of tariqa agency.

CONCLUSION

The central public squares of Senegal's contemporary Sufi settlements are paragons of the properly ordered community. Order, authority and identity are both generated and represented in these religious places. The religious, oftentimes sacred nature of these places is manifest architecturally (mosques, mausolea) as well as through the acts which occur there (prayer, pilgrimage). The Islamic identity of these places is further reinforced by their general alignment to the *qibla*. Not just proper religion, social order and authority too are promoted through the configuration of these settlements, namely through their *pénc* and grid plans.

---

22 For example, in *Sufism and Jihad in Modern Senegal* (2007), John Glover interviews some of the few surviving participants from the early years of Darou Mousty (1912-1943).

A broader historical reading of the application of the *pénc* and grid plan reveals that its association with Islam is accidental rather than original. The model was first applied to political places, not religious ones. The properly ordered community it promotes emanates more from the palatial compound of the *shaykh* than from the mosque in the middle of the *pénc*. As a settlement type, the *pénc* and grid was as amenable to the exercise of the power of nobility and the *ceddo* as it is to that of the *shaykhs*. In effect, the *shaykhs* and *tariqas* have poured the new wine of Islam into the old *pénc* and grid bottle.

Nonetheless, since the late 19th century the *pénc* and grid model has been used by the *tariqas* as a tool to implement an Islamic social and cultural agenda. Part of this agenda is to set society on the Straight Path of Islam, but it also aims to maintain the autonomy of (Islamic) society from the (secular western) state. The 'flip side' of the deployment of Islamic symbols (monumental mosques, pilgrimages) on the *pénc* is the absence of symbols of the state in these centers of community life. The authority represented in these spaces is exclusively that of the *shaykh*'s *kër* and the Sufi *tariqa*.

Figure 1, Plan of central Touba. The central square harbors the Great Mosque. There are ancillary squares in Darou Khoudoss and Darou Minam neighborhoods

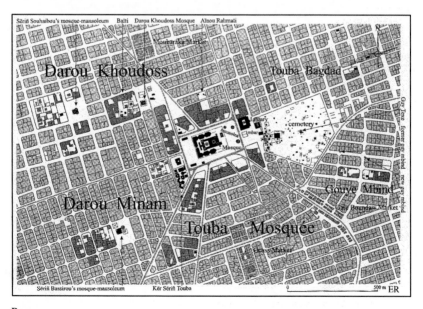

Ross

Figure 2, Darou Mousty, the second city of the Muridiyya. It was established in 1912 by Mame Tierno Birahim Mbacké (1866-1943), Sheik Amadu-Bambas' brother

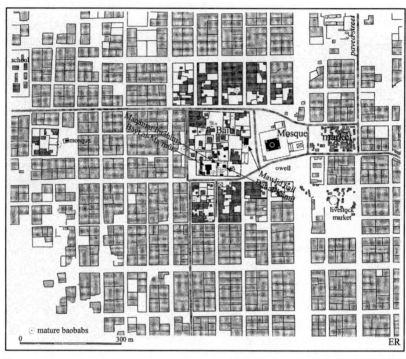

Ross

Figure 3, Plan of Boukhatoul Moubaraka neighborhood in Diourbel. The neighborhood was established by the colonial authorities in 1912 to house Shaykh Ahmadu Bamba, who was under house arrest

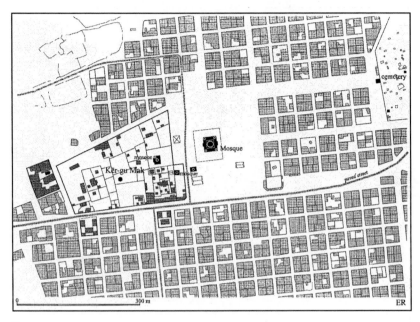

Ross

Figure 4, Plan of Taïf. Taïf was established by Shaykh Mbacké (1905-1978), eldest son of Sëriñ Mamadou Moustapha, first Caliph of the Murids

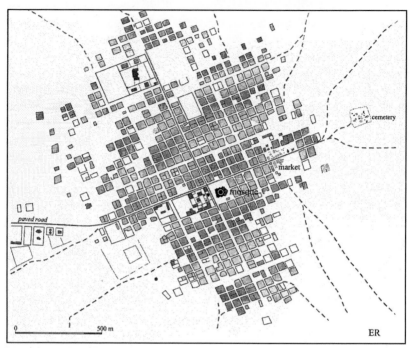

Ross

Figure 5, Plan of Taïba Niassène. Taïba Niassène was established by Tijani Shaykh Al-Hajj Abdoulaye Niass (1844-1922) sometime before 1900

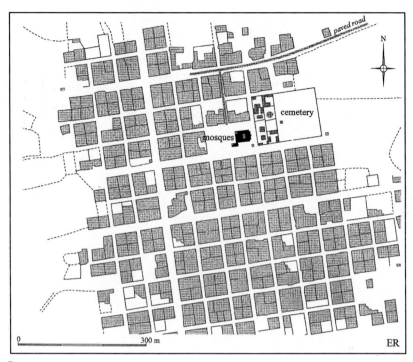

Ross

Figure 6, Plan of Ndiassane. Ndiassane was established by Qadiri Shaykh Bou Kounta (1844-1914). It is home to an important branch of the Qadiriyya

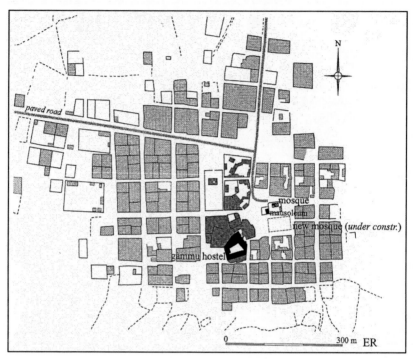

Ross

Figure 7, Plan of Cambérène, established in 1914 by Seydina Issa Rohou Laye (1876-1949), first caliph of the Layène order

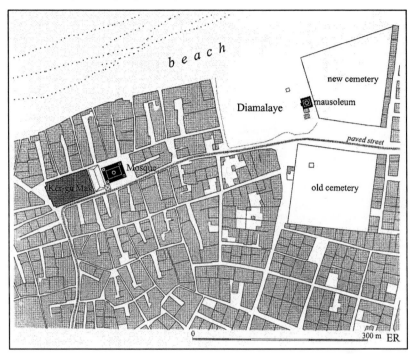

Ross

*Figure 8, Plan of Diakhaou, historic capital of the Kingdom of Sine,
16th-19th century*

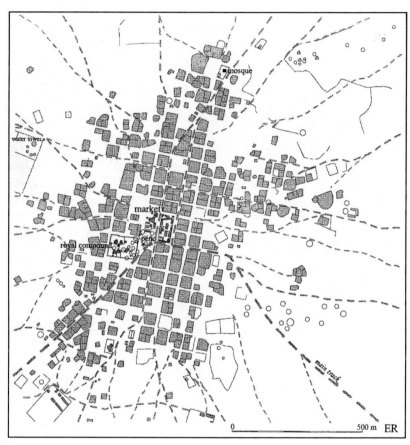

Ross

Figure 9, Plan of Lambaye, historic capital of the Kingdom of Baol, 16ᵗʰ-19ᵗʰ century

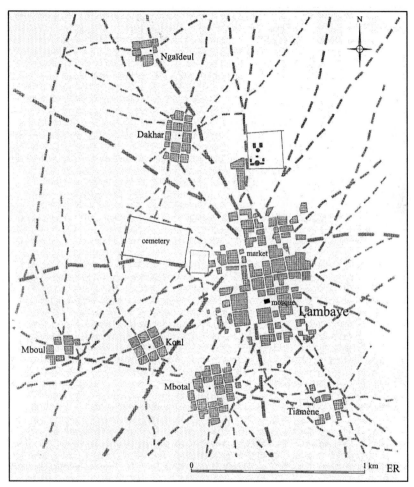

Ross

Figure 10, Plan of Ngalick, a clerical center established by the Khouma shaykhs in the 17ᵗʰ century

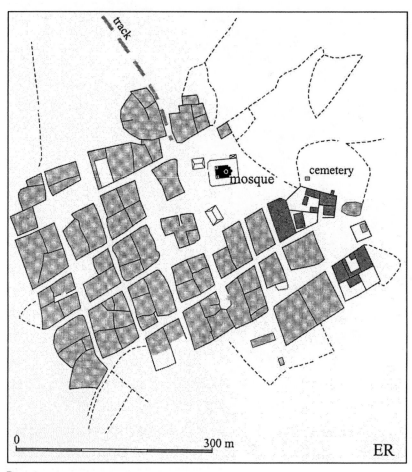

Ross

Figure 11, Plan of Ndanq, established early in the 19th century by Shaykh Bounama Kounta (1780-1843)

Ross

REFERENCES

Aïdara, Abdoul Hadir (2005): Saint-Louis du Sénégal. D'hier à aujourd'hui, Brinon-sur-Sauldre: Grandvaux.

Boulègue, Jean (1972): "Mosquées de style Soudanais au Fouta Tooro", in: Notes africaines 136, pp. 117-119.

Charles-Dominique, Paule (1995): Voyageurs Arabes. Ibn Fadlan, Ibn Jubayr, Ibn Battûta et un auteur anonyme, Paris: Gallimard.

Cissé, Youssouf Tata and Wa Kamissoko (1991): La grande geste du Mali, vol. 2, Paris: Karthala.

Copans, Jean; Couty, Philippe; Roch, Jean, and Rocheteau, G. (1972): Maintenance sociale et changements économiques au Sénégal, Paris: ORSTOM.

Copans, Jean (1980): Les marabouts de l'Arachide, Paris: Le Sycomore.

Diop, Amadou Bamba (1966): "Lat Dior et le problème musulman", in: Bulletin de l'IFAN 28:1-2, série B, pp. 493-539.

Diop, Daouda (2003): La tidjannyat mahdiste de Thiénaba Seck. Son implantation et son évolution (1875-1973). Master's Thesis: Dakar.

Diouf, Mamadou (1990): Le kayor au XIXe siècle. Pouvoir ceddo et conquête coloniale, Paris: Karthala.

Dubois, J.-P. (1975): "Les serer et la question des terres neuves au Sénégal", in: Cahiers de l'ORSTOM, Série sciences humaine 12:1, pp. 81-120.

Duchemin, G. J. (1948): "Urbanisme rural, le village de Cambérène", in: Notes africaines 39, pp. 17-18.

Fal, Arame; Santos, Rosine and Doneux, Jean Léonce (1990): Dictionnaire Wolof-français, Paris: Karthala.

Fall, Tanor Latsoukabé (1974): "Recueil sur la vie des Damel", in: Bulletin de l'IFAN 36:1, Série B, pp. 93-146.

Glover, John (2007): Sufism and Jihad in Modern Senegal. The Murid Order, Rochester: University of Rochester Press.

Guèye, Cheikh (2002): Touba. La capital des Mourides, Dakar and Paris: EN-DA-Karthala-IRD.

Mark, Peter (1995): "Constructing Identity. Sixteenth- and Seventeenth-Century Architecture in the Gambia-Geba Region and the Articulation of Luso-African Ethnicity", in: History in Africa 22, pp. 307-327.

Marone, Ibrahima (1970): "Le tidjanisme au Sénégal", in: Bulletin de l'IFAN 32:1, Série B, pp. 136-215.

Marty, Paul (1915-1916): "Les Mandingues et les peuls du Fouladou", in: Revue du monde musulman 31, pp. 448-460.

Mbacké, Khadim (2005[1995]): Sufism and Religious Brotherhoods in Senegal, Princeton: Markus Wiener Publishers.

Niang, Djibril Tamsir (1989): Histoire des Mandingues de l'ouest, Paris: Karthala.

Robinson, David (2000): Paths of Accommodation. Muslim Societies and French Colonial Authorities in Senegal and Mauritania, 1880-1920, Athens, Ohio and Oxford: Ohio University Press and James Currey.

Ross, Eric S. (2002): "Marabout Republics Then and Now. Configuring Muslim Towns in Senegal", in: Islam et Sociétés au Sud du Sahara 16, pp. 35-65.

(2006): Sufi City. Urban Design and Archetypes in Touba, Rochester: University of Rochester Press.

(2008): "Palaver Trees Reconsidered in the Senegalese Landscape. Arboreal Monuments and Memorials", in: Michael Sheridan and Celia Nyamweru

(Eds.), African Sacred Groves. Ecological Dynamics and Social Change, Oxford, Athens and Pretoria: James Currey, pp. 133-148.

Sanneh, Lamine (1989): The Jakhanke Muslim Clerics. A Religious and Historical Study of Islam in Senegambia, Lanham: University Press of America.

Sy, Cheikh Tidiane (1969): La confrérie sénégalaise des mourides. Un essai sur l'Islam au Sénégal, Paris: Présence Africaines.

A Fractured Soundscape of the Divine

Female 'Preachers', Radio Sermons and Religious Place-making in Urban Mali

DOROTHEA E. SCHULZ

INTRODUCTION

This chapter takes the notion of 'soundscape' as a starting point to examine how the adoption of new media technologies affects the experiential dimensions of religious life in urban areas of southern Mali.[1] As a country in which the majority of the population in this area converted to Islam in the course of the last hundred years, Mali's urban landscapes have been deeply shaped by the symbolic, material and social contours of West African Muslim civilization. Many material dimensions of Muslim urbanism, such as architecture, literature and (though to a lesser extent) visual forms of piety (Roberts and Nooter Roberts 2003), have received considerable scholarly attention. But the aural dimensions of urban Muslim experience, in Mali and throughout sub-Saharan Africa, have remained largely unexplored. This lack of attention to the aural is all the more surprising as audition forms an integral element of perceptual experience and constitutes a central venue for the making of everyday experience.

---

1   The article is based on research conducted in San, a town of approximately 25,000 inhabitants, and in Mali's capital, Bamako, in the period between 1998 and 2006 (altogether 22 months). I regularly participated in the two or three-weekly learning sessions of Muslim women's groups in San and Bamako, and conducted participant observation and more than 60 semi-structured interviews with participants in the Islamic renewal movement. Research was conducted in Bamanakan, the lingua franca of southern Mali, and in French.

With the notion of 'soundscape', I take up the line of inquiry pursued by a number of scholars who, since the 1950s, sought to balance prevailing scholarly assumptions about the hegemony of vision as the chief mode of perception in modernity (see Schulz 2007: 176).[2] Drawing on Zuckerkand (1956), Schafer (1977), and on the anthropological work of Steven Feld (1991, 1996), I use 'soundscape' to stress the importance of auditory space and time as interrelated parameters that shape people's everyday 'horizon of experience' (Kluge and Negt 1993).[3] I will add an analytical perspective that so far has been largely neglected in studies on auditory spaces. Whereas most authors working on soundscape have conceived of it mostly as an experiential space, I am also interested in the actors, social relations and dynamics that animate and structure it. The peculiar characteristics of a soundscape, I argue, are the result of people's struggles over accessing, occupying and defining its contours and components. Forms of social inequality and of authority are therefore at once constitutive and the result of a particular soundscape. Moreover, exploring the soundscape of urban experience, and the possibly transformative role of media technologies within it, requires sustained attention to existing institutions and patterns of sociality.

I focus on how a specific group of Muslims in urban Mali construct, experience and intervene in a 'religious soundscape', that is, an auditory space in which aural and oral modes of religious practice prevail. My analysis is inspired by Nelson's (1985, 1993) pioneering work on the importance of sound perception to Muslim religious and everyday practices, but also extends beyond her focus on Qur'anic recitation as the principal 'sound of the divine in everyday life' (Nelson 1993). We need to make room for the variety of sounds that shape Muslims' everyday life and, notably, to take account of the fact that in most places of Muslim everyday life, aural experiences of Divine presence intermingle with a cacophony of other sounds and sense impressions. How do believers deal with the fact that the sound of the divine does not come as a pristine, uninterrupted

---

2   This preoccupation echoes a long-standing tendency in scholarly research, evidenced in the once-posited argument about modernity as an essentially visual age (e.g. Levin 1993; see Erlmann 2004: intro).

3   The point is not to replace the presumed primacy of vision with – equally debatable – assumptions about auditory or other forms of sensation as primary modes of perceiving and orienting oneself within the world. Rather, we need to address different modes of perception in their interplay. The aim is to understand soundscape as a site where aural perception interacts with other modes of perception, and, through culturally and historically specific constructions of the interrelation of these modes, provides a sense of orientation (see Bull and Back 2003; Feld 1996; Corbin 1998; Connor 2004).

sense perception? Do they seek to rework the conditions of sound perception and thus the soundscape within which they move, and if so, how?

ISLAMIC RENEWAL AND THE CHANGING SOUNDSCAPE OF RELIGIOUS EXPERIENCE

The historical and political backdrop for my analysis is shaped by actors and forms of public intervention that I subsume under the label of a 'movement' of Islamic moral renewal in the urban areas of Mali's south. Over the last decades, Malian urban life has witnessed an upsurge of structures, idioms and emblems of Muslim piety that manifests in a flourishing infrastructure of Islamic proselytizing (da'wa). This development started in the early 1980s, and gained in vigor after the breakdown of President Traore's single-party rule in 1991 that paved the way for multiparty democracy and the granting of freedom of expression and other civil rights. Since then, a multitude of Muslim associations and activists have gained public prominence and audibility, calling for a return to original teachings of Islam and denouncing some local religious practices as 'unlawful innovation' (bid'a). Their positions are associated by many critics with a 'radical', 'Arab' Islam, that is, interpretations that draw inspiration from reformist trends in Egypt and Saudi Arabia that have shaped regional Muslim debate since the 1930s and 1940s. But contrary to this depiction, the representatives of Muslim moral reform articulate very diverse views on Islamic doctrine and proper Muslim practice, and position themselves in distinct ways vis-à-vis state institutions, officials and governmental politics on one side, and representatives of the religious establishment, on the other (Schulz 2003, 2006: 212-214).

Although the initiatives of supporters of Islamic renewal are in clear continuity with long-standing traditions of Muslim moral reform, certain features of contemporary Muslim activism render it distinctively novel. Of crucial relevance are the new media technologies and institutions that, following President Traoré's ouster, generated new conditions for the articulation and experience of religion in Mali's political arenas, and permeate the soundscape of public life in new ways. Another relatively novel feature is the central but contested role taken by women in the Islamic renewal movement. Since the 1980s, a steadily growing number of women in town organize themselves in neighborhood-based 'Muslim women's groups' (singular, silame musow ton[4]) to jointly engage in religious

---

4   Unless indicated otherwise, all foreign words are in Bamanakan, the lingua franca of southern Mali.

learning and other activities. Particularly striking in this respect is the rise to prominence of a number of women who, as initiators and leaders of the Muslim women's group, rely on audio tapes and local private radio stations in Mali's urban centers to disseminate their call for Islamic renewal to wider audiences. These female group leaders, deferentially called '*hadja*' by many group members, take great care in presenting themselves not as religious 'teachers' (singular, *karamɔ̀gɔ̀*), but as 'educators' who offer 'moral advice' (*ladili*).[5] In spite of this self-effacing portrayal of their own role in Islamic renewal, the group leaders confront considerable opposition and critique on the part of secularist critics, and also of some male leaders of the Islamic renewal movement. These critics dismiss the lectures of the 'radio *hadjas*' (as they sometimes call them) and criticize them for their lack of propriety and scholarly erudition. In spite of this opposition, the radio *hadjas* capitalize on the acclaim they enjoy among their female followers. By featuring regularly in religious programs on Thursday nights and Friday mornings, they do affect the auditory space of mass-mediated religious debate. Their embattled appearances on local radio illustrate some dynamics of, and also the criteria for exclusion from, the soundscape of religious experience in urban Mali.

What, then, are the historical contours of this contested soundscape and what are the stakes of participating in it? How do mass media technologies play into these dynamics and contestations? How do established notions of authority inform the role that the female leaders claim for themselves within this auditory space?

MEDIA, MEDIATION, RELIGIOUS AUTHORITY

In recent years, new scholarship has emerged on the question of how new media technologies interlock with and transform conventional understandings of religious practice and authority; and how these changes affect the relevance of religion to public life, and thereby force scholars to reconsider conventional assumptions about the 'secular' nature of modern state politics and of political modernity *tout court*.

---

5 'Moral advice' is a category of speech that older women were conventionally expected to deliver. The female leaders who present themselves as delivering 'moral advice' clearly seek to justify their public interventions by reference to this 'traditional' duty of women.

Positions taken in this literature on the 'effects' of new media technologies on religious practice can be, broadly speaking, grouped into two separate camps. On one side are scholars who, inspired by authors such as McLuhan (1994) and Castells (1996), emphasize the novelty of social processes and emotional and cognitive experiences accompanying the adoption of new media technologies; they frame these changes as a shift in social and religious praxis generated by technological innovation. Authors representative of this position employ what could be called a 'minimalist' definition of mediation. They study mediation as a process predicated on specific sets of technical devices and attendant social conventions that have come to be recognized as 'new media' (but see Sterne 2003; Gitelman 2006). Various new media, the argument goes, create new vectors of access to and participation in religious debate and interpretation; they contribute to the 'democratization' of religious knowledge acquisition and production, and thus undermine established hierarchies of interpretive authority (e.g. Anderson 1999; Turner and Volpi 2007: 8, 10-11).[6] As Eickelman and Anderson argue, participants in these circuits of religious interpretation and debate gain an awareness of the plurality of normative positions within Islam, a process these authors describe as an 'objectification' of religious knowledge (Eickelman and Anderson 1999; also see Eickelman 1992; Robinson 1993; Turner and Volpi 2007: 3, 11; Turner 2007:.117-118, 120; Mandaville 2007: 105, 108-110).

The second perspective on religion and media is formulated by authors who employ a broader, more inclusive notion of 'mediation'. Rather than highlighting novelty, discontinuity, and rupture, they are interested in the processes by which new media technologies are adopted into conventional social forms, perceptions, and protocols of religious practice. Authors such as van der Veer (1995), de Vries and Weber (2001) and Schmidt (2000), for instance, discuss the effects of new media technologies on religious practice and forms of authority by emphasizing that religion, by its very nature, always implies a process of mediation. That is, 'religious experience', as an experience of the transcendent, always necessitates a process of mediation and of 'translating' sensual experience into material, palpable, visible or otherwise 'sense-able' form.

---

6 Turner interprets this development as paradoxical, arguing that new media technologies serve religious revivalist trends (which he implicitly equates with conservative and 'fundamentalist' positions), but paradoxically also erode traditional authority (2007: 118-119). What remains unacknowledged in this perspective is that the two trends are often supported by entirely distinct groups (and generations) of actors who rely on different kinds of media and articulate different goals. Rather than pinpointing a paradox, these trends reflect a highly complex field of shifting conventions, practices and understandings of Muslim orthopraxy and correct interpretation.

What these and other authors postulate, then, is that new technologies of mass mediation, rather than introducing a fundamental break with established conventions of religious experience and authority, perpetuate earlier forms of translating the presence of the divine into believers' perceptions and daily concerns (see Meyer 2005, 2006; Stolow 2005; de Witte 2008). They stress the gradual, sometimes incomplete or incoherent, ways in which religious practice, experience, and authority change along with new technologies of mediation and the attendant forms of sociality and modes of engagement and attention these technologies enable. Common to the second body of scholarship on religion and media is an interest in understanding religion and its transformative potential as arising from, and reflecting on, a calibrated set of historical changes *and* continuities in religious practice and experience (Hirschkind 2006).

The contrasting analytical perspectives on the relationship between technological innovation, institutional reconfigurations, and changing forms of religious practice offer a useful starting place to address how the radio-mediated appearance of the 'radio *hadjas*' affect the religious soundscape of urban life in Mali. The public prominence that audio recording technologies afford these *hadjas* allow us to examine how the adoption of new media technologies affects existing forms of religious experience and authority. These questions are relevant not only to current scholarly debates on religion and media, but also to our understanding of how struggles over religious authority form an integral part of Muslim practices of place-making in societies in Africa.

As a first step toward exploring these issues, I will sketch out the material and aural contours of the soundscape within which supporters of Islamic renewal move and live. I focus on one woman, 'Mariama'. She had become one of my closest confidants over the years of my research on Islamic revival in San, a town of approximately 25,000 inhabitants, located between the rivers Niger and Bani in Mali's southwest.

SOUND BITES OF EVERYDAY LIFE IN A MALIAN TOWN

On a sunny morning in San in August 1999, I visited Mariama, a member of a local Muslim women's group, at her courtyard in San, to accompany her to the market. It was early in our acquaintance and, as she had told me beforehand, at this time of the day she would have already completed a first set of household chores, after getting up at 4:30 am to pound millet in preparation for the morning dish for her husband who was to leave for his next business trip to Kankan early that morning. After waking up her children, dressing and feeding them so that they could leave in time for the nearby *medersa* (reformed Islamic school), she had explained to me, the time for the second morning prayer would have passed, and she would finally be ready to take me to the market. During all these morning chores, Mariama had been listening to her favorite local radio station that, with the exception of Friday mornings, broadcast a program designed for women and youth that mixed call-in debates on timely topics with Malian popular music.[7]

As we left for the market, Mariama donned a second layer of clothes, comprising an ankle-length dark robe on top of the regular two-piece dress, and a prayer shawl (*kunabiri*) wrapped tightly around her shoulders, neck, and over the hairnet, making sure that nothing except her face remained visible. As we walked through the streets of her neighborhood and paved our way toward the market place located nearby, we moved through a cacophony of multiple, changing, and overlapping sound spaces. Sound bites of individual radio preachers, Qur'anic recitations and other religious sound elements intermingled with various tidbits of radio- and tape recorder-mediated sound: pop music, jingles, and word bits from various radio speakers and talk show participants. We also became privy to many other discordant sound pieces and bits of street conversations, some of which were spoken into cell phones, people laughing, shouting, yelling, calling each other across the street.

Upon our arrival at San's bustling central market square, we moved immediately to the market stands run by members of the Muslim women's group in which Mariama participated. After finishing our obligatory tour to greet fellow Muslim women, I, together with Mariama, sat down at the market stand of one of her closest friends. While we were chatting, one group member after the other stopped by for a moment and popped her head under the make-shift roof of the market stand for a casual greeting or a quick exchange of the most recent news and gossip. Yet, as relaxed as the atmosphere appeared to be, it was evident that Mariama, as well as her friend who was in charge of the market stand, felt quite uneasy about the situation. Mariama was clearly in a hurry to go home so that, as she put it, the noon call for prayer (Arabic, *adhan*) would not 'surprise' us while still in the market. Once we were back at Mariama's courtyard, I cautiously probed her about the reasons for her hurry to get home. In response, Mariama pointedly characterized the marketplace as a realm of daily life that opens the doors to *jahiliyya*, that is, the willful straying away from the path to God. She

---

7   As Mariama explained to me, she preferred to postpone her sermon listening activities (that is, her listening to audio tapes by preachers or female leaders) to the quieter and more sociable times of the day, such as the afternoon, a time when she socialized with fellow Muslim women, neighbors and relatives.

described the situation in the market as a one of 'promiscuity'; as a site for the exchange between and illicit mixing of men and women, and as a place haunted by promiscuous and jarring sound impressions that leave no room for a regard turned inward, nor for the slightest moment of contemplative, self-reflexive, and self-controlling action. For Mariama, the atmosphere of illicitness and promiscuity was epitomized by the fact that the dissonant soundscape will prevent her from hearing the sound of the *adhan* in an untainted, unaltered, and thus unmediated way. As she added disapprovingly, Qur'anic recitation could nowadays be heard "everywhere and anywhere" in public arenas that, in their jumbled juxtaposition of "noise", left no room for an "uncontaminated" experience of "God's presence in our daily life".

When I came back to Mariama's courtyard a few hours later, I found her sitting on her mat, surrounded by several fellow Muslim women, and eagerly debating a radio lecture by the leader of their Muslim women's group that they had just listened to. I must have had a puzzled expression on my face because at some point during their heated exchange, Mariama turned to me and said:

"we appear to disagree, but ultimately, we all agree on the fundamentals of our search. We seek to convince neighbors, other women, whomever we meet, that only returning to the true teachings of Islam will save us. Many people call themselves Muslims but the way they live they contribute to the strength of jahiliyya among us. ...You see, to live the example of a proper Muslim is very difficult. We strive to support one another in this effort; in our attempts to become proper Muslims, to be sociable and practice 'humanness' (*hademadenya*). Listening to Hadja's advice helps us in our daily struggles. ... If I just hear her voice talking to me, this gives me strength. Her teachings touch me profoundly; she encourages me to work on the ways in which I live and labor. That's why I try to listen to her sermons every day. When I hear the sound of her voice, it envelops and protects me; I take recourse in it and it gives me strength to keep going."

The scenes taken from Mariama's daily movements through her urban environment highlight several aspects of the soundscape that forms the backdrop of Muslim women's everyday experience. This soundscape is the very object of Mariama's practices of religious place-making, that is, of her efforts to create an environment conducive to her search for personal transformation and for the moral renewal of society. The different aural, material, social and symbolic spaces through which Mariama moves in the course of a day illustrate that media technologies interlock with the shifting physical and perceptual parameters of urban experience in multiple ways. The result of these interlocking dynamics is first, the absence of any uninterrupted, pristine religious soundscape – and experience – in most arenas of daily life. There is no room for an unmediated or distinctive experience of what Nelson (1993) refers to as 'the sound of the divine in everyday life'. Rather, the experiential space of daily life is composed of various, overlapping symbolic, material and aural space-time frames that together form the backdrop against which urban experience is generated and reflected upon. Muslim women who, like Mariama, strive for the moral transformation of society, explicitly identify this situation as one of 'promiscuity' and 'distortion' and critically remark upon the threat of *jahiliyya* they associate with this situation. Yet Muslim women feel the need to remedy this situation, and they propose to do so in three ways, all of which can be understood as practices of religious place-making. They socialize with like-minded women, thereby building a protective social sphere for their joint efforts. They draw inspiration, support and encouragement from the 'touching' lessons of their group leader. And they consciously build on the emotional comfort provided by their group activities by drawing on the immaterial, yet aurally palpable sphere of protection generated by their leader's voice. As Mariama explains, she consciously situates herself within this sound shield (in the double sense of the word) created by her *hadja's* lectures.

What, then, are the historical forms and institutions of sociability that form the backbone of Muslim women's practices of place-making?

Institutions and Practices of Female Islamic Renewal

The leaders of Muslim women's groups and other female protagonists of the Islamic renewal movement offer their 'moral lessons' on various occasions, such as the bi-weekly meetings of the Muslim women's groups and religious holidays. Muslim women's learning activities are relatively novel in scope and orientation, yet also draw on long-standing historical roots. Whereas prior to the 1970s, female religious learning was a privilege exercised by relatively few, older women from wealthy families of merchants and religious leaders[8], nowadays, Muslim women's neighborhood groups allow broader segments of the urban

---

8 Similar to other areas of the colonial French Sudan and to Northern Nigeria, these highly educated women often gained local standing as exemplars of pious conduct, verbal proficiency and oratory skills (Trevor 1975; Umar 2001). They enjoyed the privilege of leading a life withdrawn from public scrutiny and, while engaging in religious learning, substantially benefited from the support of fathers, brothers and husbands. Thanks to their knowledge – and often also organizational skills – these erudite women enjoyed considerable respect, especially if they devoted some of their time to offering religious and ritual instruction to their female 'disciples' (*kalanidenw*).

population to engage in religious learning and the acquisition of Arabic literacy. Also in contrast to historical forms of female knowledge acquisition, present-day structures of female learning are characterized by a greater degree of public visibility and audibility.

The oft-stated rationale of Muslim women's groups is to "learn to read and write Arabic", thus claiming continuity with conventional structures of female religious learning that in this area of West Africa were historically associated with individual mosques and with the teachings offered by the wives, daughters or sisters of religious scholars. A closer look at the Muslim women's groups reveal that they draw on the teaching formats of reformed Islamic schools (singular, *medersa*, see Brenner 2001). They also resemble the adult literacy classes that are sponsored by Western donor organizations, as well as the credit savings associations that mushroomed all over Africa in the wake of the Structural Adjustment Programs of the 1980s.

Most immediately, Muslim women's learning groups are the result of the expansion of Muslim organizational forms that started in the 1980s, with the support of a transnational *da'wa* movement funded by Saudi Arabia and other countries of the Arab-speaking Muslim world (e.g. Mattes 1989; Brenner 1993a, b; Otayek 1993). Similar to earlier Muslim activists' attempts to reform religious education (Brenner 2001: ch.3), this 1980s *da'wa* effort was decisive in extending opportunities to learn about religious matters and proper ritual to people who formerly would have found it difficult to access this knowledge. Growing numbers of youth from all walks of life, but also of 'younger' married women from the urban middle and lower-middle classes, were among the main beneficiaries of these changes in the infrastructure of religious education and worship.[9] But rather than simply extending knowledge acquisition to new social groups, the institutional changes initiated by local and international actors of *da'wa* had also far-reaching consequences for the sites where female Muslim leaders could engage in their moralizing activities. This is, at least, what is suggested by the earlier-mentioned, controversial reception of the lectures by the 'radio *hadjas*'.

---

9   Their activities are rooted in the reforms initiated by a younger generation of Muslims who, after prolonged stays in Saudi Arabia, Egypt and sometimes North Africa, initiated educational and other reforms to respond to the new situation established under French colonial rule. Their reformist endeavor was inspired by intellectual trends throughout the early 20th century Arab-speaking world. The interventions of this earlier generation of Muslim activists had far-reaching effects on local practices and notions of Muslim orthopraxy, and thus contributed significantly to the ongoing unsettling of conventional foundations of religious interpretive authority (Brenner 2001; Schulz 2012: ch.1, 2006; Soares 2005).

In spite of the learning efforts of the women who frequent the 'Muslim women's learning groups', many of them acquire only basic Arabic literacy skills and a rudimentary knowledge of the central tenets of Islam. Among group leaders, levels of erudition vary considerably. Apart from those who from early on had an opportunity to engage in religious learning, most group leaders limit their teachings to very general reflections on female social duties and obligations of worship. Those *tontigiw* who engage in (what they refer to as) *tafsiri* and lecture on the meaning of individual Qur'anic verses or hadiths, carefully keep to the readings of their own teachers, rather than proposing independent interpretations.

Female Islamic Renewal: The Teachings

The female leaders whose lectures, whether delivered 'live' or broadcast on local radio, are avidly followed by female supporters of Islamic renewal, present their teachings as moral lessons, and also as an interpretation (*tafsiri*) of religious texts.[10] Their lectures center on believers' individual responsibility for salvation, and that this responsibility should manifest, on the one hand, in the effort to 'understand' and appropriate the written sources of Islam, and, on the other, in the daily effort to become a pious Muslim.[11]

The *hadjas* consider their lectures to be part and parcel of their endeavor to return to more authentic modes of interpreting and living God's word. They advise their 'disciples' (*kalanidenw*) on questions of proper comportment in do-

---

10 Some group leaders hire Muslim teachers (singular, *karamògò*) to deliver the teachings. Depending on their own level of religious erudition, certain group leaders also take private lessons in tafsiri with Muslim teachers.

11 True religiosity, the hadjas often explain, may be achieved by heeding the rules of ritual worship (as illustrated by the five daily prayers) and in a number of religious and social practices relevant to the forming of pious selves and to collective wellbeing. Women should cultivate certain personal qualities that are conducive to socially responsible conduct, such as modesty (*maloya*, literally 'shame'), endurance (*sabati*, patience), and submissiveness (*munyu*). The exhortation of believers to cultivate certain ethical and emotional dispositions echoes Salafi-Sunni inspired understandings of religious subjectivity formulated by female supporters of the *da'wa* 'mosque movement'' in Cairo (Mahmood 2005). Similar to earlier trends of integrating transnational reformist thought, this trend may have entered the Malian religious field through male teachers with educational degrees from institutions in Egypt and Saudi Arabia. For a detailed discussion of the different degree to which these influences are incorporated by various activists in Mali, see Schulz 2012: ch.5).

mestic and public settings and on their duty to invite others "to embark on the path to God" (*k'ala sira ta*).

Yet in spite of the insistence of many *hadjas* that they render the timeless and unchanging God-ordained "rights and duties of women", their lessons entail many references to the repercussions of a recent, sometimes dramatic restructuring of relations between the generations and between husband and wife in town. The teachings thus reveal a tension between traditional gender morals and an emphasis on the responsibility of women for the moral renewal of society. This tension can be seen as a reflection of the new dilemmas many urban women face in the wake of limited income opportunities, a greater financial responsibility for family subsistence, and a persistent patriarchal gender ideology.

The emphasis on a Muslim woman's responsibility for collective well-being is in line with the moral role model function that elite women were historically expected to accomplish. Nevertheless, the stress on individuals' responsibility for salvation also signals a historical shift away from conceiving of Muslim identity as a family and professional identity (Launay 1992), and toward proper Muslim conduct as the result of personal decision and conviction (Schulz 2008a). As some hadjas caution their 'disciples', a woman's personal decision to 'move closer to God' may lead to a situation of conflict or tension with her own family. But, as the hadjas also insist, women need to brave this menace "for the love of God's truth". Similarly novel is the highlighting of the obligation for women to convince others to join their moral endeavor and to become public exemplars of moral excellence. The advice to adopt publicly visible signs of piety breaks with the traditional association of female religiosity with the domestic realm. Historically, women's pious lives depended on their opportunities to keep away from worldly matters. In contemporary society, many hadjas maintain, the need for moral transformation requires each and every Muslim to assume collective responsibility by making one's personal piety the object of broader, public attention and emulation (Schulz 2008b).

Mediated Authority: Contested Criteria for Legitimate Public Speech

To understand how Muslim women remake the soundscape of everyday life, closer attention is warranted to the authority that female group leaders claim for themselves, and that their followers attribute to them.

There are, broadly speaking, three categories or forms of female religious authority that historical and anthropological scholarship on 'women and Islam' in

Africa has accounted for.[12] Studies of women 'in leadership positions' (Sule and Starrett 1991) document the prestige and influence a few elite women derived historically from their affiliation with the families of the *shaykhs* and founders of individual Sufi orders (e.g. Asma'u 1997; Hutson 1997, 1999). Central to the position of spiritual guidance of these women is the special divine blessings (*baraka*) held by their family or clan and in which these women were (and still are) considered to partake. Their pious life-style and religious erudition made these women highly respected personalities in local religious fields (e.g. Constantin 1987; Coulon 1988; Coulon and Reveyrand 1990; Reveyrand-Coulon 1993; Dunbar 2000; Evers Rosander 2003; see Boyd and Last 1985). In Mali, the respect some of these women enjoyed historically in their role as educators, as examples of moral excellence, and as persons able to mediate believers' supplication to God, is illustrated by the fact that today, their tombs often serve as centers of veneration and *ziyara*, 'visits'.

Historical and anthropological studies document a second type of female authority, one that is primarily based on elite women's role as teachers and 'patrons' of social networks. Whether these women based their educational activities on their affiliation with a Sufi order and its *shaykh's* family depended on the historical and institutional context, and on the specific structuring of a Muslim discursive field (e.g. Trevor 1975; Evers Rosander 1997; Umar 2001). In nineteenth century Kano, for instance, women's educational activities were linked to having a royal family background and hence Qadiriyya affiliation (Sule and Starratt 1991; Boyd 1989, 2001). But this close connection became more tenuous in the course of British colonial occupation (Trevor 1975). In the area of the colonial French Sudan, elite women born into some leading religious clans passed on their knowledge to female-only educational circles. This convention is still evident today in Mali where a number of older women from renowned Muslim scholarly backgrounds teach in women's groups that are affiliated with certain mosques (e.g. Sanankoua 1991; also see Purpura 1997).

A third type of female authority has its origins in recent developments, notably, in women's wider access to advanced religious learning. The recent character of this authority type may be the reason why women who draw on this source of authority have received very little scholarly attention.[13] The authority of these women is based not on elite family status, but on reformed (*medersa*-style)

---

12 The three categories I identify refer to ideal types in the Weberian sense, not to neatly distinguishable forms and practices of authority.

13 Notable exceptions are Alidou (2005) and the (rather cursory) discussion by Kleiner-Bosaller and Loimeier (1994). Miran (1998, 2005); Le Blanc (1999); and Augis (2002) deal primarily with the disciples of these female 'teachers'.

school education and, very often, on a higher educational degree earned from institutions in the Arab-speaking world. In Mali, these highly educated women belong to a younger generation of Muslim intellectuals who, throughout Africa, have gained in formal political standing over the past 40 years, and who owe their growing influence to their training at institutions of higher religious learning in the Maghreb, Libya, Egypt and Syria.[14]

The leaders of the Muslim women's groups in urban Mali do not fit any of these three categories. But they are considered 'teachers' by members of their groups and are treated with much deference. What gives these *hadjas* the authority to teach 'moral lessons' and thus to affect their disciples' daily efforts of religious place-making?

Whether the leaders of the Muslim women's groups deliver 'live' or radio-mediated moral lessons, they commonly present their own role as one of 'helping' other women to gain access to the written foundation of Islam. The *hadjas* thus stress the 'rational', text-based foundations of the 'path to God' on which each Muslim needs to embark. At the same time, interactions between the *hadjas* and ordinary group members illustrate that practices of human intercession and spiritual leadership remain essential to their teacher-disciple relationship. This is exemplified in the belief in the existence of chosen individuals to whom God has granted His special blessings (*baraka*).[15]

The continued importance of notions of spiritual power and intercession manifests strikingly in the ethical significance that the 'disciples' accord to the practice of listening to their leaders' 'moral lessons', and also in the special 'moving force' that they attribute to their leaders' speech. The leadership position that *hadjas* claim for themselves is significantly rooted in commonsense assumptions about the special powers of speech and its ethically and physically moving effects on the minds and hearts of listeners (Schulz 2012). These assumptions are grounded in wider cultural perceptions of the special, transforma-

---

14 See Brenner (1993b); Otayek (1993); Cooper (1995); Alidou (2005); also see Larkin and Meyer (2006).

15 To be sure, the tension between text-centered, rational sources of religious authority on the one hand and, on the other, of a religious authority grounded in the special, God-given spiritual qualities of a leader is neither new nor unique to urban Mali. Similar tensions are evident in many regional Muslim discursive traditions influenced by the teachings and practices of mystical Islam. Nor is this tension between different sources of religious authority an issue only for female believers. Rather, what appears to be characteristic of contemporary urban Mali is that the tension between competing sources of authority comes out in more visible and public forms of female sermonizing.

tive, capacity of the voice, a capacity that tends to be conceived as a specific form of creative, but potentially also destructive power.[16]

Steven Connor (2004) insists that the different modes of sensual perception are multiply related, and that perceiving and orienting oneself within the world occurs through a combination of different senses. Connor's view of the culturally variable construction of the relationship between touch and sound experience helps illuminate conceptions of the power of voice and speech in Malian society. Regardless of considerable ethnic-cultural and regional diversity, there is a strong tendency among Malians to cherish skillful speech and also to pay attention to the specific qualities of a voice and its capacity to move listeners to action. For instance, it is a common observation that listeners spontaneously and enthusiastically react to what they consider a successful performance of professional orators and other gifted speakers, by commenting not only on the quality of his rhetoric, but also on the 'piercing' and touching quality of the voice itself. Evident in these spontaneous remarks is therefore a particular cultural construction between the tactile and sound impression a voice may leave on its subject.

The historically and culturally specific conceptualization of the performative effects of sound forms the aesthetic and perceptual architectonics on which the evaluation of the teachings of Muslim women's group leaders, and of their authority, is based. Muslim women who consider themselves disciples of a certain *hadja* often comment on her speech in ways that associate with her voice a particular capacity to 'awaken' the moral, cognitive and perceptual capacities required for personal and societal transformation. That these disciples accord to their leader and her lectures a peculiar spiritual power also manifests in many gestures and material practices in which their acts of listening to the radio-mediated 'moral lessons' of a *hadja* are embedded.

Audio reproduction and broadcasting technologies are not perceived by these listeners as a 'noise' or rupture, altering or attenuating the special, ethically and perceptually moving effects of voice. Instead, many comments of these disciples – as well as of other supporters of Islamic renewal in Mali (Schulz 2011: ch.7) – suggest that they consider audio reproduction technologies to heighten and, literally, amplify the effects of powerful speech.

Other comments, too, by women in whose company I listened to the radio sermons of their *hadja*, revealed the view that audio recording technologies, as diverse as sermon tapes and radio broadcasts, allow a *hadja's* special, divinely

---

16 For anthropological scholarship on cultural constructions of the powers of voice and speech among the Bamanakan- and Maninkakan-speaking populations of southern Mali, see Zahan (1963); Camara (1976); Kendall (1982); Wright (1989); Hoffman (1995); Schulz (2001); Diawara (2003). See, also, Stoller (1984); Irvine (1989).

granted gifts of 'giving moral lessons' to become more palpable and effective. Radio broadcasts and audio recordings were seen as enhancing the sense of emotional identification to which *hajdas* often appeal in their lectures. Both technologies of mediation support modes of interaction that allow the group leaders to establish their authority as figures of ethical guidance and as examples of moral excellence.

In this way, radio recording technologies serve to write forth the tension between the spiritual authority that followers attribute to them on the one hand, and, on the other, the insistence of many *hadjas* that their authority as radio speakers is grounded in the knowledge of texts and rules.

The spiritual authority that Muslim women attribute to their *hadjas* while interacting with them directly and while relating to them during the radio-mediated lectures, reconfirm these disciples' views of the importance of human intercession – and of the actual existence of such specially blessed spiritual leaders. The reverence with which Muslim women respond to the lectures and voice of their *hadja* reflects their understanding that individual figures of extraordinary piety and erudition have been granted God's special blessings (*baraka*) and thus yield very special capacities for spiritual guidance. That is, even if leaders and their disciples stress the importance of individual understanding and learning, and of the appropriation of written texts of Islam, what they highlight with regard to their listening practices is the special 'moving', transformative effects that inheres to a *hadja's* voice and speech.

For all these reasons, it would be hard to dismiss the authority claimed by the radio *hadjas* on the grounds that they lack the religious training and level of hermeneutic expertise that many male teachers have. Rather, if we take seriously the followers of these group leaders, we need to acknowledge that these women do indeed hold a position of authority, an authority that comes closest to the Weberian notion of charismatic authority, yet does not emanate from the special divine blessings associated with Sufi *shaykhs* and their families that scholars of Islam in Africa have sometimes associated with Weber's notion of charisma (see Coulon and O'Brien 1988).

(RE)MAKING THE PLACE OF RELIGIOUS EXPERIENCE

As intimated by Mariama during our conversation, Muslim women seek to rework the soundscape that underlies their daily experiences, to render it more conducive to their joint search for Islamic renewal. These efforts, she explained, are directed toward creating a place of "proper" religious practice and disposition.

Brian Larkin, drawing on Lefevre, argues that urban experience is importantly mediated through multiform, and historically layered, kinds of urban 'infrastructure', referring with this term to the "totality of both technical and cultural systems that create institutionalized structures whereby goods of all sorts circulate, connecting and binding people into collectivities" (2008: 6). Larkin's analytical perspective brings together the material, symbolic and economic dimensions by which urban experience is mediated and made. Also, infrastructure is always heterogeneous and multi-composite. It is made up of multiple, incongruent historical layers. Taking inspiration from Larkin's perspective, it is worth exploring in what kind of practices Muslim women engage to rework the perceptual, social, and material contours of their daily experience, with the aim of transforming their urban environment in line with their ethical search. Larkin's perspective allows us to study the role of media technologies in these practices of place-making, not in separation from, but through their integration into wider social and material processes.

One way in which Muslim women purposefully fashion their sound environment is to play one of their leader's moral lessons, thereby immersing themselves in the sounds of religious argument and debate. Yet as we have seen, the significance of the lectures offered by group leaders is not limited to the content they provide, but also resides in the medium of transmission itself, the *hadja's* voice. For female participants in the renewal movement, listening to a *hadja's* 'forceful speech' allows them to feel immersed in a soundscape generated through an at once haptic and sonic sensation, a soundscape they consider to be conducive to their experience of Divine presence in daily life. Borrowing from McLuhan's famous dictum that the 'medium is the message', we can say that for many Muslim women, the primary 'message' of a *hadja's* lecture is the medium – her voice – itself and the special, God-granted spiritual powers it conveys.

Taking their radio recorder along when moving through their courtyard was another way in which some Muslim women sought to exert control over their immediate sonic environment. Whether they listened to a sermon or to a Qur'anic recitation, this practice of – in the truest sense of the word – mobilizing sounds conducive to their ethical request, had the effect of engulfing them in a malleable yet protective experiential 'bubble', similar to what Bull describes as the effects of the mobile sound enabled by ipod consumption (Bull 2007).

Reworking the sonic and perceptual architectonics of everyday experience also involves acts that are not directly related to sound sensation. That is, Muslim women may also employ other strategies to control and remake their environment in ways that render it favorable to their search for pious transformation. For instance, I often observed how disciples often materially marked the space within which they listened to their leader's lectures and thereby transformed it into a site of religious devotion and experience. They did so by decorating the area where they place their radio post, using various religious paraphernalia and memorabilia that serve as a reminder of their leader's ethical quest and biography, such as photographs, a rosary they received from her as a gift, or a framed calligraphy.

But beyond these acts of refashioning the material and sonic elements of one's immediate environment, Muslim women also purposefully draw on their patterns of sociability to create an atmosphere that will help them "turn their regard inward" that is, concentrate on thoughts, feelings and dispositions they consider most important to their daily efforts of personal transformation. Mariama's remark already suggested that her sound experience of divine presence is intricately related to a widely shared sense of community and a spirit of solidarity. As illustrated in comments and bodily reactions by other female listeners, this sense of mutuality and sharing is reinforced, rather than disrupted, by audio recording and broadcasting technologies. Yet clearly, it is not media technologies per se that allow these Muslim women to rework and harness their sonic and perceptual environment. Rather, it is the embedding of media technologies, and of related media engagements, in practices of sociability and religious devotion that ensure a favorable soundscape.

Abdoumaliq Simone (2001) argues that contemporary urban life in Africa is characterized by the reconfiguration of 'social fields', that is, of the human relations and attendant norms of obligations that have conventionally constituted the matrix of sociality in town. In this situation, Simone maintains (following Réné Devisch 1995), religious organizations are among the most important forms of social mobilization that intervene into domains of urban life from which the state has withdrawn or has never played a significant role. Starting from Simone's observation, it is important to recognize the polyvalent significance of the forms of sociality and of joint learning practiced by Muslim women in urban Mali. That is, we need to understand these practices of sociality as integral to the endeavors of these women to refashion the urban environment within which they live and move and hence, to their practices of place-making.

As Mariama's daily activities illustrate, she and her fellow Muslim women persistently try to generate a social and experiential realm of religious devotion and ethical self-making. That is, they purposefully seek to remedy a situation they associate with moral promiscuity and *jahiliyya* by creating a social space of religiosity and ethical practice through practices and forms of sociability. They thus generate a *socially*, rather than a primarily spatially defined place for religious practice and experience. Muslim women do so by virtue of their joint listening practices and debates, and other socializing activities. Mariama's attendance of the learning sessions, as well as her engagement in other social and economic activities within the network of 'Muslim women', should be understood as part of a joint effort to remake public spaces as well as domestic domains through these forms of religious sociality.

CONCLUSION

This chapter examined the different, material and social practices by which female supporters of Islamic moral renewal in Mali seek to control and revise certain features of their daily urban environment and lived experience. For many Muslim women, creating a place conducive to their ethical endeavor importantly involves the reworking of the sonic architectonics of their daily lives. The importance these women accord to sound in everyday and religious experience comes out in their regular and reverent practices of listening to the 'moral lessons' provided by the leaders of Muslim women's neighborhood groups. Hearing and heeding the 'advice' delivered by female group leaders forms an important element in Muslim women's daily practices of religious place-making. These women's stress on aural perception as a key process by which religious places are made and unmade should prompt scholars interested in urban experiences to pay more sustained attention to the sound architectonics of life in town. Scholarship on Islam, on the other hand, could gain from greater attention to how *female* religious authority in Muslim societies is constituted both aurally and orally. Investigating the form of authority that 'radio *hadjas*' in contemporary Mali enjoy has important analytical purchase, particularly for scholarly work that seeks to understand how Muslims, in their practices of religious place-making, draw on, and are constrained by, new media technologies and engagements.

By probing the authority credentials of the radio *hadjas*, I stressed the import of processes of sensuous mediation that are supported by audio reproduction technologies and that 'translate' the spoken and heard voice into spiritual experience. My aim was to understand how sound-reproduction technologies help perpetuate conventional understandings of religious authority, and whether and how they transform regimes of authenticating religious authority and 'genuine' spiritual experience.

In Mali, radio broadcasting plays an essential role in Muslim women's place-making practices because it mediates and extends the appeal of their leaders to a broader constituency of believers. But radio broadcasting also fuels the politics of religious place-making because it adds further complexity to already existing controversies over religious authority, and over the right to speak up in public and to shape the soundscape of religious experience.

REFERENCES

Abdoumaliq, Simone (2001): "Straddling the Divides. Remaking Associational Life in the Informal African City", in: International Journal of Urban and Regional Research 25:1, pp. 102-117.

Alidou, Ousseina (2005): Engaging Modernity. Muslim Women and the Politics of Agency in Postcolonial Niger, Madison, WI: The University of Wisconsin Press.

Allen, Richard (1995): To Be Continued... Soap Operas around the World, London: Routledge.

Anderson, Jon (1999): "The Internet and Islam's New Interpreters", in: Eickelman and Anderson (Eds.), New Media in the Muslim World, pp. 41-56.

Asma'u, Nana (1997): Collected Works of Nana Asma'u, Daughter of Usman dan Fodio. Jean Boyd and Beverly Mack (Eds.), East Lansing: Michigan State University Press.

Augis, Erin (2002): Dakar's Sunnite Women. The Politics of Person. Ph.D. Thesis: Chicago.

Boyd, Jean (1989): The Caliph's Sister. Nana Asma'u (1793-1865), Teacher, Poet, and Islamic Leader, London: Cass.

(2001): "Distance Learning from Purdah in Nineteenth-century NorthernNigeria. The Work of Asma'u Fodio", in: Journal of African Cultural Studies 14:1, pp. 7-22.

Boyd, Jean; Murray Last (1985): "The Role of Women as 'Agents Religieux' in Sokoto", in: Canadian Journal of African Studies 19:2, pp. 283-300.

Brenner, Louis (1993a): "Constructing Muslim Identities in Mali", in: Louis Brenner (Ed.), Muslim Identity and Social Change in Subsaharan Africa, Bloomington: Indiana University Press, pp. 59-78.

(1993b): "La culture arabo-islamique au Mali", in: René Otayek (Ed.), Le radicalisme islamique au sud du Sahara, Paris: Karthala, pp. 161-195.

(2001): Controlling Knowledge. Religion, Power and Schooling in a West African Muslim Society, Bloomington and Indianapolis: Indiana University Press.

Bull, Michael (2007): Sound Moves. iPod Culture and Urban Experience, London: Routledge.

Bull, Michael, and Back, Les (Eds.) (2003): The Auditory Culture Reader, Oxford and New York: Berg.

Camara, Sory (1976): Gens de la parole. Essai sur la condition et le rôle des griots dans la société malinké, Paris and La Haye: Mouton.

Castells, Manuel (1996): The Power of Identity. The Information Age. Vol. 1, The Rise of the Network Society, Oxford: Blackwell Publishers.

Connor, Steven (2004): "Edison's Teeth. Touching Hearing", in: Veit Erlmann (Ed.), Hearing Cultures. Essays on Sound, Listening and Modernity, New York and Oxford: Berg, pp. 153-172.

Constantin, Francois (1987): "Condition féminine et dynamique confrérique en Afrique orientale", in: Islam et sociétés au sud du Sahara 1, pp. 58-69.

Cooper, Barbara (1995): "The Politics of Difference and Women's Associations in Niger. Of 'Prostitutes,' the Public, and Politics", in: Signs 20:4, pp. 851-882.

Corbin, Alain (1998): Village Bells. Sound and Meaning in the 19th-centruy French Countryside, New York: Columbia University Press.

Coulon, Christian (1988): "Women, Islam, and Baraka", in: Cruise O'Brien, Coulon (Ed.), Charisma and Brotherhood in African Islam, pp. 113-133.

Coulon, Christian and Reveyrand, Odile (1990): L'Islam au feminine. Sokhna Magat Diop Cheikh de la confrérie mouride (Senegal). Centre d'étude d'Afrique noire, travaux et documents 25.

Cruise O'Brien, Donal, and Coulon, Christian (Eds.) (1988): Charisma and Brotherhood in African Islam, Oxford: Clarendon Press.

de Vries, Hent and Weber, Samuel (Eds.) (2001): Religion and Media. Stanford, CA: Stanford University Press.

de Witte, Marleen (2008): Spirit Media. Charismatics, Traditionalists, and Mediation Practices in Ghana. Ph.D. Thesis: Amsterdam.

Devisch, Réné (1995): "Frenzy, Violence, and Ethical Renewal in Kinshasa", in: Public Culture 7, pp. 593-623.

Diawara, Mamadou (2003): Empire du verbe et l'éloquence du silence. Vers une anthropologie du discours dans les groupes dits domines au Sahel, Cologne: Ruediger Koeppe.

Dunbar, Roberta Ann (2000): "Muslim Women in African History", in: N. Levtzion and R. Pouwels (Eds.), The History of Islam in Africa, Athens, Oxford and Cape Town: Ohio University Press, James Currey and David Philip, pp. 397-417.

Eickelman, Dale (1992): "Mass Higher Education and the Religious Imagination in Contemporary Arab Societies", in: American Ethnologist 19:4, pp. 643-655.

Eickelman, Dale and Anderson, Jon (1999): New Media in the Muslim World, Bloomington: Indiana University Press.

Erlmann, Veit (Ed.) (2004): Hearing Cultures. Essays on Sound, Listening and Modernity, Oxford, New York: Berg.

Evers Rosander, Eva (1997): "Le dahira de Mam Diarra Bousso de Mbacké", in: E. Evers Rosander (Ed.), Transforming Female Identities. Women's Organizational Forms in West Africa, Uppsala: Nordiska Afrikainstitutet, pp. 160-174.

(2003): Mam Diarra Bousso. The Good Mother in Porokhane. Paper presented at the Workshop "Modern Adaptations in Sufi-based Islam", Centre for Modern Oriental Studies, Berlin.

Feld, Steven (1991): "Sound as a Symbolic System. The Kaluli Drum", in: David Howes (Ed.), The Varieties of Sensory Experience, Toronto: University of Toronto Press, pp. 79-99.

(1996): "Waterfalls of Song. An Acoustemology of Place Resounding in Bosavi, Papua New Guinea", in: Steven Feld and Keith Basso (Eds.), Senses of Places, Santa Fe, NM: School of American Research Press, pp. 91-135.

Gitelman, Lisa (2006): Always Already New. Media, History, and the Data of Culture, Cambridge, MA and London: MIT Press.

Hirschkind, Charles (2006): The Ethical Soundscape, New York: Columbia University Press.

Hoffman, Barbara (1995): "Power, Structure, and Mande Jeliw", in: D. Conrad and B. Frank (Eds.), Status and Identity in West Africa. Nyamakalaw of Mande, Bloomington: University of Indiana Press, pp. 36-45.

Hutson, Alaine (1997): We are Many. Women Sufis and Islamic Scholars in 20th Century Kano. Ph.D. Thesis: Bloomington.

(1999): "The Development of Women's Authority in the Kano Tijaniyya, 1894-1963", in: Africa Today 46:3/4, pp. 48-64.

Irvine, Judith (1989): "When Talk Isn't Cheap. Language and Political Economy", in: American Ethnologist 16, pp. 248-267.

Kendall, Martha (1982): "Getting to Know You", in: David Parkin (Ed.), Semantic Anthropology, London and New York: Academic Press, pp. 197-209.

Kleiner-Bosaller, Anke and Loimeier, Roman (1994): "Radical Muslim Women and Male Politics in Nigeria", in: Mechthild Reh and Gudrun Ludwar-Ene

(Eds.), Gender and Identity in Africa, Münster and Hamburg: LIT Verlag, pp. 61-69.

Kluge, Alexander; Oskar Negt (1993): The Public Sphere and Experience, Minneapolis: University of Minnesota Press.

Larkin, Brian (2008): Signal and Noise. Media, Infrastructure, and Urban Culture in Nigeria, Durham, London: Duke University Press.

Larkin, Brian and Birgit Meyer (2006): Pentecostalism, Islam and Culture. New Religious Movements in West Africa, in: E. Akyeampong (Ed.), Themes in West African History, London: James Currey, pp. 286-311.

Launay, Robert (1992): Beyond the Stream. Islam and Society in a West African Town, Berkeley etc.: University of California Press.

Le Blanc, Marie Nathalie (1999): "The Production of Islamic Identities Through Knowledge Claims in Bouaké, Côte d'Ivoire", in: African Affairs 98:393, pp. 485-509.

Levin, David Michael (1993): Modernity and the Hegemony of Vision, Berkeley: University of California Press.

Mahmood, Saba (2005): Politics of Piety. The Islamic Revival and the Feminist Subject. Princeton, Oxford: Princeton University Press.

Mandaville, Peter (2007): "Globalization and the Politics of Religious Knowledge. Pluralizing Authority in the Muslim World", in: Theory, Culture, and Society 24:2, pp. 101-115.

Mattes, Hanspeter (1989): Die islamistische Bewegung des Senegal zwischen Autonomie und Außenorientierung, Hamburg: Institut für Afrika-Kunde.

McLuhan, Marshall (1994): Understanding Media. The Extensions of Man, Cambridge, MA: MIT Press.

Meyer, Birgit (2005): "Religious Remediations. Pentecostal Views in Ghanaian Video-movies", in: Postscripts 2/3, pp. 155-181, special issue 'Mediating Film and Religion' guest-edited by Stephen Hughes and Birgit Meyer.

(2006): "Religious Revelation, Secrecy, and the Limits of Representation", in: Anthropological Theory 6, pp. 431-453.

Miran, Marie (1998): "Le wahhabisme à Abidjan. Dynamisme urbain d'un Islam reformiste en Côte d'Ivoire contemporaine (1960-1996)", in: Islam et sociétés au sud du Sahara 12, pp. 5-74.

(2005) "D'Abidjan à Porto Novo. Associations islamiques et culture religieuse réformiste sur la côte de Guinée", in: L.A.M.R.O. Fourchard (Ed.), Entreprises religieuses transnationales en Afrique de l'ouest. Ibadan and Paris: IFRA, Karthala, pp. 43-72.

Nelson, Kristina (1985): The Art of Reciting of the Qur'an, Cairo and New York: The American University Press.

(1993): "The Sound of the Divine in Daily Life", in: Donna Lee Bowen and Evelyn Early (Eds.), Everyday Life in the Muslim Middle East, Bloomington, IN: Indiana University Press, pp. 257-261.

Otayek, Réné (Ed.) (1993): Le radicalisme islamique au sud du Sahara, Paris, Talence: Éditions Karthala.

Purpura, Allyson (1997): Knowledge and Agency. The Social Relations of Islamic Expertise in Zanzibar Town. Ph.D. Thesis: New York.

Reveyrand- Coulon, Odile (1993): "Les énoncés féminins de l'Islam", in: J.-F. Bayart (Ed.), Religion et modernité politique en Afrique noire. Dieu pour tous et chacun pour soi, Paris: Karthala, pp. 63-100.

Roberts, Allen and Roberts Nooter, Mary (2003): A Saint in the City. Sufi Arts of Urban Senegal, Los Angeles, CA.: UCLA Fowler Museum of Cultural History.

Robinson, Francis (1993): "Technology and Religious Change. Islam and the Impact of Print", in: Modern Asian Studies 27:1, pp. 229-251.

Sanankoua, Bintou (1991): "Les associations féminines musulmanes à Bamako", in: L. Brenner and B. Sanankoua (Eds.), L'enseignement islamique au Mali, Bamako: Editions Jamana, pp. 105-126.

Schafer, Murray R. (1977): Our Sonic Environment and the Soundscape. The Tuning of the World, Rochester: VT: Destiny Books.

Schmidt, Leigh Eric (2000): Hearing Things. Religion, Illusion and the American Enlightenment, Cambridge, MA: Harvard University Press.

Schulz, Dorothea (2001): Perpetuating the Politics of Praise. Jeli Praise Singers, Radios and Political Mediation in Mali, Köln: Rüdiger Köppe Verlag.

(2003): "Political Factions, Ideological Fictions. The Controversy over the Reform of Family Law in Democratic Mali", in: Islamic Law and Society 10:1, pp. 132-164.

(2006): "Promises of (Im)mediate Salvation. Islam, Broadcast Media, and the Remaking of Religious Experience in Mali", in: American Ethnologist 33:2, pp. 210-229.

(2007): "Evoking Moral Community, Fragmenting Muslim Discourse. Sermon Audio-recordings and the Reconfiguration of Public Debate in Mali", in: Journal for Islamic Studies 27, pp. 39-72.

(2008a): "Piety's Manifold Embodiments. Muslim Women's Quest for Moral Renewal in Urban Mali", in: Journal for Islamic Studies, 28, pp. 26-93, Special Issue on 'Reconfigurations of Gender Relations in Africa' guest-edited by Marloes Janson and Dorothea Schulz.

(2008b): "(Re)Turning to Proper Muslim Practice. Islamic Moral Renewal and Women's Conflicting Constructions of Sunni Identity in Urban Mali", in: Africa Today 54:4, pp. 21-43.

(2011): Muslims and New Media in West Africa. Pathways to God, Bloomington: Indiana University Press.

(2012): "Dis/embodying Authority. Female 'Preachers' and the Ambivalences of Mass-mediated Speech in Urban Mali", in: International Journal of Middle East Studies 44:1, [forthcoming].

Simone, AbdouMaliq (2001): "Straddling the Divides. Remaking Associational Life in the Informal African City", in: International Journal of Urban and Regional Research 25:1, pp. 102-117.

Soares, Benjamin (2005): Islam and the Prayer Economy. History and Authority in a Malian Town, Ann Arbor: University of Michigan Press.

Sterne, Jonathan (2003): The Audible Past, Durham: Duke University Press.

Stoller, Paul (1984): "Sound in Songhay Cultural Experience", in: American Ethnologist 11:3, pp. 559-573.

Stolow, Jeremy (2005): "Religion and/as Media", in: Theory, Culture and Society 22:4, pp. 119-145.

Sule, Barbara and Starratt, Priscilla (1991): "Islamic Leadership Positions for Women in Contemporary Kano Society", in: C. Coles and B. Mack (Eds.), Hausa Women in the Twentieth Century, Madison, WI: The University of Wisconsin Press, pp. 29-49.

Trevor, Jean (1975): "Western Education and Muslim Fulani/Hausa Women in Sokoto, Northern Nigeria", in: Godfrey Brown and Mervyn Hiske (Eds.), Conflict and Harmony in Education in Tropical Africa, London: Allen & Unwin, pp. 247-270.

Turner, Bryan (2007): "Religious Authority and the New Media", in: Theory, Culture and Society 24:2, pp. 117-134.

Umar, Muhammad S. (2001): "Education and Islamic Trends in Northern Nigeria, 1970s-1990s", in: Africa Today 48:2, pp.127-150.

van der Veer, Peter (1995): "The Secular Production of Religion", in: Etnofoor 8:2, pp. 5-14.

Volpi, Frederic and Turner, Bryan (2007): "Introduction. Making Islamic Authority Matter", in: Theory, Culture and Society 24:2, pp. 1-19.

Wright, Bonnie (1989): "The Power of Articulation", in: W. Arens and Ivan Karp (Eds.), Creativity of Power. Cosmology and Action in African, Washington: Smithsonian Institution Press.

Zahan, Dominique (1963): La dialectique du verbe chez les Bambara, Paris: Mouton & Co.

Zuckerkand, Victor (1956): Sound and Symbol. Music and the External World, Princeton, NJ: Princeton University Press.

A Shrine Gone Urban

The Shrine of Data Ganj Bukhsh, Lahore, as a City within the City

LINUS STROTHMANN

INTRODUCTION

The title of this volume, *Prayer in the City*, suggests that there is something particular about the relationship between religious practice, its locality, e.g. a mosque or a shrine, and the cities they are located in. My starting point in this paper, therefore, is the question, what is a shrine in relation to a city? This is obviously not a question to be answered in general. But we can imagine the range to go from shrines that, although geographically situated in a particular city, have little connection to it or influence on it, to cities that originated in a shrine, grew around it and have become inseparable from it.

In South Asia shrines have often been seen as largely rural phenomena and until today most shrines are situated in small villages or in between settlements. This stems from a tradition of the saints to go 'into the wilderness', the space between villages, spending long periods of their lives outside of human settlements and often being buried there (Werth 1998). But with the growing population and rural to urban migration in the last century, many formerly rural shrines have become parts of cities.

One could assume that these shrines' relationships to the cities they became a part of would tend to be rather 'unspectacular', defined by little more than geographical proximity or inclusion. The contrary is the case in the example this article will explore. The shrine of the eleventh century saint Ali Hujwiri was situated outside the city of Lahore for nine out of its almost ten centuries of existence. And yet within the 80 years since it became enclosed by the city, the shrine has become not only a landmark *in* the city, but also a landmark *for* it.

This article explores the historical circumstances that eventually transformed this shrine, which was once considered as one among many, into Pakistan's largest and most complex sacred place. Besides this transformation, the complexity of the shrine is the second focus of attention. The main argument is that the shrine fulfills a number of functions for the city that cities traditionally provide for their surroundings. To develop this argument in detail I will first look at the political, economic and social dimensions of the shrine's relationship to the city. I then examine the shrine using a number of concepts used to describe and define city and urbanity. The consequences one can draw from the analogy between city and shrine for further research will be dealt with in the final section.

THE SHRINE BEFORE 1948

The shrine of Ali Hujwiri, commonly known as Data Ganj Bukhsh, was established after the saint died in 1072 AD. He had come to Lahore forty years earlier, migrating from Ghazni (today in Afghanistan) after having traveled widely throughout the Muslim world. The saint is known for his book, the Kashf Al-Mahjub, the first treatise on Sufism in Persian and the only written source available from the time, containing information about his life. The reasons for the saint to build his mosque outside Lahore and even on the opposite bank of the river Ravi are unknown. What is known is that the mosque and shelter the saint built and used in his lifetime later became the place where he was buried. Many wished to be buried near the grave, especially the saint's disciples, so for many years the shrine was a grave surrounded by other graves. During the Mogul era the shrine consisted of a small marble platform without a dome. The dome was added for the first time in 1862, a time when a new mosque was built resembling the great Badshahi Mosque in design (Shahzad 2009).

Information about the shrine from the British period is sparse. Only the shrine's name and location are given, and no information about the number of regular visitors or about the architecture and setting can be found. What can be seen in maps from this period is that the shrine was still not part of the city in 1920 but was at the brink of becoming surrounded by it.

Lahore had grown rapidly with the establishment of the British railway system in North India, but the city grew mostly to the Southeast, East and North. It was therefore not until the 1930s that the shrine became surrounded by residential areas. Since there are no written sources on what the atmosphere of the shrine was like before partition, we rely on verbal accounts, of which there are few. Those that remember the shrine remember it to be a rather quiet and peaceful place and the few available pictures of the time support this view.

INDEPENDENCE AND THE TRANSFORMATION OF THE SHRINE

In 1948 British India became independent and Lahore became part of the newly established state of Pakistan, its border to India barely 30 km away from the city. The first consequence of this was a rapid growth of the Muslim population of Lahore, part of one of history's largest migration processes.[1] The area around the shrine had been only loosely populated by both Hindus and Muslims. As the Hindus moved away, it became one of the major areas where the arriving Muslims settled down, either in houses left by Hindus, or in newly built ones. From being a shrine surrounded by a graveyard and farms only 30 years earlier, it was now part of a densely populated neighborhood, which of course affected the number of visitors.

One reason for the shrine's rapid growth in visitors during the time may have originated in the fact that the shrine of Data Ganj Bukhsh was established at a time when institutionalized orders were unknown. It is therefore open to followers of different Sufi orders and furthermore to all those Muslims who arrived in Lahore after Partition. This is unlike other shrines, such as the then much more visited shrine of Mian Mir, which is also situated in Lahore but is closely associated with the Qadiri order.

With the increasing visitors the shrine became more and more important, and along with many others, it was nationalized by 1960. The largely secularized political elite of the independence era was skeptical about many of the activities in and around shrines.[2] Therefore, a Department for Religious Affairs and *awqaf* was established in 1960 under the '*awqaf* Ordinance' (Malik 1996: 59). The De-

---

1 From an estimated population of 150,000 in 1893, the city grew to 671,659 by 1941 and to twice this size in 1961 (1,296,477) (Mauldin 1963: 66). Assuming that before partition the Muslim population was around 60% and after partition around 90%, the actual increase of Muslims in Lahore was nearly 400% in these twenty years. Current estimates (Faiza 2009: 57) suggest a population of just above 8 million, making Lahore the second largest city in Pakistan and among the 30 largest in the world.

2 For a detailed description, see Jamal Malik (1996): *Colonialization of Islam, Dissolution of Traditional Institutions in Pakistan*.

partment has the power to take over any religious endowment (= *waqf* - pl. *awqaf*). The shrine of Data Ganj Bukhsh (the shrine is often just referred to as Data Darbar) was among the first ones run by the new provincial department. In order to justify the nationalization of the shrines and to counter the criticism from the former caretakers, called *sajjada nishins*, it was necessary to show the department's willingness to accommodate the pilgrims and take care of the architecture. As part of this, a *ghulam gardish* (a shaded area around the actual tomb) was built in the early 1960s which was then extended in the early 1970s. During this period in the 70s, both Zulfikar Ali Bhutto and the department wished to further extend the shrine, as it became clear that the number of pilgrims was exceeding the capacity of the complex. But it was not until 1979 that a competition was held for a new design, to eventually enlarge the shrine to nearly five times its size.

Bhutto had shown great interest in the shrine before and, with the help of the Iranian Shah, donated a large Golden Door to it, still visible inside the Golden Gate entrance of the shrine complex today. As has been pointed out both by Katherine Ewing (1997) and Jamal Malik (1996), Bhutto's interest in shrines can be attributed to his attempt to show close relations between the socialist government and Islam, in order to counter the association between socialism and atheism. Bhutto was among the first in a long line of politicians who took great interest in the shrine. The most prominent others were Zia ul-Haq and Nawaz Sharif.

Why is this particular shrine so appealing to politicians? A major reason lies in the fact that the saint Data Ganj Bukhsh is an uncontroversial figure, as will shortly be explained. This is significant when one is vying for political support from diverse social strata. A growing sector of Pakistani society and an important part of the economic elite have been influenced by Saudi Arabian Wahhabism and other Islamic reform movements, especially in the second half of the twentieth century. Many of these reformists are especially critical about traditions and practices linked to South Asian Sufism, such as the use of drugs, alcohol, dancing or viewing the pilgrimage to a shrine (including, e.g. the circling of the grave) as small *hajj*. Furthermore, the general concept prevalent in the region, that saints can help grant wishes by mediating between people and God, is seen as blasphemy. For a politician, a strong connection to a shrine can thus have a negative impact on the support he gets from these groups. Yet in the case of Data Darbar, controversy is sidestepped since the saint himself was a critic of many such traditional practices and is not known to have practiced anything forbidden by the Qur'an. While many saints in Pakistan are known for their poems, their affection for dancing and a very open and tolerant interpretation of Islam, the contrary is the case for Ali Hujwiri, who is as much a respected scholar, as a saint. Another reason for his political appeal is that he is widely considered the most important figure to spread Islam in and around Lahore. To visit his shrine can therefore also be (or is said to be) an act of respect for the historical person rather than for an imagined 'living' saint. As an informant put it, "I come here (to the shrine), not because I believe that he can help me, or fulfill my wishes, but because he is the reason I was born a Muslim."

I will now turn to the architectural changes made to the shrine from 1982 onwards, because they changed the shrine drastically in terms of its size and functions. I see many of the changes as an attempt, especially by Zia ul-Haq and later Nawaz Sharif, to transform the shrine from a local place of veneration into a shrine serving as a national monument and political stage at the same time.

As already mentioned, the first wishes to enlarge the shrine were articulated by Bhutto and the Department of Religious Affairs and *awqaf* in the early 1970s. By the time a competition was announced in 1979, Zia ul-Haq had taken power and was now also the chairman of the committee to choose the design. From the 28 designs, four were shortlisted and after harsh critique by the general, one was deemed appropriate.

Figure 1, New Mosque and one of the Minarets as seen from the Dome of the shrine

Strothmann

It is obvious from the figure 1, showing the mosque and one minaret of the new complex, that no references to South Asian architecture were made and instead an almost futuristic look was chosen. We find a similar look in the Faisal Mosque of Islamabad, a gift from the Saudi King Faisal, built in the same period. Both projects used certain stylistic elements from other parts of the Muslim world, e.g. minarets in Turkish style at Data Darbar, or tent structures from the Bedouin nomads at Faisal Mosque. The complete lack of local architectural styles can in both cases be seen as an attempt to show that there is only one Islam and that the appearance of the building itself should therefore not reveal its location.

Figure 2 shows the layout plan of the shrine and also the larger area surrounding the shrine, including the markets facing the complex that I will discuss later.

Figure 2, Data Darbar and Surroundings 2009

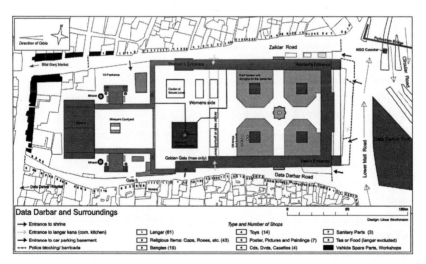

Strothmann

What did the enlargement contain and which changes came with them? The enlargement of the shrine contained first of all a new mosque and courtyard to the west of the shrine. The mosque is the third largest in Pakistan today. The complex has been made to be attractive also to those who have no relation to the saint but simply wish to pray in the new mosque, which, for example, has air-conditioning. In a second phase, a large roof garden was built to the east covering two large basements. Today the upper one, directly beneath the roof-garden is used to house a concert hall, a library, seminar rooms and a *madrassa*, as well as a police station. The lower basement is a large car park.

The huge amount of new spaces structured the shrine much more in terms of its functions. While the space in front of the grave used to be used for musical concerts, distributing food, reading the Qur'an, or listening to the lectures of a *pir* etc., now each of these activities has their specific place. With this re-allocation of space also came a much stronger control of the shrine by the administration. Thus, spontaneous concerts are now impossible. The regular sessions of *qawwali* (the most common form of music played at South Asian shrines) that take place throughout the night Thursdays at most other shrines, are now strictly confined to the afternoon time between noon and evening prayers. The administration itself grew with the complex and with time, more and more institutions settled within the complex because of the availability of space.

The growth of visitors to the shrine that originally made the enlargements necessary continued when the complex was built and after it was finished (1999). According to Katherine Ewing (1997: 88), it is in fact the only shrine in Lahore, which has gained popularity during the latter half of the 20th century, and it is considered by many to be the most important shrine of the city, or even the country. For the Department of Religious Affairs and *awqaf*, the enlargements have also been a financial success. Even though the construction of the complex was expensive and was even halted in the late 1980s due to a lack of funding, the number of visitors has increased steadily and donations made into the cash boxes placed inside the complex have risen accordingly. They have turned the complex into the main source of income for the department with a share of approximately 30% of its total annual income. Because the department is financially independent from the government of the Punjab, this shrine has become its main commitment.

Extending the shrine and the political appropriation of the place had a major influence on the relationship between the shrine and the immediate surroundings, as well as the city at large. The next three sections explore this relationship in detail.

The Economic Dimension: the Markets around the Shrine

The economic importance of the shrine for the Department of Religious Affairs and *awqaf* has already been mentioned. But apart from the donations made at the shrine, the complex itself also provides livelihood to a large number of people and over the years an important marketplace has sprung up outside the shrine. The markets around the shrine first evolved during the time when the surrounding residential areas were established. The oldest parts of the markets are found opposite the Golden Gate entrance to the south of the shrine. Almost all houses on this side of the shrine belong to the *biraderi* (in this case the extended family) of the *sajjada nishin*, the traditional caretakers. After losing control over the shrine, donations to the shrine were no longer available as a source of income and instead they now relied to a much greater extent on the shops.

Today almost all houses facing the shrine are used for shops. With an estimated number of visitors ranging between 30,000 on an average day and 60,000[3] on Thursdays and Fridays, the shrine is attracting more people than many of the bazaars around the city. The shops and their assortment can be seen in figure 2. The most prominent shops are selling *langar*. This is food, mainly lentils and rice, which is bought by the visitors of the shrine for distribution among the poor but also to other visitors of the shrine. The distribution of a *deg*, a large pot, typically takes place in front of the shop or in a specifically allocated distribution lot that is part of the shrine complex. The food is distributed in the name of the saint, and very often the distribution takes place after a wish put forward at the shrine in prayer has been fulfilled. The amount of food is extraordinary. Estimates based on how much food needs to be sold in all shops just to pay the rent for the shops and the employees show that on an average day at least ten thousand people can be served three full meals. On Thursdays and Fridays the number may be doubled. Additionally, many Lahoris bring food for distribution from home.

The social dimension of this will be discussed in detail later. For the economy of the markets the *langar* shops are the most important not only because of their number but also because they have most employees per shop, thus making this the largest labor market around the shrine. A shop always has a cook and someone standing in front of the shop offering the *langar* to passersby. Most shops also have employees walking around inside the complex with small signs showing the price for the different sizes of *degs*. The shops close to the car park entrances also have employees offering the service to the drivers waiting in line to be checked and let in to the basement.

The next important items for sale around the shrine are religious items: roses, caps that are worn inside the complex and *chaddars*, grave sheets that are thrown onto the grave. This category is followed by overpriced shops selling bangles and others selling toys. These items have little connection to practices at the shrine. The reason they are sold here is that many visitors to the shrine are families from the villages around Lahore. As shopkeepers admit, the villagers often

---

3   The numbers of visitors are based on shoe-counting at the entrances done by the administration (verbal communication).

do not know where the markets for these items can be found and thus have little choice but to accept the higher prices. Additionally the fact that the item is bought at the shrine can give extra value to it. Other categories include shops selling posters and paintings of the saint and the shrine, shops selling DVDs and CDs, mostly containing *qawwali* sessions, and a number of shops that sell food and tea. As can be seen on the map, only very few shops sell sanitary equipment. These were the typical items sold in the northern market before it was facing the complex. These shops still pay a normal rent, comparable to rents in other bazaars. All other shops pay rents that can vary from 200-800 Rs per day, depending primarily on their location (proximity to the main entrances). How high this rent is, becomes apparent when compared to rents for the shops selling mechanical spare parts in the markets adjacent to the shrine in the west. Here the rent for a shop per month can be as low as 1000 Rs thus comparable to the rent per day in the most expensive areas of the markets around the shrine.

Assuming that the market is saturated on the basis of how many shops can still give a surplus, it is possible to estimate the total economic exchange in it. For this I have calculated the number of employees, the rent paid, and a minimum surplus for all shops which adds up to a minimum of around 170 mio. Rs annually. The actual number could easily be twice as much and becomes revealing when compared to the annual donations at the shrine which amount to nearly 200 mio. Rs (July 2008 – June 2009). The money spent by visitors outside the shrine and in some way connected to the visit are thus in the range of what is donated inside the shrine.

So far I have only looked at formal employment in the shops. The number of people renting a shop or working as employees can be estimated to be around 800 to 1000. While this is an impressive number of people indirectly depending on the shrine, it is small compared to the number of people working in the surroundings in the informal sector or those depending on the shrine for daily food and shelter.

The informal employment around the shrine comprises of people selling items from carts, hawker's trays or from their hands. Many of them sell sweets or plastic bags, which are bought by people to bring *langar* home from the shrine. Additionally, criminal activities, including prostitution, kidnappings and drug dealing, secure livelihoods for a number of people, although these activities have recently declined. Then there are many people who find a new occupation on a daily basis, one day begging, the next day reselling *langar*, and the next helping drivers of cars to cross the road after leaving the car park, and asking for a couple of rupees for it. The police and administration often gloss them as beggars and drug addicts. The administration estimates that around 4000 people are permanently living in the streets around the shrine. They are considered irritating and at times have to deal with abusive treatment. On the other hand, for this very large group the shrine offers food, water, sanitary facilities and shelter from rain, cold and sun. The shrine is therefore also an important social center in the city, something the next section will show in detail.

The Social Dimension: Social Welfare and the Redistribution of Wealth in the Name of the Saint

Langar being bought in the shops around the shrine accounts for approximately half of what is distributed on a daily basis. Many Lahoris bring the food for distribution from home and many also join with work colleagues or friends to regularly distribute *langar* at the shrine. For this the work is typically divided among the members of a group so that some collect money, some buy groceries and meat, some bring the ingredients to a professional cook and some pick up the food and bring it to the shrine. For the members of such groups, organizing *langar* is as much a part of the visit to the shrine as the prayers said at the grave. In their view, the food is in fact a gift from the saint; they are only the ones helping him in his effort to secure the basic needs of the community. Because the *langar* comes from the saint ideologically, it carries blessings (*baraka*) and almost anyone coming to the shrine will therefore participate in eating *langar*, be they hungry or not, poor or rich. An important aspect of this is that no one is stigmatized for accepting the free food at the shrine. Several thousand people live off the food distributed at the shrine on a daily basis.

The shrine offers sanitation and shelter as has been mentioned, but also medical care through an associated hospital one hundred meters to the southwest of the shrine. The Data Darbar Hospital offers treatment free of charge to more than 180,000 patients annually, with almost half of them coming for eye treatment. The hospital has a growing annual budget of around 75 million Rs and among the fourteen medical dispensaries at various shrines also financed by the Department for Religious Affairs and *awqaf* in the Punjab, it is the only hospital comparable in scale and competence to government hospitals run under the Department of Health.[4]

The hospital dates back to the time when the Department took over the shrine and used one room of the shrine as a dispensary. Because there was a piece of land that belonged to the shrine but was not directly attached to it geographically, it was decided that it be used for a hospital in 1962, only two years after the

---

4   Government of the Punjab, (2009).

shrine came under government control. The reasons for attaching a dispensary and later a hospital to the shrine have to be seen in the context of the nationalization of the shrines as a policy by the newly established state:

"In the context of nationalization of religious endowments, an attempt was made, both under Ayub and later under Bhutto, to reduce the traditional religious authority of the shrineholders, by formally propagating an emancipation of the pilgrims to the shrines. In order to do so it was necessary to play down the shrine or at least to represent it as a worldly institution and thus to take away its religious character. Up to this stage the ordinary murid had no direct access to God. The saint was a mediator. The holder of the shrine had taken over the position of the saint and now functioned as the mediator between the pilgrim and the pir. The saint, and therefore the *mujawir* or *sajjadah nashin*, 'monopolized' access to God, and only through him was the path (*tariqa*) to salvation experienced. This meditating role was now supposed to be rendered superfluous through the activities of the *awqaf* Department."

"From now on every citizen, provided only that he was a 'good Muslim', was supposed to be able to enter directly into dialogue with God. Thus the saints or shrineholders acquired more mundane features and their annual feasts (arabic *'urs* literally 'marriage', i.e. the union with God) became public holidays and were consequently secularized. *The miraculous healing power of the saints was replaced by the building of hospitals in the endowments.*" (Malik 1996: 61, emph. added)

It is disputable whether the government succeeded in its effort to 'take away the religious character', and whether the hospitals actually 'replaced' the healing power of the saint. When someone is sick, their families still visit the shrines and no one sees this as a competing healing method to treatment in a hospital. The medical superintendant of the hospital puts it like this:

"You see we have a very strong belief that healing comes from God the Almighty. We (the doctors) are just playing our role. So I also pray for my health, and when I pray, I can pray in my room, I can pray in my house, I can pray in the shrine and I don´t stop the treatment [sic]." (Data Darbar Hospital, Nov. 2009)

This underlines the fact that the treatment in hospitals and the visiting of the shrines for spiritual blessing are two possibilities that are not considered contradictory, but rather as complementary to each other. It is therefore also not surprising that most patients in the Data Darbar Hospital do not make a specific connection between hospital and shrine or even see the hospital as being a part of the shrine. After all, there are many institutions, shops, streets, etc. in Lahore carrying the saint's name and the name could simply be given to the hospital because it is close to the shrine.

The connection made between the two institutions is thus largely one made by the Department of *awqaf* itself. As stated on its official website, among others, the aim of the department is:

"To make the holy places centers of social, cultural and spiritual regeneration of Muslims in accordance with the dictates of Islam." (Government of the Punjab 2009)

And the Medical Superintendant formulates it this way:

"This hospital started in a single room in 1960 in the vicinity of the shrine. Because they thought that when there is a surplus of money and the teaching of the saint is to look after the community, so how can you look after the community? By giving them health, medical facility, by giving them the teaching of Islam and by looking after their daily needs [sic]." (Data Darbar Hospital, Nov. 2009)

The hospital is thus an important institution displaying the department's aim to transform shrines into social centers and it legitimizes government control of the shrine with an Islamic ideology. While a discourse about the government control is taking place in Pakistan, for most of the people living in the area around the shrine, this aspect of the hospital is irrelevant: it is simply a hospital offering free treatment. For this treatment many patients even come from other cities, mainly because of the hospital's excellent reputation in eye operations.

Besides the hospital there are other institutions of social welfare situated around the shrine. As a reaction to a growing number of reports in newspapers about the abuse and kidnapping of children and young adults at the shrine, an NGO was established in 2001 by a social worker named Chaudry Muhammad Bashir. Although established because of the general situation in Lahore, Data Darbar was seen as central in the aim of bringing runaway children back to their families. The NGO has its main office in Iqbal Town, a part of Lahore, and additionally there are small counters near the railway station and at Data Darbar.

The counter at the shrine is a three by three meter metal lodge, placed on the Circular Road across the street from the shrine, where two social workers sit from around 5 a.m. to 10:30 p.m., sometimes also until late hours in the night. According to both these workers and the director and initiator of the NGO, on average five children are brought to them every day. This is around half of all the children the NGO picks up in Lahore. In more than 90% of the cases they are between ten and seventeen years old, most of them boys.

The boys run away from home mostly because of domestic violence. When I interviewed some of the boys at the NGO's main office, and asked why they had come to this particular shrine, they said they came to Data Darbar to pay homage. Mr. Chaudhry's view was different:

"The truth is far from this. They go there because of the food, not to pay homage. Even in their school they get this information, the boys talk about it, that there is this place, the shrine of Data Ganj Bukhsh, where there is food all the time." (NGO Office in Iqbal Town: Dec. 2009)

All children that were asked did in fact eat at the shrine and it seemed to be a major reason for them to go there, besides being one of the only places they knew in the city. None of them said that they went to the shrine in order to ask the saint for help with a problem they were facing, which is a typical answer from young adults who are from Lahore. The children come from all over Pakistan including the northern areas or places as far away as Karachi (a 24 to 30 hour train distance), but most are from the Punjab. The NGO is not related to the Department of *awqaf* and Religious Affairs or connected to the shrine's administration. Starting the NGO had nothing to do with the shrine in particular, "but it was just the place where most children go", said Mr. Bashir.

Apart from the social welfare around the shrine, there are also two institutions within the complex offering social welfare in the form of free education. One of them is a *madrassa*, with around 180-200 students, most of whom get a scholarship covering accommodation and food in addition to their classes. Another one is an industrial school for young women to learn basic crafts like sewing in order to later earn a living.

The administration of the shrine also gives out funds to young women for their marriage expenses. For this a written application can be handed in by the families on every first Monday of the month. A committee then decides which families get the money, and this leads us to the last dimension of the shrine presented in this paper. The members of this, but also of other, committees are in almost all cases from the political elite. In this particular case, for example, all members are wives of major politicians from Lahore. Often the decision on who gets the money is dependent upon the relationship between the needy families and the political party of the committee members rather than on the needs of the families.

The Political Dimension: The Shrine as a Political Stage and a Space for Defining Islam.

The circumstances under which the shrine was enlarged and the political aspect involved have already been mentioned above. Additionally, politicians have taken part in decision making at various levels. First and foremost, although the Department of Religious Affairs and *awqaf* is run by bureaucrats, the highest posts within the department are appointed by the Chief Minister of the Punjab. Secondly, a Religious Purpose Committee (RPC) consisting of politicians was set up after the shrine was nationalized to decide about long term developments at the shrine. The members of this RPC are appointed by the chairman, who in turn again is appointed by the Chief Minister of the Punjab. Currently the chairman is Ishaq Dar, a former finance minister of Pakistan and one of the highest ranked politicians within the PML-N party of Nawaz Sharif. The RPC decides upon matters that go beyond mere administration of the shrine, e.g., the decision made in 2008 to segregate genders more strictly inside the complex. They also need to approve architectural changes. How this can become an important issue becomes clear from the following example.

Until December 2009, the roof garden of the shrine consisted of four large grass patches. In most South Asian shrines, a courtyard with trees is central to the activities at the shrine. When the design for extension was made, the roof garden was to fill this gap. The grass patches were used by visitors to sit and eat, discuss and sometimes even to sleep on. Underneath the grassy areas was the *sama* hall, the basement for musical concerts. When rifts in the ceiling were discovered, they were explained as caused by the layer of soil above carrying too much water in it. When one of the large-scale donors of the shrine heard of the problem he offered to pay for the complete roof garden to be covered in marble and with the approval of the RPC, work started in December 2009. According to an informant from within the department, this was done even though there were serious concerns that the construction would become too heavy. Although officially the reason was that the marble would be easier to clean, unofficially the grassy areas had long been a 'thorn in the side' for some of the higher ranked officials, because they thought that all activities inside the complex that had a recreational rather than a religious character should be forbidden. People should visit the shrine and mosque to say their prayers, not to eat and sleep. This idea is reflected in the fact that in the month before the grass was removed, the guards of the shrine were regularly controlling the area for sleeping people and even woke them up with sticks. At prayer times they would also tell everyone resting on the patches to leave the area and go to the mosque. Even though this might not seem like a noteworthy development, it radically changes the way visitors behave at the shrine and are able to behave, and is in strong contrast to how many people imagine a visit to a shrine to be.

The decisions about what is appropriate behavior inside the complex have strong implications mainly because the shrine is visited by so many people and because it is viewed by many as the most important Pakistani shrine. Thus, activities are covered by the media, such as during the time of 'urs, the annual festival of the saint' death anniversary in the Islamic calendar.

For the department the shrine has become an important stage to clearly show what is considered right and wrong Islamic behavior. Apart from defining Islam in this way, additionally there are other institutions under the control of the department that have an influence on the national discourse on Islam. Most important in this regard is the *madrassa* mentioned before, and, linked to it, a research center publishing a quarterly magazine on Sufism. The research center also organizes the program of seminars given at the shrine during the time of 'urs. These seminars are held in the mosque throughout all three days of the festival, when an estimated 1 million people visit the shrine. Other than the *qawwali* that also takes place inside the complex but is heard only in the basement, these seminars or lectures are transmitted via loudspeakers to all areas of the complex and can even be heard in some of the streets outside. The topics of the lectures by leading Islamic clerics from Pakistan are given to them by the research officer in the research center of the shrine, paid by the Department of Religious Affairs and *awqaf*. He also edits the quarterly journal on Sufism and one of his main concerns is to make sure that neither the lectures nor the articles contain anything that could be considered sectarian. The magazine is printed by the department and is sent to all major universities in Pakistan as well as the leading scholars in the field.

This participation in the discourse on Sufism and Islam in Pakistan is not restricted to the level of academia as can be seen in regard to the students of the *madrassa*. Almost all students come from the rural areas of Pakistan and will return to their respective villages when their education at the shrine has been completed. Many will become the imam of a local mosque and thus become a multiplier for ideas brought to them in the *madrassa*. As many of the students mentioned in interviews, they were regularly confronted with practices in their hometown and villages that they now perceived as "unislamic". In many cases they were able to exert influence on such behavior at home. One example given was that the sisters and mother of one student painted their fingernails without knowing that this would make the nails underneath impervious to the ablution before prayer. Asked if their families and friends at home were willing to change or abolish practices after they had been told to do so by the students, the answers were mostly positive.

At the time of *'urs*, media attention on the shrine is at its peak and politicians also take advantage of this to show their connection to the saint. It has been common for years that the central ritual of laying a new *chaddar* on the grave at the beginning of *'urs* is done by the Chief Minister of the Punjab. He is often accompanied by a number of Ministers and the whole ritual is transmitted live on television. Additionally the shrine has been popular as a place to hold public speeches, e.g. when Nawaz Sharif returned to Pakistan in 2007 after having been exiled in 1999.

Maybe because of its close association with the Pakistani state, but most certainly because it is one of the busiest places in the city, the shrine has long been under threat of an attack by fundamentalist groups. It was hit in a twin suicide attack claiming more than 50 casualties on 1 July 2010. Although many of the fundamentalist groups generally condemn practices at the shrines, so far attacks on shrines had been an exception. The fact that Data Darbar is a shrine largely exempt from the practices that are controversial, begs the conclusion that this particular attack was one aimed at the shrine as a political space as much as a religious one.

So far we have looked at three dimensions of the shrine that of course are deeply intermingled with its religious dimension. Many of the employees of the Department of Religious Affairs and *awqaf* see themselves also as employees of the saint, helping him to help others. Likewise, there are many shopkeepers who have a long relationship with the saint. As the examples of the hospital and the groups distributing *langar* have shown, the social welfare at the shrine is also closely linked to religious beliefs and practices. The same goes for the political dimension and it is therefore important to note here that the three dimensions presented are the result rather of organizing data than of local realities. The reason that I choose to present them lies in the fact that much has been written about the spiritual and religious aspects of South Asian shrines and less about the other dimensions. These dimensions, however, lead us to rethink what a shrine is to a city. In the next section I will therefore explore how fruitful a comparison between characteristics given to cities and those we can now give to the shrine can be, in order to understand more of the complexity of a sacred place.

Classical Attributes Defining the City/Urbanity: Density, Centrality, and Heterogeneity

The most obvious and common-sense definitions of a city rely on the concepts of density and centrality and are based mostly on demographic and economic indicators.[5] Density is not only the density of population, but also of commerce, political institutions, education, entertainment and other elements. Centrality is most often measured as a relative surplus of functions by one city over another. A city relying on other cities in key sectors such as administration and education has a lower centrality than a city that can offer these to others. Lahore is known for its many colleges and universities, among them the most prestigious of the country, giving the city the highest level of centrality in this regard. But when it comes to the economic or political sector, it is ranked second to Karachi and Islamabad respectively. I will now look at how the concepts of density and centrality can be applied to the shrine of Data Ganj Bukhsh before turning to more sociological views of city and urbanity that evolved during the twentieth century.

The shrine is situated just outside the southwestern end of the Walled City. As I have already mentioned, the city grew around the Walled City, mostly to the southeast. The Mall Road built during the colonial period is generally considered the centre of the city today. Most of the important political as well as educational institutions are situated in this area. The richer residential areas of Lahore are located in the Cantonment and Defense, both to the southeast, about ten kilometers from the shrine. The Walled City and the areas around it including the Bilal Ganj area surrounding the shrine are considered poor. Many of the houses in this area used to be single family homes, consisting of a house plus courtyard. Today each house is inhabited by several families, normally occupying one story each and most of the courtyards have been sacrificed to make further residences. In terms of density, the walled city and some of the areas around the shrine can be considered the centre of Lahore.

However, as an attribute given to the shrine, density is closely linked to the *'urs* festival. During the time of the festival, approximately one million people visit the shrine, most of whom live in Lahore. A large number also camps on all available grass patches around the shrine up to one kilometer away. These tent cities have the character of temporal cities (a comparison often made, see e.g. Schielke in this volume), but at the same time everything that happens normally, happens now with much stronger intensity, be it the musical concerts, the com-

---

5   E.g. "The traditional distinction between the urban and the non-urban relied on a hierarchical organisation of density" (Segal and Verbakel 2008: 7).

mercial activities, the devotional practices or simply the amount of food distributed. In these days the city itself seems to be condensed to the area around the
shrine.

Outside the time of '*urs*, the shrine and its surrounding still have the highest
density of population, traffic, crime, and commercial activity of the city. The
markets described earlier are the only ones in Lahore open 24 hours, 7 days a
week. This indicates that the area around the shrine also has a high centrality
within the city. It is an important market not only for items related to the visit of
the shrine, but it is also one of the few places where one can find food all night.
And although crimes have decreased due to a massive police contingent appointed at the shrine, it is still one of the main magnets for informal labor, prostitution
and drug dealing. The high centrality is evident also in the domain of religion, a
fact less obvious than one might assume. Shrines of Muslim saints are an ubiqui-
ty in Pakistan, urban as well as rural. But as has been shown, the shrine of Data
Ganj Bukhsh offers on the one hand a unique stage for public appearances of
politicians and serves as a role model for other shrines. On the other hand, important institutions with regard to the discourse on Islam are situated inside the
complex.

Another example that shows the shrine's surplus in function is the *qawwali*
sessions held every Thursday afternoon. Even though they have been reduced in
length, the musicians consider the session at Data Darbar the most important of
all such sessions at shrines. "Data Darbar is the Academy of *Qawwali*" is a
common saying among them. For many it is also an important stage to get other
engagements, because people from outside Lahore come to the sessions to look
for musicians for their local shrines and festivals.

The fact that people come from all over Pakistan to get eye-treatment in the
hospital and the fact that children who run away from their families in Karachi,
Multan or Gilgit, travel all the way to Lahore in order to stay at the shrine further
exemplify the shrine's functional surplus and high centrality.

Density and centrality, although important factors for defining cities, say little about their sociological character. The sociological peculiarities of cities can
be subsumed under the notion of urbanity. In one of the most important papers
for the conceptualization of cities and urbanity, Louis Wirth wrote in 1938. "The
characterization of a community as urban on the basis of size alone is obviously
arbitrary" (1938: 4). He also suggested that "[f]or sociological purposes a city
may be defined as a relatively large, dense, and permanent settlement of socially
heterogeneous individuals" (Ibid. 8). The dimension of heterogeneity or diversity
was a new concept and focused on a characteristic difficult to measure. At first
the various different forms of labor were the main indicators for this heteroge-

neity. But with growing interest in the city as a sociological field following the Chicago School, heterogeneity became an attribute of almost everything connected with cities. Heterogeneity replaced density as a key attribute of urbanity.[6] But with growing segregation this heterogeneity has changed form. While cities like Lahore still harbor people from diverse religious backgrounds, places and classes, these people live in very different parts of the city, many of which are large gated communities.

Data Darbar stands out as one of the few places where it is possible to see the richest members of society interact personally with the poorest. This does not only happen when an industrialist distributes *langar* to the beggars, but also when he too takes part in eating *langar* with others. With few exceptions that have evolved mainly because of security concerns, anyone from any part of society can sit next to anyone else – when taking off shoes, when doing ablution, when eating or in prayer. Because the saint has not had a sufi order (see above) defining him and positioning him within the discourse of right and wrong, true and false Islam, he has maintained a sort of neutrality. In an interview with a communist activist, the saint was presented as one of the first communists, while the same saint is described by others as a pious Muslim, a friend of God, or imagined as a living *pir*, seen in dreams and visions at the shrine and putting in a good word for the pilgrim to the shrine. The shrine can therefore be regarded as a place of comunitas in Turner's (1974) sense of the term, or, to turn to more recent debates, the shrine constitutes a part of what can be called 'public space'.

Today heterogeneity has long been surpassed by notions like that of 'public place' as the major concepts for discussions among urban geographers, planners, sociologists and philosophers dealing with cities. The next section therefore looks at how some of the more recent discussions on urbanity relate to the shrine.

PUBLIC SPACE AND THE CITY AS A LANDSCAPE OF REPRESENTATIONS

Dealing also with Muslim shrines, Ahmed A. Zayed sees public places as "interactive, democratic, and meaningful places" and states that "[t]he salient feature of a public place is that it is a place owned by all people, a place in which individuals learn how to behave together" (2009: 104). This aspect of public space is extremely important to the city as is also emphasized by Segal and Verbakel:

---

6   *Urbanism without Density* is the title of an article by Segal and Verbakel (2008).

"Its role and place in the city as a space of gathering and exchange has been treated as a kind of 'glue' that holds together the city and promises to generate urban coherence and active use. Yet this notion has undergone substantial changes. Rather than a singular, continuous sphere or space, the public today is better understood as a fragmentary interplay of multiple publics and multiple groups." (2008: 8)

We can easily see how this is reflected in the shrine of Data Ganj Bukhsh: not only do many people feel that at the shrine they are somehow connected to others venerating the saint, but the space itself is also used to teach "individuals how to behave together" by the state agency controlling the place. This questions, of course, in how far the shrine is actually 'public' in the above sense, that it is 'owned by all people'. Although principally right because it is under state control, this control is to a large extent executed by individuals, be they politicians, administrators or as has been shown, industrialists who act as donors to the shrine and thus have the power to change it architecturally. These individuals' connection to the shrine is based not on a democratic vote, but is a consequence of political alliance and economic potency. On the other hand, the shrine is a place of public debate as has been shown in the example of the *madrassa* and research center, and it is even a place of conflict and contestation as the terrorist attacks have sadly shown. "The nature of the city as a clashing point for diverse subjectivities, ethnicities, corporealities and spatialities" (Amin and Graham 1997: 413) is thus evident in the shrine.

The power to define and represent is also evident in the notion of cities as "key sites of representation" (Ibid. 412) that emerged in the post-structuralist and postmodern debates in almost any field concerned with human activity. But what is represented? In the example of Data Darbar we find that a local shrine that had represented South Asian traditions architecturally, and also in terms of its inner structure and function, was changed drastically in almost all regards. The idea behind these changes was that of a unified, international Islam, and as a result, the shrine is now a somehow delocalized place. Whether or not this has been accomplished goes beyond the scope of this paper. But the shrine continues to change. Recently a proposal was made to replace the floor of the mosque's courtyard with new marble. Because they would be whiter, they would reflect more of the sunlight, thus staying cooler and more comfortable for the visitors to the shrine. The donor willing to pay for this is a regular visitor to the Prophet's Mosque in Medina, where the idea to change the floor came from. The shrine as a 'site of representation' is becoming more and more important with the growing media attention given to it, which in turn is a result of its appropriation by major Pakistani politicians.

Apart from characteristics like density, centrality, heterogeneity and the concepts of public space and that of the city as a landscape of representation, there are analogies between city and shrine that are less important and will therefore only be mentioned briefly. One is the legal status, that for a long time secured cities certain rights and was given to them because of certain functions or buildings (e.g. the presence of a cathedral in some regions of medieval Europe) and likewise is an important aspect of shrines (the status as *waqf* has legal implications). Another analogy can be found in the territorial demarcation of both cities and shrines although this has become obsolete for most cities today and not all shrines have visible boundaries to distinguish them from their surroundings.

CONCLUSION: HETEROTOPIA OR FROM SHRINE COMPLEX TO COMPLEX SHRINE

The most obvious consequence of the above analysis of an analogy between city and shrine is that a shrine is a complex place. In the same manner that the study and conceptualization of cities has evolved and become broader, the study of shrines can benefit greatly from new conceptualizations. For this it might be allowed at times to temporarily detach it from its religious, spiritual or symbolic meaning and look at the more profane or mundane features. This does not mean that they are not deeply connected and should always in the end be seen as different conceptualizations only. After all the continuing debate about cities, they are also still physical places, most of the time still densely populated, with high degrees of centrality, and so on.

Turning back to the opening question of this paper, what can we now say about the relationship between shrine and city? First of all, a shrine can become a central place for a city in various ways, reflected for example in economic indicators or in imagined landscapes. The city can rely on the shrine for social welfare or as a labor market not found elsewhere. The city is also represented in the shrine, mirrored by it and to some extent the shrine serves as the city's 'other', a space people either view as pure and holy, that constitutes almost a utopia, while for others it is a place of crimes and moral deterioration. To conceptualize this difficult relationship Foucault's classical 'definition' of heterotopia may help:

"There are also, probably in every culture, in every civilization, real places – places that do exist and that are formed in the very founding of society – which are something like counter-sites, a kind of effectively enacted utopia in which the real sites, all the other real sites that can be found within the culture, are simultaneously represented, contested, and inverted. Places of this kind are outside of all places, even though it may be possible to indicate their location in reality. Because these places are absolutely different from all the sites that they reflect and speak about, I shall call them, by way of contrast to utopias, heterotopias." (1986: 24)

While valid for many sacred places, Data Darbar is maybe not so much 'contested' as 'inverted', and even less 'outside of all places'.

Instead of one answer to the question what the shrine is to the city, we now have a number of answers. In terms of the classical definitions of city and urbanity, the shrine is something like a city within the city. In more recent discussions of what constitutes a city we can position the shrine alongside other public places, one part of a larger landscape of representations. And bringing all of this together we can also call the shrine a heterotopia.

This paper has concentrated on the shrine as a place. For most Lahoris, however, it is less a place than a representation of the saint. And the relationship between the saint and the city is maybe best described by Babsi Sidhwa in her introduction to a collection of writings on Lahore. As a Lahori, she will therefore have the last word:

"[...] the saint saved Lahore during the '65 and '71 wars with India. Sikh pilots are believed to have seen hands materialize out of the ether to catch the bombs and gently lay them to the ground. How else can one explain the quantity of unexploded bombs found in the area? They can't all be blamed on poor manufacture, surely." (Sidhwa 2005: XIII)

REFERENCES

Amin, A. and Graham, S. (1997): "The Ordinary City", in: Transactions of the Institute of British Geographers 22:4, pp. 411-429.

Ewing, Katherine (1997): Arguing Sainthood. Modernity, Psychoanalysis, and Islam, Durham and London: Duke University Press.

Mazhar, Faiza, and Jamal, Tabassum (2009): "Temporal Population Growth of Lahore", in: Journal of Scientific Research XXXIX:1, June, pp. 53-58.

Foucault, M., and Miskowiec, J. (1986): "Of Other Spaces", in: Diacritics 16:1, pp. 22-27.

Government of the Punjab: http://pportal.punjab.gov.pk retrieved on 14. Dec. 2009.

Malik, Jamal (1996): Colonialization of Islam. Dissolution of Traditional Institutions in Pakistan, Lahore: Vanguard Books.

Mauldin, Parker W. (1963): "Population and Population Policy in Pakistan", in: Marriage and Family Living 24:1, pp. 62-68.

Segal, R., and Verbakel, E. (2008): "Urbanism Without Density", in: Architectural Design 78:1, pp. 6-11.

Shahzad, Ghafer (2009): To Investigate the Forces Acting at a Religious Magnet. The Shrine in Urban Settlements and their Impact on the Immediate Surrounding. Unpublished Ph.D. Thesis: Lahore.

Sidhwa, B. (2005): City of Sin and Splendor. Writings on Lahore, New Delhi: Penguin Books.

Turner, Victor (1974): Dramas, Fields and Metaphors, Ithaca, NY: Cornell University Press.

Werth, Lukas (1998): "'The Saint Who Disappeared'. Saints of the Wilderness in Pakistani Village Shrines", in: P. Werbner and H. Basu (Eds.), Embodying Charisma. Modernity, Locality and the Performance of Emotion in Sufi Cults, London: Routledge, pp. 77-91.

Wirth, L. (1938): "Urbanism as a Way of Life", in: The American Journal of Sociology 44:1, pp. 1-24.

Zayed, A. A. (2009): "Saints (*awliya*), Public Places and Modernity in Egypt", in G. Stauth and S. Schielke (Eds.), Dimensions of Locality. Muslim Saints, Their Place and Space, Bielefeld: transcript Verlag, pp. 103-123.

SOURCES FOR INCOME AND EXPENDITURE

Chaudhry, M.T.A (Chief Administrator *awqaf* Punjab) (2009): Budget Estimates 2008-2009, Lahore *awqaf* Department, Internal Report.

Sufi Spaces in Urban Bangladesh

Gender and Modernity in Contemporary Shrine Culture[1]

GEOFFREY SAMUEL AND SANTI ROZARIO

INTRODUCTION

Sufi sacred places, generally based around the tomb (*mazar*) of a dead Sufi *pir* or holy man, or in some cases around the court (*darbar*) of a living one, are ubiquitous features of areas of Muslim population in South Asia. The largest *mazar* complexes, such as those which have grown up around the shrines of Moinuddin Chishti at Ajmer (Currie 1989, 1991; Pemberton 2000: 90-122; Moini 2004) or Nizamuddin Chishti at Delhi (Jeffery 1979; Qureshi 1995: 94-95; Pinto 1995) are very important establishments, dominating substantial areas of urban space. Bangladesh has a number of such *mazar* and *darbar*, and in this article we look at them as significant features of the urban space, in certain important ways distinctive from the rest of the city. In particular, in an urban environment that was and still largely is defined as male space, particularly in relation to religious activity, some Sufi *mazar* offer locations for specifically female religious activity. Thus we can ask, what do these spaces represent in what we could call the psychic or emotional geography of the city?

More generally, Sufi shrines can be locations where activities can take place which are not elsewhere permitted, and where people who might elsewhere be unacceptable in the urban environment can feel at home. This is particularly true of the large urban *mazar*-based complexes such as that around the Mirpur *mazar*

---

1   An earlier version of this paper was given under the title *The Sufi Mazar in Bangladesh as a Heterotopic Space. Shrines and Their Visitors* to the workshop 'Prayer in the City: Islam, Sacred Space and Urban Life', held on Friday, 26 and Saturday, 27 June 2009 at the Berlin Graduate School Muslim Cultures and Societies/FU Berlin.

in Dhaka. One might refer here to Michel Foucault's well-known if problematic concept of *heterotopic space*.[2]

"There are also, probably in every culture, in every civilization, real places – places that do exist and that are formed in the very founding of society – which are something like counter-sites, a kind of effectively enacted utopia in which the real sites, all the other real sites that can be found within the culture, are simultaneously represented, contested, and inverted. Places of this kind are outside of all places, even though it may be possible to indicate their location in reality." (Foucault 1986: 24)

Foucault's rather schematic description can be pushed too far, but it helps to capture some of the character of these sites. In particular, such shrines are significant because they are a kind of inversion or negation of the society that surrounds them. They are, or claim to be, places where the laws of ordinary logic and causation can be suspended, at least in principle. In a sense, they have to make such claims, since the principal function of a *mazar* is to provide access to spiritual power at a time of crisis. If one's life is in order, if all is going well, there is little reason to visit one of these shrines. It is when things are not going well, and access is needed to some kind of power that acts outside the everyday cycle of things, that one is likely to visit a *mazar*. In this sense, though certainly open to the general public, *mazar* operate as what Foucault refers to as 'heterotopias of crisis': "privileged or sacred or forbidden places, reserved for individuals who are, in relation to society and to the human environment in which they live, in a state of crisis: adolescents, menstruating women, pregnant women, the elderly, etc." (1986: 24).

The suspension of ordinary causality is linked to the presence of the miracle-working saint, past or present, and signaled in all kinds of ways around the shrine. Consider Pir Badr's shrine in Chittagong, where the visitor can inspect a glass case containing the broken remains of the stone upon which the saint Badr Shah floated to Chittagong, over the Bay of Bengal (Qanungo 1988: 467-470). At another famous Chittagong shrine, that of Bayezid Bostami, the visitor can view and feed the turtles in the shrine pond, who are said to be heretical teachers turned into turtles by the holy man (Qanungo 1988: 472, 482). A similar story is told about the catfish in the shrine pond at Shah Jalal's *mazar* in Sylhet. At the Mirpur *mazar* in Dhaka one can see the great tree which grew out of the walking-stick of the holy Shah Ali Bagdadi, when he came to this place to perform

---

2   See Foucault's posthumously published text *Des Espaces Autres* (*Of Other Spaces* or *Different Spaces*, Foucault (1998); for critical discussion see Johnson (2006); Saldhana (2008)).

his *chilla* or spiritual practice (Begum and Ahmed 1992: 71).[3] The fruit born by this tree are a form of *shinni* or consecrated food. Eating them is a way of taking in the blessing of the shrine.

The shrines are also places to which people can come who are not always welcome in the outside world. Beggars and the destitute are accepted at places such as the Mirpur *mazar* or Bayezid Bostami's Chittagong shrine, and may receive some food from the shrine or a little money from visitors. People who have consumed too much alcohol in this society where alcohol is against Islamic law can come to the shrine to sleep off their drink. Prostitutes and other people rejected by the morality of mainstream society are welcome here. *Faqirs* and other eccentric holy men, the *pagol* or *crazy people*[4], can come here and be tolerated. To quote Suraiya Begum and Hasina Ahmed, who carried out research in Mirpur *mazar* in the 1980s.

"*Pagals* and *mastans*[5] of different order can be seen [...]. Devotees revere them for they are believed to have acquired esoteric knowledge and extra human power. Also, they wear outlandish dresses and behave differently [...]. Beggars also sit here. They attract devotees by singing songs or by reciting *dua-darud* [prayers] and verse from the Quran." (Begum and Ahmed 1992: 71)

These are not people with whom a more respectable visitor to the shrine would normally choose to share his or her space, but all this adds to the unusual and unsettling ambience of the *mazar*. This is a place where things are not quite as normal, where the unusual and improbable might happen. This is at the base of why people might need to come to such a place. They need the improbable to happen in order to solve their personal problems. Here we can think of Foucault's analysis of heterotopic spaces as places where important transitions can take place; or Victor Turner's discussion of liminal and liminoid spaces as places of potential creativity and transformation (Turner 1969, 1982).

In the following sections of the paper, we first look briefly at research on Sufism and on Sufi shrines in South Asia in general and Bangladesh in particular.

---

3   Cf. Gardner on a local pir who walked on the water, and on Shah Jalal who used his turban-cloth as a raft (Gardner 1993a: 216).

4   Paglami can indicate psychiatric illness (cf. Bhattacharyya 1984, 1986), but pagol is also used in a part-respectful, part-affectionate way to refer to eccentric holy men and woman who are thought of as having genuine spiritual powers (cf. the crazy yogis of Tibet, or the Russian yurodivy or holy fool).

5   Here Begum and Ahmed are apparently using the term *mastan* to refer to rough or crude holy men.

Then we present some ethnographic material from two contrasting Dhaka shrines and from the famous shrine of Shah Jalal in Sylhet. Finally we present some tentative conclusions about the significance of Sufi shrines in the urban landscape of South Asia.

SUFIS IN SOUTH ASIA

As Katherine Ewing noted in her *Arguing Sainthood* (2006), which was based on fieldwork in Pakistan, 'Sufi' is a far from straightforward or unambiguous term. Kelly Pemberton similarly points to the divergence between the Sufis of the scholarly tradition, Western and Asian, and the ethnographic reality of the Indian Sufi shrines where she worked (Pemberton 2000: 11-12). Katy Gardner says much the same in relation to Bangladesh: Sufism "covers a whole spectrum of beliefs and categories" (1993a: 215), while the category of *pir* ('Sufi' teacher, healer or holy man) "covers such a broad range of characters that there is danger of it becoming meaningless" (1993a: 215).

Like many other such vocabulary items, the term 'Sufi' is ripe for postcolonial analysis, not to say deconstruction. Certainly Sufis and Sufism have between them been the basis for a considerable quantity of Western scholarship. That scholarship has a complex relationship to a variety of past South Asian practices that may or may not have been referred to in the past by practitioners or other members of their societies as 'Sufi' (cf. Pemberton 2000: 45-85). 'Sufi' is also a label that has been variously appropriated and used by contemporary practitioners, in South Asia or elsewhere. The word has also been popularised considerably in the West and globally in recent years, for example through the books of Idries Shah and other imaginative writers, through the *qawwali* singing of Nusrat Fateh Ali Khan, or through the free translations, often verging on re-creations, of Sufi poetry by contemporary American poets such as Robert Bly or Coleman Barks. A few years ago, these translations were claimed to have made the great 13th century Iranian spiritual teacher Jalaluddin Rumi into the best-selling poet in the United States.

This popular Western take on Sufism floats free of its cultural context, leading to an image of 'the Sufi' as a radical and antinomian figure who has thrown aside the apparently stifling and constricting rules of Islamic observance and Islamic law. There are indeed figures who resemble this picture within the wide spectrum of Islamic religious behavior – some of the *faqirs* at the Mirpur *mazar* might be fair enough representatives, and most big Sufi shrines have such people. In Islamic parlance, this is the type of the *qalandar*; the Pakistani term is *malang.* The world of these practitioners has been explored in considerable detail by Katherine Ewing (e.g. 1984, 1998, 2006) and Jürgen Frembgen (e.g. 1998) among others. In the specifically Bengali context, we can look at the *bauls*, religious practitioners who exist on the boundaries between Sufism and Tantric Hinduism, and present their teachings as readily in terms of Krishna and Radha as of Muhammad (e.g. Openshaw 2002; Salomon 1991), as well as a motley assortment of *pagol, marfati* and *faqir* practitioners.

While the modern Western take on Sufism often celebrates such figures, the older Western scholarly literature on Sufis, and much educated South Asian discourse today, tends to dismiss such eccentric practitioners as marginal, preferring to focus instead on a more 'genuine' Sufism represented by a series of more mainstream Sufi philosophers and scholars (e.g. Schimmel 1975; Rizvi 2003). In recent times, Sufis of this more mainstream kind, such as the great Indian scholar Ahmed Raza Khan of Bareilly (1856-1921), inspirer of the so-called Barelvi movement, often figure as 'traditionalists' noted for their resistance to modernist trends such as the Deobandi reformers and the various politically-oriented Islamist groups (Sirriyeh 1999).

It is not necessarily very useful, however, to put too much emphasis on this question of opposition to conventional Islamic practice. Nor is it particularly helpful to seek to assess particular individuals as more or less authentic versions of a genuine tradition, however defined. Defining conventional Islamic practice is far from straightforward, and Sufi orders and lineages are more characterized by variety and multiplicity than by strict fidelity to tradition. Ethnographically, one can find a wide range of kinds of practice within the general South Asian 'Sufi' ambit today, and much of it is not particularly opposed to more standard forms of Islamic practice.

At the most respectable end of the scale, one might cite many followers of the Naqshbandi-Mujaddidi lineages in Bangladesh and elsewhere in South Asia. This is the most widespread Naqshbandi tradition in South Asia, tracing its origins to the Indian Sufi teacher Ahmed Sirhindi (1564-1624). Ahmed Sirhindi – the *mujaddid alf sani,* or Renewer of Islam for the 2nd Millennium, hence the term Mujaddidi – was a close ally of the Emperor Aurangzeb in his persecutions of non-Muslims. While Aurangzeb was probably not as monstrous as he has been painted in caricatures of the Hindu right, Sirhindi was certainly no antinomian, nor are most of his followers (Rizvi 2003; Weismann 2007a). Thus it is not particularly surprising that the founders of the Deobandi *madrasas* and the Tabligh-i Jama'at revivalist movement, both socially very conservative in their orientations, had Sufi affiliations, although these movements today are strongly opposed to much of what goes on at contemporary Sufi shrines (Metcalf 2002;

Sikand 2002, 2005, 2007; Weismann 2007b). Even the Barelvi *madrasas*, which are occasionally described as 'liberal' because of their toleration of Sufi shrine culture and other popular religious manifestations, are conservative in their views on social issues (e.g. Sikan 2005).

There is also a class element here. Followers of Naqshbandi-Mujaddidi *shaykhs*, as the past associations with Mughal Emperors suggest, tended to be at the upper end of the class scale, while wandering *faqirs*, *qalandars* and *bauls* were much closer to the poor rural population. This is still true in contemporary Bangladesh, where wealthy families with Sufi inclinations are more likely to be affiliated with hereditary Naqshbandi *pir* families than with wandering *qalandars* and *bauls*. It is the poorer families too who are most likely to resort to *pirs* when they have problems in their lives: "sickness, economic crisis, marital problems, and so on" (Gardner 1993a: 215). It is only recently, and mainly among the literate middle classes and those influenced by the Tabligh-i Jama'at and similar movements, that resorting in this way to *pirs* and shrines in times of trouble has come to be seen as Islamically problematic.

SUFI SHRINES IN SOUTH ASIA

Thus Sufi shrines and the personnel associated with them can cover quite a wide range. In this paper we are dealing broadly with two rather different situations. One is the large shrine-complex built around the tomb or *mazar* of a famous Sufi figure of the past, often of the distant past. There has been considerable attention to such shrines in India and Pakistan.[6] Here we will be looking at two principal examples in Bangladesh, the Mirpur *mazar* in Dhaka and the shrine-complex of Shah Jalal in Sylhet.

Another type of shrine is that of a living Sufi teacher. These are not strictly *mazar*, since this term refers to the tomb of a dead *pir*; the term *darbar,* referring to a royal court, is often used, and can be applied to the establishment of a living or a dead saint. There has been less attention to sites such as these in the literature on India or Pakistan, with Pnina Werbner's *Pilgrims of Love* as perhaps the major contribution so far. This study is focused on an international order founded by a living Naqshbandi saint, Zinda Pir, whose headquarters is at Ghamkol Sharif in a remote valley some way from Peshawar in Pakistan's Northwest Frontier Province (Werbner 2004). In the Bangladeshi context we will be look-

---

6   See above for references to studies of the Chishti shrines at Delhi and Ajmer. Other examples include Eaton (1982) and Rehman (2009).

ing primarily at one centre of this kind, though urban rather than rural, that of Zakir Shah in Dhaka, known as the Qutub-Bagh.[7]

What both types of establishment have in common is that they constitute spaces where different rules apply to those of the everyday world outside. Both dead and living *pirs* are, conceptually at least, workers of miracles, channels through which divine grace can flow to bring about a result difficult to attain in the world outside. This can happen at any of a variety of levels, from a poor family unable to afford medical care seeking healing for a sick child, to a politician seeking re-election. In fact, the political role of Sufi shrines in Bangladesh is well known. Since the late 1980s, during the time of President Ershad, who had close associations with one particular *pir* and was well known for his patronage of *pirs* in general, most Bangladeshi politicians have made a point of staying on the right side of the main active *pirs* within the country. Ali Riaz, in his *God Willing. The Politics of Islamism in Bangladesh*, describes the shrines of these living *pirs* as "headquarters of complex social networks and places where patronage is exchanged between high-ranking people" (2004: 152).

There is certainly some validity in this comment, but our emphasis in the present paper is not so much on the high-level political networks with which *pirs* may be engaged as on the use of the spaces afforded by them for more ordinary people. We also attend particularly to the issue of gender, and ways in which Sufi *mazar* provide public spaces accessible for women in a society where such spaces are restricted.

SUFIS IN BANGLADESH

Katy Gardner's article on Sufi *pirs* in Sylhet, the region of Bangladesh from which most of British Bangladeshi population originated, gives a general introduction to the role of *pir* that applies also to the general Bangladeshi context. *Pirs* are capable of miraculous transformations and of accomplishments which ordinary men and women cannot achieve. There are however special features of the Sylheti situation, according to Gardner, and she goes on to argue for a similarity between *pirs* and successful migrants to the UK, who frequently visit their kin back in Bangladesh with lavish gifts, build large and impressive houses back in their natal villages, and display other signs of Allah's favor. Thus, in Sylhet it is "invariably" the poor who visit the *pirs*, those "who have not enjoyed the ben-

---

7   For a description of another Bangladeshi shrine focussing around a then-living saint, that of the Atroshi Pir at Faridpur see Mills (1992, 1994, 1998).

efits of migration" (Gardner 1993a: 216, 222-223, see also 1993b). Successful migrants can pray directly to God; the poor need an intermediary (1993a: 222-223). Migrants are much more comfortable with the purist forms of Islam so prominent in British Islamic discourse, those which reject the idea of intermediaries such as the supposedly miracle-working *pirs*. Migrants are also likely to reject the common village practices of worshipping Kwaz, the water-spirit, and Loki, more familiar as the Hindu goddess Lakshmi, as Hindu superstitions.

At the national level, such purist arguments can also be found, although with less intensity than among the Sylhetis, where the close association with the UK migrants has had significant effects. The Tabligh-i Jama'at, a purist missionary movement whom Gardner mentions as active among the Sylhetis, are popular throughout Bangladesh, and several million people come each year to their great annual prayer-gathering near Dhaka, the *biswa ijtema* (Riaz 2004; Rozario and Samuel 2009). However the Tabligh-i Jama'at's well-known opposition to shrine practices seems to have had limited impact in the country as a whole. The cult of *pirs* remains strong, and there was little public sympathy for those responsible for the poisoning of the fish in Shah Jalal's shrine in Sylhet in late 2003, let alone for the subsequent bombing of the shrine in January 2004. Other studies of *pirs* and shrines in Bangladesh have tended to stress the continued vitality of these practices (e.g. Begum and Ahmed 1992; Hussain 1992; Mills 1992, 1994, 1998; Ellickson 2002; Bertocci 2006).

THE MIRPUR *MAZAR*

In Ahmad Hasan Dani's Muslim Architecture in Bengal, dating from 1961, the *mazar* of Shah Ali Bagdadi at Mirpur is described as being some twelve miles from Dhaka, then still a relatively small city (Dani 1961: 230). Today the city has expanded enormously in size and population, and the *mazar* is totally surrounded by high-density living and business areas. As with many South Asian *mazar*, however, the shrine complex remains somewhat distinct from the city. The entry is marked off by an impressive modern gate, with a row of shops to either side selling religious artifacts, offerings for the shrine and other goods. Although there is an inscription here recording the building of a mosque in 1480, and the holy man to whom the shrine owes its fame is said to have died in 1577, the buildings have been completely renovated.˙

One version of the story of the shrine tells how Shah Ali Bagdadi came here via Faridpur and was allocated some land by the Mughal ruler of the time. When he arrived at Mirpur, the old mosque here was already in a very run down condition. Shah Ali went inside the mosque for his 40-day *chilla* (meditation) and shut the door behind him, leaving his stick in the ground right outside the mosque where it grew into the large tree mentioned earlier. On the 39th day, a loud noise was heard from inside the mosque. People forced open the door and found just a pool of blood. There was no sign of the *pir*, and it is believed that he became *bishal*, that is one with Allah.

When one enters the gate into the shrine compound today, one finds oneself in a large, more or less rectangular, open courtyard, perhaps 80 meters on each side. The main shrine is facing one, with the famous tree in front of it and the mosque at the right-hand side. The courtyard contains all kinds of people. There are of course always beggars, but one can also encounter eccentric holy men of the *qalandar* or *faqir* type. Here they might be referred to as *shadhu* (holy men) but also as *pagol* (crazy). On the whole women do not spend much time in this open space, though they may be among the small groups of people surrounding the holy men who set up around the courtyard on Thursday evenings. According to Begum and Ahmed, women can also be found singing and dancing here at the time of the three-day annual *'urs*. The *'urs* is the time of the saint's death, which is also his marriage to God or achievement of union with God, so it is the time of maximum emotional and spiritual intensity. It is also the time when most people come to the shrine. Begum and Ahmed also mention the presence of other socially undesirable characters at this time, such as drug addicts, drug dealers, and prostitutes.

Women are not allowed to go inside the main room of the shrine to view or touch the tomb of the saint, but they can go to an adjoining women's section. This women's section is in the form of an L-shaped verandah adjacent to the main room containing the tomb, and women can view the tomb through the tiny holes of a window opening into the room that contains it. One side of the verandah is generally occupied by visiting women and children, and the other by the female *khadem* or shrine-attendant and her assistants. Women sit facing towards the tomb, praying, crying, and talking to each other. Women try to catch a view of the tomb, or at least to touch the wall adjoining it. They get their children to touch and bow down in front of the wall, and pray. Many women tie up a piece of string onto the window grilles. These relate to the vows (*manot*) they are making in relation to their particular problems.

We have discussed the practice of *manot* at some length in another recent paper, noting there that Bangladeshi Muslim, Hindu and Christian women all take part in this practice (Rozario and Samuel: 2010). Each of the religions provides its own way of making *manots*, to Hindu deities, Christian saints, or Muslim *pirs*, but the underlying logic is the same, and as we note below it is common for people to resort to shrines or deities of religions other than their own.

It is also very common for women in all communities to make *manot* on behalf of their husbands and children. There is a kind of implicit division of religious labor across South Asian religious communities, in which men have a more public role, which in the case of Islam involves participation in the public mosque services. Women are expected to undertake a distinctive set of religious activities to do with ensuring the welfare of her husband and children, often involving fasting and other ascetic practices, and mostly based in the household. Visiting the shrine to ask for the intercession of the saint fits easily with this domestic role.

The situation in the women's section at the Mirpur *mazar* is quite informal,[8] and women share food (*shinni*) which they have brought from home, and which has been consecrated through its close physical proximity to the saint's tomb. Rozario and her friends, both of Bangladeshi Christian backgrounds, were also offered food, and told, "Eat! Eat with faith!" It was evident to Rozario that there was a common understanding among the women about why they were there – to commune with the Saint, but most of all to find some means through their contact with the saint to resolve whatever the problems were that led to their visit to the *mazar*.

The female *khadems* or shrine-attendants play a very important role for the female visitors. They listen to their problems, which are typically marital problems, fertility problems, health problems of family members, often of children, or a mother's inability to find a husband for her daughter. *Khadems* give advice but also *shinni* (sugared sweets, or flower petals) for the women to take home. Rozario was asked whether she was having marital problems, and she too got some *shinni* to take home in any case.

For women, the shrine is a particularly significant space, because it is one of the few public spaces that they can legitimately visit. In the women's section of the *mazar*, women can socialize freely with other women, and there might be a possibility, through the grace of the *pir*, of something positive happening in their lives. The shrine is an *uchila*, a way in which Allah can act to help you – *uchila* also means something like 'pretext' or 'excuse', so there is a sense that coming to the shrine gives Allah an opportunity to intervene. It is not that one necessari-

---

8 The same is true at another major Dhaka mazar, that next to the High Court, though our observations there are less extensive. Here too there is a room for women directly adjoining the room containing the tomb, with a window through which women can view the tomb.

ly *expects* something to happen, but by coming to the shrine, one is opening up a space of possibility, in which something *might* happen.

Rozario got to know one of the women whom she met at the shrine fairly well, and went round to her house on a number of subsequent occasions. Roshna, as we will call her, goes to the *mazar* often. When Rozario first met her, Roshna said she had been feeling unwell all day, since the morning, and so had come to visit the *mazar*. Most of her problems related to her anxiety about how to cope with her financial burden, in particular her children's school fees etc. Her husband was educated, so might have had a reasonable job, but he was a *marfati* or Sufi enthusiast, and his Sufi interests had led him to become somewhat neglectful of his family duties.

Roshna mentioned that she had made a vow before her youngest child and only son was born. She wanted a son very badly, having had two daughters and being financially dependent on her parents. Her mother had been angry about her third pregnancy and even asked her to get an abortion. Roshna made a *manot* (vow) and went to see a male *khadem* at a nearby Shi'a mosque, who gave her a lemon to eat. Her child, now three years old, was indeed a son, so this was a success story.

The presence of two Christian women at the *mazar* was evidently nothing unusual, and in fact *shinni* from the *mazar*, *prasad* from Hindu *pujas*, or blessed biscuits from the festival at the regional Roman Catholic shrine of St. Anthony of Padua, a few miles north of Dhaka, are all part of a common practice of the circulation of sacred foods between women. Rozario's sister in law, also from a Catholic family, asked for some of the *shinni* to take to her work place, where they would be shared among the women workers. She told a story of a Muslim woman at work whose daughter was having difficulty conceiving, but who had a child after eating consecrated food from a Christian shrine in India along with *shinni* from the *mazar* and Hindu *prasad*. The mother thanked all her colleagues for their collective effort and for their prayers to their respective deities and saints. Who knows which *uchila*, which approach to the divine, worked? St. Francis, Shah Ali Bagdadi, Goddess Laksmi, or St. Anthony? As Rozario's informants said, it does not matter, everything is in one's faith.

THE SHRINE OF SHAH JALAL, SYLHET

The *mazar* of Shah Jalal is the most popular of the many shrines of the region of Sylhet, in north-eastern Bangladesh, from which most British Bangladeshis originated. The shrine of Shah Jalal is in Sylhet town. Both shrine and town have grown very much in recent years, in large part because of the flow of money from expatriate Sylhetis in the UK. Shah Jalal is the most significant religious figure of Sylhet, and his name is omnipresent in the British Bangladeshi community, with mosques, cultural centers and businesses throughout the UK named after him. His story is connected with the Muslim conquest of the region and the conversion of the population to Islam, a process in which the saint and his followers are supposed to have played a key role (Eaton 1993: 73-76, 212-213).

Today Shah Jalal's *mazar* is the wealthiest and most important shrine in Bangladesh. As with the Mirpur *mazar*, the shrine, once at the edge of the small town of Sylhet, is now surrounded by a substantial modern city. As at the Dhaka shrine, the shrine is entered through a large gate, which delimits the space of the shrine from the surrounding town. This main gate is at the end of a street of shops selling religious goods, and again opens out into a principal courtyard, on the far side of which is a set of stairs leading through a domed building to the tomb of Shah Jalal, which is on a small hill, in the open air, and covered by a canopy. A series of buildings surrounds the courtyard, with the tank containing the famous catfish, restocked after their poisoning in 2003, in another smaller courtyard to the right. Smaller gates delimit the shrine compound in other directions.

The *mazar* gets plenty of visitors, especially on Thursdays and Fridays, and the small mosque that Dani described in 1961 (238-241 and pl. LXXXIV) has now been incorporated into a large multi-story building. Rozario first visited Shah Jalal in January 2008 with the British Bangladeshi parents of a child suffering from a life-limiting genetic condition. She knew the parents from the UK, and they had been planning to visit this *mazar* for a long time. They had also planned to visit the famous *mazar* of Khwaja Moinuddin Chishti at Ajmer in India. Rozario has visited twice since, and Samuel has been once.

Unlike the situation at the Mirpur *mazar*, the women's enclosure at Shah Jalal is not adjacent to the tomb itself, but down in the courtyard at the foot of the hill where the tomb is situated. There is also a separate women's mosque area in one of the buildings near the main gate. As at the Mirpur *mazar*, women pray, bow down and kiss the floor, but often also stand up and put their heads against the wall to pray. The women's enclosure is less private than at Mirpur, and the atmosphere was more formal when Rozario visited, with none of the casual and relaxed interaction between women that she noted at the Mirpur *mazar*. There are nevertheless clearly-delimited female spaces at the shrine, and opportunities for both socializing and religious activity.

THE QUTUB BAGH *DARBAR* AND *'URS*, DHAKA

As noted earlier, the involvement of living *pirs* in politics has a long history in South Asia as elsewhere. While generally described in spiritual terms, such relationships had political advantages for both sides. They helped to secure political legitimacy for rulers, while providing material support to *pirs* and their shrines. The first two governments of independent Bangladesh (that of Shaykh Mujibur Rahman, 1972-75, and of General Ziaur Rahman, 1975-81) gave little attention to the *pirs*, but the military government of General Hussain Mohammed Ershad, which lasted from 1982 to 1990, marked a major involvement of the *pirs* in politics. Ershad in fact became famous for his devotion to Sufi holy men, particularly the Atroshi *pir* of Faridpur (Hazrat Maulana Hashmatullah, 1910-2001; see Mills 1994, 1998). The *pir* of Atroshi was himself a disciple of the Enayetpuri *pir*, Hazrat Mawlana Khwaja Yunus Ali (1886-1952), a follower of the Naqshbandi-Mujaddidi tradition. The Enayetpuri *pir* and his disciples founded a series of Sufi teaching centers and shrine-complexes, many of which remain prominent in the religious and political landscape of contemporary Bangladesh.

The Atroshi *pir* himself founded a political party, the Zaker Party (cf. Mills 1998: 48), but it has failed to achieve any significant electoral success in the period since the fall of the Ershad regime, and was a minor member of the Awami League electoral alliance in the last (December 2008) election. Living *pirs* vary considerably in their involvement in politics today, but another offshoot of the Enayetpuri tradition, Zakir Shah, has established a significant presence in Dhaka and evidently has good political connections. We visited this *pir* in January 2008, shortly after his organization, Qutub Bagh, held an *'urs* in a central Dhaka location, and also met with some of his followers in Dhaka and London. We also visited the *'urs* in Dhaka the following year, when it had moved to an even larger and more prominent location just off Farmgate, a central shopping and commercial area in Dhaka. According to a report in *Probe Magazine*

"[Zakir Shah] has three darbar sharifs at present. One is on a 40-bigha stretch of land in Trishal of Mymensingh. It is eight years old. Hazrat Zakir Shah took this over from the Enayetpur Peer sahib. Another darbar sharif is in Narayanganj. This was constructed in 1986 on a 12-bigha plot of land. And lastly, four years ago, his darbar sharif was built on a five katha plot at 36 Indira Road. It is still under construction.

How does this peer have such huge darbar sharifs and in so many places? Says Liaqat Ali [MM Liaqat Ali Swapan, President of the Urs Organization Committee], 'It is simply for the sake of spreading the religion. The more darbar sharifs baba has, the more followers he gathers. This will not remain in the country alone, but spread all over the world.'

Who generally come to the darbar sharif? 'Ministers, advisors, secretaries, army majors, doctors and rickshaw-wallas, everyone comes to touch baba's feet. They come with all sorts of ailments and baba cures them. I came to him in that way too, but now I have the privilege to serve him. When I call him 'baba', I received immense peace of mind.'"[9]

Certainly Zakir Shah's establishment on Indira Road, also in central Dhaka, was both large and well appointed, and Zakir Shah and his followers made a point of telling us about various politicians, including ex-President Ershad and the then Foreign Minister of Thailand who had visited Zakir Shah. The emphasis around Zakir Shah's court is less on Sufi teachings than on the transfiguring presence of the living *pir* himself. We were told by several followers (*murid*) of how merely being in the same room as him and looking at him brought one to a state of peace, and how he could give his *murid* whatever it was that they wished for, such as for example the birth of a child.

Thus Zakir Shah's *darbar* functioned much like a traditional *mazar*, in that it was appropriate and expected for people to come to the *pir*'s presence with their problems, in the hope that they would be solved through their contact with the *pir*'s miracle-working powers. How far this expectation was shared by the thousands of people who crowded into the city-centre park where the *'urs* took place it is hard to know. The park too was marked off very clearly for the duration of the *'urs* as a specific and different kind of space, sacralized by the presence of the *pir* and by his discourses.

CONCLUSION

In conclusion, we return to this question of the special kind of space that is created in the city by Sufi shrines and activities. In Katharine Ewing's *Arguing Sainthood*, she talks about the way in which the inner experience of the Sufi is defined by Sufi poetry and writings:

"The inner experience of a Sufi requires a Muslim society ordered according to the principles dictated by God. It is not that the interior is a reality that must be exposed at all costs. In contrast to the Cartesian notion that the inner self, the 'I,' is an entity more real, more essential than the phenomenal world and the body that houses that self, for these Sufis the

9   http://www.probenewsmagazine.com/index.php?index=2&contentId=3469, (accessed 24 August 2009).

inner experience is not an entity but a space that exists only within a properly constructed framework." (2006: 243)

Ewing's argument here is that, according to the Sufi writers such as the 12th century Persian court poet San'ai, being a Sufi implies the full observance of Islamic forms and practices. This is not, as a Westerner might suppose, a superficial obedience concealing some kind of inner essence which transcends such conventional forms. Rather, external observance is a framework that enables the Sufi to engage in private with the chaos of inner experience and so makes spiritual progress possible.

Perhaps one could say that these Sufi urban spaces act, or acted in the past, as a kind of externalization of the inner experience of which Ewing is talking. Instead of inner psychic experience being a space held within the framework of a properly disciplined religious practice, we here have a physical space that is held, in principle at least, within a properly disciplined religious society. Visitors come to these places because the tension between their personal life experiences and what is happening in that properly disciplined society is too great for them to hold, and the shrine offers ways of mediating and coming to terms with that tension, and the promise too of a material solution to one's problems.

If the *mazar* offers an opportunity to reconfigure one's psychic experience, this might be true in one sense for the troubled and often poverty-stricken men and women who come to the Mirpur *mazar* or Shah Jalal in search of healing and solutions to their other problems (cf. Samuel 2010). It would be true in a somewhat different sense for those who become followers of the *pir*, and who see themselves as embarking upon a journey to develop this world of inner experience within themselves. Here they encounter and have to come to terms with a place that encompasses much of what is repressed and dismissed by the society outside it, but is at the same time firmly held within the bounds of that society. The *mazar*, to return to Foucault's concept of the heterotopia, is a tolerated space where other spaces within society are "simultaneously represented, contested and inverted" (1986: 24).

We began this chapter by referring to Foucault's concept of the 'heterotopia of crisis'. He suggested that such heterotopias were being increasingly replaced by what he called 'heterotopias of deviation' (1986: 25). The *mazar* is both, though like all heterotopias it has a specific function, or set of functions, delimited by the particular society of which it forms a part (1986: 25). We close with some reflections on the transformations of the *mazar* in recent years.

Certainly, to return to the question of the self, the inner psychic world, and its transformations, patterns of the self in South Asia are increasingly open to change. In Bangladesh, as in Pakistan, the ordered and hierarchical world of the extended family is progressively breaking up to be replaced by an increasingly self or nuclear-family oriented urban society. Both modern scientific discourses, and the claims of new kinds of Islam more at home in the modern world, weaken and contest the magical mode of thinking on which the Sufi *mazar* and *pir* depend.

In an earlier chapter of her book, Ewing comments on an encounter between her university-trained Pakistani research assistant and a series of *malang, qalandar*-type practitioners. For her assistant, a 'modern' Pakistani, the *malang* were by definition criminals and frauds, but at the same time he could not entirely resist the idea that they might have genuine powers and put them to evil use. Ewing suggests that "the abject is an object of desire and temptation as well as revulsion" (2006: 227)[10]. It raises central and critical concerns (sex, death, supernatural power) that cannot be entirely suppressed or rejected:

"The qalandar is at the furthest extreme from the middle-class subject – the profoundly 'not-Me.' Yet the qalandar is painfully close, one of the grounds on which both everyday understandings and subjectivity itself rest. […] The qalandar lives at the border of social being, at the edge of the imaginary. The presence of the abject invites the subject to self-constitution through the exclusion of the abject as 'not-Me.' Yet the power of this signifier of abjection indicates that the middle-class individual, even one who is university educated and fully embedded in the 'modern' world, is not fully 'subject' to modern discourse." (2006: 229)

Ewing's comments are suggestive and intriguing, particularly in relation to a place such as the Mirpur *mazar*, where the local equivalents of the *qalandar* are much in evidence. They suggest how 'Sufi spaces' can retain a distinctive and even uncanny feeling for people who have on the surface at least rejected such ideas altogether. One can also imagine how in a situation of crisis (health, employment or whatever) in which the solutions offered by modernity fail to work, such people might be tempted to resort to the world of the Sufi shrine with its ambiguous yet potent forces.

The power associated with a more 'ordered' location such as that of the living *pir*, Zakir Shah, is less evident and immediate. Zakir Shah's presence is not at all antinomian or transgressive, and his personal style if anything communi-

---

10 Ewing's use of the category of the 'abject' here carries Kristeva's sense of 'abjection,' of those things that evoke disgust and repulsion because they are "[…] what disturbs identity, system, order. What does not respect borders, positions, rules. The in-between, the ambiguous, the composite" (Kristeva 1982: 4).

cates an aura of Islamic orthodoxy and propriety. At the same time, Zakir Shah is defined by his followers as a man of power and a worker of miracles, and one does not quite know when one visits his *darbar* precisely what one is coming into contact with, or what effect it may have for good or bad. This is not a normal space, and it retains an aspect of unpredictability and uncertainty compared to, for example, the home, the office or the mosque.

Ewing's Pakistani research assistant was at a certain point along a process of change which is enveloping his whole society, and which is moving in an uncertain direction. Much the same is true of Bangladesh today. It is by no means clear that the overall direction of movement in Bangladesh is towards secular modernity, but as we have noted elsewhere is undoubtedly coming to include elements of the Western-style individualism that has characterised modernity in many parts of the world (e.g. Rozario 2007).

The tension between outer respectability and inner experience works differently in a fully individualistic, Western-style society, since the basis of such a society is precisely the image of the transcendent ego imposing its will on the external world and somehow getting the best deal it can out of life. In a context such as this, Sufi urban spaces may certainly continue to exist, but may lose some of its ability to facilitate inner transformation and healing.

The future of the unique context which some *mazar*, such as that at Mirpur, provide for spontaneous female religious community may also be in question. The growth of women's prayer groups linked to organizations such as Tabligh-i Jama'at or Jama'at-i Islami is providing alternative and more 'respectable' modes for female religious sociality (cf. Huq 2009; White 2010), and one could imagine that these might in part at least take over from the *mazar* context.

So far, though, the specific kinds of urban space associated with the *mazar* and *'urs* seem to be maintaining themselves in Bangladesh, though their psychological meaning may well be undergoing reconfiguration, and may well transform in interesting ways as, perhaps, Western models of the self themselves transform in relation to a changing world.

REFERENCES

Begum, Suraiya and Ahmed, Hasina (1992): "Beliefs and Rituals in a Shrine in Bangladesh", in: J. Social Studies 53, pp. 68-95.

Bertocci, Peter J. (2006): "A Sufi Movement in Bangladesh. The Maijbhandari Tariqa and its Followers", in: Contributions to Indian Sociology (n.s.) 40, pp. 1-28.

Bhattacharyya, Deborah P. (1984): "Desire in Bengali Ethnopsychology.", in: Contributions to Asian Studies 18, pp.73-84.

(1986): Paglami. Ethnopsychiatric Knowledge in Bengal. South Asian Series No. 11, Syracuse.

van Bruinessen, Martin, and Howell, Julia Day (Eds.) (2007): Sufism and the 'Modern' in Islam, London: I.B. Tauris.

Currie, P.M. (1989): The Shrine and Cult of Mu'in al-Dīn Chishti of Ajmer, Delhi: Oxford University Press.

(1991): "The Pilgrimage to Ajmer" [Excerpt from Currie 1989.], in: T.N. Madan (Ed.), Religion in India, Delhi: Oxford University Press, pp. 237-247.

Dani, Ahmad Hasan (1961): Muslim Architecture in Bengal, Dacca: Asiatic Society of Pakistan.

Davidson, Joyce, and Milligan, Christine (2004): "Editorial. Embodying Emotion Sensing Space. Introducing Emotional Geographies", in: Social and Cultural Geography 5, pp. 523-532.

Davidson, Joyce; Smith, Mick, and Bondi, Liz (Eds.) (2007): Emotional Geographies, London: Ashgate.

Eaton, Richard M. (1982): "Court of Man, Court of God: Local Perceptions of the Shrine of Baba Farid, Pakpattan, Punjab", in: Contributions to Asian Studies 17, pp. 44-61.

Eaton, Richard M. (1993): The Rise of Islam and the Bengal Frontier, 1204-1760, Berkeley and Los Angeles: University of California Press.

Ellickson, Jean (2002): "Local Saint vs. Contemporary Reformer. Religious Trends in Bangladesh", in: S.M. Nurul Islam (Ed.), Contemporary Anthropology. Theory and Practice, Dhaka: Jahangirnagar University and The University Press Limited, pp. 197-210.

Ewing, Katherine P. (1984): "The Sufi as Saint, Curer and Exorcist in Northern Pakistan", in: Contributions to Asian Studies 18, pp. 106-114.

(1998): "A Majzub and his Mother. The Place of Sainthood in a Family's Emotional Memory.", in: P. Werbner and H. Basu (Eds.), Embodying Charisma. Modernity, Locality and the Performance of Emotion in Sufi Cults, pp. 160-183.

(2006 [1997]): Arguing Sainthood. Modernity, Psychoanalysis and Islam, Durham, NC and London: Duke University Press.

Foucault, Michel (1986): "Of other Spaces", in: Diacritics 16 Spring, pp. 22-27.

(1998): "Different Spaces", in: J. D. Faubion (Ed.), Aesthetics, Method, and Epistemology. Essential Works of Michel Foucault, 1954-1984, volume 2, London: Allen Lane, pp. 175-186.

Frembgen, Jürgen Wasim (1998): "The Majzub Mama Ji Sarkar. A Friend of God Moves from one House to Another.", in: P. Werbner and H. Basu (Eds.), Embodying Charisma. Modernity, Locality and the Performance of Emotion in Sufi Cults, pp. 140-159.

Gardner, Katy (1993a): "Mullahs, Migrants, Miracles. Travel and Transformation in Sylhet", in: Contributions to Indian Sociology 27:2, pp. 213-235.

(1993b): "Desh-Bidesh. Sylheti Images of Home and Away", in: Man 28:1, pp. 1-15.

Huq, Maimuna (2009): "Talking Jihad and Piety. Reformist Exertions among Islamist Women in Bangladesh", in: Journal of the Royal Anthropological Institute 15:1, pp. 163-182.

Hussain, Naseem Akhter (1992): Women in a Bangladesh Village. Sources of Female Autonomy. Ph.D. Thesis: Australia.

Jeffery, Patricia (1979): Frogs in a Well. Indian Women in Purdah, London: Zed Press.

Johnson, Peter (2006): "Unravelling Foucault's 'Different Spaces'", in: History of the Human Sciences 19:4, pp. 75-90.

Kristeva, Julia (1982): Powers of Horror. An Essay on Abjection, New York and Chichester: Columbia University Press.

Metcalf, Barbara Daly (2002): Islamic Revival in British India. Deoband, 1860-1900, New Delhi: Oxford University Press.

Mills, Samuel Landell (1992): An Anthropological Account of Islamic Holy Men in Bangladesh. Ph.D. Thesis: London.

(1994): "The Atroshi Urus", in: J. Social Studies 63 (January), pp. 83-106.

(1998): "The Hardware of Sanctity. Anthropomorphic Objects in Bangladeshi Sufism", in: P. Werbner and H. Basu (Eds.), Embodying Charisma. Modernity, Locality and the Performance of Emotion in Sufi Cults, pp. 31-54.

Moini, Syed Liyaqat Hussain (2004): The Chishti Shrine of Ajmer. Pirs, Pilgrims, Practices, Jaipur: Publication Scheme.

Openshaw, Jeanne (2002): Seeking Bāuls of Bengal, Cambridge: Cambridge University Press.

Pemberton, Kelly (2000): Women, Ritual Life, and Sufi Shrines in North India. Ph.D. Thesis: Columbia.

Pinto, Desiderio (1995): Piri-Muridi Relationship. A Study of the Nizamuddin Durgah, New Delhi: Manohar Publishers and Distributors.

Qanungo, Suniti Bhushan (1988): A History of Chittagong. Vol. 1. From Ancient Times down to 1761, Chittagong: Dipankar Qanungo.

Qureshi, Regula Burckhardt (1995): Sufi Music of India and Pakistan. Sound, Context and Meaning in Qawwali, Chicago and London: University of Chicago Press.

Rehman, Uzma (2009): "Sacred Spaces, Rituals and Practices. The Mazars of Saiyid Pir Waris Shah and Shah 'Abdu'l Latif Bhitai", in: Catharina Raudvere and Leif Stenberg (Eds.), Sufism Today. Heritage and Tradition in the Global Community, London: I.B. Tauris, pp. 137-157.

Rizvi, Saiyid Athar Abbas (2003): A History of Sufism in India. Vols. 1 and 2, Delhi: Munshiram Manoharlal.

Riaz, Ali (2004): God Willing. The Politics of Islamism in Bangladesh, Lanham, MD, New York and London: Rowman & Littlefield.

Rozario, Santi (2007): "Outside the Moral Economy? Single Bangladeshi Female Migrants", in: The Australian Journal of Anthropology (TAJA) 18:2, pp. 154-171.

Rozario, Santi and Geoffrey, Samuel (2009): "Secularism or Islamic Modernism? Young Bangladeshis in the UK and in Bangladesh", in: Paper for Diasporas, Migration and Identities. Crossing Boundaries, New Directions, CRONEM Conference, June 11-12, Centre for Research on Nationalism, Ethnicity and Multiculturalism, University of Surrey.

(2010): "Gender, Religious Change and Sustainability in Bangladesh", in: Women's Studies International Forum 33, pp. 354-364. (Special Issue edited by Santi Rozario and Geoffrey Samuel, From Village Religion to Global Networks: Women, Religious Nationalism and Sustainability in South and Southeast Asia.)

Saldhana, Arun (2008): "Heterotopia and Structuralism. Environment and Planning D", in: Society and Space 40, pp. 2080-2096.

Salomon, Carol (1991): "The Cosmogonic Riddles of Lalan Fakir", in: Arjun Appadurai, Frank J. Korom and Margaret A. Mills (Eds.), Gender, Genre, and Power in South Asian Expressive Traditions, Philadelphia: University of Pennsylvania Press, pp. 267-304.

Samuel, Geoffrey (2010): "Healing, Efficacy and the Spirits", in: Journal of Ritual Studies 24:2, pp. 7-20. (The Efficacy of Rituals Part II, Special Issue edited by William S. Sax and Johannes Quack.)

Schimmel, Annemarie (1975): Mystical Dimensions of Islam. Chapel Hill, NC: University of North Carolina Press.

Sikand, Yoginder (2002): The Origins and Development of the Tablighi Jama'at (1920-2000). A Cross-country Comparative Study. India and Great Britain: Orient Longman.

(2005): Bastions of the Believers. Madrasas and Islamic Education in India. New Delhi: Penguin.

(2007): "The Reformist Sufism of the Tablighi Jama'at. The Case of the Meos of Mewat, India", in: M. van Bruinessen and J.D. Howell (Eds.), Sufism and the 'Modern' in Islam, London: Tauris, pp.129-148.

Sirriyeh, Elizabeth (1999): Sufis and Anti-Sufis. The Defence, Rethinking and Rejection of Sufism in the Modern world, Richmond: Curzon.

Turner, Victor W. (1969): The Ritual Process, London: Routledge and Kegan Paul.

(1982): "Liminal to Liminoid, in Play, Flow, and Ritual. An Essay in Comparative Symbology", in: Victor Turner (Ed.), From Ritual to Theatre. The Human Seriousness of Play, New York: PAJ Publications, pp. 20-60.

Weismann, Itzchak (2007a): The Naqshbandiyya. Orthodoxy and Activism in a Worldwide Sufi Tradition, Routledge Sufi Series, 8, London and New York: Routledge.

(2007b): "Sufi Fundamentalism between India and the Middle East", in: M. van Bruinessen and J.D. Howell (Eds.), Sufism and the 'Modern' in Islam, London: Tauris, pp. 115-128.

Werbner, Pnina (2004): Pilgrims of Love. The Anthropology of a Global Sufi Cult, London: C. Hurst & CO.

Werbner, Pnina and Basu, Helene (Eds.) (1998): Embodying Charisma. Modernity, Locality and the Performance of Emotion in Sufi Cults, London and New York: Routledge.

White, Sarah. C. (2010): "Women's Empowerment and Islam in Bangladesh", in: Women's Studies International Forum 33, pp. 354-364. (Special Issue edited by Santi Rozario and Geoffrey Samuel, From Village Religion to Global Networks. Women, Religious Nationalism and Sustainability in South and Southeast Asia).

Contributors

Catherine B. Asher is a Professor of Art History at the University of Minnesota and author of any articles and several books, including *The Architecture of Mughal India* (Cambridge University Press, 1992; revised version 2001) and *India before Europe* (co-authored with Cynthia Talbot, Cambridge University Press, 2006). She co-edited *Perceptions of South Asia's Visual Past* (with Thomas Metcalf, Oxford and IBH and the American Institute of Indian Studies, 1994). She serves on several boards, for example the 'College Art Association Task Force on Governance', the editorial board 'Medieval Encounters' and the advisory board of *'Muqarnas'* (Harvard Publication on Islamic Art).

Johara Berriane is doctoral student of social anthropology and Islamic studies at the 'Berlin Graduate School of Muslim Cultures and Societies' (BGSMSC). She is presently researching the transnational impact and different meanings of the shrine of Ahmad al-Tijani in Fez/Morocco.

Patrick Desplat is lecturer of social anthropology at the University of Cologne. His research is on Islam in Africa, in particular Ethiopia, and migration in the Indian Ocean. He received his Ph.D from the University of Mainz, published as *Heilige Stadt – Stadt der Heiligen. Ambivalenzen und Kontroversen islamischer Heiligkeit in Harar, Äthiopien* (R. Koeppe, 2010). A further book, *Muslim Ethiopia* (co-edited with Terje Østebø), is forthcoming with Palgrave. Currently he is doing research on (im-)mobility and masculinity in Madagascar.

Simon Hawkins is social anthropologist and received his Ph.D from the University of Chicago. He has published widely on Tunisia, including the topics Islam, gender, language and cosmopolitanism. Currently he is an assistant professor of Anthropology at the University of Arkansas-Little Rock, Department of Anthropology at the Franklin and Marshall College.

Eric Ross is Associate Professor of Geography at the Al Akhawayn University, Morocco. He obtained his Ph.D. in Islamic Studies from the Institute of Islamic Studies, McGill University and has written on urban spaces and tourism in Senegal. His publications include *Sufi City. Urban Design and Archetypes in Touba* (University of Rochester Press, 2006) and *Culture and Customs of Senegal* (ABC-Clio Publishers, 2008).

Santi Rozario is reader in the School of History, Archaeology and Religion at Cardiff University, and obtained her Ph.D in social anthropology from the University of New South Wales, Australia. Rozario has undertaken extensive research in Bangladesh, India, Nepal and Sri Lanka and the UK. Her books include *Purity and Communal Boundaries* (Zed Books, 1992; revised version University Press Limited, 2001), *The Daughters of Hariti. Childbirth and Female Healers in South and Southeast Asia* (edited with Geoffrey Samuel, Routledge, 2002) and *Return Migration in the Asia Pacific* (edited jointly with Robyn Iredale and Fei Guo, Edward Elgar, 2003). Rozario's latest book, *Genetic Disorders and Islamic Identity among British Bangladeshis*, is to be published shortly by Carolina Academic Press. A further book, *Bangladesh in Transition, 1985-2010. Studies on Women, Gender and Development* is forthcoming with University Press Limited.

Geoffrey Samuel is Professor and director of the 'Research Group on the Body, Health and Religion' at Cardiff University. Among his publicatiosn are *Mind, Body and Culture* (Cambridge University Press, 1990), *Civilized Shamans* (Smithsonian Institution Press, 1993), *Tantric Revisionings* (Ashgate, 2005), and *The Origins of Yoga and Tantra* (Cambridge University Press, 2008), as well as the edited volumes *Healing Powers and Modernity in Asian Societies* (with Linda H. Connor, Bergin and Garvey, 2001) and *The Daughters of Hariti* (with Santi Rozario, Routledge, 2002).

Samuli Schielke research fellow and head of the junior research group 'In Search for Europe. Considering the Possible in Africa and the Middle East' at the ZMO, Berlin. He received his Ph.D at the University of Amsterdam, and worked as post-doctoral researcher at the ISIM and the University of Mainz. His main research focus is on Egypt and he published widely on *mawlids* as well as the ambiguities of morality, religiosity and aspiration. His publications include the edited volume *Dimensions of Locality. Muslim Saints, their Place and Space* (with Georg Stauth, 2008) and the monograph *Hatit'akhkhar 'ala al-thawra: Daftar yawmiyat 'alim anthropologia shahid al-thawra (You'll be late for the*

Revolution. The Diary of an Anthropologist who Witnessed the Egyptian Revolution, in Arabic, transl. Amr Khairy, Cairo: Dar al-Nafisa, 2011).

Dorothea E. Schulz is Professor of social anthropology at the University of Cologne. She received her Ph.D. from Yale University and her Habilitation degree from the Free University Berlin. She taught at Cornell University and Indiana University before moving to her current position at the University of Cologne. Her research, publications, and teaching are centered on the anthropology of religion, political anthropology, Islam in Africa, gender studies, media studies, and public culture. Her publications include *Perpetuating the Politics of Praise. Jeli Praise Singers, Radios and Political Mediation in Mali* (R. Koeppe, 2001), *Muslims and New Media in West Africa. Pathways to God* (Indiana University Press, 2011), and *Culture and Customs of Mali* (ABC-Clio Publishers, 2012).

Georg Stauth had academic positions, lectureships and professorships at the Universities of Alexandria and Cairo (Egypt), Adelaide and Geelong (Australia), Oxford/St. Antony's College (England), Singapore, Bielefeld, Essen and Mainz (Germany). Among his publications are *Die Fellachen im Nildelta* (F. Steiner, 1983), *Nietzsche's Dance* (with Bryan S. Turner, Blackwell, 1988), *Islam und westlicher Rationalismus* (Campus, 1994), *Islamische Kultur und moderne Gesellschaft* (transcript, 2000) and three volumes of *Ägyptische heilige Orte* (all transcript, 2005, 2008, 2010).

Linus Strothmann is doctoral student at the 'Berlin Graduate School of Muslim Societies and Cultures' (BGSMSC). His research focus is on the Sufi Shrine of Data Ganj Bakhsh in Lahore, Pakistan as place of sacred space and sacred exchange.

Jörn Thielmann is executive director of the 'Erlangen Centre for Islam and Law in Europe' (EZIRE) at the Friedrich-Alexander-University in Erlangen-Nürnberg. He received his Ph.D. in Islamic Studies from the University of Bochum with a research on the Egyptian *hisba*, published as *Nasr Hamid Abu Zaid und die wiedererfundene hisba* (Ergon, 2003). He edited *Islam and Muslims in Germany* (with Ala Al-Hamarneh, Brill, 2008).

Karin Willemse is Assistant Professor of History of Africa and of Gender and Islam at the Erasmus School for History, Cultural and Communication of the Erasmus University Rotterdam, the Netherlands. She obtained her Ph.D. in 2001 from Leiden University based on her dissertation entitled *One Foot in Heaven.*

Narratives on Gender and Islam in Darfur, West-Sudan, which was published by Brill (2007). She is writing on narrative analysis and on transformation in the relations between religion, ethnicity, gender, youth and citizenship in Sudan and South Africa.

Katharina Zöller is lecturer for African History at the University Bayreuth and doctoral student at the 'Bayreuth International Graduate School of African Studies' (BIGSAS). She is currently researching Muslim networks and local orders between eastern Congo and Tanganyika, 1920s-1960s.